G000140123

MAXIMUM WINDOWS 2000® SECURITY

Anonymous

SAMS

201 West 103rd St., Indianapolis, Indiana, 46290 USA

Maximum Windows® 2000 Security

Copyright © 2002 by Sams Publishing

All rights reserved. No part of this book shall be reproduced, stored in a
retrieval system, or transmitted by any means, electronic, mechanical, photo-
copying, recording, or otherwise, without written permission from the publisher. No patent liability is assumed with respect to the use of the information
contained herein. Although every precaution has been taken in the preparation
of this book, the publisher and author assume no responsibility for errors or
omissions. Nor is any liability assumed for damages resulting from the use of
the information contained herein.

International Standard Book Number: 0-672-31965-9

Library of Congress Catalog Card Number: 00-109550

Printed in the United States of America

First Printing: December 2001

04   03   02   01   4   3   2   1

Trademarks

All terms mentioned in this book that are known to be trademarks or service
marks have been appropriately capitalized. Sams Publishing cannot attest to
the accuracy of this information. Use of a term in this book should not be
regarded as affecting the validity of any trademark or service mark.

Warning and Disclaimer

Every effort has been made to make this book as complete and as accurate as
possible, but no warranty or fitness is implied. The information provided is on
an "as is" basis. The authors and the publisher shall have neither liability nor
responsibility to any person or entity with respect to any loss or damages aris-
ing from the information contained in this book.

ACQUISITIONS EDITORS
Betsy Brown
Shelley Johnston Markanday

DEVELOPMENT EDITOR
Steve Rowe

MANAGING EDITOR
Charlotte Clapp

COPY EDITOR
Pat Kinyon

INDEXER
Chris Barrick

PROOFREADER
Plan-It Publishing

TECHNICAL EDITORS
Rob Blader
L.J. Locher

TEAM COORDINATOR
Amy Patton

INTERIOR DESIGNER
Anne Jones

COVER DESIGNER
Anne Jones

PAGE LAYOUT
Gloria Schurick

Overview

Contents

Part III   Windows 2000 Networking   129

8   Windows 2000 Network Security Architecture   131

Lead Author

Anonymous is a reformed hacker and programmer who lives in southern California with his wife, Michelle, and a half-dozen computers. He currently runs an Internet security consulting company and is at work building the world's largest computer security archives. He also moonlights doing contract programming for several Fortune 500 firms.

Contributing Authors

Mark Burnett is a writer and consultant specializing in IIS and Windows 2000 security. He is the original founder of Xato Network Security and is currently the Managing Editor of the *IIS Security Insider* newsletter. He regularly contributes articles to several online security portals, and his extensive research in Windows 2000 security gives him unique insight into the protection of Windows-based servers.

L.J. Locher began working with mainframe and personal computers in the mid 1980s, and has since been employed as a network administrator, programmer, and security consultant for mainframe systems and PC LANs. Now a full-time author and editor, L.J. has contributed to numerous books and articles for various publishers, including Microsoft Press and *Windows 2000 Magazine*.

Chris Doyle is CEO/Managing Consultant for Coneth Solutions, a leading IT consulting firm based in California's central valley that specializes in collaboration, directory, messaging, and security solutions. He has more than 10 years of industry experience helping clients achieve their business goals through effectively leveraging IT technologies. He holds a bachelor's degree in English and many industry certifications from vendors such as Cisco, Compaq, HP, and Microsoft. Visit Chris and Coneth Solutions online at http://www.coneth.com.

Chris Amaris is the Chief Technology Officer and cofounder of Convergent Computing, a consulting firm based out of the San Francisco Bay Area. He has more than 15 years experience consulting for Fortune 500 companies, leading companies in the technology selection, design, planning, implementation and troubleshooting of complex Information Technology projects. He specializes in security, performance tuning, network/systems management, infrastructure migration, and messaging. A Windows 2000 MCSE, Novell CNE, Banyan CBE, and a Certified Project Manager, he is also an author, contributing writer, or technical editor for a number of technical books.

Rand Morimoto has been in the computer industry for more than 20 years and, as a Premier level member of the National Speaker Association (NSA), is world-renowned for public speaking and authoring books on networking technologies, communication, and security. He is an author for Sams Publishing and Osborne McGraw with a number of top-selling books. Each year, he travels to dozens of countries to speak at conferences and conventions around the world on subjects ranging from electronic commerce, mergers and acquisitions, e-Outsourcing, Internet security, and electronic messaging. He is also an advisor to the White House setting domestic policy on electronic commerce and communications.

Dedication

For Harlie, my sister...
For you, I stopped the clocks. I wound down the money machine. I bade the planets come to rest and
commanded that all the winds fall silent, merely so that I could hear you.
I still hear you now, laughing, as you rush through the trees in our garden.

—Anonymous

To Craig, who is always there for me.

—L.J. Locher

To my wife, Deborah, and our girls, Kaleigh and McKenna.

—Chris Doyle

I would like to dedicate this book to my wife, Sophia, and our five children, Michelle, Megan, Zoe,
Zachary and Ian. May the world be a more secure place when they grow up.

—Chris Amaris

I dedicate this book to Bandit the beagle, my best buddy for 14 years.

—Rand Morimoto

Acknowledgments

The following persons were indispensable: The Right Reverend Harry Reginald Hammond, Michael Michaleczko, Scott Lobel, Walter Zebrowski, David Fugate, Andrew Marsh, Alex Brittain, Marty Rush, Lisa McCarthy, and John Sale. Additionally, my deepest thanks to a superb editing team: Mark Taber, Scott Meyers, Shelley Johnston, Randi Roger, Rob Blader, and Pat Kinyon.

—Anonymous

I would like to thank my wife for her belief in me to succeed and thank my daughters, Kaleigh and McKenna, for sharing their inspiring outlook on life with me. A special thanks to our extended family for all the assistance they give us throughout the year. I would also like to thank Betsy Brown, Steve Rowe, and Neil Rowe for the publishing opportunity with Sams and for their support throughout the book-writing process.

—Chris Doyle

I would like to thank my co-author and mentor, Rand Morimoto, for showing me that the only limitations are those that we impose on ourselves.

—Chris Amaris

I want to thank my wife, Kim, and our two children, Kelly and Andrew, for their patience and their support as I had my head down at my computer to do the writing for this book.

—Rand Morimoto

Tell Us What You Think!

As the reader of this book, *you* are our most important critic and commentator. We value your opinion and want to know what we're doing right, what we could do better, what areas you'd like to see us publish in, and any other words of wisdom you're willing to pass our way.

You can e-mail or write me directly to let me know what you did or didn't like about this book—as well as what we can do to make our books stronger.

Please note that I cannot help you with technical problems related to the topic of this book, and that due to the high volume of mail I receive, I might not be able to reply to every message.

When you write, please be sure to include this book's title and author as well as your name and phone or fax number. I will carefully review your comments and share them with the author and editors who worked on the book.

E-mail: webdev@samspublishing.com

Mail: Mark Taber
            Associate Publisher
            Sams Publishing
            201 West 103rd Street
            Indianapolis, IN 46290 USA

Introduction

While security of a networking environment is at the forefront of everyone's mind, with vast outbreaks of viruses and attacks on electronic commerce and Web servers occurring regularly, it's obvious that few organizations are doing much to truly implement a fully secured network. This book was written to help IT Professionals prioritize the implementation of security in their organizations and guide them through the actual steps it takes to implement security in their networking environments.

Because security holes are created and exploited in all aspects of a Windows 2000 network (from desktops to servers, from remote access users to LAN-based users, and from Web servers to file and print servers), this book addresses all areas of security for a Windows 2000 environment.

When we outlined the book to identify key areas of secured networking that would be of most interest for IT Professionals, we came to the consensus that the following areas would be of most value in a real-world environment:

- Clarification of common terms relating to network security
- Planning and design steps to prepare for a secured environment
- Recommendation of test tools that can assist in exposing existing security holes
- Step-by-step processes to configure and update a Windows 2000 networking environment to lock down the security of the infrastructure
- Operation of perimeter analysis tools to test for weaknesses of a presumably secured environment
- Logging and monitoring procedures to track the intrusion or breach of security when all other security measures fail

To organize the extensive areas of information, this book is divided into five major parts.

Part I, "Introduction to Windows 2000 Server Security," has three chapters that introduce basic hacking techniques that are used and outlines the general areas an organization should secure. Specific tools are identified in Chapter 3, "The Hacker Toolkit," that both implement and test security processes.

Part II, "Windows 2000 Server Security Basics," walks the reader through the installation and configuration of a secured Windows 2000 server, along with core security implementation tips, tricks, and techniques. Key to all secured environments is a tight password security plan, therefore an entire chapter (Chapter 6, "Password Security") has been dedicated specifically to password-level security.

Part III, "Windows 2000 Networking," covers the major topics of security architecture and implementation. This starts with the background of the network security architecture built into Windows 2000 and progresses to specific network protocols, client configurations, and Windows services most relevant to secured communications and networking. Several security terms are introduced and clarified in Chapter 10, "Trojans and Backdoors," such as Trojans, Backdoors, Worms, and Malicious Code. Not only are these terms identified and defined, but the more common versions are specifically examined with steps intended to clearly outline how to secure your networking environment from security attacks.

This part of the book continues with chapters focused on implementing security policies that help administrators of the network define user, group, site, and organizational security standards and practices based around specific areas of secured access and secured communications configurations. These policies are so important to organizations looking to create best practices based on secured networking operations that an entire chapter is dedicated to cover business-level secured networking systems and controls (Chapter 12, "Security Policy and Configuration").

These policies are then expanded to include very explicit methods of protecting Web servers (Chapter 14, "Protecting Web Services") and other common publicly accessed Internet servers (Chapter 15, "Protecting Other Internet Services") with key methods of implementing security. Security implementation, validation tools, and test procedures are highlighted to help IT Professionals identify holes in their networking environment, as well as produce extensive reports through the use of both built-in and third-party monitoring and logging tools.

Part IV, "Privacy and Encryption in a Windows 2000 Environment," expands on new technologies built into Windows 2000, such as IPSec (Chapter 20, "IPSec") and Virtual Private Networking (VPN) technologies (Chapter 21, "Virtual Private Networking"), along with the certificate of authority server system that provides integrated support for add-ins, such as SmartCard and CardKey technologies. These technologies create envelopes of security that can be extended beyond just the Windows 2000 servers to include remote and mobile desktops, laptops, and even Web-based kiosks and terminals. Examples are provided to help the IT Professional implement these technologies to add privacy through encryption standards in a full end-to-end secured networking environment.

Part V, "Maintaining Windows 2000 Server Security," covers the maintenance components of the Windows 2000 network that takes in account logging and monitoring of network events that can be used to provide both proactive and reactive intrusion detection schemes. While it is every organization's goal to prevent intrusion to a network, the only way to truly provide full security is to continually monitor and validate that unauthorized access has not occurred.

Because security of a full networking environment covers an extremely broad range of topics (from hardware, to servers, to internetworking), security consultants from around the country were assembled to write key portions of this book that matched their level and area of expertise. It is our hope that you find this book a valuable resource in your implementation of security in your Windows 2000 networking environment, so that your organization does not easily fall victim to the liability and the embarrassment caused by an unwanted breach of enterprise security.

Introduction to Windows 2000 Server Security

PART

I

IN THIS PART

Hacking Windows 2000 Servers

IN THIS CHAPTER

A *hacker*, in the traditional sense, is an individual with exceptional programming or systems knowledge. Such an individual is able to manipulate a system or programming language in a way that the designer might not have originally intended. At one time, it was a favorable thing to be considered a hacker, because it implied that one had extraordinary knowledge of computer systems.

However, when hearing the word *hacker*, most people imagine an individual who penetrates computer systems with malicious intent. Unfortunately, the media misuse of the word hacker has evolved the term so much that the original meaning is hardly ever used. Many would prefer the term *cracker* or *attacker* to refer to these malicious characters but, for our purposes here, we will use the term in its most popular sense—one who uses his or her knowledge to circumvent security measures to access a network resource. Our definition includes those hackers with bad intent as well as those with good intent. Whatever the intent, it is all about breaking in.

> **NOTE**
>
> A malicious hacker is often referred to as a *black hat* hacker, while a hacker who does so to further security research is referred to as a *white hat* hacker. Of course, there are many who are somewhere in between, referred to as *gray hat* hackers.

There are many motivations to break into a Windows 2000 server. Some do it to for personal gain, others do it as a security audit, while still others do it for nothing more than the thrill of the challenge. But whether your motivation is malevolent or benevolent, it is important to know what the other side is doing. If your motivation is one of bad intent, you should know what the security administrators are doing to protect their servers. If your intentions are good, it is equally important to know what is happening at the opposite end. This chapter should be beneficial to both the hacker and the system administrator.

After people discover I have any kind of hacking skills, it does not take long for them to beg me to teach them everything I know. I try to refer them to the many tutorials on the Internet, but most people want the quick rundown that will get them hacking in 30 minutes or less. The truth is that there are no quick results when it comes to hacking. It requires constant learning and a tremendous amount of patience.

So, giving up on the quick lesson, people ask me at least where do they start? The answer for that is simple—start anywhere. In other words, start with any Windows exploit and learn everything you can about it. Then go on to the next one and learn everything you can about that one. Eventually you will have an arsenal of knowledge that you can pull from as needed.

To learn how to hack Windows 2000, you should:

- Know the OS
- Know its weaknesses
- Know the tools

By now, most people who had any desire to hack have already given up. Only those who are genuinely interested will go and spend the time to actually learn the stuff. That is the difference between a real hacker and a *script kiddie*. A *script kiddie* is someone who hacks with some pre-made tool or script he or she found on the Internet, hardly even understanding what he or she is doing or what to do where the tool leaves off.

Unfortunately, because of the abundance of automated hacking tools, script kiddies are very common. Furthermore, there are so many servers still vulnerable to very old exploits that script kiddies are able to successfully hack many servers. But to an experienced system administrator, a script kiddie is not much of a threat. One advantage to system administrators is that script kiddies typically are easy to detect and track down.

A more many experienced hacker knows the operating system he is attacking. He knows the strengths and weaknesses of the system and knows how to exploit them. He also knows the tools at his disposal and knows which tools to use and when to use them.

What Makes Windows 2000 Vulnerable

Windows has traditionally had a bad reputation when it comes to security. Many network administrators simply will not use it because of this reputation. The truth is that any operating system can have security weaknesses if configured improperly. Windows 2000 itself is not inherently weak and, with proper configuration, can be very secure. Still, every system has its strengths and weaknesses. The following are the main factors that make Windows 2000 vulnerable:

- The users (including the system administrator)
- The quest for openness
- The difficulty in monitoring effectively
- Its size and complexity
- Weak out-of-the-box installations

User Weaknesses

Users are the primary weakness in any operating system, but because Windows 2000 is easier to use, there is a larger base of beginner users. This is also true for the system administrators. Windows 2000 makes it so much easier to learn how to become a network administrator that many who have little or no experience in areas such as network protocols and security are becoming network administrators.

Even worse, many smaller companies cannot afford a full-time system administrator, so they offload that task to one of their users who seems to know the most about Windows. As a result, people have weak passwords, vulnerable services are left running, and hotfixes are not installed.

As you become familiar with the common user weaknesses, you will get a feel of how to exploit those weaknesses.

The Openness of Windows

Windows is a product that makes considerable money for Microsoft. To keep making money, Microsoft must maintain dominance in the operating systems market. That means that Windows has to do more than competing operating systems, and that usually means that Microsoft must constantly add new Windows features. These features are often focused on things such as interoperability, integration, and extensibility. As these features are added, Windows becomes more open for application development, network connectivity, and communications. The problem with openness is that each new service presents a whole new set of security issues that must be dealt with. And often, the programmers who are writing code with openness in mind are not thinking of the security risks involved. The mindset for openness is in direct contradiction with the mindset for security.

For example, to expand the reaches of its COM technology, Microsoft created a service called Remote Data Services (RDS). This service allowed users to do great things involving remote data access, but also opened up a very big security hole that allowed anyone on the Internet to run just about any command they wanted on a Windows NT server. Certainly the developers of RDS did not imagine that their data service would be used to hack so many Windows servers that year.

If you look at some of the services available in a default Windows 2000 install, it makes you wonder how many holes we will see in the future. Some of the services that make me uncomfortable are

- Internet Connection Sharing
- NetMeeting Remote Desktop Sharing
- Remote Access Auto Connection Manager
- Remote Registry Service
- Terminal Services
- Intersite Messaging

The Difficulty of Monitoring Effectively

Another problem plaguing Windows 2000 is the lack of quality monitoring tools. Windows 2000 does have the Event Log, but in my experience, few system administrators actually review their event logs on a regular basis.

The problem is that the average system administrator will open the Event Viewer and see a huge number of security-related events, some audit success and some audit failures, with meaningless codes, such as 529, 681, and 577. The large number of entries along with their ambiguity makes it difficult to spot intrusions from the Event Viewer. Even if you do make sense of it, the Event Viewer often does not log relevant information, such as a remote IP address.

I have run many penetration tests on Windows 2000 computers and the system administrator was never even aware of what I had done. I often ask system administrators if they would know if they were hacked and, if so, how would they know? Most often, they admit that they would not know they were hacked. When I ask them when was the last time they looked at their Event Logs, the answer is usually more than a few months, if ever.

In Windows 2000, without the help of third-party software, it is often difficult or unclear how to answer questions such as the following:

- Who is connected to my computer at this very moment?
- When was the last time someone logged in using Terminal Services?
- How many bad password attempts have been made against an account?
- Is someone else logged in with my account from another computer right now?
- Does someone else have shares mapped to my computer right now?

Clearly, it is difficult to know if you are under attack without good monitoring. And, although there are third-party tools for monitoring different aspects of Windows 2000, no single tool will make up for Windows 2000's shortcomings. One must use a variety of tools to be able to get the complete picture.

As long as Windows 2000 is difficult to monitor, a hacker might feel that his or her intrusions are not going to be spotted. And chances are he or she will be right. Proper system monitoring can be accomplished, but it does take an extra effort that most system administrators do not bother doing.

NOTE

Learn more about the Windows Event Log in Chapter 22, "Log Monitoring and Analysis."

The Size and Complexity of Windows 2000

There was a time not many years ago when an operating system fit on a single-sided 360KB floppy disk. In contrast, Windows 2000 is a huge operating system with tens of millions of lines of code. Couple that with the fact that a good portion of that code is not much more than a year or two old. With so much code and so much of it new code, there is much room for the discovery of holes that could compromise the system's security. And there are plenty of people out there constantly hammering away at Windows 2000 searching for those holes.

When it comes to security, complexity is never good. A hacker can easily exploit the complexity of Windows 2000. For example, if a hacker was to place a Trojan file in the WINNT directory named something official-sounding, such as `tapi.exe`, it would be easy for it to go unnoticed among all the many other system executables located there. Similarly, if such an application showed up running in Task Manager, it might not cause alarm. The reason is that many administrators do not recognize the names of many of the applications that are running anyway. It is very similar to the concept that if you carry a clipboard and look like you know where you are going, you can get into just about any secured building you want. An executable that looks legitimate is too often blindly dismissed as legitimate. With the constant growth and change of Windows 2000, it is not difficult at all for a hacker to take advantage of that complexity and sneak by unnoticed.

Weak Out-of-the-Box Installations

Although Windows 2000 is much more secure out-of-the-box than Windows NT 4 was, all systems have the same default settings when they are first installed. Installing Windows 2000 is a two-step process. First you install the operating system, and then you go through and harden it. *Hardening* is the process of shutting off services and changing settings to make the operating system less vulnerable to attack. The problem is that so many administrators neglect to perform this hardening process, leaving the system exposed to a number of attacks. For that reason, a system might have something such as World Wide Web Publishing Service running and the user might not even be aware of it. If the user is not aware that it is running, he or she certainly is not watching Web logs for intrusions. The same is true for a number of other Windows 2000 services.

The first Windows 2000 hotfix (MS00-006) was released on January 26, 2000, a month before Windows 2000 had even arrived in stores. This hotfix addressed a bug that allowed any remote user to view sensitive files on a Web server using any Web browser. Despite the fact that this issue is well over a year old at the time of this writing, thousands of Web servers on the Internet (including those belonging to many large companies) are still vulnerable to this bug. It is so easy to neglect the hardening process that many systems are installed without going through that second step. With the right tools, it does not take long to identify those systems that are not kept up-to-date. If you scan a system and discover a vulnerability that is well over a year old, chances are that nothing after that was fixed either.

> **NOTE**
>
> Learn more about installing Windows 2000 in Chapter 5, "Installing Windows 2000: The First Step Toward Security."

Knowing the Tools

Hacking, like many things, is much more effective if you have a good collection of the right tools. There are plenty of hacking tools available, but finding the right tools is the hard part. Any good hacker has a good arsenal of tools he has collected or built himself over the years. To be a good hacker, it is essential that you know what tools are available and how to use them.

Tools could take the form of Windows or console applications. They could also be scripts or simply just batch files. Tools could also include Web sites that make online applications available that are useful for hacking. Whatever form they take, as you learn about Windows 2000 weaknesses, you should also focus on gathering (or building) the tools to exploit those weaknesses. In Chapter 3, "The Hacker Toolkit," we will discuss specific tools that you can put in your toolbox to get you started.

One important aspect of collecting tools is knowing when not to use them. Many script-kiddie tools often create easily spotted patterns on a network or in system logs. Knowing which tools are easily spotted and which ones are not is a big part of the tool-gathering process.

Although there are many tools produced that are created specifically for hacking, Windows 2000 has many built-in tools that are also important to identify. Some of these tools include the following:

- `net.exe`   Can be used to discover system and network information and make network connections
- `nbtstat.exe`   Can be used to display NetBIOS name tables of a remote system
- `tftp.exe`   Can be used to transfer files to or from a hacker's system
- `telnet.exe`   Can be used to access connected networks

You should take the time to dig through Windows 2000 to see what other tools are available to you. In addition, the Windows 2000 Resource Kit contains a wealth of tools that will also be useful in hacking Windows 2000. The best part of learning how to exploit the built-in tools is that they are already installed on the system you are hacking, eliminating the often difficult step of getting your tools onto a remote system.

Tools are such an important part of hacking that you can typically judge a hacker's skills by his collection of tools.

> **NOTE**
>
> Learn more about hacker tools in Chapter 3.

Summary

The ability to hack Windows 2000 is by no means something that can be acquired overnight. By knowing the operating system, learning the weaknesses, and finding the tools to exploit those weaknesses, you will gradually gain a mastery of Windows 2000. You will be able to penetrate just about any system many times, doing so in just a few minutes. Even better, if your ultimate goal is to protect Windows 2000 by learning how to break it, you will be so much more adept than someone who has never actually broken in will ever be.

Whether your goal is to break Windows 2000 or to protect Windows 2000, you have to obtain the kind of street smarts that you can only get by actually using the techniques and tools acquired through your constant learning.

Windows 2000 Server Security Features

IN THIS CHAPTER

Windows 2000 Security Features

Windows 2000 has come a long way in security features compared to the original release of Windows NT. In the last few years, security protocols have matured and the operating system has been through much public scrutiny. In this chapter, we will discuss many of the security features available in Windows 2000 and how they contribute to increasing overall system security.

For a server to be secure, the operating system must have a number of built-in security features. However, the features do not make the system more secure if the administrator does not make use of them. This chapter introduces the security features in Windows 2000 so that the administrator can take advantage of what is available. The rest of this book will address each of these features in more detail and explain exactly how they can be used to increase overall system security.

Enhanced Access Control

Unless you're new to computers, you've likely experienced some form of security breach, even if you were never aware of it. Indeed, it wasn't that long ago that most desktop operating systems offered little or no security, and users could access one another's files on a whim.

The last decade or so changed this as networking became more prevalent at the consumer level. Heightened public awareness—spawned by wild stories about computer hackers—engendered a healthy suspicion in most users. This, in turn, prompted software vendors to gradually incorporate security features in their products to meet public demand.

The Internet plays a significant role in this shift of public consciousness. Hence today, most network operating systems offer a feature called access control. Loosely defined, *access control* is any technique or mechanism that lets you selectively grant or deny users access to system resources, files, folders, directories, volumes, drives, services, hosts, networks, and so on.

Windows 2000 centrally vests all administrative power in a single account called `Administrator`. The `Administrator` is Windows 2000's equivalent of Unix's root or NetWare's Supervisor. As administrator, you control everything, including the following:

- *User accounts*—Who can log on and access your system's resources
- *Authentication*—How the system uniquely identifies users and verifies their identities
- *Objects*—Who can access registry settings, files, directories, folders, libraries, applications, and computers
- *Peripherals*—Who can access printers, scanners, cameras, and other accessories
- *Network policy*—Which users, workgroups, domains, computers, and networks can access your system

Windows 2000's User and Accounts

Windows 2000's user and account system somewhat resembles models common to Unix and Novell NetWare. In Windows 2000, user and account information is stored in a database referred to as Active Directory. With Active Directory, each account is a separate entity with a separate username, a separate password, and separate access rights. Windows 2000 logically segregates these users so that you can selectively and incisively apply access rules.

Windows 2000 segregates users this way partly for security's sake, and partly to impose order in a potentially chaotic environment. Put another way, you might find it useful to imagine your Windows 2000 system as a community. This community consists of users and administrators.

As your community grows, it becomes more complex. Users generate their own files, install their own programs, and so on. To maintain order, Windows 2000 segregates user directories and creates unique user profiles. Each user is given a home directory and hard disk space. This location is separate from system areas (see Figure 2.1).

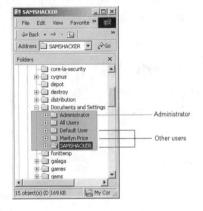

FIGURE 2.1

The Documents and Settings directory and subdirectories, where Windows 2000 stores user files by default.

Inside a user's home directory, Windows 2000 stores user-specific application data, cookies, network favorites, desktop folders, local settings, documents, and so forth. Each time a user creates a document, the system suggests that the user store it in his or her *My Documents* directory (see Figure 2.2).

2

WINDOWS 2000 SERVER SECURITY FEATURES

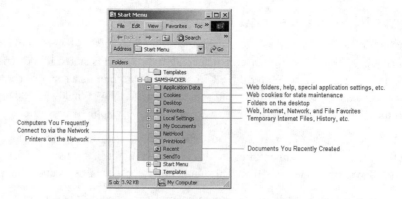

FIGURE 2.2

A typical Windows 2000 user's home directory and its subdirectories.

This prevents normal user activity from affecting the file system at large. Moreover, it provides each user with some measure of privacy. As you'll later learn, users own their files and, unless they specify otherwise, other users cannot access them. This concept is known as *Discretionary Access Control*.

Discretionary Access Control (DAC)

One central theme in Windows 2000's security is Discretionary Access Control (DAC). Discretionary Access Control lets you control the degree to which each user can access files and directories (see Figure 2.3).

FIGURE 2.3

The Administrator can allow or deny access to files and specify exactly which ways a user can access those files.

As depicted in Figure 2.3, you can specify precisely how users A, B, and C access the same files in a directory. User A, for example, can read those files, write to (or create) new files, modify existing files, list the contents of the directory, and execute any of the files. In contrast, User B can only read from those files and write to (or create) new files and finally, User C cannot access them at all.

However, that's very refined control and, often it's overkill. The Microsoft Windows 2000 development team recognized that many organizations are divided into departments (and multiple users in those departments often need access to the same files). Consequently, Windows 2000 lets you lump users into groups where they all have similar or identical permissions (see Figure 2.4).

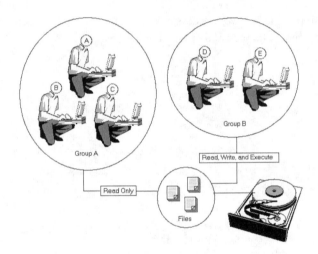

FIGURE 2.4
Groups are collections of users that have similar access rights.

As depicted in Figure 2.4, members of Group A have only read access, whereas Group B has read, write, and execute access. Such group-level management comes in handy when you have many users (and various user subsets need similar or identical access privileges). Windows 2000 has a number of built-in groups, such as Administrators and Backup Operators, to assist in the classification of users.

But Windows 2000 access control allows you to control much more than file access. For example, an administrator can control which users can

- Backup and restore
- Create pagefiles
- Create shared objects

- Debug programs
- Generate security audits
- Load or unload device drivers
- Log on as a batch process
- Shutdown the computer

These access control mechanisms, if used properly, can allow an administrator to control Windows 2000 security down to the finest detail.

Enhanced Network Control

Windows 2000 also provides network access control or the ability to selectively allow or deny hosts the ability to connect to one another (see Figure 2.5).

FIGURE 2.5
You can use Windows 2000 network access control to specify who has access to the server.

As depicted in Figure 2.5, you can enforce very refined domain access rules. User A cannot log in to the network at all, User B must be using a particular workstation before he or she can log in, and User C has no restrictions—he or she can log in to the domain freely from wherever he or she likes.

NOTE

Learn more about Windows 2000's network access control in Chapter 16, "TCP Filtering and Firewalls."

IPSec and VPNs

Network access control ensures that only authorized workstations can connect to your system. This is certainly very useful. However, the mere fact that only authorized systems can connect does not, in itself, prohibit unauthorized users from viewing your data.

As you'll read later in the book, even when unauthorized users cannot connect, they can still capture and view data traveling over your network. This type of attack is called sniffing. In *sniffing*, attackers surreptitiously intercept, monitor, and record network traffic for later perusal. To protect against this, you must conceal your data before and during transport.

For this, Windows 2000 uses IPSec (Internet Protocol Security), which lets you build *Virtual Private Networks* or VPNs. VPNs are exactly what their name implies: private networks. These are *virtual* in so far as they exist wholly as private communication channels within public networks like the Internet. VPNs use the Internet as a communications conduit between two or more machines that support IPSec cryptographic services. Such services encrypt data transiting between two or more points, thus armoring a session's traffic. Traffic encrypted this way is scrambled beyond human recognition and, thus, defeats the nosey attacker (who reaps digital garbage for his efforts). IPSec also can encrypt traffic on your private LAN, protecting all data that crosses your network.

The IPSec approach is advantageous for several reasons. First, as we'll discuss, sniffing is difficult to detect because sniffers leave no (or precious little) evidence of their existence. Additionally, IPSec is architecture independent, transparent, and simple to configure. These features, when measured against features of other proprietary encryption systems, make IPSec quite attractive. Enabling a computer with IPSec demands little or no intervention from users.

IPSec in Windows 2000 supports several encryption algorithms, including

- *The Data Encryption Standard (DES)*—DES uses a 56-bit key, which, for transient sessions, is suitable (and meets U.S. export regulations)
- *Triple DES (3DES)*—3DES uses stronger encryption (two 56-bit keys), which is optimal for relatively short, transient sessions (and meets U.S. standards for high-security, domestic environments).

2

WINDOWS 2000 SERVER SECURITY FEATURES

> **NOTE**
>
> Learn more about IPSec in Chapter 21, "Virtual Private Networking."

Kerberos

Network access control and IPSec, when used in concert, guarantee that only authorized work-stations can connect and that their traffic is impervious to electronic eavesdropping. This is fairly advanced security for many purposes. However, network access control and encrypted communications are not the only security measures that should be taken. Conditions will arise where these controls might fail to sufficiently protect your data.

For example, suppose that an attacker already has unrestricted access to a trusted or authorized workstation. Network access control won't keep him out (after all, he does have the right workstation address) and IPSec will merely protect his session from sniffing. In high security environments, therefore, network access control and IPSec are not enough; you need to authenticate not merely the machine, but the user, too.

Enter Kerberos, a system designed expressly for such situations. RFC 1244 (now superseded by RFC 2196) states:

> "Kerberos, named after the dog that in mythology is said to stand at the gates of Hades, is a collection of software used in a large network to establish a user's claimed identity. Developed at the Massachusetts Institute of Technology (MIT), it uses a combination of encryption and distributed databases so that a user at a campus facility can login and start a session from any computer located on the campus. This has clear advantages in certain environments where there are a large number of potential users who might establish a connection from any one of a large number of workstations."

Kerberos, therefore, superbly addresses the problem of an attacker coming from a trusted workstation. Without proper Kerberos authentication, the attacker will be rejected.

NOTE

Learn more about Kerberos in Chapter 19, "Privacy and Encryption in a Windows 2000 Environment."

Advanced Authentication Support

In addition to Kerberos, Windows 2000 supports other authentication methods, including some that have only recently been in wide public use. Two we'll cover here are

- General session authentication
- Public Key Cryptography

Session Authentication

So far, we've mentioned various authentication schemes. Some, like network access control mechanisms, authenticate machines. Others, like Kerberos, authenticate users. Still other mechanisms exist that expressly authenticate sessions.

A *session*, for our purposes, is any live exchange between a client and server, either on a local socket or between hosts over a network. For example, the series of exchanges between your Web client and a Web server to complete an electronic transaction in sum constitutes one session.

Such a Web session—without additional security measures—is negotiated largely through Hypertext Transfer Protocol (HTTP) and other protocols common to internetworking. However, because HTTP is a stateless protocol, and because it passes text openly (without encryption), it can neither remember your settings or protect your data. Newer protocols, such as SSL, have been developed that maintain session state and encrypt data.

But this is only one step in securing a connection or session. Another is to maintain session integrity. Session integrity is not as much about protecting data as it is about verifying the data's source or destination. With session integrity, you ensure that the source you started with remains consistent throughout the session's duration.

Network security specialists designed session integrity techniques to defeat an attack called *session highjacking*. Loosely, session highjacking is where attackers seize control of a session midstream, insert themselves therein, and subsequently masquerade as legitimate participants. Absent some express mechanism to detect changes in a session participant's identity, Web servers have no way to defend against highjacking. This type of attack is also sometimes called a *man-in-the-middle attack*.

To obtain high assurance of session integrity, Windows 2000 supports several encryption algorithms, including some we've already briefly discussed, such as DES and 3DES. However, it also supports two specialized algorithms for session integrity—MD5 and SHA1.

MD5: A Message Digest Algorithm

Message Digest Algorithms (MD5) belong to a family of one-way hash functions called *message digest algorithms* and was originally defined in RFC 1321 as follows:

> "The algorithm (MD5) takes as input a message of arbitrary length and produces as output a 128-bit "fingerprint" or "message digest" of the input. It is conjectured that it is computationally infeasible to produce two messages having the same message digest, or to produce any message having a given pre-specified target message digest."

MD5's offer high assurance and are particularly well-suited—and often used—for testing file and session integrity. Windows 2000 supports MD5 for several session types, including those based on Challenge Handshake Authentication Protocol (CHAP) and Extensible Authentication Protocol (EAP), and extensions to the Point-to-Point Protocol (PPP).

SHA1: The Secure Hash Algorithm

The Secure Hash Algorithm (SHA1) is a 160-bit algorithm often used in defense environments. For example, the Department of Defense historically required that all DoD managed systems adhere to the Multilevel Information System Security Initiative (MISSI) and use only products cleared by the same.

One MISSI-cleared product in particular—the Fortezza card, a PCMCIA card that provides an extra layer of security to electronic mail sent from DoD laptops—uses SHA. SHA is also incorporated into the Secure Data Network System Message Security Protocol, a message protocol that provides security to the X.400 Message Handling environment.

Finally, SHA1 is used in conjunction with the Digital Signature Algorithm (DSA) to generate digital signatures that verify human identities and are not used for file encryption.

Public Key Cryptography

In addition to authentication systems previously mentioned, Windows 2000 supports a powerful and flexible architecture called *Public Key Cryptography*. Public Key Cryptography (PKC) is a system based on *key pairs*.

In any PKC transaction, two keys exist:

- *The public key*—A key available to the general public or less often, a select group. This key generally resides on a *key server* and consists of a plain text dump of its encrypted value.
- *The private key*—A key held by the key owner and unpublished. Only this private key's owner can decrypt a message encrypted to its corresponding public key.

PKC has become exceedingly popular of late, chiefly due to its high reliability and assurance. Some of the strongest encryption systems available to civilians are based on PKC, including Pretty Good Privacy (PGP).

PGP is a free PKC system that lets you create private keys and create, manage, publish, and revoke public keys. A PGP public key looks like digital garbage to the human eye, scrambled and unintelligible.

For example

```
-----BEGIN PGP PUBLIC KEY BLOCK-----
Version: PGPfreeware 6.5.2 for non-commercial use
mQGiBDlrEj4RBADx06Gfza7GlIXuslMe49iq5m73DrdEMg29ZYFRylPAyE2ESftU
nhH+oNCnwKNLhomk1rLulgaeCrBhhBH78dNPdDIWOf+5GmmKkcfTqhQ1BSfY9z4P
vaoHMuDsX7TreqHuWZnRUSAPa8kTJHz9cT6WY5PMqxSd84vRASjroud2mQCg//86
mqka2pq9U/xNEOcvlOuAZy0D/1+2Htbddeyj0X/VQU9hn2vY1qWkMRG5IH9I/xnn
OvhGYaM2PtXk9KoNVbJ4r39qQhf8+Y9L4RbQ43OT3ohl25bhlqehgXGmalJtWvrL
Cc60fMIFrby/lbjGa9Sw4D47gtt8E7BZCuuFcnfVJ9dBJGCN21jgmXHiHJDC2gfV
```

```
Mh/WBAC3ZASs0jh1JBuYCWm9srb5Nkpu6ZENe4f+gOrgi1zOvzEGAVUy2XUOKpVt
R9HTTWigfAGnmN7FIXTsdzGj2byyHzJQPn4umkvRETLTNYaVVNIvwXq5Q54o1/oh
dkEflpoqkf5I6wocM4tNps2Y9HOtPZT0YYb15UHbnKXvIjdNDLQvV2lsbGlhbSBS
YW5kb2xwaCBSb3llcmUgSUlJIDxvc2lyaXNNAcm95ZXJlLm51dD6JAE4EEBECAA4F
AjlrEj4ECwMCAQIZAQAKCRAUg3vs7lip9uFBAJ91Ddghb1YF65mzEfnfCxAX50/c
dgCgkMQtcIhp/k3Ir7iblcU4Xs6lnzW5BA0EOWsSPxAQAPkYoH5aBmF6Q5CV3AVs
h4bsYezNRR8O2OCjecbJ3HoLrOQ/40aUtjBKU9d8AhZIgLUV5SmZqZ8HdNP/46HF
liBOmGW42A3uEF2rthccUdhQyiJXQym+lehWKzh4XAvb+ExN1eOqRsz7zhfoKp0U
YeOEqU/Rg4Soebbvj6dDRgjGzB13VyQ4SuLE8OiOE2eXTpITYfbb6yUOF/32mPfI
fHmwch04dfv2wXPEgxEmK0Ngw+Po1gr9oSgmC66prrNlD6IAUwGgfNaroxIe+g8q
zh90hE/K8xfzpEDp19J3tkItAjbBJstoXp18mAkKjX4t7eRdefXUkk+bGI78KqdL
fDL2Qle3CH8IF3KiutapQvMF6PlTETlPtvFuuUs4INoBp1ajFOmPQFXz0AfGy0Op
1K33TGSGSfgMg71l6RfUodNQ+PVZX9x2Uk89PY3bzpnhV5JZzf24rnRPxfx2vIPF
RzBhznzJZv8V+bv9kV7HAarTW56NoKVyOtQa8L9GAFgr5fSI/VhOSdvNILSd5JEH
NmszbDgNRR0PfIizHHxbLY7288kjwEPwpVsYjY67VYy4XTjTNP18F1dDox0YbN4z
ISy1Kv884bEpQBgRjXyEpwpy1obEAxnIByl6ypUM2Zafq9AKUJsCRtMIPWakXUGf
nHy9iUsiGSa6q6Jew1XrPdYXAAICEADM5o/u1WIAp6O28XOS45dUJza+GgVIS8i/
a8K+JRM3nIYom/axSxadHbXayp5ECc6h+lfPGTsc+LIr2i5tZmOTblYAPcc7azNY
4gXK2d/IyzfAyUdzYtHXQv9HnKsuyQ7dUfUDd19bgzZ/9lYWGCjUwZZmOfacz4HJ
ZxoPltpHM9j3L92RicmT+Y+4cZTKy1k2roD4KCkuqovn+6d0dJwB91Fieq3gBSRK
H71klssQMHVthk5rk1CwQHTYe+EwJcwtbJv5n5OeABOp6MMnp6MikggtM61X4vu4
nPCFdmcaAAxJZJ3e2WlV3y0/dca+DhHqLpoeo8cxtZa5xSMcPgzqvBR/XGvwbsHG
Tfvw/zzMo6zsxljwn6h5L+X1DTt3/ILZ+G1ZWufboYBRXcxHNxFAQRbk1lKdgEA0
kbM9yb0AfYv98CxeDAr+HUXyMAb2ogAcfk3NdhJFB2D2gqKVppwgtRjDhVarhSjy
ddBHqPhL06PJxM0vQmEfzpodLZe/Pm/036D0iSog9wtOwOLzlgifKkRZ90a3X/rL
5FyzoeRBKrdkomQB/zjfyJ7dDPG3djwLwEfET/JL2ySxbQf09mbN2386kZvO2CIt
MGBr5x1PvtP0qpuh5QVlpLMqI0Dv8XS17Uqq4S26icXIRCdrY0+2vgd1D4pjFV+v
Fcmpnpc3XokARgQYEQIABgUCOWsSPwAKCRAUg3vs7lip9pbeAKCqTbaKMC2z9COi
zQcDAsel/uYQLwCg3+OJIpvqkp66LcMIocROiPBCyr0=
=jKHd
-----END PGP PUBLIC KEY BLOCK-----
```

However, when you feed this key to a PKC-enabled application, it uniquely identifies its owner by his or her e-mail address. After you encrypt the data to this public key (and send it to the recipient), the key's owner applies his or her corresponding private key and decrypts the data.

PKC systems introduce an interesting advantage not available in many network-based encryption systems. In standard encryption systems, users or applications often must transmit or exchange private keys or passwords across the network. This invites attack because attackers can intercept such keys and passwords and crack them at their leisure. This represents risk because, as we'll discuss later, time is often a significant factor.

For example, many encryption systems rely on relatively small or characteristically "weak" keys or passwords. Such systems, for short sessions, are suitable and often sufficient, because the time necessary to transfer a password leaves attackers a very narrow window. If attackers cannot intercept the password or key within the specified time, they lose out.

However, if the attackers *can* grab the password or key and transport it to a safe environment, they could theoretically take days or weeks to crack it without risking discovery. And, while keys are generally unique and used only once (though passwords are not), attackers can concentrate purely on cracking the underlying encryption system used (rather than the specific key itself). If the attackers determine this, any key generated in a similar way is vulnerable to attack.

PKC systems eliminate this possibility in two ways. First, users transmit only one half of the puzzle in PKC systems. The private key remains forever hidden and the public key is essentially useless. Moreover, PKC algorithms rely on and produce impossibly large numbers that make an attacker's brute force and key searching attacks essentially useless (or if not useless, probably futile).

Summary of Windows 2000's Advanced Authentication Methods

Windows 2000's use of these encryption mechanisms (DES, 3DES, MD5, SHA1, Kerberos, and PKC) results in support for a diverse set of authentication mechanisms, including the following:

- With biometric systems, it's possible to have Windows 2000 authenticate users via fingerprint or retinal scan data.
- Encrypted and authenticated network logons.
- Encrypted Web sessions and secure electronic commerce.
- Remote Authentication Dial-in User Service (RADIUS) is a system commonly used by Internet Service Providers (ISPs) to authenticate and manage user dialup connections.
- You can use Windows 3000 in conjunction with smart card authentication.

File System Encryption

So far, the authentication methods we have mentioned will prevent certain types of attacks, but what if someone decides to just grab your whole server when no one is looking and walk out with it? A good defense when someone has gained access to your server is to implement the Encrypting File System (EFS).

The *Encrypting File System* is a service that encrypts your data so that other users cannot access it, even if they have physical access to the system. EFS allows you to encrypt individual files or folders or encrypt an entire folder tree. This encryption guarantees that only the file's owner can read the data that has been encrypted.

But Microsoft went the extra mile in making EFS a seamless part of the file system. If you've ever used file encryption mechanisms, you know that encryption can be a laborious process. Often, you must open a third-party encryption application, load the target file, and manually encrypt it. And, when you want to access the file later, you must first load it (again), decrypt it, and then open it in its native application.

In typical Microsoft ease-of-use tradition, EFS doesn't merely encrypt files; it makes their encryption transparent. That is, you can encrypt files and subsequently work with them as you normally would; Windows 2000's underlying system handles subsequent decryption automatically, thus enabling you to work without worrying about manually encrypting and decrypting the data.

But keep in mind the drawbacks of having the encryption so transparent. First of all, because the encryption is transparent, it would be easy to overlook encrypting some files and not be aware that they are not encrypted. Furthermore, if someone has your system password, he or she can have full access to any of the encrypted files.

Because the process of encrypting and decrypting data is CPU-intensive, another drawback of having an encrypted drive is that performance will suffer somewhat. The extent of this performance drop depends on your particular hardware configuration.

2

WINDOWS 2000 SERVER SECURITY FEATURES

NOTE

Learn more about EFS and file encryption generally in Chapter 19.

Logging

If you use the security controls mentioned so far, you will achieve a basic level of security:

- Users and groups will have restrictive permissions.
- Windows 2000 will allow only authorized workstations to connect.
- Windows 2000 will encrypt all network traffic.
- Windows 2000 will authenticate your users.
- Even if attackers get in, your files will be encrypted.

If you get that far, you'll have better security than many Windows 2000 servers now online. However, even this might be insufficient. Sadly, even when you diligently apply all security controls, newfound vulnerabilities sometimes surface. Hackers quickly exploit these opportunities by attacking as many machines as possible before the hole is patched.

Alas, Windows 2000 can't predict when your host will next come under attack, but it can record the attacker's movements. Windows 2000 has extensive system logging capabilities.

Briefly, *logging* is any procedure by which an operating system or application records events as they happen.

It's difficult to say when logging first became a staple procedure in computing, but it hails from the discipline of programming. Even when you write a relatively simple program, it's useful to have diagnostic information on hand, such as the following examples:

- Whether the program faulted and, if so, when and why.
- The program's UID or PID.
- Who has used the program and when.
- Does the program perform tasks in the way you want it to?

In a security context, logging serves a different purpose: to preserve a record of an attacker's evil deeds. Logs provide the only reliable evidence that an intrusion has occurred. The process of keeping track of user actions on a system is called *auditing*.

An administrator can tell Windows 2000 to log or audit all of the following event types:

- Account logon events
- Account management events
- Directory service access
- Logon events
- Object access
- Policy changes
- Privilege use
- Process tracking
- System events

Although there are some shortcomings with the Windows 2000 Event Log, many of these can be overcome with third-party software. The Event Log does have good auditing features and plays an important role in system security.

> **NOTE**
>
> Learn more about logging in Chapter 22, "Log Monitoring and Analysis."

Summary

All the aforementioned mechanisms constitute individual components of Windows 2000's security architecture. Taken alone, none will sufficiently safeguard your data from the myriad of cracker attacks. However, when used in concert, they constitute a comprehensive, powerful, and holistic approach to network security.

The Hacker Toolkit

IN THIS CHAPTER

Some hackers like to think that you are not cool if you use tools. They think that anyone who uses a tool to hack is nothing more than a *script kiddie*. Perhaps at one time that was the case, but nowadays, it's all about having the coolest tools. Script kiddies will be script kiddies with or without tools; it's not the scripts that make them script kiddies.

Tools automate the tedious work of being a hacker. They extend a hacker's skills and allow scripted attacks to be scheduled for later or run from a remote system. Sure, much of what a hacker can do does depend on his own knowledge and skills, but a hacker does depend on having the right tools. The master hacker is one who has mastered his tools.

This chapter's title implies that it is only about tools for malicious hackers. Nevertheless, it is equally important for a system administrator to build a good collection of tools. Like the rest of this book, many of the concepts mentioned in this chapter are just as useful for the administrator as for the hacker. There is certainly nothing wrong with a system administrator keeping his own hacker's toolkit to protect his network.

Types of Tools

Tools come in many shapes and forms. In this chapter, I use the word in the broadest sense to include just about anything that automates the process of hacking. Hacking tools fall into the following basic categories:

- Windows tools
- Win32 Console tools
- Non-Windows 2000 tools
- Scripts
- Web-based tools

Windows Tools

Windows tools are easy to learn and use and have their definite strengths. Having access to the Windows UI facilities certainly can make a tool very flexible and can allow for better reporting of the tool's output. But a Windows interface is not always the best when it comes to hacking. It is difficult to script a Windows application, and even more difficult to automatically send the output of one tool as the input to another tool. It is best to see Windows tools for what they are and use them when they make the most sense. When they do not make sense, you should know which tools would make sense for that particular scenario.

Win32 Console Tools

Console tools play a big role in the hacking process. Console tools are text-based tools that are run in a command prompt window. They are smaller, easier to script, simpler, and simply more elegant solutions for hacking. With console tools, you can pipe, redirect, chop, trim, sort, or whatever you want with the output and then send the output to another tool for further action. Moreover, sometimes when you hack a remote system, all you have is a command prompt to work with. If you do not have the right console tools, you will never get much farther than that. If you think you want to be a hacker, you need to learn how to spend time at a command prompt.

As an example of what you can do with console tools, consider the following command:

```
C:\>for /f "tokens=1*" %i in ('fscan -eq -p 80 10.120.1.1-254') do @ping |
➥ nc -v -n %i 80 | Find /i "Server"
(UNKNOWN) [10.120.1.202] 80 (?) open
Server: Microsoft-IIS/5.0
(UNKNOWN) [10.120.1.203] 80 (?) open
Server: Microsoft-IIS/4.0
(UNKNOWN) [10.120.1.206] 80 (?) open
Server: Microsoft-IIS/4.0
(UNKNOWN) [10.120.1.207] 80 (?) open
Server: Microsoft-IIS/5.0
```

The purpose of this script is to locate all Web servers on a given IP address range and determine what type of Web server software is installed. The command scans a range of IP addresses for Web servers listening on port 80 by using the `fscan` TCP/IP port scanning utility. It then loops through the results of `fscan` and extracts the IP addresses. It then feeds the IP addresses to Netcat through a pipe (|) so that Netcat can determine the Web server type, and then feeds those results to `find.exe` through another pipe (|) to parse out and display the server header string. It's hard to accomplish something like that with a Windows-based tool. To try this script on your own, visit `http://www.foundstone.com` to obtain fscan and `http://www.atstake.com/` to obtain Netcat.

Non-Windows 2000 Tools

Unfortunately, sometimes the best Windows hacking tools were not written for Windows. Linux and other Unix-based operating systems have a number of great tools that never made it to the core Windows 2000 command set. Fortunately, a number of those utilities have been ported to the Win32 platform and are readily available and free to use. Even the Unix basics, such as `sed`, `awk`, `grep`, and others can make a Windows 2000 command prompt competitive with other operating systems. You should also grab Cygwin, available at `http://www.cygwin.com` so that you can compile other Unix tools on your Windows 2000 system. Unfortunately, not every Unix tool has been ported or will work in Windows 2000, so you might just want to give up on ported tools and install an entire Unix-based system.

3

THE HACKER
TOOLKIT

Scripts

Scripts are text files that contain a set of sequential instructions that are sent to a script interpreter for processing. Many scripting languages, such as VBScript, are just lean versions of full programming languages, such as Visual Basic. Scripts are sometimes preferable to full-blown applications because they are easy to write, portable, and can easily be modified as needed. Some scripting languages, such as Perl, work well on a variety of different operating systems with little or no modification of the scripts themselves.

> **NOTE**
>
> For information on VBScript, see the VBScript User's Guide available at http://msdn. microsoft.com/library/default.asp?url=/library/en-us/script56/html/ vbstutor.asp. For information on using Perl on the Win32 platform and to download a Perl scripting environment for Win32, visit Active State at http://www.activestate.com/.

Web-Based Tools

Some people build Web-based hacking tools and make them available for public use. There are a number of Web sites that provide valuable applications for both hacking and security. The best thing about these tools is that they provide anonymity for the hacker and they provide an outside view of your network for the network administrator. The drawback is that the really good tools get so many complaints from people getting scanned that they usually do not last long. As a result, it seems like most of the online tools sites do not do much more than trace routes and DNS lookups. Nonetheless, the tools are out there if you know how to find them (and keep finding them when they die).

The Hacker's Toolkit

As you begin to build your toolkit, you should consider how you install each tool. By default, many Windows-based installation programs want to install to the Program Files directory. The problem with that is that every time you reinstall Windows, you will often have to reinstall all your programs as well. The better solution is to have a directory dedicated to your tools. After installing a tool, figure out what support files it uses (such as .dll or .ocx files) and place them all in the same directory as the program. This defeats the purpose of having shared Windows components, but it does make your tools directory more self-contained and portable. Administrators can use the depends.exe program to locate the supporting .dll and .ocx files that are required by an .exe file to accomplish creating a tool directory. depends.exe is installed with the Windows 2000 Resource Kit or Visual Studio 6.0.

One thing that can be a nuisance with console tools is that they must be located in a directory that is in your PATH environment variable for them to be run from any command prompt. However, you do not want to put too many directories in the PATH environment variable because that can affect performance. To deal with this, you might want to create a directory below your toolkit directory that is included in the PATH variable. Place copies of your most common tools in that directory, so that you can launch them as needed. This common directory is also a good place to put batch files and scripts as you collect or build them.

It is important to remember to protect your tools directory by making sure you are the only one with permissions to those files. If someone is attacking your own computer, you certainly do not want to give them the advantage of having your entire hacking toolkit.

One other significant tool that we have not mentioned so far is *information*. As you go about learning and developing your hacking skills, you will gather documents, essays, tutorials, URL links, and other reference material. You might find that your hacking toolkit directory is a good place to organize this material by subject. Having all your tools and information in a central location just makes you that much better a hacker.

Finding Tools

There are countless hacking tools and hacking tool Web sites on the Internet. Finding the tool is not the hard part; it's finding a good tool that is difficult. There are some very good tools on the Internet, but there are also just as many tools that are totally worthless. Being able to find tools is only half the battle. You certainly do not want to fill your toolkit up with junk.

One tip for finding tools is to pay close attention to what other hackers and security experts are recommending. Just make sure that they are recommending it because they actually use it, not just because they heard about it from someone else. Every hacker (and security expert) has a core set of favorite tools they use on a daily basis. Find out what those tools are because they will usually be the best tools.

Another tip is to look for old DOS freeware collections. These sites usually contain superb console-based tools that have long since been forgotten in the age of Windows. See `http://dosware.nfo.sk/` for some useful batch file utilities. Still another place to look is with Internet server packages. For example, many DNS and Mail servers install a number of useful console diagnostic utilities that turn out to be just as useful for hacking. Resource kits and development kits from Microsoft are always packed full of often-overlooked networking and Windows 2000 utilities. Spend the time to discover what is in each of those kits.

You should also closely monitor all the standard security and hacking tool sites on the Internet. Usually when a tool is released, it makes it to those sites first.

NOTE

The following are some of the bigger tool sites to monitor:

`http://www.securityfocus.com`

`http://packetstorm.security.com`

`http://neworder.box.sk`

No matter how you look for the tools, never stop looking. New tools are created every day, so you should be out there looking for them every day.

What to Look For

When looking for tools, there are certain characteristics and features that you should watch for. Some tools might seem useful, but that does not mean they will be well-suited for a hacker's toolkit. Some features you should watch for are

- Stealthiness
- Size
- Portability
- Speed

Tool Stealthiness

One thing that distinguishes script kiddies from real hackers is that script kiddie attacks are so easily detected by the tools they use. Many tools out there generate so much network traffic and produce so many log file entries that even beginner administrators will recognize the attack. Some security auditing tools were created for auditing networks and do so quite well, but these tools were meant to audit your own systems and therefore are not very stealthy, in other words their actions are not easily hidden. These tools make no attempt to conceal their actions and are easily detected on the other end. There are also a number of freeware CGI scanners available, but using one of those scanners could easily produce several hundred Web server log entries. And in a Web server log, several hundred HTTP 404 File Not Found errors will stand out like a sore thumb.

What follows is a small portion of a Web log after being scanned with the CGI scanning tool Whisker (`http://sourceforge.net/projects/whisker`):

```
2001-08-20 15:36:07 10.220.10.1 GET /Default.htm - 200
2001-08-20 15:36:07 10.220.10.1 GET /cgi-bin/aglimpse - 404
2001-08-20 15:36:07 10.220.10.1 GET /cgi-bin/AnyForm2 - 404
```

```
2001-08-20 15:36:07 10.220.10.1 GET /cgi-dos/args.bat - 404
2001-08-20 15:36:07 10.220.10.1 GET /scripts/iisadmin/bdir.htr - 404
2001-08-20 15:36:07 10.220.10.1 GET /cgi-bin/campas - 404
2001-08-20 15:36:07 10.220.10.1 GET /carbo.dll - 404
2001-08-20 15:36:07 10.220.10.1 GET /cgi-bin/Count.cgi - 404
2001-08-20 15:36:07 10.220.10.1 GET /cgi-bin/faxsurvey - 404
2001-08-20 15:36:07 10.220.10.1 GET /cgi-bin/finger - 404
2001-08-20 15:36:08 10.220.10.1 GET /cgi-bin/handler - 404
2001-08-20 15:36:08 10.220.10.1 GET /cgi-bin/htmlscript - 404
2001-08-20 15:36:08 10.220.10.1 GET /cgi-bin/jj - 404
2001-08-20 15:36:08 10.220.10.1 GET /cgi-bin/man.sh - 404
2001-08-20 15:36:08 10.220.10.1 GET /cgi-bin/nph-test-cgi - 404
2001-08-20 15:36:08 10.220.10.1 GET /cgi-bin/pfdispaly.cgi - 404
2001-08-20 15:36:08 10.220.10.1 GET /cgi-bin/phf - 404
2001-08-20 15:36:08 10.220.10.1 GET /cgi-bin/php.cgi - 404
2001-08-20 15:36:08 10.220.10.1 GET /search97.vts - 404
2001-08-20 15:36:09 10.220.10.1 GET /cgi-bin/test-cgi - 404
2001-08-20 15:36:09 10.220.10.1 GET /cgi-bin/textcounter.pl - 403
2001-08-20 15:36:09 10.220.10.1 GET /cgi-win/uploader.exe - 404
2001-08-20 15:36:09 10.220.10.1 GET /cgi-bin/view-source - 404
2001-08-20 15:36:09 10.220.10.1 GET /cgi-bin/webdist.cgi - 404
2001-08-20 15:36:09 10.220.10.1 GET /cgi-bin/webgais - 404
2001-08-20 15:36:09 10.220.10.1 GET /cgi-bin/websendmail - 404
2001-08-20 15:36:09 10.220.10.1 GET /cgi-bin/www-sql - 404
2001-08-20 15:36:09 10.220.10.1 GET /mall_log_files/order.log - 404
2001-08-20 15:36:10 10.220.10.1 GET /quikstore.cfg - 404
2001-08-20 15:36:10 10.220.10.1 GET /orders/mountain.cfg - 404
2001-08-20 15:36:10 10.220.10.1 GET /orders/orders.txt - 404
2001-08-20 15:36:10 10.220.10.1 GET /Admin_files/order.log - 404
2001-08-20 15:36:10 10.220.10.1 GET /cfdocs/expeval/openfile.cfm - 404
2001-08-20 15:36:10 10.220.10.1 GET /_vti_pvt/authors.pwd - 403
2001-08-20 15:36:10 10.220.10.1 GET /_vti_pvt/service.pwd - 403
2001-08-20 15:36:11 10.220.10.1 GET /_vti_pvt/users.pwd - 403
2001-08-20 15:36:11 10.220.10.1 GET /iisadmpwd/ - 404
2001-08-20 15:36:11 10.220.10.1 GET /iissamples/ - 404
2001-08-20 15:36:11 10.220.10.1 GET /iisadmin/ - 404
2001-08-20 15:36:11 10.220.10.1 GET /iishelp/ - 404
2001-08-20 15:36:11 10.220.10.1 GET /msadc/samples/ - 404
```

3

THE HACKER
TOOLKIT

As you can see, not only do the log entries stand out because of all the 404s, the requests are somewhat alphabetical and they are all submitted within a few seconds of each other. When checking out a tool, be sure you know what kind of traffic and log file entries it will generate. If there is no way of avoiding the traffic and log entries, the tool should at least have an option to perform the scan very slowly and should have support for proxy servers to help avoid tracing the scan back to you.

Tool Size

When it comes to hacking, the smaller your tools, the better. Because you will normally want to move your tools onto remote computers, you want to find the smallest tools for the job. Sometimes, having plentiful features is good, but sometimes a more trimmed-down tool is more appropriate for the job. Many tools have source code available. If so, you might be able to go through and rip out unnecessary code to make it smaller. You should also use executable compression utilities (explained later in the chapter) to bring your tools down in size.

Tool Portability

If you are installing a tool on a remote computer, you normally do not have the luxury to run a graphical installation program to get the tool installed. You should select tools that can easily be transported to other computers. Pick those tools that do not require a bunch of support files, and especially try to avoid those that require runtime modules or a script interpreter.

Tool Speed

Obviously, you always want your software to run as quickly as possible, but in the case of hacking tools, a fast tool can make a huge difference. For example, if you are cracking passwords, a tool that cracks an extra 100,000 passwords per second could potentially cut days off a brute-force attack. But keep in mind that speed is not always good. As I mentioned earlier, you also want to watch for tools that you can slow down if necessary.

Tools for Your Tools

Sometimes having good tools is not enough. There are tools out there that can enhance your tools in one way or another. These tools for your tools fall into various categories:

- Compilers, Interpreters, and Runtimes
- Compressors
- Converters
- Encryptors
- Hex Editors
- Chainers and Wrappers
- Virus Scanners

NOTE

Most of these tools (along with other categories) can be found at `http://www.suddendischarge.com`.

Compilers, Interpreters, and Runtimes

If you are going to be putting together a toolkit, you are going to need a compiler at some point. Many good hacking tools are distributed as source code and must be compiled before they can be used. You should have compilers for the most common languages, such as C, C++, Assembly, Delphi, and Visual Basic. Some of these compilers are free, but others you must buy. You should also try to keep on-hand script interpreters, such as Windows Scripting Host, Perl, and TCL. Finally, many executables require runtimes to work properly. You should collect the most common runtime modules because you will most likely need them.

Executable Compressors

Executable compressors perform compression and optimization on an executable to make it use less disk space. This makes it easier to transport a tool to a remote location or allows you to fit more tools onto a floppy disk. Compressors add code to the executable to make the decompression process transparent so the tool can run normally without any manual intervention. Compressors normally do not cause any problems with the executable and add little performance overhead, so it is usually worth the effort to compress all of your most common tools.

What follows is a directory listing of the tool Netcat before and after compression:

```
01/03/1998  03:37p          59,392 nc.exe
01/03/1998  03:37p          30,208 nc.compressed.exe
```

As you can see, the size of the compressed executable file is nearly half the size of the original, with hardly any loss of performance.

Another example of an effective compression tool is Petite, available at `http://www.un4seen.com/petite/`. Petite provides both a GUI and command line version of the utility that can be used as a shell extension in Windows Explorer or in the Visual C++ compilation process.

Encryptors

Sometimes, you must conceal the contents of your tools. For example, if you place a Trojan on a remote computer, you might want to evade detection by a virus scanner, or you might want to conceal what the tools actually do, if ever discovered. For that, you will need a good executable encryptor. An *executable encryptor* is a tool that encrypts a program and adds code to unencrypt the program when run. Like compressors, encryptors run transparently and are unencrypted automatically. Some encryptors also allow you to require a password to run the program, protecting it even further. An example of an encryptor program is Stealth Encryptor, available at `http://www.tropsoft.com/stealth/`. This is an encryption tool that will encrypt files for personal privacy or malicious tasks.

Converters

Converters change a tool from one format to another. These tools might convert a batch file to an executable, a .com file to an .exe file, or an executable to an ASCII format. Sometimes, the format of your tool needs to be changed for one reason or another. These tools accommodate that change. For example, suppose that you want to send a binary executable file to a remote computer via a URL. Because URL's cannot contain binary data, you can convert the executable to ASCII instead and then include it without any problems.

Hex Editors

Hex editors are tools that allow you to edit the contents of a binary file in its native format. One particular use for a hex editor is to use it to change hard-coded strings in a tool. For example, a tool might send a packet that includes a string that might trigger an intrusion detection system on a remote computer. To avoid that, you can open the tool in a hex editor and modify the string as needed.

Chainers and Wrappers

Chainers are tools that combine several executables into a single file. They are called chainers because when the file is executed, each individual file that was included is run in sequence. A wrapper is a tool that takes a command, along with any command-line parameters and other input, and wraps it into a single executable. For example, to get the NetCat tool to run as a remote command prompt, see the following command-line syntax:

```
Nc.exe -v -L -p 23 -t -e cmd.exe
```

However, with a wrapper, one could take the executable along with all the arguments and execute it with a single command. The usefulness of this is that sometimes, when trying to execute a remote command through a Web server or using the Scheduler service, extra parameters can make things a bit more difficult.

Virus Scanners

Knowing how hackers are, it is always a good idea to check out a tool before first running it. There are a number of commercial and freeware virus scanners that will do the job very well.

Another technique is to set up some kind of packet filtering firewall or network monitor to see if any data is being sent from your computer. See Chapter 10, "Trojans and Backdoors," for more information on Trojans.

Building Tools

Although there are many hacking tools publicly available, you might not be able to find the right tools at times. Or you might be able to find the tools out there, but you find that you need something that you can tweak if necessary. In those cases, it is often better if you can just build your own custom tools. Sure, building tools requires extra knowledge of scripting or programming, but those are skills that are indispensable to both hackers and system administrators.

Scripting Your Own Tools

Scripts are sets of instructions that are processed by a command or script interpreter. Scripting languages are fairly easy to learn and are often available on most platforms. The complexity of the scripting language determines how long it takes to learn, but also largely determines how much can be done with it. There are several types of scripting languages, ranging from simple batch files to full-blown script interpreters.

Batch Files

Batch files are nothing more than a series of console commands saved in a text file that execute as if they were typed at a command prompt. Batch files add some looping and conditional processing capabilities that you cannot accomplish at a command prompt. Although batch files are somewhat limited, they can be very powerful. Learning how to write batch files is an important skill for both the hacker and the administrator.

Windows Scripting Host

Windows Scripting Host (WSH) is a script interpreter included with Windows 2000. WSH scripts are far more powerful than batch files, but require more effort to learn. By default, WSH supports scripts written in VBScript and JScript, but support can be added for languages such as PerlScript, TCL, Python, and others.

WSH is a powerful language that can automate hacking as well as administration activities. It is fairly easy to learn and is somewhat extensible through COM objects. It is also well-suited for working with remote systems.

The following code is a VBScript example that displays the current user, computer name, and domain:

```
Dim objNet
Set objNet=CreateObject("WScript.Network")
```

```
wscript.echo "Username:    " & objNet.UserName & vbcrlf & _
             "Workstation: " & objNet.ComputerName & vbcrlf & _
             "Domain:      " & objNet.UserDomain
```

VBScript is useful in enough situations that it is well worth the effort to at least learn the basics of how to use it. If you are hacking a Windows 2000 server, VBScript tools are nice because you know the remote system will already have WSH installed. Even though WSH is installed by default, it's not always a safe bet that the Windows Script Host will be enabled. Due to the recent outbreak of viruses exploiting VBScript files, some administrators have disabled the file associations in Windows Explorer that link files with .vbs, .vbe, .js, and .jse extensions with the script engine.

Perl

Perl is a language that has its roots in Unix-based environments but has been gaining much support from Windows NT and 2000 administrators. With the proper modules installed, Perl can do just about anything that can be accomplished with any other programming language. Perl is a powerful language that is well-suited for network applications, and Perl scripts often run unmodified on a number of applications. Perl has a large user base, so finding code samples on the Internet is not much work.

Perl is an elegant and powerful programming language, but it is a bit complex and, therefore, takes some effort to learn. But once mastered, it is a great language for building hacking tools.

Other Scripting Languages

There are many other scripting languages available that can be helpful. Each one has its strengths and weaknesses. Some languages are more suitable for specific tasks than others. For example, some languages are well suited for Windows networking tasks, while others are better suited for TCP/IP communication. It is important to know the strengths and weaknesses of each scripting language.

Building Compiled Tools

Although scripting languages are very powerful, some things can only be accomplished with a full programming language. Compiled applications have the benefit of being portable, fast, and standalone (with the exception of occasionally requiring runtime support files). Compiled tools also have the added benefit of not revealing your source code if you want to distribute your tools. One disadvantage of compiled programs is that if poorly designed, they can crash and potentially affect system stability. Some examples of languages that can produce compiled executables are

- C and C++
- Visual Basic

- Delphi
- Assembly Language

One drawback of compiled tools is that they will only run on the operating system for which they were compiled.

The Basic Tools

While making your own tools is an important skill, it's certainly easier to just collect the tools that others have already built. There are thousands of tools available, so this list is hardly a representation of what is out there. It is nothing more than a small sampling of tools that I have discovered myself. Table 3.1 lists some of these tools.

TABLE 3.1   Basic Hacking Tools

Tool	Tool Information
Fscan	Developer: Foundstone, Inc. Licensing: Freeware Location: `http://www.foundstone.com` Description: Although there are port scanners out there with more features, FScan is a very fast command-line port scanner and is by far my personal favorite.
John the Ripper	Developer: Solar Designer Location: `http://www.openwall.com/john` Licensing: Freeware Description: Although originally a Unix password cracker, John now cracks NT LanMan password hashes. John's best features are that it is extremely fast and has flexible rules syntax.

TABLE 3.1 Continued

Tool	Tool Information
L0phtCrack	Developer: L0pht Heavy Industries Location: `http://www.securitysoftwaretech.com` Licensing: Demo Description: Probably the most useful Windows password cracking tool. Includes the ability to dump passwords from remote systems, as well as grab them by sniffing the network. Besides being costly, L0phtcrack also has the disadvantage of not being easy to install and run on a remote system.
lsadump2	Developer: Todd Sabin Location: `http://razor.bindview.com` Licensing: Freeware Description: An essential tool for dumping the contents of the LSA secrets on a system once you have Administrator access.
Netcat	Developer: Weld Pond Location: `http://www.atstake.com` Licensing: Freeware Description: A self-proclaimed TCP/IP Swiss Army knife. A reliable tool that you will use frequently.
PipeUpSam	Developer: Maceo Location: `http://www.dogmile.com` Licensing: Freeware Description: A tool that exploits the "Service Control Manager Named Pipe Impersonation" vulnerability (MS00-053) to dump the hashes from the local SAM database. Does not require Administrator access.
Pwdump2	Developer: Todd Sabin Location: `http://razor.bindview.com` Licensing: Freeware Description: Another excellent tool from Todd Sabin that dumps the password hashes from the SAM database whether or not `SYSKEY` is installed.
SolarWinds Management and Discovery Tools	Developer: SolarWinds.net, Inc. Location: `http://www.solarwinds.net` Licensing: Demo Description: A fast and capable set of scanning tools useful for sweeping ranges of IP address for DNS and SNMP information.

TABLE 3.1 Continued

Tool	Tool Information
SuperScan	Developer: Foundstone, Inc. Licensing: Freeware Location: `http://www.foundstone.com` Description: Another excellent port scanner from Foundstone. This one works as fast as FScan but offers a Windows interface.
ToWhom	Developer: Xato Network Security, Inc. Location: `http://www.xato.net` Licensing: Freeware Description: A tool similar to the WhoIs utility but that also allows lookups by IP address.
Whisker	Developer: rfp.labs Licensing: Freeware Location: `http://www.wiretrip.net/rfp` Description: An extremely useful CGI scanner written in Perl. Works well on multiple platforms and can be customized with little effort.

Summary

This chapter has introduced the reader to the hacker's toolkit. There are a variety of tools that are a part of the toolkit, including Windows-based, command-line tools scripts and custom code. The ability to combine these tools and use them effectively is also another component in the toolkit that the hacker must develop on his or her own. Understanding programming and scripting languages is also another essential skill that both hackers and administrators should develop.

A list of tools has been provided in this chapter that will hopefully expand your own toolset. Many of the remaining chapters in this book discuss methods that help administrators protect their networks from attacks. Consider using the tools provided in this chapter to test the security of your own systems as you tighten their access.

Windows 2000 Server Security Basics

PART
II

IN THIS PART

Hacking Windows 2000: Getting Started

IN THIS CHAPTER

Although there are many who would prefer that I not teach people how to hack Windows 2000, learning how to hack is a positive step toward making your network more secure. One could not possibly expect to be able to protect a network when unfamiliar with the tools and techniques being used every day by both skilled and unskilled hackers. My belief is that the better hacker you are, the better your own security is.

Recently, I was involved in an incident response job where an e-commerce site was hacked. The client called me explaining that one of the network administrators noticed some new files on the system, and that the owner of those folders was the Internet user account. I immediately suspected that someone had used the IIS Unicode attack against the client's e-commerce site's Web server. The IIS Unicode exploit allows an attacker to enter a particular URL into any Web browser and execute commands on the IIS Web server. I have performed the exploit many times myself, because it is an excellent demonstration I can do for my clients. I know that the command prompt will run with the limited permissions of the Internet user account, and any directories created using that exploit will show the Internet user account as the owner. It turned out that the files on the system were some of my favorite hacking tools that I would have used if I were hacking that system. Clearly, knowing how I would have hacked that system gave me insight as to what the real hacker had done.

Consider the following advantages of openly teaching people how to hack:

- System administrators are better able to identify unusual activity on their network.
- Software vendors are better able to fix flaws in their software.
- Software vendors are better able to learn from the mistakes of others.
- The balance of knowledge is no longer on the side of the hackers.

There is just no better way to protect your network than to learn how people are hacking it. Every exploit mentioned in this book can be avoided with a good security policy and proper network configuration. Since the beginning of time, people have had the belief that suppressing information will make us a moral society, but immorality has always found its way. The same is true with hacking. The information on how to hack is already widespread, except, up until now, it was only in the hands of the bad guys. This is no longer the case. Information security philosophy now subscribes to the concept that releasing information regarding vulnerabilities is better than withholding it.

The people who will appreciate this approach are the people who look to see where the security cameras are when they enter a bank, but will never rob one, and the people who have figured out the formula for the codes on their phone card but have never committed phone fraud. Not the least, it is for those who took apart most of the household electronics in their home before they were eight.

This chapter will teach you how to hack a system by exposing its weaknesses and taking the system apart, one piece at a time, to expose potential weak security spots. The concepts and methods used in this chapter can be used to hack Windows 2000, as well as other operating systems. If you are a network administrator, this information will make you a better administrator. On the other hand, if you have no interest in security but just want to learn how to hack Windows 2000, this chapter will benefit you also.

Finding Networks

The first step in hacking is to find something to hack. Many script kiddies will randomly scan large blocks of addresses just to find vulnerable servers. More skilled hackers, who might be looking for something in particular, will scan a targeted list of networks. The most dedicated hackers (and perhaps the most dangerous) will target a specific company in search of something specific that company has or to cause some form of damage to that company. This last category of hacking is the role we will assume in this chapter.

To hack a company, you must first know what IP addresses it is using. Many companies will locate their Web server with a third-party hosting or collocation company and have a totally separate network that goes to their offices. Some hackers might want to attack the Web server, but a better approach is to track down the company's home network where it is probably most vulnerable.

The process of finding networks is relatively straightforward:

- Lookup the IP addresses of known servers.
- Discover other DNS names and look up their IP addresses.
- Discover if the company has IP addresses registered in its name.
- Scan ranges of IP addresses to discover the associated DNS names.
- Discover if the company owns other domain names.

Looking Up IP Addresses

Domain Name System (DNS) is the system on the Internet that translates a DNS name, such as `www.microsoft.com`, to an IP address, such as `207.46.230.219`. The reason for this process is that DNS names make more sense to humans, but IP addresses are necessary for one computer to know how to contact another. As a hacker, knowing IP addresses is important, because most companies have a contiguous block of IP addresses assigned to their network. If you can discover one IP address in that block, it's not difficult to discover the extent of a company's network.

We begin the network discovery process by looking up DNS names to get their corresponding IP addresses. Looking up addresses can be accomplished with the `NSLookup.exe` tool that is included in both Windows 2000 Professional and Server. DNS lookups can be done from a Windows 2000 command prompt as follows:

```
C:\>Nslookup www.got-hacked.net
Server:  ns.got-hacked.net
Address:  10.83.155.2
Name:     www.got-hacked.net
Address:  10.83.155.3
```

In this example, when someone wants to browse to `http://www.got-hacked.net`, the computer will perform a DNS lookup and return the IP address associated with this URL. You will usually know at least the Web address of a company, so you can start by looking up that address. You might also know other common addresses, such as FTP and e-mail addresses. You can begin to look up each of these name sources and begin to compile a list of known IP addresses. But keep in mind that just because a DNS name resolves to an IP address does not mean that the IP address will resolve back to the same DNS name. An IP address can have several DNS records pointing to it. Sometimes, the name you get on a reverse DNS lookup can give you some insight to the victim's network configuration, as in the following example:

```
C:\>nslookup mail.got-hacked.net
Server:  ns.got-hacked.net
Address:  10.83.155.2
Name:     mail.got-hacked.net
Address:  10.83.155.1
C:\>nslookup 10.83.155.1
Server:  ns.got-hacked.net
Address:  10.83.155.2
Name:     gateway.got-hacked.net
Address:  10.83.155.1
```

Looking at those results, we see that the DNS name `mail.got-hacked.net` maps to the address `10.83.155.1`, but that same address, when looked up, maps to `gateway.got-hacked.net`. What this confirms for us about the victim network is that they are most likely protected by a firewall. The firewall is most likely the `gateway.got-hacked.net` server. That firewall is either hosting the mail server, which is quite unlikely, or it's proxying the mail communication from the Internet to the mail server behind the firewall. We can continue to confirm our suspicion with further NSLOOKUP commands for the company Web server and other Internet services they might provide. If they all point back at the 10.83.155.1 address, we would be safe to say our suspicion is correct. Something we still don't know is where the mail server is located. The mail server could be located on a DMZ network or on the internal network with other servers we might want to break into.

NOTE

A DNS name can also have multiple addresses assigned to it. This is referred to as *round-robin DNS*. When one DNS name points to multiple IP addresses, the DNS server will load balance the network traffic by alternating which address to which the DNS name points. To see a round robin in action, try performing an NSLOOKUP on a well-known URL, such as `www.microsoft.com` as shown next. What you will see is a list of many IP addresses all linked to the WWW record for `microsoft.com`. The DNS server will return a different IP address for each name looked up for the WWW record. This will provide load balancing between the Web servers.

```
C:\>nslookup www.microsoft.com
Server:  ns.coneth.com
Address:  192.168.1.3

Non-authoritative answer:
Name:    www.microsoft.akadns.net
Addresses:  207.46.197.100, 207.46.230.218, 207.46.197.102, 207.46.230.220
Aliases:  www.microsoft.com
```

Discovering DNS Names

By now, you should have at least a few IP addresses on your list, but those addresses are public knowledge and the most obvious addresses to attack. To discover other DNS names for a company, you must do a little more digging through a process known as a zone transfer.

A *zone transfer* is a method that name servers use to synchronize their DNS data. However, if it is not properly secured, a DNS server will dump all DNS information for a domain—including private DNS information—to anyone who asks for it. This gives the hacker a big advantage and is a great place to start looking for DNS names.

Most organizations that are concerned with security do specify the systems allowed to request zone transfers, but there are still many open DNS servers on the Internet. Those network administrators with the benefit of an IDS system should monitor zone transfers on their DNS servers on TCP port 53 to prevent against attack. Refer to Chapter 15, "Protecting Other Internet Services," for information on securing Windows 200 DNS servers.

To perform a zone transfer, we will use two tools starting with `host.exe`.

`host.exe` is a tool used to query a name server for DNS information. When used with the `-a` option, it will dump all information about the domain, including the record count and all records. Using the `ls` command with the `-d` switch (dump all records to screen) from the

NSLOOKUP utility will provide similar output if you do not have access to the `host.exe` utility. The output from the `host.exe -a` command is as follows:

```
C:\>host -a got-hacked.net
Using domain server 10.102.18.1
Trying null domain
rcode = 0 (Success), ancount=5
got-hacked.net       3600 IN A        10.102.18.150
got-hacked.net       3600 IN MX       10 mail.got-hacked.net
Additional information:
ns1.got-hacked.net     3600 IN A        10.102.18.1
ns2.got-hacked.net     3600 IN A        10.102.18.2
lab2.got-hacked.net    3600 IN A        10.102.18.14
mail.got-hacked.net    3600 IN A        10.102.18.100
you.got-hacked.net     3600 IN A        10.102.18.41
```

By default, `host.exe` will query the local name server. However, your local name server will not have the information for an outside domain you might want to hack. To get that information, you must use another tool, nslookup.exe, which is included with Windows 2000. By using the `set` command, you can request that only NS or name server records be returned. After you have the name server records, use the `set` command again to ask for the A records for the name servers. The query for the A records will then return the IP addresses for the name servers. See the following syntax on how to use NSLOOKUP to locate the name server IP addresses:

```
C:\>nslookup
> set type=NS
> got-hacked.net
Non-authoritative answer:
got-hacked.net   nameserver = ns1.got-hacked.net
got-hacked.net   nameserver = ns2.got-hacked.net
> set type=A
> ns1.got-hacked.net
Server:  [192.168.1.3]
Address:  192.168.1.3
Name:    ns1.got-hacked.
Address:  10.102.18.1
```

After finding the name server address, add it to the command line as follows:

```
C:\>host -a got-hacked.net 10.102.18.1
```

This will allow you to see all the DNS records from any domain that allows zone transfers. However, some domains do not allow zone transfers, but they still must allow name lookups.

In that case, some smart guessing will sometimes turn up a few names. This is also where the tool Shat comes into play.

Shat is a tool that will take a list of common hostnames (such as www or FTP names) and query the DNS server until it finds a match. The tool will go through as many DNS names as are provided in the hostnames.txt file that is included with Shat. People are predictable, so this type of attack is actually quite effective in discovering new names. For example, if a company has a router on its network, it will normally name it *router*, as in router.example.net.

> **NOTE**
>
> To locate a copy of host.exe visit http://bind8nt.meiway.com/ download.cfm and download the ISC BIND 8.2.4 for NT4/W2K: DNS Utilities. To get a copy of Shat, visit http://www.xato.net.

Discover Registered IP Addresses

After you have a number of IP addresses, you should check to see who actually owns them. This can be done one of several ways. One method is to query the whois search engine located at http://www.arin.net. Another method is to use the previously mentioned ToWhom.exe tool.

When passed an IP address, ToWhom.exe will do a reverse lookup to determine the owner of that address. For example, if we determine that the address www.networksolutions.com is located at 216.168.224.69, we would enter the following command:

```
C:\>towhom.exe 216.168.224.69
Network Solutions, Inc. (NETBLK-NSI-NETBLK1) NSI-NETBLK1
                    6.168.224.0 - 216.168.255.255
```

If you use the Web-based whois search at http://www.arin.net, you can enter a company name and determine what IP addresses are registered in its name.

For example, if you enter a query for Federal Bureau of Investigation, you get the following results:

```
Federal Bureau of Investigation (NET-FBI) FBI
                    205.229.233.0 - 205.229.233.255
Federal Bureau of Investigation - CJIS (NET-ITN) ITN
                        153.31.0.0 - 153.31.255.255
Federal Bureau of Investigation - FBI Academy (NET-NCAVC) NCAVC
                        192.84.170.0 - 192.84.170.255
Federal Bureau of Investigation - FBI Laboratory (NET-CHEMTOX) CHEMTOX
198.190.209.0 - 198.190.209.255
```

By looking at the preceding results, we can see four distinct blocks of IP addresses, none of which are in the same block as the FBI's Web site:

```
c:\>nslookup www.fbi.gov
Non-authoritative answer:
Name:    www.fbi.gov
Address:  32.96.111.130
```

Scanning IP Ranges

Most TCP port scanners will also return DNS names of the addresses that they scan. By looking at the DNS results, you can usually determine the extent of the network you are targeting. Scanning ranges of IP addresses also fills in all those blanks that you have not already figured out up to this point.

```
C:\>fscan -qne 192.168.1.1-254
The -qne options are described in the help as follows:
-q     - quiet mode, do not ping host before scan
-n     - no port scanning - only pinging (unless you use -q)
-e     - resolve IP addresses to hostnames
```

The interesting thing about these command-line options is that you are telling the fscan command not to ping the host and to not perform any port scanning either. In other words, you are not doing anything other than looking up the DNS names of each address in that range. No packets will actually be sent to any of the IP addresses listed on the command. You can download the fscan.exe port scanner from Foundstone at http://www.foundstone.com.

Discovering Other Domains

With a little searching, you can sometimes determine other domains that a company owns. By looking at whois records, you will often see that one or more of the contacts have a different domain. For example, consider this portion of a whois record for example.com:

```
Registrant:
Internet Assigned Numbers Authority (EXAMPLE-DOM)
   4676 Admiralty Way, Suite 330
   Marina del Rey, CA 90292
   US
   Domain Name: EXAMPLE.COM
   Administrative Contact, Technical Contact, Billing Contact:
      Internet Assigned Numbers Authority  (IANA)   iana@IANA.ORG
```

If you look at this record, you will see that example.com is, in fact, owned by IANA.ORG. If you look up example.net and example.org, you will see that they too are owned by IANA. The logic behind this is that a company usually must have an e-mail address when it registers its domain, so it uses an address for a domain other than the one it is registering.

Using these techniques, you can often map out a good portion of a company's public network. As you play around, you will find other ways of discovering IP addresses and DNS names.

Consider the following potential sources of IP addresses and DNS names:

- Logfiles and other statistics
- Partners and Web developers
- E-mail headers
- HTTP referrer headers
- Search engines

Finding Windows 2000 Servers

After you have determined what networks you will be targeting, you can begin to determine which of those IP addresses are assigned to Windows 2000 systems. There are several ways to find out if a system is running Windows 2000.

If the victim system is running a Web server, you can look at the HTTP Server header for the Web site to discover the operating system used on the server. This can be accomplished using the NetCat tool, seen as nc in the following command:

```
C:\>ping | nc www.got-hacked.net 80 | Find /i "Server"
Server: Microsoft-IIS/5.0
```

The reason for piping ping into nc.exe is because the output results of ping contain an extra carriage return that causes the Web server to respond with the correct host headers. Responses that return Microsoft-IIS/5.0 are Windows 2000 servers.

Perhaps a better way to discover what a Web server is running is to visit http://www.netcraft.com. Netcraft collects statistics on Web server software and has a form to query what a particular site is running.

In a similar manner, checking FTP and Mail server banners could reveal the operating system. But if a system is not running any of these services, sometimes a port scan will reveal the operating system.

Table 4.1 is a list of TCP port signatures that you will see on various Windows operating systems.

TABLE 4.1 TCP Ports Signatures by Operating System

Operating System	TCP Port Signatures						
	135	139	389	445	464	593	636
Windows 95		X					
Windows 98		X					
Windows 98SE	X	X					
Windows NT4	X	X					
Windows 2000	X	X		X			
Windows 2000 Domain Controller	X	X	X	X	X	X	X

Based on this chart, you can get a good idea what operating systems exist on a network by scanning for a few basic ports. But keep in mind that this process will not be perfect. Depending on the system configuration, it might have more or fewer ports open than listed in Table 4.1. Furthermore, some ports might be blocked by firewalls and packet filtering software.

Another way to identify the operating system is by using the OS fingerprinting features of NMAP, which is available for download at http://www.insecure.org. NMAP is a Linux port scanning utility that can be used to identify the operating system type. Many great hacking tools are only available for Linux, so it's a must to master both Linux and Windows 2000 to become a master hacker.

Finally, a very good way to identify operating systems is by using Simple Network Management Protocol (SNMP). SNMP is a protocol that uses UDP port 161, which is rarely blocked at a firewall. To make things worse, Windows 2000 installs with a default community string of public, so that anyone can retrieve information from a system as long as they pass the system a matching community string in the SNMP request.

A community string is a string of characters assigned to the server's SNMP configuration that tells the server to only communicate with other devices over the SNMP protocol that have a matching community string. The string is configured on the system by the administrator, and most organizations never change the default setting of public. Some systems have a read community string and write community string, such as Cisco routers and Novell Netware servers. With these systems, the default read string is public and the default write string is private.

To scan for operating systems using SNMP, I would recommend either using SNMPSweep from SolarWinds.net or the snmputil.exe tool from the Windows 2000 Resource Kit. SNMPSweep is a Windows-based tool that scans a range of IP addresses and returns any SNMP information it is able to collect.

If you prefer doing things from a command prompt, `snmputil.exe` is the way to go. Although the Object Identifier (OID) number is somewhat cryptic, you can write them to a script and not have to remember them. The following command will query the system for its description:

```
snmputil walk 10.250.111.61 public .1.3.6.1.2.1.1.1.
Variable = system.sysDescr.0
Value    = String Hardware: x86 Family 6 Model 8 Stepping 3 AT/AT COMPATIBLE -
➡Software: Windows 2000 Version 5.0 (Build 2195 Uniprocessor Free)
```

By looking at the results of that command, you can see that it gives you plenty of information, including the Windows version and build.

Another way to discover Windows 2000 servers is to use a tool named `nbtscan.exe`. Nbtscan scans for NETBIOS name servers (WINS servers) on a local or remote network. Most Windows networks use WINS to locate network services in routed TCP/IP networks. All systems register themselves in the WINS database, which allows other Windows machines to find servers and services on the network. The `nbtscan` utility is similar to the `nbtstat` utility that is installed on all Windows systems except that `nbtscan` allows the user to pass a range of IP addresses to the command rather that just a single address. The following sample shows `nbtscan` in use:

```
C:\> nbtscan 192.168.1.0/24
192.168.1.3     MTNDEW\WINDEV              SHARING DC
192.168.1.4     MTNDEW\LIZZIE             SHARING
192.168.1.5     MTNDEW\TESTING
192.168.1.9     MTNDEW\WIZ                SHARING U=FRIEDL
```

Notice in the far right column of the output that the command states additional information about the machine. The word SHARING indicates the machine has the Windows File and Print Sharing service loaded. The U= indicates the username that is currently logged onto the system. `nbtscan` will also indicate if the server has IIS, Exchange Server, Domain Controller services, or Lotus Notes running on the server. For documentation and a free download of `nbtscan`, visit `http://www.unixwiz.net/tools/nbtscan.html`.

As you develop your skills, you will begin to discover a number of other ways to track down Windows servers. If you are a system administrator, you should regularly check your network to see how much information it reveals about itself.

Finding Open Services

After you have uncovered a list of Windows 2000 servers, it is time to figure out how to exploit those servers. There are a number of ways to exploit a server, but you should first attempt those that give you the most control with the least effort.

Some services that you might want to exploit are (in order of preference):

- Windows Networking (also known as NetBIOS)
- Web Services
- Terminal Services (or other remote control software)
- Other public Internet services

Windows Networking

Microsoft networking, also known as Windows networking, is what Windows computers use to communicate with each other. Windows networking has been around for some time and many of the peculiarities of protocols, such as NetBIOS, still present security risks on a Windows network. Although we will discuss Windows networking in more detail in Chapter 9, "Network Protocols, Clients, and Services," it is important to know the impact of being able to exploit it.

Essentially, if you can access a server via Windows networking, you have a huge head start on hacking that server. If you have administrator access to even one computer on a network, you can probably exploit that to gain access to the entire network, even if the rest of it is behind a firewall.

Windows networking is obviously the most preferable way to compromise a system and, unfortunately, so many Windows networks are configured incorrectly that they are often the easiest to break into.

Depending on how the servers and domain are configured, the Windows networking ports are identified by TCP ports 139 and 445. Port 139 is the traditional NetBIOS port, whereas port 445 is for Windows networking using native TCP/IP.

The following example demonstrates how to scan or open Windows networking ports using `fscan.exe` (available at `http://www.foundstone.com`):

```
C:\ >fscan -p 139,445 10.146.18.1-254
FScan v1.12 - Command line port scanner.
Copyright 2000 (c) by Foundstone, Inc.
http://www.foundstone.com
 Scan started at Thu Apr 26 07:06:34 2001
10.146.18.39      139/tcp  lab2
10.146.18.39      445/tcp  lab2
10.146.18.56      139/tcp  exchange
10.146.18.56      445/tcp  exchange
10.146.18.102     139/tcp  TestW98
10.146.18.103     139/tcp  TestNT4
10.146.18.104     139/tcp  Win2kPro
10.146.18.104     445/tcp  Win2kPro
 Scan finished at Thu Apr 26 07:06:53 2001
 Time taken: 508 ports in 18.797 secs (27.03 ports/sec)
```

Looking at the results of this scan, we can see that there are several systems open for Windows networking. If we ignore the hostnames of the machines, we can narrow down or determine the OS version based only on the open ports. We can deduce that `lab2 exchange` and `Win2kPro` are Windows 2000 systems because they are listening on TCP port 445. Windows 2000 machines use port 445 to communicate over SMB with machines that do not use NetBT. Only Windows 2000 systems support this feature. `TestW98` and `TestNT4` are not listening on TCP port 445 and are, therefore, either Win9x or Windows NT 4.0 machines. Refer to Chapter 9 for more information on Windows Networking, TCP/IP, and Netbios over TCP/IP (NetBt).

Web Services (IIS)

Internet Information Server (IIS) has traditionally been a problem area for Windows servers. If not configured correctly, IIS can provide numerous entry points to a system. The problem with running a Web server is that you cannot just block the port to a Web Server with a firewall, because you want legitimate traffic to be able to connect to that server. Another problem is that, by default, IIS installs extra samples and ISAPI components that most Web sites do not need. For example, there is the default Web site that is used to show off some of the new features in IIS. Because everyone has a copy of this site, hackers all over the world can scrutinize it. If a breach is made, the same attack can be used on thousands of systems all over the world, because most systems still keep the default Web site enabled. Many IIS exploits have come from attackers hitting those default sites, so, unless you take the time to clean things up, you will most likely be vulnerable to a number of attacks.

Another problem is that when IIS is running, there is no user interface feedback to let the user know it is running. Therefore, it is easy for a user to have IIS running and not realize it. Such a situation would be even more dangerous because if a user does not realize that IIS is running on his machine, he certainly is not going to take the time to keep it patched and review the Web logs. As is often the case, the attacker might very well know more about the system than the user.

IIS can be exploited in a number of ways yielding everything from simple file viewing to full remote command access. If left unpatched and unsecured, it can be as big a problem as having Windows shares exposed to the Internet.

To scan a network for Web services and see what they are running, you can use `fscan.exe` and `what.exe` (available at `http://www.xato.net`). The following syntax is an example command to scan for Web services listening on TCP port 80. The `fscan` command is used to locate servers on the network that respond to port 80, and then the syntax uses the `what.exe` Perl script to determine what network services are running.

```
C:\>for /f "tokens=1,2*" %i in ('fscan -eq -p 80 10.15.100.1-254') do @what.exe %I
10.15.100.156:  Microsoft-IIS/5.0
10.15.100.159:  Microsoft-IIS/5.0
```

```
10.15.100.160:   Microsoft-IIS/4.0
10.15.100.161:   Apache/1.3.9 (Unix) mod_perl/1.20
10.15.100.178:   Novell-HTTP-Server/3.1R1
10.15.100.180:   Microsoft-IIS/5.0
```

what.exe can also be used to scan one particular host to see what it is running:

```
C:\>what.exe www.microsoft.com
www.microsoft.com:   Microsoft-IIS/5.0
```

Terminal Services

Terminal Services is something that was originally introduced with NT4 as a separate OS version. On Windows 2000, Terminal Services are built in. Terminal Services allow a user to access a Windows 2000 system remotely. In remote administration mode, this can potentially be a very big security risk, especially if someone has already found an administrator password by some other means.

Scanning for open terminal servers is similar to scanning for Windows networking ports:

```
C:\ >fscan -p 3389 10.146.18.1-254
FScan v1.12 - Command line port scanner.
Copyright 2000 (c) by Foundstone, Inc.
http://www.foundstone.com
 Scan started at Thu Apr 26 07:06:34 2001
10.146.18.39      3389/tcp   lab2
10.146.18.39      3389/tcp   lab2
10.146.18.56      3389/tcp   exchange
10.146.18.56      3389/tcp   Win2kPro
```

To connect to a terminal server, you can install the Terminal Services client located at %SystemRoot%\System32\clients\tsclient\ or use the Citrix ICA client (http://www.citrix.com).

Evading Detection

The techniques I have explained so far do not involve much more than port scanning the network you have targeted. Some would consider this to be nothing more than doorknob rattling, while others would consider it an actual intrusion to be reported. As far as the actions described so far being legal, there was a recent court decision where it was decided that because a port scan alone does not result in a compromise of data, it is not illegal. See http://www.securityfocus.com/news/126 by Kevin Poulsen for more information. Either way, if your goal is to compromise a network, you want to leave as few traces of your activity as possible.

One major advantage on the side of the hacker is that Windows 2000 does not have any logging functions for TCP/IP connections. Without third-party software or hardware, all port scans will go unnoticed and never be recorded. At one time, third-party firewall and intrusion detection software was rare on a Windows-based network, but recently, personal firewalls on individual workstations have become more common. Keep this fact in mind, because any packet you send to the target network that gets logged is potential evidence of your activity.

Intrusion detection is the process of watching network traffic in an attempt to recognize intrusion attempts. An intrusion detection system (IDS) is software that automates this process by comparing network traffic to a database of known attack signatures. Although not perfect, IDS software is a tremendous asset in protecting a network.

There are some steps that can be taken to reduce the chances of being detected by an IDS:

- Be familiar with what is logged.
- Bounce, proxy, and relay.
- Go slow at first until you know you are not being watched.
- Watch for tracing.
- Overload the target to hide your tracks.
- Clean up your mess.
- Destroy the credibility of the evidence.

Be Familiar with What Is Logged

Simply put, you cannot avoid being logged if you do not know what is being logged. Get familiar with the system's capabilities to know what is and what is not logged. For example, if you are using a file viewing exploit on IIS, the first file you should view is the current Web log to see how much of your exploit is showing up in the logs. Sure, they might notice strange activity, but they might not be logging extended information, such as parameters passed to scripts and executables.

Bounce, Proxy, and Relay

Bouncing, proxying, and relaying are methods of using one computer on the Internet to perform network operations on your behalf. The effect is that the target will see connections from this other computer and not from yours. This process can involve multiple layers of proxies to further complicate the process of tracking you down. If possible, avoid ever using your own IP address, even to browse to the target's Web site. You might even want to go as far as setting a temporary rule in your firewall to explicitly block traffic to that network to avoid any accidental connections.

Find Web pages that perform port and DNS scans, keeping in mind that they too will probably have logs of your visit. Also, keep an arsenal of resources that you can use to protect your identity. This might involve using hacked Unix shell accounts or Windows Terminal Servers to hide you. Many public Internet servers unknowingly aid thousands of hackers every day in avoiding detection.

> **NOTE**
>
> There are countless ways to conceal your identity through proxying. Visit the Web site `http://www.cotse.com/privres.htm` for further information on these techniques.

Go Slow at First Until You Know You Are Not Being Watched

Evading detection is more than just hiding your IP address. If possible, you do not want network administrators to be alerted of your presence. Performing a full port scan is a quick way to trigger alerts. Before performing a port scan, it is sometimes better to keep the number of connections down at first until you are more confident that the victim administrator does not have intrusion detection software running. The best way to do this is to scan for the most commonly blocked ports to see how they are handled. On a Windows network, the best port to scan is TCP port 139.

Netcat is the ideal tool for simple port probing. To check a port with Netcat, enter a command such as the following:

```
C:\>nc -vz 10.167.92.8 139
example.net [10.167.92.8] 139 (netbios-ssn): connection refused
```

Based on the type of protection the victim administrator has, you will get a variety of results. Some packet filtering systems block unauthorized packets, while others will simply drop them. If the packet is dropped, you will get a TIMEDOUT message as the result. But, if you are lucky, you will get the following message:

```
 (UNKNOWN) [10.167.92.8] 139 (?) open
```

If you see this, connections are not being blocked and perhaps not being logged. It's not a perfect rule, but it's usually a safe bet that if the victim administrator knows enough to log port 139 connections, he or she would also know enough to block them too.

Even as you perform the full port scans, you might want to use the delay features that many scanning utilities have. A very slow port scan is surely more difficult to detect than a very fast one.

There is one interesting aspect of this that you might want to consider. There are so many script kiddies blatantly scanning so many networks that some networks are quick to ignore them. More than once I have seen an administrator react to a port scan alert by saying, "Oh, its just some script kiddie." Perhaps having the ability to look dumb is smarter than looking smart.

Watch for Tracing

When scanning a network, it is important to use intrusion detection software on your end. That way, if a network administrator is alerted to your activity and attempts to discover who you are, you will know about it. For example, you might scan a system and then pick up a `ping` or a `tracert` from that IP address. If you do, chances are that you have been discovered.

Overload the Target to Hide Your Tracks

If you know that the target is running an intrusion detection system, all might not be lost. It is possible to flood the IDS with spoofed intrusion events so that your own attacks are essentially lost in the crowd. If a network administrator is suddenly faced with over a thousand intrusion events in less than thirty seconds, chances are you will be in and out before he has a chance to sort things out. Obviously, this is not a stealthy form of attack, but there are times when you have no other choice.

Spoofed attacks can also help if you have already been detected and you want to affect the credibility of the log files.

Clean Up Your Mess

Despite your best efforts to conceal your actions, some logging will take place. It is important to go back and remove any traces of your activity. This is not always so easy. For example, IIS Web logs cannot be modified until they are cycled, usually every 24 hours. Therefore, it is necessary to leave a back door open so that you can get back into the system the next day to remove those log entries. Some of the back door utilities that can provide continued access are discussed in Chapter 10, "Trojans and Backdoors." Backdoor utilities generally rely on an open port in the firewall to come through so they will not be useful in all situations. Also, many IDS systems scan for the ports used by the common backdoor utilities. Other things to remember are to delete any files you created and change the datestamp of any files that you modified. If you fail to do this, the network administrator can easily pinpoint the date and time you were on the system. It should be noted that file integrity checking systems that use hashes on files, such as Tripwire and centralized logging systems, used on the victim network can foil your clean up attempts.

The bottom line is that unless you make an effort to avoid detection, chances are good that eventually you will get caught. It is easy for a hacker to feel invincible and get lazy. I know hackers who have compromised so many systems that it feels like no one is watching. Most of the time, no one is watching.

Summary

If you are a network administrator, you can try the hacking attempts described in this chapter on your own network systems. Most network administrators would be surprised to find out how easy it is to compromise a system while the victim system's administrator is at the console working on the system.

There are many ways to penetrate a Windows 2000 server. The methods discussed here are only a small introduction to the most common and most dangerous methods. Network administrators must be aware that a separation must be made between a private network and the Internet. Normally that separation is a packet filtering firewall that separates the two. Unfortunately, many Windows systems are connected directly to the Internet with absolutely no protection from the world.

If you own such a system, chances are that your IP addresses will be scanned many times each day. If that system has been unprotected for some time, chances are that it has already been compromised.

Perhaps it takes a good scare to get people to think about security. For many, learning exactly what hackers can do will give them that scare. On the other hand, many network administrators still see this knowledge as damaging to their network and will attempt to suppress it. Nevertheless, hacking will find its way.

Installing Windows 2000: The First Step Toward Security

IN THIS CHAPTER

Some of the biggest mistakes in security are made as early as when the Windows 2000 installation CD-ROM is first placed into the CD-ROM tray. Security preparations need to be made as early as possible, even before you tear the shrink wrap off the Windows 2000 Server packaging. The choices you make at installation will have a long-lasting affect on your server's overall security.

Pre-Installation Considerations

Before installing any Windows 2000 server, you should take a few minutes to plan an installation strategy. The questions you should ask yourself at this point are

- What role will this server play on my network?
- What services will this server need to run?
- What method will be used to install the operating system?
- How will the disks be partitioned?
- Who will have local and remote access to this server?
- How many network interfaces will be required?
- Will the system be standalone or part of a domain?
- Will network protocols beside TCP/IP be required on the system?
- Will the system need to use WINS or DNS for name resolution services?

Knowing the answers to these questions will help you make smart security decisions throughout the installation process. In addition, in the next few sections, you will cover some pre-installation items that need to be considered as you prepare for a Windows 2000 installation. Items such as physical security, scripting, logging your installation, determining server roles, clean installations, installation choices, and file system are sometimes overlooked or not considered heavily, but can provide for more efficient and better-secured installations. Chapters 12, "Security Policy and Configuration," 14, "Protecting Web Services," and 15, "Protecting Other Internet Services," also address strategies and steps to use when hardening the operating system that can be used on both public and privately accessible servers.

Physical Security

One great weakness with Windows 2000 (and most other operating systems) is that if someone gets physical access to the system, he or she will eventually get full access to all the resources on the system. Physical security is the process of securing the physical computer itself. It is a step that's easily overlooked, both at install time and after, but a step that is as important as the rest.

The following are some tips to physically secure the system:

- Install case locks as well as other locks that prevent the system from being removed.
- Put high-security servers in locked cages or locked rooms.
- If possible, eliminate unnecessary removable media.
- Install biometric security devices, such as fingerprint scanners.
- Install physical security devices, such as smart card readers.
- Password protect the system BIOS.

One item that needs further discussion is removable media. Any removable media presents the opportunity for someone to remove media and insert another media, such as a bootable CD-ROM. Simply stated, the person can bypass operating system controls by booting to an alternate operating system on another device. Since the server is now under control of the alternate operating system, access controls set by the original operating system are not enforced. It is preferable to not put any removable media on a sensitive system and instead use portable USB devices to install software or transfer data.

NOTE

Visit `http://home.eunet.no/~pnordahl/ntpasswd/` for an example of how to reset any password on a Windows 2000 system by booting from a Linux boot disk.

Note also that setting a password on the system BIOS really does not do much to secure the system. This is because one can easily reset the password via jumpers on the motherboard. However, that does require having access to the motherboard.

TIP

Also, if you do use a BIOS password, make sure it is only to protect the settings, not to keep the system from booting. If the system reboots at 3 a.m., it might sit there waiting for hours for someone to go up to the console and enter a password.

Installation Scripts and Templates

One good rule to follow is that if you want to do something more than once, it might save you time to make a script for it. A script could include anything from a simple batch file to a complex WSH script. Even if the batch file is nothing more than one or two commands with the proper arguments, it is worth saving. Creating scripts can also be extended into the realm of Windows 2000 installations and the security plan you design for your new installation.

One way scripting can help in a Windows 2000 install is via unattended installation files. During the unattended installation, the setup program receives answers to the Windows 2000 setup questions from a file called unattend.txt that the administrator has pre-configured. You should consider using an unattended installation to keep everything consistent, especially in terms of your security plan. The unattend.txt file is a good place to enforce an installation security strategy and to make sure nothing is overlooked. Included on the CD-ROM is a unattend.txt installation script that installs absolutely nothing but the basic operating system. The unattend.txt file can be modified so it can automatically configure items such as which components are installed, the system name, as well as most Windows 2000 setup options that can be manually configured during setup. The Windows 2000 Resource Kit is also a valuable resource to use to help build unattended installations and set the installation parameters. If the administrator needs to install five or more servers, using an unattended installation can also be a major saver.

Other scripts and templates to consider are as follows:

- Group policy templates
- IPSec policy templates
- Security configuration templates
- Hotfix installation scripts
- IIS configuration scripts
- Post-installation hardening scripts

Many of the Group Policy settings can be configured through the Security Configuration Tool Set covered in Chapter 12. The Security Configuration Tool Set can be used to apply Group Policy and general domain and domain controller policies to standardize the security configuration on the Windows 2000 network. Information on IIS configuration scripts can be found in the Internet Information Server Resource Kit.

Other hardening scripts can be configured manually by the administrator to automate many of the settings covered throughout this book through Registry files (`.reg`), batch files (`.bat`), or other scripting languages supported by WSH. For the latest information on WSH, refer to the Microsoft Developer Network scripting site at `http://www.msdn.microsoft.com/library/default.asp?url=/nhp/Default.asp?contentid=28001169`.

Scripts keep things consistent and eliminate the single greatest obstruction to security—the human factor. Despite our efforts to be a smart species, humans simply make too many mistakes. We do things like lose our car keys and miss our exits on the freeway. We are much better off having a script that will run the same way every time. For example, if the installer sets the local administrator password to "password" during the installation, possibly for convenience purposes, and then forgets to change the local administrator password before putting the system on a public network, it won't be too long before the system is breached. Scripting the password change or at least scripting a message box reminder to change the password can help eliminate this oversight.

Keeping a Log

Even if you are able to script most of the installation, you should always keep an installation log of everything you do to a server. The log should be a straightforward list of the date, time, and what you did.

Logging what you have done to a server will not only save you more times than you can imagine, it will give you credibility if anything ever came up that questioned your installation procedure.

The following is a portion of an example installation log:

Server Installation Log for WSRV-E-T-1

2:13 AM	Started unattended install.
2:28 AM	Ran `hotfixes.bat`.
2:29 AM	Ran `post-install.bat`.
2:38 AM	Installed IIS.
2:44 AM	Ran `harden-iis.bat`.

| 2:47 AM | Changed administrator password. |
| 2:48 AM | Removed the CD-ROM from the CD-ROM drive. |

Again, humans make mistakes, so it is good to keep a log of what you did, because you might not remember what you did the next day, especially if you really are installing a server at 2:00 AM.

The Windows 2000 setup program keeps its own log of the installation at the root of the drive where the OS is installed. For custom scripts, the administrator must create his or her own function that will log the changes made to the system. This can be done through VBScript with the `FileSystem` class and basic text file manipulation commands in the scripting language. For information on VBScript, see the VBScript User's Guide available at

`http://msdn.microsoft.com/library/default.asp?url=/library/en-us/script56/html/vbstutor.asp`.

Server Roles

The role a server will play on the network will make a big difference in your installation strategy. If possible, each server should have a single, well-defined role. You do not want a weakness in one service to be used to compromise another service. For example, a system might be an external Web server or an internal terminal server, but never both. After you have a clearly defined role, every security decision you make must be based on that role.

It is difficult to decide what things to install if you do not know what the computer will be doing. You should not even install Windows 2000 on a system until you have a specific use for that system. Refer to Chapters 14 and 15 for the specifics on configuring DNS, FTP, Mail, and Web servers that will be publicly accessible.

Starting Clean

As you prepare a system for installing Windows 2000, you should make sure that all the hard drives are completely clean. You should not install over any other previous Windows versions and you should not create a dual boot system. Previous versions of Windows can create security holes, and extra stuff on the hard drive just makes it more difficult to manage what is on the system. If you must upgrade the systems, refer to Chapters 12, 14, and 15 for information on hardening the operating system.

Dual boot systems can allow a user to bypass the operating systems security checks on file access. For example, if there are two copies of the operating system on the machine, booting the second operating system will put the files under the second operating system's control and not the first, while the second operating system is loaded. If permissions to the files are allowed in the second operating system, the file is accessible, even if that user is denied access to the file in the first copy of the operating system.

> **NOTE**
>
> Dual boot systems should only be used in lab environments and not on production servers and workstations.

Another problem with previous data on the hard drive is that it could contain a virus or Trojan that could potentially destroy your new installation. If the system's security is important enough (or you are paranoid enough), you might even want to consider using a brand new unopened hard drive for the Windows 2000 installation.

> **NOTE**
>
> It is a good idea to never install any software on top of a previous version. You should completely remove the old version and then install the new one as if it were a completely new installation.

Installation Methods

There are a number of ways to install Windows 2000. Some of the most common are

- Installing from a bootable CD-ROM
- Installing from a bootable floppy, which reads from the CD-ROM
- Using Remote Installation Service
- Copying a hard drive image of a previous install

Each method has its advantages and disadvantages. You should consider the security ramifications of each method and take steps to avoid any vulnerabilities the installation process might introduce. For example, if you are using Remote Installation Service that deploys a Windows 2000 image across the network, the server must be connected to a network. In general, it is recommended that you install the server totally disconnected from any network. However, if you take precautions to keep the server on a private, trusted network connection, you will be able to reduce that security risk.

Other security concerns are the integrity of the source installation files. You must protect those files so that they are not corrupted with Trojans. These files should be secured that only Administrators have write access.

The File System

The partitions and file system you choose at installation are difficult to change later, so you should choose them carefully before starting the setup. Generally, you should never use any file system besides NTFS. There are very few exceptions to that rule. Some computer manufacturers require a FAT partition for diagnostic utilities, so in those cases, you have no choice.

The decision on how to partition your drives is not so simple. In general, you can create the following partitions:

- System partition
- Administrative partition
- Data partition
- Internet services partitions

The system partition is the partition that contains the operating system and any installed program files. The size of this partition depends on how much software you plan to install, and it will take some practice to determine what size works best for you.

The administrative partition is where any administrative tools and data will be stored. Log files and system monitoring data should also be installed on this partition. This partition should contain a secured Program Files directory for sensitive administrative software. This entire partition should be highly secured and properly audited.

The data partition (or user partition) is where any databases and other general data are stored. This would also be a good location for user directories. This partition should be secure with carefully selected permissions.

For Internet services, you can create a unique partition for each one that involves any kind of file system access. For example, you might have one partition for the Web root and a separate partition for the FTP root.

The purpose of creating so many different partitions is, first, that it is easier to manage the security of things in well-defined containers, and, second, in the event the system is compromised using through Internet services, the damage can be controlled by limiting the Internet Services to access only to a single partition.

Table 5.1 demonstrates an example partition layout.

TABLE 5.1 Example Partition Layout

Drive Letter	Name	Size
C:	System	2.5GB
D:	Users	5.0GB
E:	Admin	1.0GB
F:	WebRoot	1.0GB
G:	FTP Root	250MB

The Installation Process

At this point, you are ready to actually begin the setup process. As the setup program begins, one of the first screens you will see is the disk partitions screen. Create the partitions as you had planned, and proceed to format the partitions.

After partitioning and formatting is complete, the system will reboot and you will enter the graphical portion of setup. Although most of the information you enter will be obvious, several important steps need to be done correctly for maximum security.

First, when Setup asks for a name and organization, you should consider the impact of someone being able to discover this information. My personal preference is to simply enter Organization in the organization box and Name in the name box. The same is also true for the computer name. You should come up with a name to properly identify the system, but you should not identify the role of the system. For example, it is very common for someone to assign system names, such as WEBSERVER, WIN2kSERVER, EXCHANGE, and so on. These names reveal information about the server's role and save the attacker an extra step in having to get that information. Another common poor choice for a hostname is using *NSx* to name DNS servers where *NS* stands for name server and *x* is usually a digit indicating the DNS servers number. The number 1 is usually the primary DNS server, and the number 2 is a secondary DNS server.

Another significant item is the administrator password. Select a strong password that will be used during the installation process. It is okay to write this password down because it will be changed after installation is complete.

Finally, when you select the workgroup or domain, again be careful about the naming conventions you use. If the system is going to be a standalone server, you might want to consider renaming the workgroup from the default name Workgroup to something unique. This does not add a great deal of security, but, along with everything else, it makes a system that is non-identifiable and builds a foundation for a secure system.

Selecting Windows Components

One of the more important rules in Windows 2000 security is that you should never install something unless you have a specific immediate use for it. At some point during setup, you will be asked what Windows 2000 components you want installed. You should uncheck all options except a very few basic allowed. We will first create a secure minimal installation, and then later add other components as we need them. The process of keeping things at a minimum is so important that you should resist the temptation to install any other components at this point. Adding unnecessary components is not recommended because the configuration of these components is usually left as the default, and many attackers know the default settings. Adding unnecessary utilities will make the system easier to launch future attacks from in the event it is compromised.

Unfortunately, some component's files are installed, although they might not be running as active services. For example, every Windows 2000 server will have the Trivial FTP client (tftp.exe) located in the system directory. If you will not be doing TFTP file transfers, the file should be deleted from the system (or at least properly secured). To secure the file, create a Tools group and grant this group access to the file. Next, remove all other groups including Everyone, Administrators, and the SYSTEM account from the Access Control List (ACL) of the file. The minimalist strategy for installing components and services can save more servers from attack than many other security practices. If there is a question whether you should install something or not, you should always choose to not install it. If it turns out you need it later, just pop in the installation CD-ROM and add it.

The only items that you should ever check to install during setup (and only if you have a specific need for them) are

- WordPad
- Calculator
- Character map
- Paint
- Volume control

If you are using an unattend.txt file, use the following settings for the Components section of the file to prevent Accessories and IIS components from being installed:

```
[Components]
accessopt = off
calc = off
```

```
certsrv = off
certsrv_client = off
charmap = off
cluster = off
deskpaper = off
dialer = off
fp = off
freecell = off
hypertrm = off
iis_common = off
iisdbg = off
iis_doc = off
iis_ftp = off
iis_htmla = off
iis_inetmgr = off
iis_nntp = off
iis_nntp_docs = off
iis_pwmgr = off
iis_smtp = off
iis_smtp_docs = off
iis_www = off
indexsrv_system = off
LicenseServer = off
media_clips = off
media_utopia = off
minesweeper = off
mousepointers = off
mplay = off
msmq = off
mswordpad = off
netcis = off
netoc = off
objectpkg = off
paint = off
pinball = off
rec = off
reminst = off
rstorage = off
solitaire = off
templates = off
TSClients = off
TSEnable = off
vol = off
```

The whole point of installing nothing up front is so that you take one item at a time, install it, and then go through the steps of securing it before moving on. The process of securing many of the additional components through this method is covered throughout this book, and especially in Chapters 12, 14, and 15 that specifically focus on security policies and securing Internet services. If you follow this procedure, it is less likely that you will have something installed and running insecurely without your knowing it.

Networking Components

When you get to the networking phase of the setup process, allow Setup to install your network adaptor, but uncheck all network components for now, unless you need them to complete the setup process. It is best to configure the networking components last so that the system is not vulnerable to network-based attacks before you get it secured. After setup is complete, and updated with the latest service packs and hotfixes, you can go back and add only those components that you will be using on your network. If you install the networking components, your system can now potentially be seen by others on the network (and possibly the Internet). Moreover, a computer that can be seen is a computer that can be attacked.

Service Packs and Hotfixes

After finishing the setup process, the next thing to consider is applying service packs and hotfixes. Anyone who administers Windows servers is familiar with the headaches of keeping up with the endless flow of security bulletins coming from Microsoft. Indeed, any software is going to have security bugs, especially when you take into consideration the many security exposures of being connected to the Internet. However, keeping up with hotfixes is necessary to keep security at a maximum, but keeping abreast of these fixes and packs can be just plain difficult.

The process of keeping up with everything can be a time-consuming and often confusing process. You must consider which fixes are applicable for any particular server. This is complicated by the fact that Microsoft security bulletins are sometimes quite defensive and vague. Even after understanding the hotfixes, one must then come up with a good way to deploy them across the enterprise. Unfortunately, as long as there is software, there will be hotfixes for that software.

The Difference Between Service Packs and Hotfixes

For each major version of Windows, Microsoft releases a service pack about every six months. Service packs have been well tested and there is little reason not to install them. Hotfixes, on the other hand, are temporary interim fixes for dealing with specific issues until the next service pack is released. Hotfixes have not gone through a lengthy testing process and, therefore, carry some risk of causing problems with your server. You should be a bit more selective about installing hotfixes, but normally you are reasonably safe. The best strategy is to test hotfixes on non-production servers before installing them on systems that are more critical.

System administrators have many different philosophies when it comes to hotfixes. Some will religiously apply every available fix, while others will never touch a system that is already working well. There are systems out there that have 99.9999+% uptime, but that is only because they are running the same software that was originally installed ten years ago. The proper way to approach the problem is to balance the benefits of a hotfix to the risks of introducing new bugs. I imagine that some hotfixes are nothing more than the software version of duct tape and bailing wire, and even Microsoft warns against using all hotfixes unless specifically needed. Ultimately, because they have not been fully tested, the effects of installing a hotfix are for the most part unknown.

The question is really one of whether you really need the update or not. Often, the security benefits of a hotfix far outweigh the risks of applying the fix. However, if the hotfix applies to a service or function that you are not using, and uptime on a server is extremely important, you might be better off not applying it. You might also be able to find a workaround that will protect you from the vulnerability without having to apply the fix. Uninstalling Service Packs and hotfixes can also leave the system in an unstable state, so make sure you are confident that you need the fix before applying it.

To know whether you should apply the hotfix or not, you might have to research the issue. For every hotfix, there's a knowledge base article ID (also known as a Q-number, because the numbers are something like Q172653). These articles will explain more details about how the hotfix affects the system. Keep in mind, however, that Microsoft's interest is to protect their reputation, so the articles might not come right out and say what the vulnerability really is. Nevertheless, if the bug was discovered by someone outside of Microsoft, he or she will usually publish his or her own advisory that will have much more detail. There will also usually be a discussion on the common security-related mailing lists, such as Bugtraq and focus–ms (see `http://www.securityfocus.com`).

Slipstreaming Service Packs

Windows 2000 has a new feature that allows you to *slipstream* a service pack into the main installation source. This means that the service pack files will be integrated into the original Windows 2000 distribution files. When this slipstreamed distribution is installed, the service pack will automatically be there when Windows 2000 setup is complete.

To slipstream a service pack into Windows 2000, first create a directory on a computer where the new distribution will be stored. In this example, we will create a directory named Win2k on the C drive. From a command prompt, type the following:

```
C:\>md C:\Win2k\i386
```

Next, copy all files and subdirectories from the i386 directory on the Windows 2000 CD-ROM into the new distribution directory on your hard drive. If your CD-ROM drive was assigned the D drive letter, you would enter the following command:

```
C:\>xcopy d:\i386 c:\Win2k\i386 /e
```

If you downloaded the full service pack from Microsoft's Web site, you received a compressed .exe file. To configure the slipstream installation, the compressed file must be uncompressed and expanded into individual files and placed into a directory. Use the -x switch to extract the contents to a directory on the hard drive as shown in the following syntax:

```
C:\>sp2network.exe -x
```

When prompted, enter a directory name, such as **c:\win2k\SP2**.

At this point you will have two directories, one for the original Windows 2000 installation and one for Service Pack 2. To integrate the two, enter the following command:

```
C:\>win2k\sp2\update.exe -s:c:\win2k\i386
```

If you have the service pack on a CD-ROM , enter the following command, assuming the D drive is your CD-ROM:

```
C:\>d:\i386\update\update.exe -s:c:\win2k\i386
```

The distribution located at `C:\Win2k\i386` now includes the service pack as part of the installation. You can use that new distribution to install Windows 2000 and the service pack as one. Note that this method does have its drawbacks. First of all, it does make CD-based installations more difficult to perform (you must now build a custom CD-ROM for installation), but if you only perform network-based installations, this will not be a problem. Second, because the service pack cannot be uninstalled if it is slipstreamed, you might want to wait until it has had some time to be tested before integrating it into all of your installations.

Automating Hotfixes

Hotfix installation can also be automated in the event that multiple fixes need to be applied at the same time. The batch file described in this section will loop through the directory it's installed in and execute all .exe files with Q as the first character. The command line switches used keep the installation running in silent mode with no backup of the original files and no reboot after each fix is applied. Use the following syntax to create the batch file to apply the hotfixes:

```
@echo Installing hotfixes...
@for %2 %%f in (Q*.exe) do  @echo %%f && @%%f -n -z -q -m
```

Save this batch file as **hotfixes.bat** and place it in the same directory as all of the hotfixes you have downloaded. You can then either run this batch file manually after installing Windows 2000, or you can have it installed as part of an unattended installation.

To make it a part of an unattended installation, you must

- Update your distribution folder containing the hotfix files.
- Modify the `unattend.txt` file to install the additional hotfixes.

If you have a network distribution folder for your Windows 2000 installation, you can update it to include the hotfix files by creating a subdirectory named `\$OEM`. During installation, the setup program automatically checks the `\$OEM` directory and any files in this subdirectory will be copied to the target computer for installation. When the installation is complete, the `\$OEM` directory will be deleted. Copy all hotfix files, as well as the `hotfixes.bat` file we created to the `\$OEM` subdirectory.

Next, you must modify your `unattend.txt` file to copy and then install these hotfixes. If you do not already have an `unattend.txt` file, you can create one using the Setup Manager utility that is included with the Windows 2000 Resource Kit.

In the `unattend.txt` file, locate the `OemPreinstall` parameter under the [Unattended] section. If the parameter is not there, go ahead and add it. The `OemPreinstall` line should read as follows:

```
OemPreinstall = Yes
```

This switch will cause all the files located in the `\$OEM` directory and all its subdirectories to be copied to the target computer.

After setup is complete, run the `hotfixes.bat` file we created. To instruct Setup to do that, you need to locate (or add) the `[Commands]` section in `unattend.txt` and add the following line:

```
[Commands]
hotfixes.bat
```

When setup is complete, the batch file will run and install each of the hotfixes located in that same directory.

It is important to remember that no Windows 2000 system should ever be accessible from the Internet (or any other untrusted network) until all service packs and hotfixes have been applied. The single most common reason for Windows 2000 servers being compromised is that they are not up-to-date on their service packs and hotfixes. You can bet that if you have a public server, such as a Web server, it will regularly be probed to see if you have applied the most recent fixes. If you have not applied these fixes and patches, chances are that your server could soon be compromised.

Post-Installation Cleanup

After the setup process is complete, it is necessary to take a few more steps to clean up some leftover items. First, you should locate and delete any log files, temporary files, and uninstall files created during setup. The primary reasons for performing this cleanup are

- To remove files that might contain setup passwords or other sensitive information
- To free up disk space
- To remove unused programs that might pose a threat to the server
- To make the system more manageable by reducing the number of files

Much of this cleanup can be accomplished using the System Cleanup tool located under the Accessories group of the Start Menu (shown in Figure 5.1). This tool will delete the following files:

- Downloaded program files
- Temporary Internet files
- Recycle bin files
- Temporary files

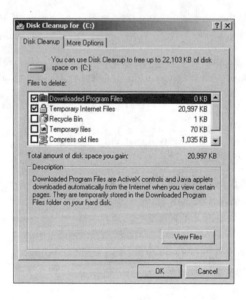

FIGURE 5.1

The Disk Cleanup tool.

After that is finished, you should search your hard drives for files with the `.log` filename extension. Most of these can be safely deleted, and those that cannot are generally locked and cannot be deleted anyway.

At this point, you might also want to consider removing the uninstall files for all the hotfixes. These files are located in your `%systemroot%` directory and are normally not needed after you are sure that a hotfix is working well on your system. It is normally not a good idea to leave them around too long, because you certainly do not want anyone removing hotfixes from your system, and also because they might contain versions of executable that have known vulnerabilities. To remove hotfix uninstall information, you must first delete the directory located under `%systemroot%\winnt`. For example, the directory might be named `C:\winnt\$NtUninstallQ262694$`. You must also remove the registry reference to the uninstall so that it no longer appears under the Add/Remove Programs component of Control Panel. To do that, use `regedit.exe` to browse to `HKEY_LOCAL_MACHINE\SOFTWARE\Microsoft\Windows\CurrentVersion\Uninstall\` and remove the appropriate key for the hotfix.

Post-installation cleanup is also where you want to go through the system and remove those files that you will not be using and pose a potential threat being on a server. These are the items mentioned earlier in this chapter that Setup installs by default without any option to not install them. Although each system will have different requirements, the following are examples of files that might pose a threat because they can be used to modify the system or compromise additional systems in the event the server you are installing is compromised:

- `telnet.exe`
- `tftp.exe`
- `ftp.exe`
- `cmd.exe`

Certainly, some of these files are indeed important components of some systems, but you must take some steps to make sure they are not used inappropriately. For example, Telnet can be used to probe other servers for vulnerabilities, while TFTP and FTP can be used to upload malicious code or scripts that can be run under cmd to destroy the system or probe for weaknesses in other servers. If you must keep these files on your system, you might want to consider implementing one or more of the following strategies:

- Enforcing strong permissions to only allow administrators (excluding the built-in SYSTEM account) to access these files
- Relocating the files to another location besides the default, such as the administrative partition mentioned earlier
- Renaming the files to something besides their default name
- Auditing the execution of these files

Although it is not recommended to do these things as common practice on every system, this combination of good security and a little obscurity can go a long way on critical servers. A final option might be to simply move the sensitive executables to removable media, such as a CD-ROM that can be inserted when needed.

As a final step to the cleanup stage, you might want to walk through the system directories and look for extra, unneeded, or sensitive files.

Post-Installation System Backups

The first thing that should ever be done to a system after installation, and before configuration, is to perform a complete system backup to tape. This backup might be necessary if anything happens during the rest of the configuration process. It is not uncommon to mess something up during configuration and have to start over from scratch. For example, it is possible to implement policies that will lock everyone out of the system, even the system administrator. This backup will also serve as a baseline if any system files get modified or replaced while installing other applications. This backup is the only completely untainted backup you will ever make, so it might be wise to keep it around permanently.

After installing your applications, hardening the OS, and configuring the system for your needs, you will also want to make one more backup to tape. This backup is the final backup to be made before the system goes into production. So it might be prudent to keep this one around permanently, as well. These backups are the only baseline you will have for judging what has happened to your file system since installation. Both of these backups should be clearly labeled as permanent (that is, not to be overwritten) and properly secured in a locked cabinet.

Installation Wrap-Up

The final step you should take at this point is to change the administrator password and reboot the system. This simple step is very critical, and yet it is one that is most often overlooked. This password is the most important password on the system and, if discovered, the entire system can be compromised. After installing Windows 2000, some remnants of the administrator password might exist on the system, and these pose a threat. Furthermore, if you commonly use the same password during setup, or if your unattend.txt file uses a common password, this is your opportunity to make that system unique.

Because many systems are members of a domain, it is easy to overlook the local administrator password. This local password is very rarely used, but it is equally important to manage it along with the rest of the passwords on your network. If you manage many systems, you will probably want to document this password in a secure area, along with the date it was set.

Your final entries in your installation log should always be that you completed the setup, removed any CD-ROMs, and changed the administrator password.

After the system is installed, it's time to install anti-virus software and other third-party management and security tools. Refer to Chapter 10, "Trojans and Backdoors," for more information on tools and strategies to protect your systems from malicious code attacks.

Summary

Although some of these processes seem tedious, following a strict installation procedure can eliminate many of the weaknesses common to Windows 2000 servers. Windows 2000 has had a bad reputation when it comes to security, but it is not all Microsoft's fault. People who install and maintain the systems are also at the root of many security problems, so it is crucial that we follow a rigid installation process. It is important to automate as much of the process as possible. It is also important that system administrators understand what happens during Windows Setup. It is wise not be lazy and careless with any of the steps mentioned in this chapter. Finally, it is crucial that you write down what you did.

Windows 2000 is used for everything from Mom-and-Pop Web sites to advanced military operations. If you require Windows-based operating systems, Windows 2000 is a solid choice. So, you must take the proper steps to secure it. Whether you are protecting your top-secret pie recipe or protecting an entire country, the foundation for security starts when you first boot up to that familiar "Welcome to Windows 2000 Setup" screen.

Password Security

IN THIS CHAPTER

You've partitioned your drives, installed Windows 2000, and created users and groups. Your next step is to address the most important security issue of all—password security.

Indeed, password security is so critical that your system will never truly be safe without it. Unfortunately, because the biggest weakness with passwords is the human factor, passwords across your enterprise will never be completely secure. Therefore, in addition to applying all the proper tools, you'll eventually find yourself educating local users in password policies.

Passwords are a single point of failure in your network security. If someone gets the right password, he or she can gain full control of every resource on your network. Many network intrusions are the result of easily guessed or poorly protected passwords. Password security requires initially selecting good passwords and then taking the proper steps to keep those passwords secure.

Keeping your passwords secure often means resisting the urge to be careless with your passwords, which will sometimes inconvenience and possibly even offend others. When I sit down at a keyboard to type in a password, I wait for others to look away before typing. Some take offense to that because it implies I do not trust them. On the other hand, I always extend them the courtesy of looking away when they need to type in their passwords. Eventually, people get the idea that I am just following good password security practices.

Inside Windows 2000 Passwords

After a hacker has a password, many of your security efforts are in vain. If you only allow administrators access to a certain file, that accessibility extends to anyone with an administrator password. After a hacker has the right password, it no longer matters what limits you have set on your network. With your password, a hacker essentially becomes you. Having a bad password is like handing over the keys to the place to any stranger who passes by.

Even without the human factor, our passwords are still vulnerable to a number of other attacks. A password might be very strong, but it loses its strength as time goes on as password cracking techniques improve. There are a number of ways to crack Windows 2000 passwords, and they usually require no more than a decent PC and a little patience. Let's take a look at some older and current NT password technologies to gain a better understanding of NT passwords.

Windows NT passwords have suffered from several security setbacks since their inception. Much of Windows Networking technology is based on Microsoft's first network operating system, LanManager. Windows NT used much of the LanManager authentication and password mechanisms when it was first released, and some of that technology is still present today in Windows 2000. *LanManager* (LM) passwords were the first passwords to be cracked in Windows networking history. Microsoft's LM authentication splits a password into two 7-character hashes. This has the effect of reducing the password into two smaller passwords that are easier to crack. LM passwords are also limited, because they do not distinguish between upper and lower-case letters, greatly reducing the number of possibilities when performing a brute-force password attack that attempts to try random passwords until a match is found.

NTLM authentication, on the other hand, uses all 14 characters in the password hash (see more on hashes later in the chapter in the "What Are Hashes?" section) and supports both upper and lower-case letters. Nevertheless, because the hashes can be sniffed on the network, they too can still be cracked, given enough time and the proper tools.

NTLMv2 is even more secure because it computes a 128-bit key space, making it more difficult to crack. It provides separate keys for message integrity and confidentiality, and makes use of the HMAC-MD5 algorithm for further message integrity. Unfortunately, NTLMv2 is a highly proprietary protocol that was introduced in later Windows NT service packs. Windows 2000 also uses NTLMv2 when communicating with Windows NT 4.0 systems. Furthermore, NTLMv2 still provides no anti-replay protection and still carries with it some of the older in-transit attacks.

> **NOTE**
>
> A replay or in-transit attack is when a challenge/response packet is recorded using a network sniffer and played back later to appear as if the user had authenticated with a valid password. Essentially, playing back the hash is the same as entering an actual password. It is sometimes referred to as *passing the hash*.

Finally, in Windows 2000, Microsoft has implemented the Kerberos standard that provides integrity, confidentiality, and allows authentication of both the client and the server. Kerberos is compatible across many platforms and products and is an open standard that has undergone much scrutiny. Despite the strengths of Kerberos, most networks still have older clients that do not support Kerberos, such as Windows 9.x and Windows NT clients; therefore, Windows 2000 machines must still authenticate using LM, NTLM, or NTLMv2. Backwards compatibility in Windows 2000 means that the problems of LM and NTLM are not gone yet. The hashes are still there for the taking.

What Are Hashes?

Most modern operating systems, including Windows 2000, have made reasonable efforts to secure system passwords. For Windows 2000 to know if you have typed in a correct password, it must have something to which to compare your password. Rather than storing the password itself or even an encrypted form of the password, it stores what is called a hash of the pass-word. A *hash* is simply an algorithm that is applied to the password to produce a result called a *message digest*. This message digest hash is a one-way function that is nearly impossible to reverse. It is possible to reverse the function but, in practice, it would take either millions of computers or millions of years, so it is considered the same as if it were impossible. This hash is stored in a secure portion of the registry referred to as the SAM. When Windows 2000 authenticates, it runs your password through the same algorithm to see if it gets the same result as the stored hash. If it does, it lets you in. Even if someone was able to retrieve these hashes, the encryption is irreversible, so they cannot be used to produce passwords.

On the surface, this hashing technique seems like a great way to protect your passwords, but because the algorithms used to create the hashes are widely known, they are still vulnerable to an offline, brute-force attack. In other words, it can still be cracked. There are tools that will pass millions of passwords through the same hashing process and then compare the results until it finds a match.

Cracking Windows 2000 Passwords

Although the word *cracking* implies the process of breaking something such as *cracking a code*, the term has expanded to include other methods, such as blind brute-force attacks and guessing. Often, someone will use the word to refer to the general process of discovering a user's password.

To a hacker, it really doesn't matter what method you use to get the password as long as you get it. Because having a password is often the transition from probing a network to entering a network, it is normally one of the first goals in hacking a Windows 2000 server. Anything up to that point is simply a means to achieve that goal.

There are a number of ways to crack passwords—exploiting weaknesses in protocols, software, and social engineering. Social engineering is the process of conning a person into giving the hacker the password or giving the hacker enough information about the user to make highly educated guesses to crack the password. This might include the user's car type, family names, dog's name, and so on. The resources that are available to you largely determine the method you use. Applying several different methods is even more effective and will usually produce better results.

The Art of Guessing

The biggest weakness with passwords is that a human is usually creating them. Most people simply are great at coming up with bad passwords. In fact, many people will use blank pass-words or use their login name (or some form of it) as their passwords. People are also not

6

very good at creating true randomness with their password creation and, if asked to produce a list of random passwords, that list will clearly exhibit some form of a pattern. People also have difficulty remembering things, so they select passwords that are easy to remember or they write them down so that they do not forget them. Finally, people are predictable and like to do things the same way day after day, week after week, month after month. For example, if a user's password is "rover1" and he or she is forced to change the password, he or she will most likely select a variation of the number attached to "rover," such as "rover2."

Armed with this knowledge, the hacker is already well along in discovering a password. Guessing passwords is a skill and, in some ways, even an art that many hackers possess. Just knowing a few rules and watching for patterns, one can easily cultivate this skill.

In analyzing hundreds of thousands of actual passwords, the following are some patterns I have seen emerge:

- More people will use the number 0 to replace the letter O than people who will substitute the number 3 for the letter E.
- If including numbers in their passwords, people are more likely to add them at the end rather than put them at the beginning or in the middle.
- When using numbers in a password, most people will use the numbers 1, 2, 7, or 9.
- People like to use dictionary words or passwords that contain dictionary words.
- People type the same words at the same rate and tempo, so if the password is the same as the username, one would clearly hear that they were typed the same.
- Most people have one or two favorite passwords they use across many systems.

Brute-Force Attacks

A *brute-force* password attack is a primitive form of attack that is performed by using an automated tool that tries many passwords in an attempt to discover the correct one. Passwords are eventually discovered if the attack is run long enough, but that might involve testing billions of password combinations to find the correct one. Even though these attacks are time consuming and resource intensive in terms of CPU cycles, they are often quite effective in producing passwords.

Although brute-force attacks can be performed against a Windows 2000 service, slow network connections and account lockouts usually make those types of attacks ineffective. The most effective method is to obtain the password hashes themselves and perform an offline attack.

There are several forms of password guessing attacks, but they are all essentially the automatic discovery of passwords through the process of elimination. The following are the main types of password guessing attacks:

- *Common Passwords*—An attack that checks for a small number of common passwords. Some of these would include a blank password, the user's login, test, admin, password, 123456, and qwerty. These attacks are often performed across many computers or networks and are set to not trigger account lockouts by keeping the number of attempts low. With this form of brute-force attack, rather than attempting large numbers of passwords against a few accounts, a few passwords are tested against a large number of accounts.

- *The Dictionary Attack*—An attack performed by attempting to login with every word in a supplied dictionary or word list. These attacks can be performed online against a network service or offline using password hashes and a password-cracking tool. Dictionary attacks can be very effective against weak passwords, but all it takes is adding a number to your password to foil them.

- *The Brute-Force Attack*—An attack performed by sequentially trying every combination of letters in the alphabet, numbers, and punctuation symbols. It is usually not a very effective attack, and the length of time to crack a password is sometimes measured in billions of years.

- *Hybrid Dictionary/Brute-Force Attack*—A brute-force attack that intelligently combines dictionary words with combinations of letters, numbers, and punctuation. By using a dictionary in this method, the chances of getting a valid password are improved, and it can greatly reduce the time required to complete the attack.

The effectiveness of a brute-force attack is largely determined by the wordlist supplied and the software used to perform the crack. Most password crackers apply rules to make more intelligent password guesses. A user might select a password like vacati0n99 and feel as if he or she has selected a good password. However, going through nearly a million passwords per second, the password can be easily cracked because it combines a word from the English dictionary with a numeric string. Most decent cracking tools can create word combinations well beyond the limits of the average user's imagination or patience. Even when users get somewhat creative with their passwords, cracking tools can often prevail.

Foiling Brute-Force Attacks

Three factors determine how fast a brute-force cracking tool can crack a password:

- *Character Set*—By including upper and lower-case letters, numbers, and punctuation symbols, the number of password combinations is dramatically increased. By doubling the range of characters used, you are doubling the amount of time it will take to crack the password.

- *Processor Power*—The processor speed and the number of processors determines how many passwords are cracked per second. By doubling the number of processors involved in the process, you cut the cracking time in half.

- *Password Length*—The number of password combinations increases exponentially for each digit in password length.

NOTE

The formula for determining how long it would take to brute-force a password is (Number of Possible Characters^Length)/Speed. So, to crack a 6-character password that uses only lowercase letters on a computer that can do a million passwords per second, the formula would be (26^6)/1,000,000, or about 309 seconds.

Increasing the character set and using numbers and symbols in a password increases the time it will take to crack the password. But the biggest advantage that can be gained is by increasing the size of the password. If you select a password that uses the full range of printable characters, every time you increase the password length by one character, you increase the complexity by nearly 100 times. In other words, if it takes a cracker a week to crack a six-character password, he or she would need 100 computers to crack a seven-character password in the same amount of time. To crack an eight-character password in the same amount of time would require 10,000 computers. A hacker can get faster computers and more of them but, clearly, adding a few characters to the length of the password gives the user a huge advantage.

We have all heard calculations about how a password of any certain length could take billions of years to crack. A 14-character password that uses the full range of printable characters has 5,646,733,123,551,140,000,000,000,000,000 possible combinations. I wouldn't even know how to say that number, but obviously it would take many lifetimes to crack. However, that number is somewhat misleading. That number is the absolutely worst case scenario in cracking the password. There certainly is a (very, very) small chance of guessing that password on the first try. Obviously, the password itself is going to determine how long it takes to get cracked. For example, if a cracking tool goes through each letter of the alphabet starting at the beginning, the password *aaaaaa* will be cracked much sooner than the password *zzzzzz*. If the cracking tool starts at the end of the alphabet, the reverse would be true.

Furthermore, as I mentioned earlier, most cracking tools use rules to greatly increase the likelihood of finding a password by trying the most likely combinations first. In practice, many passwords can be cracked within 24 hours and even the stronger passwords are often cracked within 30 days. As time goes by, passwords have more likelihood of being cracked. Therefore, despite all your efforts to have strong passwords, it is still necessary to change them regularly. This is because as long as people can find your password hashes, they can perform brute-force attacks on your password. Most organizations that are concerned about security force password changes every 30–45 days. A warning is usually given to the user 10–15 days prior to the password's expiration. About half of the users change the password when they get the warning to stop the annoying dialog box from popping up every time they log on. The other half will change their passwords a few days prior to the expiration or when the password expires.

Finding Password Hashes

When breaking in to a Windows 2000 server, the first goal would probably be to find password hashes. Although Windows 2000 has stronger password encryption, it still stores the old LanManager password hashes for backwards compatibility. If we can dump those hashes, we can feed them into a password cracker and just wait for the results.

Windows 2000 stores the password hashes in a database called the Security Account Manager (SAM). Although Windows 2000 now uses Active Directory for storing domain passwords, any Windows 2000 system that is not a domain controller still maintains a SAM for local accounts. The SAM itself is a part of the registry that is stored in the `%SystemRoot%\System32\Config` directory. To crack AD passwords stored in Windows 2000 Domain Controller servers, administrative rights to the domain are required to retrieve the password hashes to crack the passwords. For more information on Active Directory security, refer to Chapter 11, "Active Directory."

There are a number of ways to obtain the hashes in the SAM:

- Steal the SAM file itself (or a copy of it).
- Access the SAM registry keys.
- Exploit running code.
- Sniff hashes on the network.

Stealing the SAM

Because Windows 2000 locks the SAM file itself, it is not possible to copy it while Windows 2000 is running. However, if you are able to boot from another operating system and access the NTFS partition that contains the SAM, it is free for the taking. Winternals Software (http://www.winternals.com) makes utilities that can be used to boot from a floppy disk and access the NTFS partition.

> **NOTE**
>
> There is a tool called the Offline NT Password Editor that allows you to boot from a boot disk and change passwords on a system. You cannot retrieve the old passwords, but you can replace them with new ones. It certainly is not a conspicuous way to hack a server, but if you lose your administrator password, it can probably save your job. You can get the tool at http://home.eunet.no/~pnordahl/ntpasswd/.

Normally, you don't need to go through that much work to grab a SAM file. Whenever the NT Repair Disk Utility (rdisk.exe) is run with the /s option, a backup of the SAM is placed in the %SystemRoot%\Repair directory. This backup copy is compressed, but it can be expanded using expand.exe.

It is also possible to find copies of the SAM on system backups or emergency repair disks if they are available. Even if the SAM has been encrypted with SYSKEY, the latest password crackers will be able to retrieve the passwords.

Accessing the SAM Registry Keys

Because Windows 2000 has tight access restrictions on the SAM registry keys, only the System account has access to them. Some have talked about a trick of using the Scheduler service to launch a copy of Regedt32.exe in the System context to be able to access the keys, but there is an easier way. The administrator, having all power, can simply change the permissions on those keys to allow administrator access.

PWDump3 (http://www.ebiz-tech.com/html/pwdump.html) is a utility that can be used to dump password hashes from the registry. LC3 (http://www.@stake.com/research/lc3/download.html) can be used to crack the hashes after they are obtained.

Unfortunately, dumping the SAM directly from the registry requires administrator access to accomplish, and, if the SAM is encrypted (either Windows NT 4.0 with SYSKEY or Windows 2000 by default), the hashes must be decrypted using PWDUMP3. Older versions of PWDUMP do not support Windows 2000 or SYSKEY. Administrator access is required to obtain the hashes from PWDUMP3.

Exploiting Running Code

One way of getting past the problem of the hashes being encrypted is to circumvent the encryption process altogether. PWDump3, a utility written by Phil Staubs and Erik Hjelmstad (http://www.ebiz-tech.com/html/pwdump.html) accomplishes this by tapping into lsass. exe's address space (and therefore its user context) and injecting its own code. By doing this, PWDump3 is able to see the unencrypted hashes just as the system itself would see them.

PWDump3 does require administrator or system access, but it can be used in combination with other exploits to gain that access.

Another utility exploits the Service Control Manager Named Pipe Impersonation Vulnerability (MS00-053) to elevate permissions to gain access to the SAM. This vulnerability, discovered by Guardent, Inc. (http://www.guardent.com) allows malicious code to predict the next named pipe name and exploit that to elevate access to that of system. An exploit demonstrating this named PipeUpSAM.exe is available at http://www.dogmile.com/files/. This exploit does not work on encrypted SAM hashes, but it can be run without administrative privileges.

Sniffing Passwords on the Network

One of the weaknesses of NTLM and LM authentication is that Windows 2000 authentication packets can be sniffed on the network. LC3 has the ability to watch for these packets and gather password hashes that it sees. But to accomplish this, you must be on the same network segment as the system you want to attack.

There are also ways to trick someone into trying to connect to your computer via Telnet or another service that uses NTLM authentication. After the user's credentials are passed to your computer, the password hashes can then be sniffed. One way that can be accomplished is by sending out an e-mail with a disguised link to your computer. After the recipient clicks the link, his or her computer will attempt to authenticate to yours via NTLM, exposing his or her password hashes.

Cracking Password Hashes

After you have gathered the password hashes you need, you must feed them into a password cracking tool to begin a dictionary or other brute-force attack.

The following are some tools for cracking password hashes from Windows 2000:

- *LC3* `http://www.@stake.com/research/lc3/download.html`
- *John the Ripper* `http://www.openwall.com/john/`
- *Advanced NT Security Explorer* `http://www.elcomsoft.com/antexp.html`

Note that some of these tools will not work directly with SYSKEY encrypted passwords (which is the default with Windows 2000). To overcome that, you must use PWDump2 to get the unencrypted hashes and then feed those into the program. The problem is that encrypted password hashes look just like the unencrypted password hashes, so you need to make sure you are feeding the tool the correct hashes.

Protecting Passwords Through Security Policy

Windows 2000 Server provides hardened password security not available in Windows NT4. If you previously used Windows NT 4.0, you know that SP2 introduced `Passfilt.dll`, a DLL that provides at least minimal proactive password checking.

Windows 2000 enforces the following policies:

- Windows 2000 will reject any password that contains either part or all of your full name or your username.

- Windows 2000 will reject any password that doesn't contain characters from at least three of the following classes: English uppercase, English lowercase, Westernized Arabic numerals, and non-alphanumeric characters (such as the @ symbol).

- Windows 2000 will reject any password that isn't at least six characters long.

If you're using Windows 2000 Server, take advantage of these features, because they greatly complicate an attacker's task. To enable `Passfilt.dll`'s proactive password features for your domain, do the following:

1. Go to the Active Directory Users and Computers MMC snap-in, choose your specified domain object, and click Properties.

2. Choose Group Policy.

3. Choose Default Domain Policy, Edit.

4. Choose Group Policy Object Policy, Computer Configuration, Windows, Settings, Security Settings, Account Policies, Password Policy.

5. Choose Passwords Must Meet Complexity Requirements and set it to Enabled.

Password policies can also be set using the Local Security Policy, Domain Security Policy, and Domain Controller Security Policy MMC Snap-ins on the Administrative Tools section of the Start menu, as shown in Figure 6.1.

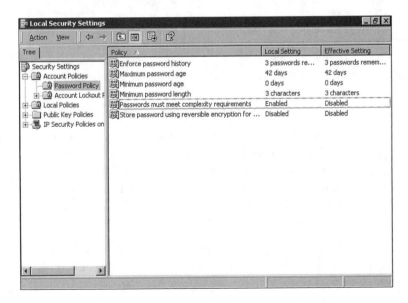

FIGURE 6.1

Setting password policies using the Local Security Settings MMC Snap-in.

NOTE

For more information, please see HOWTO: Password Change Filtering & Notification in Windows NT, `http://support.microsoft.com/support/kb/articles/Q151/0/82.ASP`.

Protecting Passwords Through User Education

Password security is an ongoing battle between system administrators and users. But with a smart password policy, administrators can accomplish good password security and users can still remember their passwords.

Part of the problem is that so many system administrators believe the myth that a password like *krP4@sWq* is a strong password. In fact, there are plenty of password generators out there that will spit out millions of unique passwords like that. The problem is that totally random passwords are simply difficult to remember. And a password that is difficult to remember is not a good password at all.

Another myth is to replace the letter O with the number 0. That was a good trick at one time but, as we discussed earlier, most password crackers will look for things like that. A better technique would be to replace the letter O with something completely different, such as the percent sign (%).

Yet another myth that can lead to bad passwords is telling users not to write them down. In my opinion, that leads to users selecting simpler passwords that are easier to remember. I tell users to write the password down if they need to, but to be sure to keep the paper concealed and destroy it as soon as they have it memorized. Users will be much more willing to make strong passwords if they can have it on a piece of paper for a few days.

An even better technique is to let users use a password storage utility. Password storage utilities allow a user to enter many passwords in a small application where they can later be retrieved. Access to the program is protected by a single master password that the user must remember. They are not a perfect solution, but they certainly are much more secure than writing passwords on paper. There are many password storage utilities available, including Xato's Quagmire utility on the CD-ROM included with this book.

To make users comfortable with long complex passwords, you must make it easy for them to remember long passwords. The following are some tricks for making passwords easier to remember:

- *Create pronounceable words*—If you use random letters, at least make them pronounceable. A word like *baramopoto* is not an English word, but a user can pronounce it,

6

making it easier to remember. The key here is that the user needs to remember just one word rather than a bunch of individual non-related letters.

- *Use repetition*—People like repetition, and it certainly makes a password easier to remember. The passwords *clip/clip/clip* and *vera-vera-* are easy to remember because the same elements are repeated.

- *Bracket words*—One way of getting users to use symbols in their passwords is to teach them how to bracket words. For example, instead of using the password *red apple*, they should use the password *(red)[apple]*.

- *Let users know what is valid*—Many users do not realize that you can use characters, such as spaces or other punctuation, in their passwords. Something as simple as a space and a period can make a password much stronger. In Windows 2000, if you can type it on the keyboard, it is a valid password character.

- *Embed words*—Although dictionary words by themselves are not good for passwords, they can be useful for remembering passwords. If combined with other techniques, even meaningful words like a spouses name can be just as strong as a random string of characters. The benefit is that words are easier to remember and users often can type a word faster than a random string of characters. To test this, try typing the password *#Hfk5Lpa6Rw* and then try typing the password *=totally-54-total=*. The second one is much easier to type, making it harder for an onlooker to watch your fingers.

- *Use common formatting conventions*—One of my favorite password tips is to have users make passwords look like real things such as URLs, e-mail addresses, file paths, math formulas, programming statements, phone numbers, bogus dates, and so on. For example, passwords like *Not8@example.com*, *www3.Got-Hacked.net*, *%systemroot%\repair\sam.*, and *March 40, 2022* are very good passwords. They are long, contain characters from a number of character sets, and, best of all, they are easy to remember.

- *Use smileys*—Its not too hard to teach a user to add a smiley, or emoticon, such as *:-)* to the end of his or her password. For a list of smileys, check out `http://www.randomhouse.com/features/davebarry/emoticon.html`.

Despite these techniques, you might still find that, because people are so predictable, they might still have a hard time selecting random passwords. Because people like patterns so much, their passwords will eventually follow the same patterns. To combat this problem, it might be useful to use a tool such as Xato's Pafwert tool, which can be found at `http://www.xato.net`. This tool generates completely random passwords but uses techniques such as those listed in this chapter to make them easier for users to remember.

The best effort you could make to educate your users is to practice these rules yourself when creating passwords.

Password Synchronization with Existing Unix Systems

Five years ago, as the operating system wars raged, the notion of Windows and Unix working seamlessly was heresy. Not anymore. Today, users and administrators recognize that different operating systems excel at different tasks. The key is to skillfully exploit each operating system for its unique characteristics and integrate.

Integration can occur smoothly or not-so-smoothly at various levels. Garden-variety networking and file sharing are good examples. Windows NFS clients can attach to exported Unix file systems, while Linux boxes (using Samba) can access Windows' file and print services. These are major achievements in integration. However, sometimes, integration at more mundane levels—such as authentication—can be difficult.

For this, Microsoft developed a password synchronization system that works (in most cases) in both directions and on the following Unix flavors:

- Digital Tru64—bi-directional
- HP-UX 10.3+—bi-directional
- IBM AIX 4.2—unidirectional (from WINDOWS 2000 to AIX)
- Red Hat Linux 5.2+—bi-directional
- Solaris 2.6+—bi-directional

The Microsoft software suite that accomplishes this is Windows Services for Unix (which, incidentally, includes such things as the Korn shell and many Unix utilities).

Microsoft's answer to the password synching problem is interesting. It achieved integration through a combination of Pluggable Authentication Modules (PAMs) on Unix and Windows 2000 services.

PAMs are tools that allow you to alter how Unix applications perform authentication without actually re-writing and compiling them. Most interesting of all, PAMs support many eclectic authentication schemes and free you from traditional Unix authentication methods.

Today, PAMs exist for a multitude of applications, servers, clients, and operating systems, including, but not limited to, IMAP, Kerberos, LDAP, Netscape Web server, NetWare, PHP, S/Key, SAMBA, SQL, ssh, TACACS+, and many others.

In the Windows 2000 Windows-to-Unix and Unix-to-Windows password synchronization system, Windows responds to messages generated by a Unix PAM. Windows services receive this transmission at the same moment the user executes `passwd` (the Unix password-changing tool). As soon as the user changes his or her password, the Windows service grabs the encrypted password, decrypts it, and uses the resulting text string to change the local password.

If your network requires integration that close, you must get Windows Services for UNIX. To learn more (and download the system), go to `http://www.microsoft.com/windows2000/sfu/sfu2wp.asp`.

Miscellaneous Password Issues

Table 6.1 identifies some peripheral password issues to be aware of in WINDOWS 2000 and earlier releases, especially when using third-party software or add-ons.

TABLE 6.1 Windows Password Issues

Issue	Discussion
Broker FTP	TransSoft Broker FTP server is an ftpd implementation for Windows. Version 4.7.5 stores its passwords in plaintext. Solution: go to `http://www.transsoft.com/` and upgrade.
CA eTrust	eTrust, CA's intrusion detection system) stores its password and key in `HKLM\Software\ComputerAssociates\SessionWall\1.0\Security`. Reportedly, the password is XOR'd. Check your version to be certain. If true, get an upgrade (.1.4.5+) from CA at `http://www.ca.com/`.
DTS Password Hole	SQL Server supports Data Transformation Service packages that can schedule database actions. In 7.0, unless you previously followed stringent security procedures, local users (programmers) can obtain the password. Learn more and get the patch at `http://www.microsoft.com/technet/security/bulletin/ms00-041.asp`.
GNU Emacs Hole	Emacs is a CLISP-based Unix editor for both text and binary files. Emacs versions for Windows prior to 20.6 store user passwords in memory in a history facility. This allows local attackers to obtain and reuse passwords. Upgrade at `ftp://ftp.gnu.org/gnu/emacs`.
Lotus Domino	Domino versions 4.6-R5 produce weak passwords and, under some conditions, expose those passwords to the network. This hole is critical. As a quick fix, migrate to stronger HTTP passwords or visit Lotus at `http://www.lotus.com/` for more information.
Microsoft Money Hole	Microsoft Money 2000 and 2001 both store user passwords in plaintext under certain conditions. Microsoft assures that "... The vulnerability only affects Money data stored on the user's local computer—it does not affect the security of Money's online services in any way." Hmmm. If you use Money at work or any other shared environment, see Microsoft Security Bulletin MS00-061 immediately and get the patch at `http://www.microsoft.com/technet/security/bulletin/MS00-061.asp`.

TABLE 6.1   Continued

Issue	Discussion
NetZero Hole	NetZero provides free Internet access. In early releases, the asterisk-masked password, when pasted into a regular text document, reveals itself. Check yours and if you confirm this, upgrade. Visit NetZero at `http://www.netzero.com/`.
PostgreSQL Hole	PostgreSQL is a free, open-sire SQL database system common to Linux but available for other platforms, including Windows. PostgreSQL stores various passwords in plaintext that are readable by users and root. To upgrade or for more information, go to `http://postgresql.readysetnet.com/`.
QNX Crypt	Certain releases of QNX OS (for embedded systems) use a faulty crypt function. Go for more information and the patch at `http://qdn.qnx.com/support/bok/solution.qnx?9619`.
RAS Caching Hole	Remote Access Service (RAS) and Routing and Remote Access Service (RRAS) both cache your security credentials, including your password, even when you tell them not to. If you find this condition to be true, go to `http://www.microsoft.com/technet/security/bulletin/ms99-017.asp` to learn more and obtain the patch. This link also provides additional links to general information on password caching.
Restoration Password	If you used the Configure Your Server applet, your Directory Service Restore Mode password could be null. Certainly, only users with physical access to the server can exploit this vulnerability. However, under such conditions, this is a critical hole. Check it now and also see `http://www.microsoft.com/technet/security/bulletin/MS00-099.asp`.
Samba Logfile Hole	Samba provides CIFS/SMB/NetBIOS services and is commonly used to integrate Linux, Unix, and Windows. The Samba `cgi.log in /tmp` stores easily crackable logins and passwords. This is more of an issue for Unix folks, but if you run both operating systems, be aware. Check out `http://www.samba.org` for more information. Also: no matter how much you'd like to disable Win98 password encryption for use with Samba, don't do it.
Sawmill Hole	Flowerfire Sawmill earlier than 5.0.22 generates easily cracked passwords, thus allowing attackers to view statistics on your site. Not a dramatic hole, but you should address it. Solution: Upgrade. Refer to `http://www.flowerfire.com/sawmill/` to obtain an upgrade.

TABLE 6.1 Continued

Issue	Discussion
Share Level Password	Though this isn't a Windows 2000 problem, it's prevalent on many Windows networks and affects 95, 98, and Me. The Share Level password (for file and print sharing) is weak, and remote attackers can get local shares. Get the patch at `http://www.microsoft.com/technet/security/bulletin/MS00-072.asp`.
Shiva Access Manager	Shiva Access Manager stores LDAP passwords in a plaintext world-readable file (`radtac.ini`). This could allow attackers expanded directory access. Check `radtac.ini` for plaintext entries and if you find them, upgrade. Visit `http://www.intel.com/network/shiva/` for information on obtaining an upgrade.
SIMS	Sun Internet Mail Server (SIMS) stores passwords in plaintext, in a world-readable file. This could allow an attacker to seize control of mail accounts or eventually, the mail server itself. Upgrade. Visit `http://www.iplanet.com/products/sun_internet/home_2_1_1i.html` information on obtaining an upgrade.
SQL 7.0 SP	Under certain conditions, after you install SQL Server 7.0 Service Packs 1 and 2, the Server Pack password will commit to disk in plaintext. Check the `%TEMP%\sqlsp.log` and `%WINNT%\setup.iss` files. If either sport plaintext passwords, go to `http://www.microsoft.com/technet/security/bulletin/ms00-035.asp` to learn more and obtain the patch.
SQL Enterprise Manager	SQL Server 7.0 Enterprise Manager can, under certain conditions, expose passwords to attackers. Note that this is only so when you're not using Windows authentication. Hackers can obtain the password with password cracking utilities that they pass over an asterisk-masked password field. When they pull away, the system reveals the password. Use Windows authentication (which you should anyway), read more, and get the patch at `http://www.microsoft.com/technet/security/bulletin/MS00-041.asp`.
SQL Server 7.0 Install	The administrative password for SQL Server 7.0 exists in plaintext in the `sqlsp.log` file while you're doing SP installations. To learn more and obtain the patch, go to `http://www.microsoft.com/technet/security/bulletin/MS00-035.asp`.
Tumbleweed MMS	Tumbleweed Messaging Management System (MMS) is an e-mail security and management tool common in enterprise environments. In several releases (4.5 and 4.6) the system's default administrative password is null. Upgrade or obtain the "SA Password" patch at `http://thompson.tumbleweed.com/Support/support.asp`.

There are many other password issues constantly being discovered. Visit `http://www.securityfocus.com` for a good list of current issues.

Maximum Password Security

In this chapter, we have covered many techniques for selecting and protecting passwords. But there are times when we have to go through extreme measures to protect our passwords. The following are some more techniques that should satisfy even the most paranoid system administrators:

- *Alternate between left- and right-hand letters*—By choosing passwords that alternate between hands, it is more difficult for someone to watch you type your password. Also, learn to type so that your hands are above the keyboard to better conceal what you are typing.

- *Do not try to type too fast if someone is watching you*—When typing your password too fast, you can make errors requiring you to type your password all over again, giving the other person another chance to watch you.

- *Always look at the screen to make sure you are in the right field before typing your password*—It doesn't do much to conceal your password if you type it in the User Name field.

- *Be careful about which keys you use in your password*—Some keys, such as the space-bar, have distinct sounds that a well-trained hacker can distinguish.

- *Use the keyboard to camouflage your password*—If you suspect someone is listening to you type your password, type in extra characters followed by the backspace key so they cannot determine the length of the password. In fact, you could just do that always to make it part of the password itself.

- *Use acceptable characters*—It might be tempting to use high-ASCII characters in your password using combinations such as ALT+255. Keep in mind that while you are making your password extremely difficult to crack, some keyboards, such as laptop keyboards, will not always let you enter those characters.

- *Check your command-line tools*—Some characters, such as quotes or spaces, will not work when entering a password with certain command-line tools. Some tools will interpret those characters as having a special meaning and not include them as part of the password. Test out your common command-line tools before using those special characters in your passwords.

- *Vary your characters*—Typing a password on the number pad is fast, but you have pretty much given away the fact that your password is only numbers.

- *Enforce password complexity requirements in Windows 2000*—Forcing password complexity is inconvenient for the end user but it's one of the best defenses available today.

- *Train yourself how to remember very long passwords without ever having to write them down*—It is an indispensable skill that you certainly can learn.

- *Learn how long it would take to crack your password*—With this information, be sure to change your password before that much time passes.

- *Schedule password days*—Several times a year, go through and change every password for every account on every device attached to your network. Be sure to include easily-overlooked passwords, such as those on routers, online Web accounts, domain registration passwords, and local administrator passwords on each workstation. Hackers like to keep several passwords on hand in case one changes. By changing them all at once, you might be able to lock them out completely.

Summary on Password Security

Good password security is the best asset your network could have. Conversely, bad password security is the best asset a hacker could have in attacking your network. If you take the proper steps to train your users and properly manage your passwords, it will make other exploits much less effective. By involving users in the process of how to make their passwords stronger, they will become more aware of password security issues and will be more willing to participate in your efforts.

Windows 2000 Services

7

IN THIS CHAPTER

In Windows 2000, a service is essentially a program that runs at startup independent of any user. Most of the functions a server performs, such as file sharing, are run as services. Most services run with SYSTEM privileges. SYSTEM is a special account that the operating system uses to perform priveledged operations on the system. Most services are started before any user logs in to the system. Running in the background, services normally do not allow user interaction, and most of their communication with the user is through entries in the event log.

Services have their benefits and their disadvantages. The benefits are clear:

- Services do not require a user to log in at the console to begin execution.
- Services run independent of any user logged in to the console.
- Services have sufficient privileges to perform any system operations.
- Services can be configured to run at startup and automatically restart if they fail.

However, consider the disadvantages:

- Because most services have SYSTEM privileges, exploiting a service often results in obtaining SYSTEM privileges.
- Because services do not interact with the desktop, a user sitting at the console is normally not aware if a service is started.
- Services can be confusing, and it is not always clear if a service should be running.

In this chapter, we will discuss some service strategies and review the security ramifications of each Windows 2000 service.

Understanding How Services Work

Because services run independently of the user, they are controlled by a process named the *Service Control Manager* (SCM). The SCM knows about all services installed on a system and which ones are currently running. It also makes sure that autostart services are run at startup, and it handles user requests to start and stop services.

When Windows 2000 is started, the SCM determines which services must be started, and it logs each one in to the system to obtain a security token. Although most services will log in as SYSTEM, a service can be set to log in as any locally authorized user provided the user account has the Log on as a Service right assigned to them in the Domain Security Policy MMC Snap-in found under the Administrate Tools. Assigning a user account to run the service can be accomplished by using the Services MMC Snap-in found under the Administrative Tools. By selecting a service and viewing its properties, an administrator can set the user account the service runs under, as shown in Figure 7.1. By default, every service that comes with Windows 2000 is automatically installed to run as SYSTEM. Normally, when it comes to security, you run an application with *least privilege*. That means that only the minimal set of privileges required to accomplish the task should be assigned. However, SYSTEM is an account with full access to everything, so giving every service that kind of access clearly breaks the rule of least privilege.

The alternative is to spend the time to create service accounts that have lesser privileges and set each service to use those accounts. However, because creating and managing those accounts is a headache that most administrators would rather not deal with, permissions are rarely changed from the default. Furthermore, it is difficult to know if reducing a service's permissions will cause the service to stop functioning, and most administrators do not have the time to research each individual service.

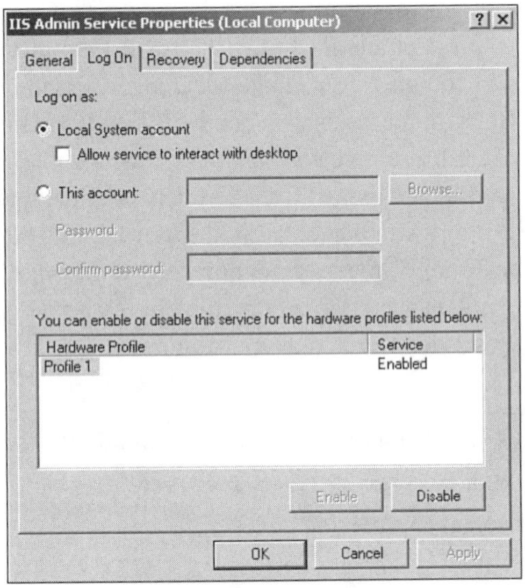

FIGURE 7.1
Services can be set to log in as local system or a specified account.

To add to this problem, auditing the SYSTEM account yields countless event log entries and does not allow you to distinguish between the activities of different services.

Rather than going through the trouble of giving each service its own logon and experimenting with the rights of each, we control services in other ways. We make sure that only administrators can start services, remove unsafe services, and make sure that the SYSTEM account cannot access certain files, such as cmd.exe. Sure, there is a certain amount of exposure by running services as SYSTEM, but with some things, the amount of work does not warrant the returned benefit.

Windows 2000 Services

Understanding each Windows 2000 service and shutting off unnecessary services will keep your server more secure than creating accounts for each service. If you carefully choose which services you run on a server, you can significantly reduce that server's exposure to attack. In the following list, you will discover some of the most common services and some risks they might pose. Keep in mind that just because I recommend not using a service does not mean that the service poses a direct security risk. The strategy here is to reduce risk by not running services unless they are specifically being used for a needed purpose.

Alerter Service

The Alerter service notifies users of administrative alerts (disk failure, space allocation problems, and so on). It works in conjunction with the Messenger Service, which receives and routes Alerter messages. Because unseasoned users might not recognize the difference between legitimate and illegitimate Alerter service notifications, someone might be able to trick a user into thinking he or she is getting a message from a system administrator. This type of attack, known as a *social engineering attack*, can result in the user taking some action based on what message was received. For example, the user might receive a message requesting their password to perform system maintenance or correct a problem. As a rule, you should probably restrict reception of Alerter service alerts to administrators.

> Service ID: Alerter
>
> Description: Notifies selected users and computers of administrative alerts
>
> Executable: `%SystemRoot%\System32\services.exe`
>
> Risks: Potential for social engineering attack

Application Management

The Application Management service provides communicates with Active Directory to assign, publish, and remove applications installed on the system through Group Policy. If your organization is not deploying applications through Goup Policy, it is best to disable the service.

> Service ID: AppMgmt
>
> Description: Provides software installation services such as Assign, Publish, and Remove
>
> Executable: `%SystemRoot%\System32\services.exe`
>
> Risks: No known risks

Boot Information Negotiation Layer

This service is used with the Remote Installation Service (RIS), and should not be running unless the organization installs the operating system through RIS. The service does not pose a security risk, but it is not required and is a waste of system resources.

Service ID: BINLSVC

Description: Provides the ability to install Windows 2000 Professional on PXE remote boot-enabled client computers

Executable: `SystemRoot%\System32\tcpsvcs.exe`

Risks: No known risks

Browser

The Browser service keeps a list of computers on your network and supplies the list to programs as they request it. This service is not required and in some cases, such as with a Web server, it should not be running.

Service ID: Browser

Description: Maintains an up-to-date list of computers on your network and supplies the list to programs that request it

Executable: `%SystemRoot%\System32\services.exe`

Risks: Reveals information about a network

Indexing Service

The Indexing Service indexes documents and document properties on your disks and stores the information in a catalog so you can later search it. The indexing service has been the source of numerous vulnerabilities on IIS Web servers and should not be enabled on public servers unless specifically used.

Service ID: cisvc

Description: Indexes files on the hard drive

Executable: `%SystemRoot%\System32\cisvc.exe`

Risks: Has been prone to vulnerabilities in the past.

Refer to the following security bulletins for more information on how the Indexing Service has been exploited in previous compromises:

- *Microsoft Security Bulletin MS01-033*—Unchecked Buffer in Index Server ISAPI Extension Could Enable Web Server Compromise at `http://www.microsoft.com/technet/treeview/default.asp?url=/technet/security/bulletin/MS01-033.asp`.

- *Microsoft Security Bulletin MS01-025*—Index Server Search Function Contains Unchecked Buffer at `http://www.microsoft.com/technet/treeview/default.asp?url=/technet/security/bulletin/MS01-025.asp`.

ClipBook

The ClipBook Service supports ClipBook Viewer, which allows pages to be seen by remote ClipBooks. This allows users to clip and paste text and graphics over network connections. Unless you use this feature, disable the service. A summary of a potential vulnerability using the ClipBook can be found at `http://www.securiteam.com/windowsntfocus/5TP022A2AW.html`.

Service ID: ClipSrv

Description: Supports ClipBook Viewer, which allows pages to be seen by remote ClipBooks

Executable: `%SystemRoot%\System32\clipsrv.exe`

Risks: Potential for remote access to ClipBook pages

Distributed File System

Allows you to create a single logical drive that is distributed across several locations on a network. Although there are no known vulnerabilities, it is something that should be turned off unless needed.

Service ID: Dfs

Description: Manages logical volumes distributed across a local or wide area network

Executable: `%SystemRoot%\System32\Dfssvc.exe`

Risks: No known risks

DHCP Client

The DHCP Client manages network configuration by registering and updating IP addresses and DNS names. Although DHCP is not considered an insecure service, it is recommended to assign a static IP address to servers to prevent potential attacks against the DHCP protocol.

Service ID: DHCP

Description: Manages network configuration by registering and updating IP addresses and DNS names

Executable: `%SystemRoot%\System32\services.exe`

Risks: No known risks

Logical Disk Manager Administrative Service

This service is used to manage logical disks. It is recommended that you should set it to start manually. The service will start itself when needed by the operating system. The service can be set to manual startup by using the Services MMC Snap-in found under the Administrative Tools. By selecting a service and viewing its properties, an administrator can set the Startup type to Manual.

> Service ID: dmadmin
>
> Description: Administrative service for disk management requests
>
> Executable: `SystemRoot%\System32\dmadmin.exe /com`
>
> Risks: No known risks

Logical Disk Manager

This is the Logical Disk Manager Watchdog Service, a service that manages dynamic disks. This service is required by the operating system to run. This service's startup settings should be left set for automatic startup.

> Service ID: dmserver
>
> Description: Used to manage logical disks
>
> Executable: `%SystemRoot%\System32\services.exe`
>
> Risks: Logical Disk Manager Watchdog Service

DNS Server

The DNS Server service answers Domain Name System (DNS) name queries. Although there are no known risks with the Windows 2000 DNS Server, DNS servers in general have been the source of many vulnerabilities and the service should be used with caution. Refer to Chapter 15, "Protecting Other Internet Services," for a discussion of potential DNS vulnerabilities and instructions on securing a Windows 2000 DNS server.

> Service ID: DNS
>
> Description: Answers query and update requests for Domain Name System (DNS) names
>
> Executable: `%SystemRoot%\System32\dns.exe`
>
> Risks: No known risks, but opens a TCP port to listen for requests

DNS Client

The DNS Client service can be useful for caching DNS lookups for logging or an intrusion detection system. This service can speed DNS lookups, but does pose a security risk, because an attacker can view the contents of your DNS cache and determine Internet sites that you have recently visited. To view the contents of your DNS cache, type the command `ipconfig / displaydns`.

Service IDDnscache

Description: Resolves and caches Domain Name System (DNS)

Executable: `%SystemRoot%\System32\services.exe`

Risks: No known risks

Event Log

The Event Log logs administrative event messages from the system as well as running programs. Although limited in features and still suffering from a few bugs, it can be useful for intrusion detection and system monitoring. This service should be enabled, especially on stand-alone servers.

Service ID: Eventlog

Description: Logs event messages issued by programs and Windows

Executable: `%SystemRoot%\System32\services.exe`

Risks: No known risks

COM+ Event System

This system provides automatic distribution of events to subscribing COM components. For more information on COM+ and to obtain a COM+ spy program, visit `http://www.rollthunder.com/news1v2n2.htm`. If this service is not used by any of your installed software, the COM+ Event System and System Event Notification Service can be disabled.

Service ID: EventSystem

Description: Provides automatic distribution of events to subscribing COM components

Executable: `%SystemRoot%\System32\svchost.exe -k netsvcs`

Risks: No known risks

Fax Service

This manages fax sending and receiving. It's not required or recommended for a server, unless it is specifically designated as a fax server.

Service ID: Fax

Description: Helps you send and receive faxes

Executable: `%SystemRoot%\system32\faxsvc.exe`

Risks: No known risks

Single Instance Storage Groveler

This service is used with the Remote Installation Service and is not required unless using the Remote Installation Service.

> Service ID: Groveler
>
> Description: Scans Single Instance Storage (SIS) volumes for duplicate files, and points duplicate files to one data storage point, conserving disk space
>
> Executable: %SystemRoot%\System32\grovel.exe
>
> Risks: No known risks

Internet Authentication Service

This service is used to authenticate dial-up and VPN users. Obviously, this service should not be used on anything but dial-up and VPN servers.

> Service ID: IAS
>
> Description: Enables authentication, authorization and accounting of dial-up and VPN users. IAS supports the RADIUS protocol.
>
> Executable: %SystemRoot%\System32\svchost.exe -k netsvcs
>
> Risks: No known risks

IIS Admin Service

The IIS Admin service allows for administration of IIS services through the Internet Services Manager MMC panel. This service is required if you are running any Internet services. If the server is not running any Internet Services, you should uninstall Internet Information Server from Control Panel, Add and Remove Programs and the IIS Admin service will also be uninstalled.

> Service ID: IISADMIN
>
> Description: Allows administration of Web and FTP services through the Internet Information Services snap-in
>
> Executable: %SystemRoot%\System32\inetsrv\inetinfo.exe
>
> Risks: No known risks

Intersite Messaging

Intersite Messaging is used with Active Directory replication and is not required or recommended for anything except Active Directory servers.

7

WINDOWS 2000
SERVICES

Service ID: IsmServ

Description: Allows sending and receiving messages between Windows Advanced Server sites

Executable: `%SystemRoot%\System32\ismserv.exe`

Risks: No known risks

Kerberos Key Distribution Center

This domain service provides Kerberos Authentication Services (AS) and Ticket-Granting Services (TGS). This service works in conjunction with Active Directory on a Domain Controller, and cannot be stopped. This service should not be running on anything but a Domain Controller.

Service ID: kdc

Description:Generates session keys and grants service tickets for mutual client/server authentication

Executable: `%SystemRoot%\System32\lsass.exe`

Risks: No known risks

Server

This service provides RPC support and file, print, and named pipe sharing. This service is implemented as a file system driver and handles I/O requests. The service does not need to be running unless you plan on sharing files or printers over a Windows network.

Service ID: lanmanserver

Description: Provides RPC support and file, print, and named pipe sharing

Executable: `%SystemRoot%\System32\services.exe`

Risks: Exposes system file and printer resources if not properly secured.

Workstation

This service provides network connections and communications. It works as a file system driver and allows a user to access resources located on a Windows network. This should only be running on workstations and servers on an internal network secured behind a firewall. It should be disabled on any server that is accessible to the Internet.

Service ID: lanmanworkstation

Description: Provides network connections and communications

Executable: `%SystemRoot%\System32\services.exe`

Risks: Some standalone servers, such as Web servers, should not participate on a Windows network.

TCP/IP Print Server

This service allows remote Unix users to access a printer managed by a Windows 2000 server using the TCP/IP protocol. This service has had some vulnerabilities and, because it opens a port to the Internet, is not recommended unless the network is separated from the Internet by a firewall. Refer to the following article that discusses a potential issue with the TCP/IP Print Server by using malformed print requests available at `http://support.microsoft.com/support/kb/articles/Q257/8/70.ASP?LN=EN-US&SD=gn&FR=0&qry=tcp/ip%20printing&rnk=17&src=DHCS_MSPSS_gn_SRCH&SPR=WIN2000`.

> Service ID: LDPSVC
>
> Description: Provides a TCP/IP-based printing service that uses the Line Printer protocol
>
> Executable: `%SystemRoot%\System32\tcpsvcs.exe`
>
> Risks: Has had vulnerabilities and opens a listening port

License Logging Service

Manages licensing information for a site. This service should not be used on anything but a domain controller.

> Service ID: LicenseService
>
> Description: Domain License Management
>
> Executable: `%SystemRoot%\System32\llssrv.exe`
>
> Risks: No known risks

TCP/IP NetBIOS Helper Service

Allows for NetBIOS communications over TCP/IP networks. This service should be disabled unless required for compatibility with an older version of Windows. Refer to Chapter 9, "Network Protocols, Clients, and Services," for more information on Netbios and Netbios over TCP/IP (NetBT).

> Service ID: LmHosts
>
> Description: Enables support for NetBIOS over TCP/IP (NetBT) service and NetBIOS name resolution
>
> Executable: `%SystemRoot%\System32\services.exe`
>
> Risks: Exposes system to NetBIOS weaknesses, such as NTLM authentication.

Messenger Service

The Messenger Service (not to be confused with MSN Messenger Service or other instant messenger services) sends and receives messages transmitted by administrators or by the Alerter service. This service is not required and should be disabled.

Service ID: Messenger

Description: Sends and receives messages transmitted by administrators or by the Alerter service

Executable: `%SystemRoot%\System32\services.exe`

Risks: No known risks

NetMeeting Remote Desktop Sharing

This service allows authorized users to remotely access your Windows desktop using NetMeeting. This service should be disabled because it has much potential for vulnerabilities. For remote desktop access, use Terminal Services instead.

Service ID: mnmsrvc

Description: Allows authorized people to remotely access your Windows desktop using NetMeeting

Executable: `%SystemRoot%\System32\mnmsrvc.exe`

Risks: Exposes a potentially insecure service

Distributed Transaction Coordinator

The Microsoft Distributed Coordinator Transaction Coordinator (MS DTC) provides a transaction coordination facility via the OLE Transactions protocol, and coordinates transactions that are distributed across two or more databases, message queues, file systems, or other transaction protected resource managers.

Service ID: MSDTC

Description: Coordinates transactions that are distributed across two or more databases, message queues, file systems, or other transaction protected resource managers

Executable: `%SystemRoot%\System32\msdtc.exe`

Risks: No known risks

FTP Publishing Service

File Transfer Protocol (FTP) is not a secure protocol and the FTP publishing service can be a great security risk if not properly secured. This service should be disabled unless specifically providing file sharing via FTP. If used, it should be carefully secured and monitored. Refer to Chapter 15 for information on securing the FTP Publishing Service.

Service ID: MSFTPSVC

Description: Provides FTP connectivity and administration through the Internet Information Services snap-in

Executable: `%SystemRoot%\System32\inetsrv\inetinfo.exe`

Risks: No known risks with Microsoft's FTP server. In general, FTP is an insecure service. See Chapter 15 for more information.

Windows Installer

The Windows Installer Service manages software installations. This service is useful for installing and repairing software applications.

Service ID: MSIServer

Description: Installs, repairs and removes software according to instructions contained in .MSI files

Executable: `%SystemRoot%\System32\msiexec.exe /V`

Risks: No known risks

Network DDE

This service provides Dynamic Data Exchange traffic transport and security. Network DDE is not required for most applications and should be set to manual startup.

Service ID: NetDDE

Description: Provides network transport and security for dynamic data exchange (DDE)

Executable: `%SystemRoot%\System32\netdde.exe`

Risks: Accepts DDE requests over the network

Network DDE DSDM

This service stores a database of shared conversations so that when a Network DDE share is accessed, the shared conversation is referenced, and security checks determine if the requester can be granted access. This service should be set to start manually.

Service ID: NetDDEdsdm

Description: Manages shared dynamic data exchange and is used by Network DDE

Executable: `%SystemRoot%\System32\netdde.exe`

Risks: No known risks

Net Logon

The Net Logon service supports pass-through authentication of account logon events for computers in a domain. This service should not be used on standalone servers that should not be part of a domain, such as Web servers.

7

WINDOWS 2000
SERVICES

Service ID: NetLogon

Description: Supports pass-through authentication of account logon events for computers in a domain

Executable: `%SystemRoot%\System32\lsass.exe`

Risks: Can be used to relay brute-force password attempts

Network Connections

This service manages objects in the Network and Dial-Up Connections folder, in which you can view both local area network and remote connections. This service can be set to start manually because it will start itself when needed.

Service ID: Netman

Description: Manages objects in the Network and Dial-Up Connections folder, in which you can view both local area network and remote connections

Executable: `%SystemRoot%\System32\svchost.exe -k netsvcs`

Risks: No known risks

Network News Transport Protocol (NNTP)

The Network News Transport Protocol (NNTP) is used to provide a news server service, such as USENET. When building an NNTP server, follow the steps to harden the operating system included in Chapter 15. NNTP servers should be installed in a DMZ network and be treated like other Internet services, such as FTP, Mail, and Web. It is not recommended to configure NNTP servers on private networks. Any server on an inside network should have the NNTP service uninstalled or disabled.

Service ID: NntpSvc

Description: Transports network news across the network

Executable: `%SystemRoot%\System32\inetsrv\inetinfo.exe`

Risks: No known risks

File Replication

The File Replication service (FRS) replicates files, system policies, and logon scripts across servers in a domain. The service can also be used to replicate data for Distributed File System (DFS) sets.

Service ID: NtFrs

Description: Maintains file synchronization of file directory contents among multiple servers

Executable: %SystemRoot%\System32\ntfrs.exe

Risks: No known risks

NTLM Security Support Provider

This service provides security to remote procedure call (RPC) programs that use transports other than named pipes (Windows 3.x, for example). The service appears in the service list once Client for Microsoft Networks is installed.

Service ID: NtLmSsp

Description: Provides security to remote procedure call (RPC) programs that use transports other than named pipes.

Executable: %SystemRoot%\System32\lsass.exe

Risks: NTLM password hashes are vulnerable to offline brute-force attacks.

Removable Storage

This service manages removable media, drives, and libraries. The service can be enabled as needed.

Service ID: NtmsSvc

Description: Manages removable media, drives, and libraries

Executable: %SystemRoot%\System32\svchost.exe -k netsvcs

Risks: No known risks

Plug-and-Play

This service manages device installation and configuration and notifies programs of device changes. I have successfully run a system without this service, but booting up takes much longer and some services, such as Remote Access Service, will not work. This service is probably best set to automatic.

Service ID: PlugPlay

Description: Manages device installation and configuration and notifies programs of device changes

Executable: %SystemRoot%\System32\services.exe

Risks: No known risks

IPSEC Policy Agent

This service manages IP security policy and starts the ISAKMP/Oakley (IKE) and the IP security driver. The IPSEC Policy Agent retrieves the IPSEC policy from Active Directory or the local registry.

Service ID: PolicyAgent

Description: Manages IP security policy and starts the ISAKMP/Oakley(IKE) and the IP security driver

Executable: `%SystemRoot%\System32\lsass.exe`

Risks: No known risks

Protected Storage

This service provides protected storage for sensitive data, such as private keys, to prevent access by unauthorized services, processes, or users. This service is required.

Service ID: ProtectedStorage

Description: Provides protected storage for sensitive data, such as private keys, to prevent access by unauthorized services, processes, or users

Executable: `%SystemRoot%\System32\services.exe`

Risks: No known risks

Remote Access Auto Connection Manager

This service automatically dials network connections when a request is made for a remote network address. This service is only required if using dial-up network connections.

Service ID: RasAuto

Description: Creates a connection to a remote network whenever a program references a remote DNS or NetBIOS name

Executable: `%SystemRoot%\System32\svchost.exe -k netsvcs`

Risks: No known risks

Remote Access Connection Manager

This service manages dial-up network connections. The service should only be running if the server is supporting Routing and Remote Access Services (RRAS).

Service ID: RasMan

Description: Creates a network connection

Executable: `%SystemRoot%\System32\svchost.exe -k netsvcs`

Risks: No known risks

Routing and Remote Access

This service offers routing services in local area and wide area network environments. The service should be only used on remote access points such as VPN servers. If configured incorrectly, this service could allow unauthorized access to a network.

Service ID: RemoteAccess

Description: Offers routing services to businesses in local area and wide area network environments

Executable: `%SystemRoot%\System32\svchost.exe -k netsvcs`

Risks: Could allow unauthorized network access if configured improperly

Remote Registry Service

This service lets authorized administrators manipulate registry entries on remote hosts. This service is required for some functions, such as remote performance monitoring, but is not recommended if not specifically needed.

Service ID: RemoteRegistry

Description: Allows remote registry manipulation

Executable: `%SystemRoot%\System32\regsvc.exe`

Risks: Can potentially expose registry if not secured properly

Remote Procedure Call (RPC) Locator

This service lets RPC-enabled applications register resource availability and lets clients find compatible RPC servers. This service should only be running on a domain controller.

Service ID: RpcLocator

Description: Manages the RPC name service database

Executable: `%SystemRoot%\System32\locator.exe`

Risks: No known risks

Remote Procedure Call (RPC)

This service calls services available on remote computers and is used for remote computer administration. This service is required on any Windows 2000 system.

Service ID: RpcSs

Description: Provides the endpoint mapper and other miscellaneous RPC services

Executable: `%SystemRoot%\System32\svchost -k rpcss`

Risks: Can expose system information

QoS Admission Control (RSVP)

This service provides managed bandwidth control to guarantee access to network services. This service should be enabled if you use the Windows QoS features.

Service ID: RSVP

Description: Provides network signaling and local traffic control setup functionality for QoS-aware programs and control applets

Executable: `%SystemRoot%\System32\rsvp.exe -s`

Risks: No known risks

Security Accounts Manager

The Security Accounts Manager (SAM) stores security information for local user accounts for authentication purposes. This is a required service.

Service ID: SamSs

Description: Stores security information for local user accounts.

Executable: `%SystemRoot%\system32\lsass.exe`

Risks: Although there are a number of ways to obtain SAM data, the SAM service itself does not pose a risk.

Task Scheduler

This service schedules a program to run at a later designated time. With NT4, only administrators could schedule tasks and all tasks ran as SYSTEM. With Windows 2000, any user can schedule a task that will only run under their own user context. This service should be disabled unless there are jobs that need to be scheduled.

Service ID: Schedule

Description: Enables a program to run at a designated time

Executable: `%SystemRoot%\System32\MSTask.exe`

Risks: No known risks

RunAs Service

This enables starting processes under alternate credentials, one of Microsoft's responses to the Trojan problem. Using RunAs, you can run a process as administrator while logged in as a non-privileged user. This service should be left enabled.

Service ID: seclogon

Description: Enables starting processes under alternate credentials

Executable: `%SystemRoot%\System32\services.exe`

Risks: No known risks

System Event Notification

This recommended service tracks system events such as Windows logon, network, and power events.

> Service ID: SENS
>
> Description: Tracks system events such as Windows logon, network, and power events. Notifies COM+ Event System subscribers of these events.
>
> Executable: `%SystemRoot%\System32\svchost.exe -k netsvcs`
>
> Risks: No known risks

Internet Connection Sharing

This provides sharing of one machine's Internet connection with several others, for example to share a DSL or cable modem connection. This service should be disabled because it could allow users to use an unauthorized Internet connection, bypassing the organization's proxy and monitoring services.

> Service ID: SharedAccess
>
> Description: Provides network address translation, addressing, and name resolution services for all computers on your home network through a dial-up connection
>
> Executable: `%SystemRoot%\System32\svchost.exe -k netsvcs`
>
> Risks: No known risks

Simple TCP/IP Services

These services run several basic TCP/IP services, most of which are not considered secure. Opens TCP ports 7, 9, 13, 17, and 19. Simple TCP/IP Services is not installed by default and is not recommended to be installed. If it is installed, it can be removed from Control Panel, Add/Remove Programs, Add/Remove Windows Components, Networking Service and uncheck the option for Simple TCP/IP Services.

> Service ID: SimpTcp
>
> Description: Supports the following TCP/IP services: Character Generator, Daytime, Discard, Echo, and Quote of the Day
>
> Executable: `%SystemRoot%\System32\tcpsvcs.exe`
>
> Risks: Runs several insecure services on various TCP ports

Simple Mail Transport Protocol (SMTP)

Provides outgoing Internet mail service. This service can be useful but should be limited to only be accessible from the local host or network.

Service ID: SMTPSVC)

Description: Transports electronic mail across the network

Executable: %SystemRoot%\System32\inetsrv\inetinfo.exe

Risks: E-mail spoofing or relaying

SNMP Service

The Simple Network Management Protocol (SNMP) is not a secure protocol and, by default, is set to use public as its community string. The SNMP service reveals sensitive information about a Windows 2000 server and should only be used on an internal network.

Service ID: SNMP

Description: Includes agents that monitor the activity in network devices and report to the network console workstation

Executable: %SystemRoot%\System32\snmp.exe

Risks: Reveals sensitive information about a server

SNMP Trap Service

The SNMP trap service receives SNMP messages sent from other SNMP agents. The SNMP trap service should be used only on internal networks and should not be exposed to the Internet.

Service ID: SNMPTRAP

Description: Receives trap messages generated by local or remote SNMP agents and forwards the messages to SNMP management programs running on this computer

Executable: %SystemRoot%\System32\snmptrap.exe

Risks: No known risks

Print Spooler

The print spooler is used to spool print jobs so that an application does not have to wait for a file to print. Unless the server is handling print queues, this service should be disabled.

Service ID: Spooler

Description: Loads files to memory for later printing

Executable: %SystemRoot%\System32\spoolsv.exe

Risks: No known risks

Performance Logs and Alerts

This service handles performance logs and alerts. This service is useful for both system and network monitoring.

> Service ID: SysmonLog
>
> Description: Configures performance logs and alerts
>
> Executable: `%SystemRoot%\System32\smlogsvc.exe`
>
> Risks: No known risks

Telephony

This service provides for telephony and IP based voice connections. This service should not be enabled unless you use such features on your LAN.

> Service ID: TapiSrv
>
> Description: Provides Telephony API (TAPI) support for programs that control telephony devices and IP-based voice connections on the local computer and, through the LAN, on servers that are also running the service
>
> Executable: `%SystemRoot%\System32\svchost.exe -k tapisrv`
>
> Risks: No known risks

Terminal Services

Terminal Service provides remote desktop access through TCP/IP connections. This service can be dangerous, especially if system passwords have already been compromised. Access to this service should be strictly limited by IP address (at the firewall or using IPSec) and should be closely monitored.

> Service ID: TermService
>
> Description: Provides a multisession environment that allows client devices to access a virtual Windows 2000 Professional desktop session and Windows-based programs running
>
> Executable: `%SystemRoot%\System32\termsrv.exe`
>
> Risks: Potential remote desktop access, potential brute-force attack exposure

Terminal Services Licensing

Terminal services licensing is used to manage client licenses when using Terminal Services in application server mode. This service is required when the server is running Terminal Services in Application Server Mode. It is not installed unless Terminal Services has been installed in Application Server Mode.

Service ID: TermServLicensing

Description: Installs a license server and provides registered client licenses when connecting to a Terminal Server

Executable: `%SystemRoot%\System32\lserver.exe`

Risks: No known risks

Trivial FTP Daemon

Trivial FTP (TFTP) is not a secure service and should be used sparingly and only on a local trusted network. TFTP provides no form of user authentication or identification.

Service ID: TFTPD

Description: Implements the Trivial FTP Internet standard, which does not require a user name or password. Part of the Remote Installation Services.

Executable: `%SystemRoot%\System32\tftpd.exe`

Risks: Potential unauthorized file access.

Telnet

Allows a remote user to log on to the system and run console programs using the command line—the Microsoft Telnet server. Telnet is not a secure protocol and passwords are sent across the wire in plaintext. Furthermore, if NTLM authentication is enabled, NTLM password hashes can also be discovered. Telnet should be used sparingly and access should be tightly controlled at the firewall.

Service ID: TlntSvr

Description: Allows a remote user to log on to the system and run console programs using the command line

Executable: `%SystemRoot%\System32\tlntsvr.exe`

Risks: Potential for unauthorized remote command-line access, passwords and hashes sent unencrypted across the network

Utility Manager

The Utility Manager starts and configures accessibility tools. Disable this service unless you require use of the accessibility tools.

Service ID: UtilMan

Description: Starts and configures accessibility tools from one window

Executable: `%SystemRoot%\System32\UtilMan.exe`

Risks: No known risks

Windows Time

This service sets the system clock from a network time server. This service is only required on Windows 2000 Domain Controller services because the authentication protocol Kerberos depends on accurate time to validate users. It can be disabled on any other machine.

Service ID: W32Time

Description: Sets the computer clock

Executable: `%SystemRoot%\System32\services.exe`

Risks: No known risks

World Wide Web Publishing Service

Provides Web site services accessible anonymously from the Internet. This service exposes many vulnerabilities, especially with a default configuration. This service should never be run without first being hardened. See Chapter 14, "Protecting Web Services," for more information on hardening Web services.

Service ID: W3SVC

Description: Provides Web connectivity and administration through the Internet Information Services snap-in

Executable: `%SystemRoot%\System32\inetsrv\inetinfo.exe`

Risks: Numerous file access, remote command execution, denial of service, and other risks

Windows Management Instrumentation

The Windows Management Instrumentation (WMI) service provides system management information. It is essentially a Web-Based Enterprise Management (WBEM) compliant tool to collect and associate management data from a wide range of disparate sources. WMI is a useful administrative tool, but it is also useful for gathering information. The service should not be enabled if you are not specifically using it.

Service ID: WinMgmt

Description: Provides system management information

Executable: `%SystemRoot%\System32\WBEM\WinMgmt.exe`

Risks: Potential for exposing sensitive system information

Windows Internet Name Service (WINS)

WINS is Microsoft's name service for NetBIOS networks. Native Windows 2000 networks do not rely upon WINS. WINS can expose information about network users and computers and should be disabled. If enabled, it should be limited only to local network use.

Service ID: WINS

Description: Provides a NetBIOS name service for TCP/IP clients that have to register and resolve NetBIOS-type names

Executable: `%SystemRoot%\System32\wins.exe`

Risks: Potential for revealing sensitive system information

Summary

This chapter discussed how Windows 2000 Services work and provided an overview of the function of each service. All services are not required and, when building a secure system, it's best practice to disable unnecessary services. This is especially true when servers will be made accessible over the Internet. Later chapters, such as Chapters 14 and 15 of this book, discuss disabling specific services to build a hardened Windows 2000 configuration to support Internet Services that will further build on the knowledge provided in this chapter.

Windows 2000 Networking

PART

III

IN THIS PART

Windows 2000 Network Security Architecture

IN THIS CHAPTER

You can secure your file system on a Windows 2000 machine by encrypting it and applying permissions to it. Unfortunately, these features only protect your file system locally, because, when an authorized user accesses them from another machine in the network, the machine on which the files are stored transmits them across the wire in clear text. Consequently, this leaves your network vulnerable to intruders and unauthorized users bent on intercepting confidential information from your organization.

Fortunately, the Windows 2000 operating system includes technologies that enable you to secure data as you transmit it across the wire, and to protect network systems and services from unauthorized access. These technologies, which I discuss in more detail in the following section, include

- Active Directory
- Kerberos
- Internet Protocol Security (IPSec)
- Public Key Infrastructure (PKI)

Active Directory

The Active Directory directory service has a fundamental relationship with the incorporated Windows 2000 security model. Active Directory stores all of the domain's security policy information, as well as security policy information for overall domain management. To use all of the security features of the Windows 2000 operating system, you must use the improved NTFS file system that comes with Windows 2000.

Security Descriptors

Administrators can manage properties on objects in the domain by setting permissions, assigning ownership, and monitoring user access. Not only can administrators control access to a specific object, they can also control access to specific attributes of that object. You call objects with associated security attributes *securable objects*. Active Directory uses a security descriptor to define the security attributes of a securable object. The security descriptor is important because it contains information about the object's primary group and about the owner of the object.

The security descriptor contains two access control lists (ACLs), the system ACL (SACL) and the discretionary ACL (DACL). The SACL defines the type of auditing to record for an object. This means that the SACL contains information in reference to various audited access events for a particular object, such as a successful or a failed attempt to access that object. The DACL contains information about who is permitted access to a particular object and what type of access to grant. For example, an administrator can configure a security descriptor for a specific user account object to enable that user to read employees' e-mail addresses, but not their home telephone numbers.

Attributes for objects are set by choosing Start, Programs, Administrative Tools, Active Directory Users and Computers, right-clicking the object on which you want to set attributes, choosing Properties, the Security tab, clicking the Advanced button, and then editing the desired permission entry. Figure 8.1 illustrates the Permission Entry dialog box for the Read Personal Information permission of a user account.

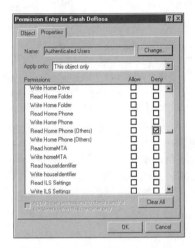

FIGURE 8.1
The Permission Entry dialog box.

Security Principals

Groups, user accounts, and computer accounts are directory objects (called *security principals*) that Active Directory uses to do the following:

- Perform domain authentication.
- Permit or deny access to domain resources.
- Audit actions performed with computer accounts and user accounts.
- Administer security principals.

When you establish a trust relationship between two Windows 2000 domains in different forests, you can grant access to resources within the internal domain to security principals from the external domain. The trusting domain's Active Directory creates a foreign security principal to represent each of the security principals from the trusted external domain. You should never change any of the properties of foreign security principals.

8

NETWORK
SECURITY
ARCHITECTURE

Computer Accounts

For computers to join a Windows 2000 domain, a domain administrator must create a unique computer account for each computer. The computer account provides a means for authenticating and auditing the computer's access to the network and to the domain resources. You use Active Directory Users and Computers to maintain, create, disable or delete computer accounts. Information, such as the computer's role in the domain and the operating system in use, is stored in the computer account.

You can create computer account names on the domain controller in two ways:

- The person performing the installation can create the computer account name on the local machine during the installation process of Windows 2000 Professional or Server. If the computer account name does not yet exist on the domain controller, the domain controller will ask the installer to present domain administrator credentials. If the installer has those credentials, he can create the computer account name on the domain controller. The installer cannot create the computer account name on the domain controller without presenting valid domain administrator credentials.

- The domain administrator can create the computer account name by using the Active Directory Users and Computers console on the Windows 2000 domain controller. This is done by choosing Start, Programs, Administrative Tools, Active Directory Users and Computers. Next, you expand the domain name in the console tree, right-click Computers, point to New, and then click Computer.

Netlogon

After the domain administrator creates the computer account name on the domain controller, the machine attempts to validate its computer account. The computer accomplishes this by first sending a local Netlogon request, and then sending a unicast Netlogon request to all of the domain controllers in the trusted domain list. A secure channel is established between the machine and the first domain controller that validates its Netlogon request. The secure channel is only established after both the requesting computer and the domain controller are certain that the other has correctly identified itself through its computer account. After the secure channel is established, user account logon requests can successfully pass from the computer to the domain controller.

Active Directory and Interoperability

Active Directory supports standards to ensure interoperability of the Windows 2000 environment with previous versions of the Windows operating system, as well as with a variety of products from other vendors. Active Directory is a Lightweight Directory Access Protocol (LDAP) version 3-compliant directory service and is defined in RFC 2251 "Lightweight Directory Access Protocol (v3)." All access to Active Directory objects occurs through LDAP, and Active Directory uses LDAP to enable interoperability with other LDAP-compatible client applications. If an administrator grants the appropriate permissions to you, you can use any LDAP-compatible client to access and modify information in Active Directory. Read about RFC 2251 at `http://www.ietf.org/rfc/rfc2251.txt`.

> **NOTE**
>
> Read more about the basics of Active Directory at `http://www.microsoft.com/windows2000/guide/server/features/dirlist.asp`.

Kerberos

Microsoft has replaced NTLM with Kerberos v5 as the fundamental security protocol. The Kerberos protocol provides the means for authenticating the identities of security principals on your network. Kerberos performs this authentication by using conventional DES cryptography.

> **NOTE**
>
> For backward compatibility purposes, Windows NT LAN Manager (NTLM) and Secure Sockets Layer (SSL) protocols are still supported.

How Does the Kerberos Authentication Process Work?

The Kerberos authentication process works in the following manner:

1. A client sends a request for credentials for a specified server to the authentication server.

2. The authentication server encrypts the credentials with the client's key and then transmits the package back to the client. The credentials consist of two items: a ticket for the server and a temporary encryption key, called the *session key*. The ticket contains both the identity of the client and a copy of the session key.

3. The client transmits the ticket, which the authentication server has encrypted with its own key, to the specified server.

4. The specified server can then use the session key to authenticate the client, because the client and that server now share the session key. Conversely, the client can use the same session key to authenticate the server. The two machines can use the session key to encrypt further communication between them during the same session.

The implementation of the Kerberos protocol depends on one or more authentication servers running on machines that you have physically secured. The authentication servers maintain a database of security principals and their secret keys. These code libraries implement the Kerberos protocol and provide encryption for your enterprise.

> **Note**
>
> It is always advisable to physically secure the servers on the network to keep them locked away from malicious users and intruders.

Identity Verification and Integrity

The security principals use credentials to verify the identity of each other in a transaction, preserve privacy of the transactions, and ensure the integrity of the transactions exchanged between them.

To verify the identity of the security principals in a transaction, the client transmits the ticket in clear text (except for the sessions key, which is always encrypted) to the server. Because an attacker can intercept and attempt to replay the ticket, additional information (called the authenticator) is included to prove the identity of the security principal to whom the ticket was issued. The sending machine encrypts the authenticator in the session key, which includes a timestamp. The timestamp proves that the client recently created the transaction and that an intruder is not replaying it. Because the sending machine encrypts the authenticator in the session key, it proves that the sender is the one possessing the session key. The client and the server are the only security principals that know the session key.

The security principals also use the session key to guarantee the integrity of the transactions exchanged between them. They accomplish this by generating and transmitting a collision-proof hash of the sending machine's transaction, keyed with the session key. This ensures the privacy and integrity of the transaction that the client and the server are transmitting between themselves. This approach detects both message stream modification attacks and replay attacks. A *replay attack* occurs when an attacker copies and replays a given transaction. *Message stream* modification attacks occur when an attacker modifies message traffic in transit.

Kerberos and Interoperability

A Windows 2000 domain controller provides authentication for clients running implementations of RFC 1510 Kerberos. This includes clients running operating systems other than Windows 2000. Unix clients and servers can have Active Directory accounts and can, therefore, obtain authentication from a Windows 2000 domain controller.

Win32 client applications, and operating systems other than Windows 2000, that are based on the Generic Security Service Application Program Interface (GSS-API) can obtain session tickets for services within a Windows 2000 domain.

NOTE

Learn more about the Kerberos Network Authentication Service (V5) by reading RFC 1510 at `http://www.ietf.org/rfc/rfc1510.txt`.

Internet Protocol Security (IPSec)

When you use IPSec, it defines the use of end-to-end encryption that results in the protection of all network communication generated between participating machines within the network. What this means is that, if you use this technology, your confidential information will remain confidential as it travels across the wire to another machine in the network. IPSec is your main line of defense against private network, internal, and external attacks levied against your network.

Windows 2000 provides predefined IPSec policies that provide for a range of security levels with which to secure your network's data.

Predefined Policies

You select one of the predefined IPSec policies, or define your own policy in the Local Security Policy console for the local machine and in the Domain Security Policy console for domain-wide policies. You run either of these consoles on the domain controller by choosing Start, Programs, Administrative Tools and then clicking either Local Security Policy or Domain Security Policy, depending on the type of policy you need to set. Figure 8.2 illustrates the Domain Security Policy console.

8

NETWORK
SECURITY
ARCHITECTURE

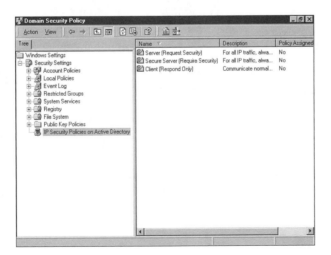

FIGURE 8.2

The Domain Security Policy console.

The predefined IPSec policies are

- *Client(Respond Only)*—You use this policy on machines that don't need secure communications most of the time. This policy enables a machine on which it is active to respond appropriately to a request for secured communications by another computer.

- *Server (Request Security)*—You use this policy on machines that require secure communications most of the time. When this policy is active, the machine will accept unsecured traffic, but will always attempt to secure additional communication security by requesting IPSec from the sending machine. If the other machine isn't IPSec-enabled, the communication between the two machines will be unsecured.

- *Secure Server (Require Security)*—This is the most stringent predefined IPSec policy and is used for machines that always require secure communications. When this policy is active, the machine will reject any unsecured incoming communications, and will always secure the outgoing communications. This policy does not allow unsecured communication, even in a peer-to-peer network.

IPSec Encryption Requirements

Internet Key Exchange (IKE) encryption protects the security negotiation between machines, and the IPSec component of TCP/IP uses encryption to protect data packets. IKE and Windows 2000-based machines must be able to use DES encryption to protect the negotiation and to secure traffic using the IPSec packet format.

IPSec policies permit using 3DES, a stronger encryption algorithm. The advantage of using 3DES is that it uses a longer key length than DES, which, in turn, provides a higher security for your enterprise. To be able to use 3DES on Windows 2000-based machines, you must have the High Encryption Pack installed on every machine that will use 3DES encryption to perform the 3DES algorithm. If a machine receives a 3DES communication and that machine does not have the High Encryption Packed installed, the 3DES setting in the encryption policy on that machine will be automatically set to the weaker DES.

IPSec and Interoperability

When the high security and overhead of 3DES is not necessary, and for interoperability with other products and operating systems, your list of security methods must include DES. Otherwise, the machine that you are trying to communicate with (or that is trying to communicate with you) might not be able to reach a common security agreement with your machine. Depending on the security policy in place on your machine, this might result in failure of the communication.

> **NOTE**
>
> Learn more about IPSec in Chapter 21, "Virtual Private Networking," and by reading RFC 2401 "Security Architecture for the Internet Protocol" at `ftp://ftp.isi.edu/ in-notes/rfc2401.txt`.

Public Key Infrastructure (PKI)

PKI is a system made up of registration authorities, such as certification authorities and digital certificates, that use public key cryptography to verify and authenticate the validity of each client involved in an electronic transaction. The following features are included in the PKI.

Certificates

A *certificate* is a collection of digitally signed data issued by an authority that vouches for the identity of the certificate holder. A certificate holder can be any number of entities including users, certificate authorities (CAs), and services and devices that users need to access on the network. An entity can possess more than one certificate because certificates are issued for more than one purpose. One common purpose for a network certificate is the private key issued to network users for the Encrypting File System (EFS). If you use EFS certificates, you should archive them in a secure place so that you or the EFS Recovery agent can recover the encrypted data of a lost key.

Windows 2000 certificates use the X.509v3 standard certificate format. The X.509v3 certificate includes information about the entity to which the certificate is issued, the Certificate Authority (CA) issuing the certificate, and information about the certificate itself, such as the entity's name, public key, and public key algorithm. Administrators manage certificates through the Certificates console. You add the Certificates console to the Administrative Tools menu by doing the following:

1. Click Start and then click Run.
2. The Run dialog box appears. In the Open drop-down combo box, type `mmc /a` and then click OK.
3. The Microsoft Management Console (MMC) appears, as shown in Figure 8.3. Click the Console menu and then click Add/Remove Snap-in.
4. The Add/Remove Snap-in dialog box appears, as shown in Figure 8.4. Click the Add button.

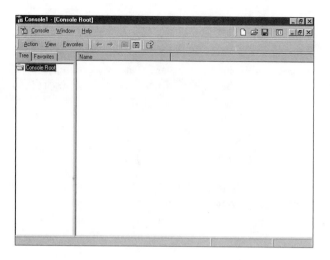

FIGURE 8.3

The Microsoft Management Console (MMC).

FIGURE 8.4

The Add/Remove Snap-in dialog box.

5. The Add Standalone Snap-in dialog box appears, as shown in Figure 8.5. In the Available Standalone Snap-ins list box, click Certificates and then click the Add button.

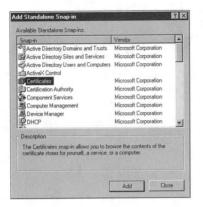

FIGURE 8.5

The Add Standalone Snap-in dialog box.

6. The Certificates Snap-in dialog box appears, as shown in Figure 8.6. You have three options for managing certificates on this page—My User Account, Service Account, and Computer Account. Click the corresponding radio button for the desired option and then click the Finish button.

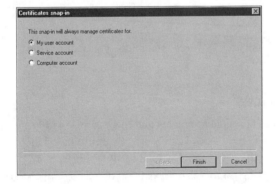

FIGURE 8.6

The Certificates Snap-in dialog box.

7. Click the Close button in the Add Standalone Snap-in dialog box.

8. In the Add/Remove Snap-in dialog box, the Certificates snap-in should be listed. Click OK.

9. "Certificates" is now listed in the console tree of the MMC, as seen in Figure 8.7. Click Console and then choose Save As.

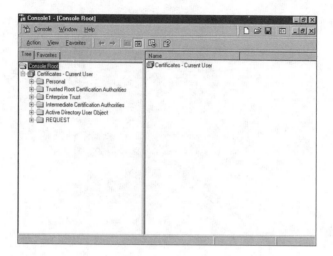

FIGURE 8.7
Certificates console added to the MMC.

10. The Save As dialog box appears. In the File Name text box, type `Certificates` (or a description that you would like to see listed in the Administrative Tools menu) and then click the Save button.

11. Exit the MMC.

When you click the Administrative Tools menu now, you will see the Certificates console listed.

Certificate Services

The Certificates Services component creates and manages CAs in Windows 2000. The responsibilities of an enterprise CA includes issuing certificates to individual, computers, and organizations and vouching for the certificate holders' identity. Enterprise CAs can issue certificates for purposes such as logging on to a Windows 2000 domain using a smart card and securing e-mail using Secure Multipurpose Internet Mail Extensions (S/MIME.) A CA in a Windows 2000 enterprise can either be a CA you created by installing Windows 2000 Certificate Services or it can be a remote third-party CA, such as VeriSign (`http://www.verisign.com/`).

A Windows 2000 enterprise CA requires that you install Active Directory on your domain controller. The enterprise CA uses your Windows 2000 user account credentials as proof of identity when you request a certificate from the enterprise CA. The CA presumes that you are who Active Directory says you are.

CA Roles

A CA can function in four separate roles. The role you assign to a CA determines what the CA's certificates are used for, and the role is assigned during the installation process. The four roles are as follows:

- *Enterprise Root CA*—The enterprise root CA is at the top of the certificate chain and serves as the root CA for the entire enterprise. The enterprise root CA can issue certificates for users, computers, and subordinate CAs. When enterprise subordinate CAs also exist in your enterprise, the enterprise root CA will normally issue only subordinate CA certificates. The enterprise root CA self-signs its certificate, asserting that it is the root. Active Directory access is required for the enterprise root CA.

- *Enterprise Subordinate CA*—Subordinate CAs are used for a number of reasons. Your organization might have different policies for issuing certificates, depending on an entity's organizational role. Your organization might have geographical divisions, and the network connectivity between these sites might require multiple subordinate CAs at each site to meet usability requirements. Subordinate CAs can be used to administer and separate policies and to ease the workload on a single CA in your enterprise.

  The enterprise subordinate CA requires that the enterprise root CA has issued a CA certificate to it. After the root CA issues the CA certificate, the subordinate CA can issue certificates to users, computers, and other subordinate CAs in the enterprise. Active Directory access is required for the enterprise subordinate CA.

- *Stand-Alone Root CA*—The stand-alone root CA behaves like a stand-alone server. There is an advantage to using this type of CA role. You can keep the CA separate from your network so that it is secure from network-born attack attempts. The stand-alone root CA doesn't have to participate in Active Directory, but it can.

- *Stand-Alone Subordinate CA*—A CA in this role can only issue certificates to users. A stand-alone subordinate CA doesn't have to participate in Active Directory, but it can.

Certificate Templates

Certificate templates are pre-defined templates that specify the content of certificates based on their intended usage. There are a number of certificate templates included with the Windows 2000 Certificate Services, listed in Table 8.1.

TABLE 8.1   Windows 2000 Certificate Templates

Certificate	Purpose
Administrator	You issue this certificate to users for code signing, certificate trust list (CTL) signing, ncrypting file system (EFS), secure e-mail, and client authentication.
Authenticated Session	You issue this certificate to users for client authentication.

TABLE 8.1   Continued

Certificate	*Purpose*
Basic EFS	You issue this certificate to users to use with the Encrypting File System.
Computer	This certificate is issued to computers for client authentication and server authentication.
Code Signing	You issue this certificate to users for code signing.
Domain Controller	This certificate is issued to computers for client authentication and server authentication.
EFS Recovery Agent	You issue this certificate to trusted users that you assign as EFS Recovery Agents for encrypted file recovery.
Enrollment Agent	You issue this certificate to trusted users that you assign as Certificate Request Agents.
Enrollment Agent (offline request)	You issue this certificate to trusted users that you assign as Certificate Request Agents.
IPSec (offline request)	This certificate is issued to computers to enable Internet Protocol security.
IPSec	This certificate is issued to computers to enable Internet Protocol security.
Router (offline request)	This certificate is issued to computers and routers for client authentication.
Smart Card Logon	You issue this certificate to users for client authentication.
Smart Card User	You issue this certificate to users for client authentication and to secure e-mail.
Subordinate Certification Authority	This certificate is issued to computers and is permitted to perform all certificates functions.
Trust List Signing	You issue this certificate to users for certificate trust list signing.
User	You issue this certificate to enable users to use the Encrypting File System, to secure their e-mail and for client authentication.
User Signature Only	You issue this certificate to users for client authentication and to secure e-mail.
Web Server	This certificate is issued to computers for server authentication.

When you install a new enterprise CA, by default, only seven certificates are available to issue. They are the Administrator, Basic EFS, Computer, Domain Controller, EFS Recovery Agent, User, and Web Server certificates. You can select additional certificate templates that the enterprise CA can issue by performing the following steps.

1. Click Start, choose Programs, Administrative Tools, and then click Certification Authority.
2. The Certification Authority console appears, as shown in Figure 8.8. Expand the CA in the console tree.

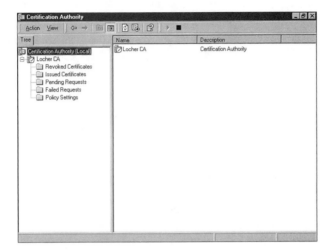

FIGURE 8.8

The Certification Authority console.

3. In the console tree, click Policy Settings.
4. To issue additional certificate templates, click the Action menu, choose New, and then click Certificate To Issue.
5. The Select Certificate Template dialog box appears, as shown in Figure 8.9. Select the new certificate template from the list box that you want to use, and then click OK.

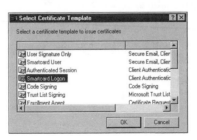

FIGURE 8.9

The Select Certificate Template dialog box.

You have added the new certificate template to the list of available templates that you can issue.

Smart Card Support

A smart card is a portable, tamper-resistant, integrated circuit plastic card that an individual, or a group of individuals, owns and that provides security solutions for tasks, such as client authentication and securing e-mail. You can think of the smart card as a small computer in itself because it can perform advanced security functions, such as storing certificates and cryptographic keys, and has the ability to perform cryptographic algorithms. Microsoft is taking steps to make it easier to incorporate smart cards into everyday desktop computer use. One such way is the integration of smart cards with development tools, such as Microsoft Visual Studio and Microsoft Visual Basic. If you are designing an application that requires a form of authorization or security, smart cards might be a solution for you.

Unfortunately, it is still not possible to secure logins to the Windows 95 and Windows 98 platforms. If you need to use smart cards in your enterprise, you should use either Windows 2000 or Windows NT 4.0.

In the Windows NT 4.0 platform, the smart card replaces the GINA.DLL (Graphical Identification and Authentication) with one that is smart card aware. The most common use of the GINA.DLL is to communicate with an external device, such as a smart card reader. The purpose of the GINA.DLL is to provide customizable user identification and authentication procedures. The GINA is loaded early in the boot process because it operates in the context of the Winlogon process. By default, GINA delegates the secure attention sequence (SAS) event monitoring to Winlogon, which then receives and processes the CTL+ALT+DEL SAS.

The Windows 2000 platform has built-in technology for smart cards and certificate-based logons. Therefore, in Windows 2000, the smart card contains the certificate and associated private key. Upon request for a logon, the server sends a challenge to the smart card. In turn, the private key stored on the smart card signs the challenge and then returns the result and the certificate to the authentication server. The authentication server verifies the information and checks on the validity of the certificate from Active Directory. In Windows 2000, the RAS dial-up client can also be smart card enabled.

In both of these methods, instead of seeing the usual logon window requesting the user's username and password, the user will see a window that states Please Insert Your Smart Card. After the user enters the correct PIN for the smart card, the smart card extracts the username, password, and domain name and then transmits that information to the authentication server.

There are significant advantages for using a smart card over traditional methods of authentication.

- If a user has multiple passwords, the smart card can remember all of them for him, protected by a single PIN.

- Using a smart card makes the password more secure because the user doesn't need to know the password and so can't write it down or share it with others. In addition, an administrator can initialize the card with a very strong password that any ordinary person would find difficult to remember.

- If the smart card is able, it can perform the symmetric or the asymmetric cryptographic algorithms on the card so that the key doesn't appear in the desktop, making it difficult for a malicious program to sniff it out.

Public Key Policies

Public key policies are set by administrators in the Windows 2000 Group Policy console. Administrators use public key policies to

- Have computers automatically submit requests to an enterprise CA for certificates and then install the issued certificate

- Manage recovery policies for the Encrypting File System (EFS)

- Establish common trusted CAs and certificate trust lists

You open Group Policy in a number of ways, depending upon what action you want to perform.

- If you need to apply a Group Policy to a site, you open Group Policy by choosing Start, Programs, Administrative Tools, Active Directory Sites and Services. Expand Services in the console tree, and then choose Public Key Services. Apply the desired Group Policy.

- If you need to apply a Group Policy to a domain or an organizational unit, you open Group Policy by choosing Start, Programs, Administrative Tools, Active Directory Users and Computers. Right-click the domain or organizational unit to which you want to set Group Policy for, and then click Properties. In the Properties dialog box, click the Group Policy tab. This dialog box gives you options to create, add, edit, or delete Group Policy.

- If you need to apply a Group Policy to the local machine, you can add the Local Group Policy console to the Administrative Tools menu.

You add the Local Group Policy console to the Administrative Tools menu by doing the following:

1. Click Start and then click Run.

2. The Run dialog box appears. In the Open drop-down combo box, type `mmc /a` and then click OK.

3. The Microsoft Management Console (MMC) appears. Click the Console menu and then click Add/Remove Snap-in.

4. The Add/Remove Snap-in dialog box appears. Click the Add button.

8

NETWORK SECURITY ARCHITECTURE

5. The Add Standalone Snap-in dialog box appears, as shown in Figure 8.10. In the Available Standalone Snap-ins list box, click Group Policy and then click the Add button.

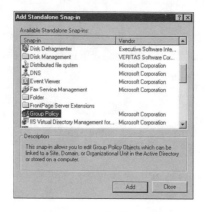

FIGURE 8.10

The Add Standalone Snap-in dialog box.

6. The Select Group Policy Object dialog box appears, as shown in Figure 8.11. Click the Finish button.

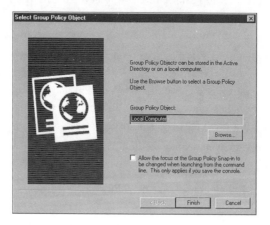

FIGURE 8.11

The Select Group Policy Object dialog box.

7. Click the Close button in the Add Standalone Snap-in dialog box.

8. In the Add/Remove Snap-in dialog box, the Local Computer Policy snap-in should be listed. Click OK.

9. Local Computer Policy is now listed in the console tree of the MMC, illustrated in Figure 8.12. Click Console and then click Save As.

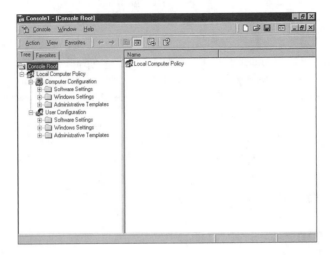

FIGURE 8.12
Local Computer Policy console added to the MMC.

10. The Save As dialog box appears. In the File Name text box, type `Local Computer Policy` (or a description that you would like to see listed in the Administrative Tools menu) and then click the Save button.

11. Exit the MMC.

When you click the Administrative Tools menu now, you will see the Local Computer Policy console listed.

Although it isn't necessary to use public key policy settings to deploy a public key infrastructure in your enterprise, it does give you additional control when you establish CAs.

PKI and Interoperability

Because Windows 2000 Certificate Services uses the industry-standard X.509v3 certificate formats, these services operate with products and technologies that support the use of public key cryptography and PKI.

NOTE

Learn more about the basic architecture of PKI by reading RFC 2459 "Internet X.509 Public Key Infrastructure Certificate and CRL Profile" at `ftp://ftp.isi.edu/in-notes/rfc2459.txt`.

The X.509v3 standard also adheres to existing PKI Internet interoperability standards established by the Internet Engineering Task Force (IETF). The IETF working group responsible for defining the basis of an interoperable PKI is PKIX (Public-Key Infrastructure X.509). Visit the PKIX site for a host of information and links related to PKI at `http://www.ietf.org/html.charters/pkix-charter.html`.

Public Key Cryptography Standards (PKCS) are a set of crytpgraphic message standards that were developed and maintained by RSA Laboratories (`http://www.rsasecurity.com/`). These standards provide a basic framework for cryptographic interoperability. Windows 2000 Certificate Services use two of these standards:

- PKCS #7, "Crptographic Message Syntax Standard." You can find this document at `http://www.rsasecurity.com/rsalabs/pkcs/pkcs-7/`.

- PKCS # 10, "Certification Request Syntax Standard." You can find this document at `http://www.rsasecurity.com/rsalabs/pkcs/pkcs-10/`.

Understanding Workgroups

A workgroup (also called a peer-to-peer network) is a small collection of Windows machines (made up of ten or fewer machines) all located in the same general area. Machines in a workgroup are thought of as peers because they are all equal and do not require a server to manage network resources. In the workgroup network model, computers communicate directly with each other. Each user determines which resources and data he or she will share. This model is difficult to administer in any but the smallest network, and it lacks centralized control. You would only want to set up your network as a workgroup if there are less than ten computers and those computers don't store sensitive data because the centralized security policies offered in domains don't exist here.

Understanding Windows 2000 Domains

You create a Windows 2000 domain when you create the first domain controller in a network. A domain can't exist without at least one domain controller, and a DNS domain name identifies each domain controller. Understanding domains includes understanding the domain structure, domain servers, and types of domains.

Domain Structure

Trees, forests, trusts, and organizational units make up the Windows 2000 domain structure. Each of these is discussed in this section.

Trees

A tree is a set of one or more domains with contiguous names. A single tree is a contiguous namespace. In a contiguous namespace, each domain name inherits the name of the domain ahead of it in the hierarchy. Figure 8.13 illustrates a tree with a contiguous namespace.

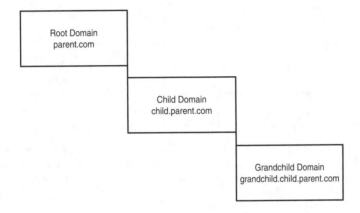

FIGURE 8.13

Single tree with three domains forming a contiguous namespace.

The first domain created in a domain is the tree root domain. When you create additional domains in the same domain tree, you call them *child* domains. A domain immediately above a child domain in the same domain tree is its parent. Domains in a contiguous namespace have contiguous DNS domain names. The domain names form in the following ways:

- The domain name of the child domain appears at the left of the parent domain name. A period separates the two names, for example, `child#1.parent.com`.

- When there are more than two domains in the tree, each domain's parent name is to its right in the domain name, for example, `child#2.child#1.parent.com`.

It is important to understand that the parent-child relationship between domains in a domain tree is a trust relationship and a naming relationship only. Administrators in a parent domain are not automatically administrators in a child domain, and child domains do not automatically inherit policies from a parent domain.

Forests

Forests are groups of trees with noncontiguous namespaces. All members of the forest have transitive Kerberos trust relationships with each other, as long as the Windows 2000 domain is running in Native mode. The trees in the forest share the same configuration, schema, and Global Catalog. A Global Catalog is created automatically on the first domain controller that

8

NETWORK
SECURITY
ARCHITECTURE

you create in the forest. It stores a full replica of all objects in the directory for its host domain and a partial replica for all other domains in the forest. Figure 8.14 illustrates a forest with two domain trees.

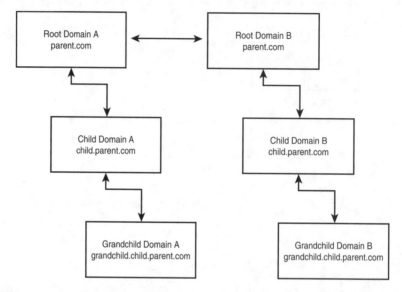

FIGURE 8.14
One forest with two domain trees.

Trusts

A trust relationship is a mechanism by which a domain controller in one domain can authenticate users in another domain. In Windows NT 4.0 domains, all trusts were non-transitive. In other words, each trust was a one-way relationship that you had to explicitly establish. You had to establish two separate trust relationships (one for each direction) in order for two domains to trust each other.

Windows 2000 permits transitive trusts within the same forest. *Transitive trusts* are always two-way trusts. When you create a child domain, Windows 2000 automatically creates a transitive trust between the child domain and the parent domain. However, transitive trusts don't exist at all until you remove all Windows NT domain controllers from the domain and then explicitly switch the Windows 2000 domain from mixed to native mode. This is because Windows 2000 does not permit transitive trusts in mixed mode.

Organizational Units

Organizational units are similar to domains in that they also are containers for network objects, such as resources and user accounts. Unlike domains, they don't require domain controllers and they don't mark security boundaries. In fact, they create a means to provide organization within a domain without the need for additional domain controllers and security policies.

Domain Controllers

In Windows 2000, the concepts of primary and backup domain controllers are history. Each domain controller has equal authority over the domain. If any one domain controller should go down, the others will continue to authenticate and administer the domain. Any domain controller can initiate a change to the domain and then replicate that change across the domain.

Another change that Windows 2000 has introduced to domain controllers is the role of operations masters. An operations master is a domain controller in an Active Directory domain that performs one or more special roles. The domain controllers assigned to these roles perform single-master operations. *Single-master operations* are operations that the domain does not permit to occur at different places in the domain at the same time. The domain controller that controls a particular operation owns the operations master role for that operation. The domain controller who owns a particular role can transfer ownership of that role to another domain controller. There are five operations masters roles in Windows 2000 domains.

- *Domain naming master*—The domain naming master controls domain addition and removal in the Active Directory forest. This master ensures that a new domain name is unique to the forest. There is only one domain naming master in a forest.

- *Infrastructure master*—Infrastructure changes, such as deleting or moving objects, occur on the infrastructure master. When you rename, move, or delete a member of a group, the infrastructure master is responsible for updating the group in its database. Updating this information is important so that all of the members of a domain know the new name or location of the member, or that the member has been deleted. There is only one infrastructure master in each domain.

- *PDC emulator*—The PDC emulator is the former PDC in a Windows NT 4.0 or NT 3.51 domain that has been migrated to Windows 2000. The new Windows 2000 domain controller retains the role of the PDC to maintain compatibility with Windows NT 4.0 and NT 3.51 servers that are still operating as BDCs in the NT domain. The Windows NT BDCs perceive the updated domain controller as the PDC and replicate from it. Only one PDC emulator can exist per Windows 2000 domain.

- *Relative ID master*—The relative ID master allocates RID sequences to each domain controller in its domain. Windows 2000 assigns Relative Identifiers (RIDs) any time a domain controller creates a user, computer, or group object. A RID is a unique security ID (SID) that consists of the domain's SID plus a unique RID that the relative ID master assigns. There is only one relative ID master in each domain in the forest.

8

NETWORK
SECURITY
ARCHITECTURE

- *Schema master*—The schema master controls all modifications and updates to the schema. The schema master replicates a copy of the schema to all domain controllers in the forest. There is only one schema master in the forest.

Modes of Operation for Windows 2000 Domains

Because Windows 2000 domains are capable of supporting both Windows NT 4.0-based servers and workstations within Windows 2000 domains, there are two possible modes of Windows 2000 domains.

Mixed Mode

A mixed mode domain is a domain with a mixture of Windows NT 4.0 and Windows 2000 domain controllers. Mixed mode provides the maximum backward compatibility with previous versions of the Windows operating system. Mixed mode only relates to the authentication infrastructure, the domain controllers, of a domain. When you decide to migrate your Windows NT 4.0 servers to Windows 2000, the PDC must be migrated first. After you have converted all of your Windows NT 4.0 servers to Windows 2000, you can convert to native mode. However, after you make the conversion to native mode, you cannot switch the domain back to mixed mode later.

Native Mode

A native mode domain is a domain that consists solely of Windows 2000 domain controllers and that you have explicitly switched to native mode operation. As soon as you upgrade to native mode, Windows NT 4.0 domain controllers will no longer be able to function in the domain. However, Windows NT 4.0 member servers and Windows NT 4.0, 98, and 95-based clients will continue to work without problems in the Windows 2000 native mode domain.

You should be aware that as long as you have legacy clients and servers running in the Windows 2000 domain, you need WIN servers for NetBIOS name resolution. Also, you shouldn't shut off NetBIOS over TCP/IP on machines running Windows 2000 until the network consists entirely of Windows 2000 machines, because legacy machines will be unable to communicate with the Windows 2000 machines. Legacy machines rely on NetBIOS calls for network communication.

Switching from Mixed to Native Mode

When you have upgraded or taken offline all Windows NT 4.0 BDCs, you can switch the network to Windows 2000 native mode. To switch to native mode, log on to a Windows 2000 domain controller with an administrator account, and do the following:

1. Click Start, choose Programs, Administrative Tools, and then choose Active Directory Domains and Trusts.

2. The Active Directory Domains and Trusts console appears. Right-click the domain you want to convert to native mode, and then click Properties.

3. The Properties dialog box appears with the General tab selected. Notice in the Domain Operation Mode information box, that the mode is mixed mode. In the General tab, click the Change Mode button.

4. An Active Directory dialog box appears. The dialog box asks if you are sure you want to change the domain to native mode. If you are sure that you want to make this change, click the Yes button. The domain controller makes the change immediately.

5. Click OK to close the Properties dialog box, and then exit Active Directory Domains And Trusts.

Your Windows 2000 domain is now running in native mode.

Interoperability and Heterogeneous Network Features

Today's network environments are, more often than not, heterogeneous. Many networks rely on a number of network operating systems that must interoperate with each other as well as newer intranet client/server environments and with legacy applications and operating systems. Microsoft supports key standards to ensure that the Windows 2000 operating system interoperates with existing technologies. Some of these standards include the following:

- *Client Services for Netware (CSNW)*—CSNW is included with the Windows 2000 Professional package and enables Windows 2000 clients to make connections to resources on machines running NetWare versions 2.x, 3.x, and 4.x servers.

- *File Server for Macintosh (MacFile)*—MacFile enables Macintosh clients and Windows 2000 clients to share files with each other. This service enables administrators to design a directory on a Windows 2000 machine as a Macintosh-accessible volume, handle permissions, and ensure that Macintosh filenames are legal NTFS names.

- *IPX/SPX/NetBIOS Compatible Transport Protocol (NWLink)*—NWLink is packaged with both Windows 2000 Server and Windows 2000 Professional. NWLink enables connectivity between computers running NetWare and those running Windows 2000. NWLink is an implementation of the internetwork packet exchange (IPX), sequenced packet exchange (SPX), and NetBIOS protocols that Novell networks use.

- *Services for NetWare version 5.0 (SFN5)*—SFN5 provides directory synchronization with NDS and Netware 3.x binderies, NetWare file and print server emulation software, and tools to help you migrate NetWare directory information and files to Windows 2000 server.

- *Services for UNIX 2.0 (SFU2.0)*—SFU2.0 provides a Network Information Service (NIS) server, a NIS to Active Directory migration wizard, a network file system (NFS) server, client and gateway support, username mapping support, and password synchronization.

- *TCP/IP Support*—Windows 2000 supports standards-based TCP/IP. Built-in support for Domain Name System (DNS), Dynamic Host Configuration Protocol (DHC), BOOTP, and remote procedure call (RPC) ensures that the Windows 2000 operating system can provide the necessary infrastructure to manage heterogeneous networks.

Further Reading on Windows 2000 Network Security and on Windows 2000 Interoperability

The following is a list of books and Web sites related to the subjects of Windows 2000 network security and Windows 2000 interoperability.

- *Windows 2000 Security.* Roberta Bragg. New Riders Publishing, 2000. ISBN: 0735709912.

- *Configuring Windows 2000 Server Security.* Thomas W. Shinder and D. Lynn White. Syngress Media, Inc., 1999. ISBN: 1928994024.

- *Windows 2000 Security Handbook*, Philip Cox and Tom Sheldon. McGraw-Hill Professional Publishing, 2000. ISBN: 0072124334.

- *Microsoft Windows 2000 Security Handbook*, Jeff Schmidt. Que, 2000. ISBN: 0789719991.

- *Windows NT/2000 Network Security (Circle Series)*, E. Eugene Schultz. New Riders Publishing, 2000. ISBN: 1578702534.

- *Windows 2000 Security: The Definitive Guide*, Richard Schwartz. John Wiley & Sons, 2001. ISBN: 0471387851.

- *UNIX and Windows 2000 Interoperability Guide*, Alan R. Roberts. Prentice Hall, 2001. ISBN: 013026332X.

- Windows IT Security (formerly NTSecurity.net) `http://www.ntsecurity.net/`.

- *An Introduction to the Windows 2000 Public Key Infrastructure*, `http://www.microsoft.com/WINDOWS2000/library/howitworks/security/pkiintro.asp`.

- *Windows 2000 Magazine Online*, `http://www.winntmag.com/`.

- *LabMice.net—The Windows 2000 Resource Index*, `http://www.labmice.net/`.

- *Windows 2000 Installation Security Checklist*,
  `http://www.labmice.net/articles/securingwin2000.htm`.

- *Systems Migration & Interoperability*,
  `http://www.microsoft.com/windows2000/library/interop/default.asp`.

Summary

This chapter covered some of the key concepts that relate to Windows 2000 network security. You also learned about Windows 2000 interoperability with other products and operating systems.

8

NETWORK
SECURITY
ARCHITECTURE

Network Protocols, Clients, and Services

IN THIS CHAPTER

This chapter focuses on networking theory and the main networking protocols and services that Windows 2000 uses for network communication. This chapter focuses specifically on TCP/IP and Netbios over TCP/IP (NetBT) protocols because they are most often the primary protocols used in Windows 2000 networks. This chapter also provides information on the higher-level protocols that Windows networks use to communicate and the name resolution services Windows 2000 machines require to locate one another on the network.

The purpose of this chapter is to provide some background knowledge of networking and protocols before the reader progresses to other chapters in the book where this knowledge is assumed. Later chapters in the book that cover topics such as denial of service attacks and the IP Sec protocol assume the reader is well versed in TCP/IP.

Open Systems Interconnection (OSI) Reference Model

The Open Systems Interconnection (OSI) model is a conceptual model that defines how software applications on different computers communicate with one another across a network. The OSI model is composed of seven layers, each of which has a unique responsibility in the communication process. Because each layer has its own responsibility, the layers are independent of one another, and modifications at one layer do not affect modifications at another layer. The OSI model was developed in 1984 by the International Standards Organization (ISO) and has become the standard architectural model for networking communications. The layers are as follows:

- Application Layer (7)
- Presentation Layer (6)
- Session Layer (5)
- Transport Layer (4)
- Network Layer (3)
- Data Link Layer (2)
- Physical Layer (1)

The lower levels in the model (1–4) handle the data transport across the network, while the upper layers (5–7) focus on application data. When communication occurs within a system, each layer communicates with the layer directly above and below. When communication occurs between systems, the request is sent down through the model to the physical layer. On the destination system, each layer communicates directly with the same layer or peer layer on the sending system, as seen in Figure 9.1.

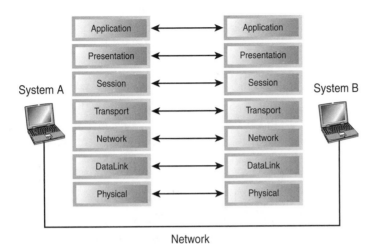

FIGURE 9.1

OSI model layers communicate directly with the same layer on the destination machine.

Each layer in the model has a Service Access Point (SAP) that allows the information to be moved between the layers on the sending system. As the information travels down the model, each layer encapsulates the higher level's information by appending header and trailer information to the higher level's data. The peer layer on the destination system will read the header and trailer information when the information arrives. The peer layer on the destination system removes the header and trailer information and the information is passed up to the next layer in the model through the SAP. This process continues through each layer in the model until the data reaches the application layer.

OSI Model Layers

The following sections discuss the individual layers of the OSI model and their responsibilities. The sections also discuss the layers' data format and addressing types.

Physical Layer

The physical layer is responsible for initiating, maintaining, and deactivating connections between systems. Voltage, frequency, maximum distance, and timing are all specified in the physical layer. Physical layer connections can either be the physical LAN or WAN connections. Examples of real-world implementations of the physical layer include the following:

- Ethernet
- IEEE 802.3
- 100BaseT

- Token Ring/IEEE 802.5
- FDDI

Data Link Layer

The data link layer is responsible for reliable transmission of data across the physical layer. The data link layer is responsible for physical addressing of systems, flow control, error notification, and frame sequencing. At the data link layer, error notification notifies the network layer that an error has occurred. The flow control at the data-link layer ensures that the receiving device's buffer is not overflowed by the sending system. The data format that is transmitted at the data link level is referred to as a *frame*. Frames can arrive out of order from the sending device, and the data link layer is responsible for reordering the frames.

The data link layer was subdivided into two sub-layers by the IEEE, as shown in Figure 9.2. The two sub-layers of the data link layer are the MAC sub-layer and the LLC sub-layer. The LLC sub-layer is defined in the IEEE 802.2 specification and is designed to allow multiple upper layer protocols to share a single physical layer connection. The 802.2 specification allows both connection-oriented and connectionless services in the higher layers and defines the number of fields in the data link frames.

FIGURE 9.2
Subdivision of the data link layer.

The MAC sub-layer manages access to the physical layer media. The IEEE MAC specification defines a MAC address as a standard, so devices on the network can uniquely identify one another at layer 2. MAC addresses are burned into the network adapter and uniquely identify both the manufacturer and the machine. A MAC address is 48 bits long expressed as 12 hexadecimal digits. The first 6 digits identify the manufacturer, and the last 6 digits uniquely identify the network interface. At the data link layer of the OSI model, the addressing space used to identify the devices is referred to as a *flat address space*. This means that all machines are viewed as individuals and have equal access to the media. There are no network addresses that define groups of machines, and there is no concept of routing at the data link layer.

Network Layer

The network layer introduces the concept of hierarchical address spaces and routing. Addressing at the network layer is logical versus the physical addressing that takes place at the data link layer. The administrator assigns the logical addresses instead of being burned into the network adapter by the manufacturer like the data-link layer. Hierarchical address spaces have the advantage of grouping addresses into blocks and then routing data between the blocks of addresses. This allows for each block of addresses to have its own physical segment of media allowing for more bandwidth for each system. Protocols at the network layer are responsible primarily for routing, but some are also used for network status and error information. Routing protocols at the network layer include: RIP, OSPF, EIGRP and BGP. The unit that is transmitted across the network at this layer is referred to as a *packet.*

Transport Layer

The transport layer implements reliable data transmissions and is responsible for flow control, multiplexing, error checking, and error recovery. Virtual sessions are established and maintained between systems at this level through processes such as the TCP three-way handshake. Flow control is implemented and can automatically adjust transmission levels based on network conditions. Data is error checked, and if errors are discovered, the receiving system can request a retransmission from the sending system. The unit of data that transmitted over the network at the transport layer is referred to as a *segment.* The best example of a transport layer protocol is TCP.

Session Layer

The session layer establishes, maintains, and terminates communication sessions between presentation layers on separate systems. The session layer transmits service requests and service responses between applications. An example of a session layer protocol is AppleTalk's Zone Information Protocol (ZIP).

Presentation Layer

The presentation layer is responsible for data coding and conversion of application level data. The purpose of the presentation layer is to make sure data is readable when it arrives at the destination system. Presentation layer services include data formats, compression, and encryption. Presentation layer data formats include ASCII, EBCDIC, MPEG, GIF, and TIFF.

Application Layer

The application layer is the highest level in the OSI model and is the layer closest to the end user. Data transmission units at the application layer are referred to as *messages.* Software applications that have a communication component access the application layer to send messages to the application layer on the destination system. Examples of application layer protocols include FTP, SMTP, and Telnet.

Connection and Connectionless Services

Networking communication generally involves two types of communications—connection-oriented and connectionless communications. Connection-oriented traffic is used for reliable transmission of data across the network and requires a session between two systems be established and maintained for the duration of the session. Connection-oriented data transmissions include three phases—session establishment, data transmission, and session termination. Connection-oriented data transmission determines the path the data will take before the transmission begins. Connection-oriented transmissions are used for applications that cannot tolerate delays or packet resequencing. Connection-oriented services do come with a penalty in that the connection management requires additional overhead on the sending and receiving systems. Real-time applications, such as traditional voice and video applications, generally use connection-oriented data transfers because the data must arrive to make sense to the end user. The reader should note that the implementation of many modern streaming voice and video applications do use UDP for data transfer, which is a connectionless protocol. This seems to make this example confusing unless you consider the fact that the streaming client is buffering the data to make sure the sound presented to the user is heard in order. If the buffering wasn't occurring in the UDP-based application, the transmission would be garbled. Theoretically, voice and video applications need connection-oriented service.

Connectionless services do not require that a specific session be established to transmit data. Connectionless services assume that there is a permanently established link, and that the data transmission will get there. Connectionless traffic is used when 100 percent reliable data transmission (zero packet loss) is not required and applications can tolerate delays and out of order packets. Connectionless data transmissions carry less overhead and are more flexible in that they can use dynamic path selection. Data-based applications typically use connectionless data transmissions.

TCP/IP

TCP/IP has become the standard internetworking protocol on corporate LANs and is well suited for LAN and WAN communication. TCP/IP is a suite of protocols that provide network, transport, and application layer protocols. It was first developed in the mid 1970s by the Defense Advanced Research Projects Agency (DARPA) to establish a packet-switched network to link research computers. TCP/IP was incorporated into BSD UNIX distributions that were used to build the first Internet computers.

TCP/IP has four layers in its networking model. TCP/IP identifies the application, transport, network, and physical layers of the OSI reference model. Figure 9.3 shows how the TCP/IP protocol stack maps into the OSI reference model.

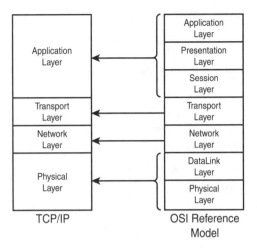

FIGURE 9.3
TCP/IP and the OSI reference model.

TCP/IP is managed by the Internet community through public papers called Request for Comments (RFCs). The RFCs eventually become Internet Drafts and work their way to becoming official standards through refinements at the proposed and draft standard levels. The following sections discuss the basics of the main TCP/IP protocols. Many of the protocols discussed are used in security exploits covered in later chapters. This section is meant to familiarize the reader with the way these protocols operate and some of the key fields used in these protocols.

Internet Protocol (IP)

The Internet Protocol (IP) is a layer 3 or network layer protocol in the TCP/IP stack. IP was defined in RFC 791 and is responsible for providing connectionless service across the network and for providing fragmentation and reassembly of packets to support different physical media with different maximum transfer unit sizes (MTU).

IP packets contain the following fields:

- *Version*—Indicates the IP version number. The current version is 4, but IP v.6 is in use in some networks. If the system cannot handle the version, it discards the packet.
- *IP Header Length*—Length of the header information so the receiver knows when the header information ends and data begins.
- *Type of Service*—Specifies how the upper layer wants IP to handle the information based on the segment's importance.
- *Length*—Indicates the total length of the packet, including the header and data.

9

PROTOCOLS,
CLIENTS, AND
SERVICES

- *Identification*—Includes a unique identifier that is used to reassemble fragmented packets.

- *Flags*—The flag field indicates whether the packet cannot be fragmented by setting the Don't Fragment bit (DF) or if the packet is already fragmented by setting the More Fragments bit (MF).

- *Fragment Offset*—Contains the position of the fragment in the completed message.

- *Time to Live*—The amount of time the packet can remain on the network before it is discarded.

- *Protocol*—This designates the destination layer 4 protocols. Common protocols are TCP (6), ICMP (1) and UDP (11).

- *Header Checksum*—Checksum information for header information.

- *Source Address*—The source system's IP address.

- *Destination Address*—The destination system's IP address.

- *Options*—Supports options, such as security.

- *Data*—The contents of the packet to be passed to the next layer.

IP defines a hierarchical addressing scheme that makes the routing of packets through the internetwork possible. The IP address is a 32-bit address that is displayed in dotted decimal notation. The address is grouped in blocks of 8 bits and is divided into two sections—network and host. The network section identifies a particular network, similar to the way a zip code identifies a group of areas in the postal system. The host portion of the address identifies a particular host on a particular network in the same way that a street address identifies a house within the postal system.

The IP address ranges are grouped into classes as follows: A, B, C, D, and E. The valid IP address ranges for each class are shown in Figure 9.4. These address ranges are the ranges that are available on the Internet.

Address Class	First Octet Decimal
Class A	1–126
	127 (Reserved For LoopBack)
Class B	128–191
Class C	192–223
Class D	224–239
Class E	240–254

FIGURE 9.4

IP addresses and classes.

In the late 1990s, as the Internet boom took off, IP addresses were beginning to become scarce. RFC 1918 was introduced to allow ranges of addresses considered private to be used inside an organization's network behind a firewall or other device that prevents packets with the private source addresses from leaving the network. The private address ranges are as follows:

- 10.0.0.0 /8 (255.0.0.0)
- 172.16.0.0 /12 (255.240.0.0)
- 192.168.0.0 /16 (255.255.0.0)

The private address ranges are considered non-routable addresses on the Internet. Most Internet routers can be configured to drop packets with a destination address from the private address range. Many network attacks discussed later in this book use addresses from the private address range as the source address when launching Internet-based attacks. Using a private address allows the attacker to hide the location from where the attack is launched.

To make the most out of the number of networks and hosts within an IP address range, a subnet mask is used. A *subnet mask* defines where the network portion of the IP address ends and the host portion begins. So instead of having one network with 254 hosts, an administrator can configure two networks with 126 hosts on each network. This section of the chapter does not cover IP addressing to the level of detail of how to subnet an internetwork, but the reader should understand that the first address in the address range that the subnet mask defines is called the *network address*, and the last address in the range is called the *broadcast address*. Notice in the previous subnetting example that when the address space was subnetted into two networks, two host addresses were lost. This is due to one additional address being used for the network address and one being used for the broadcast address, because we created two networks.

You should note that subnet masks could be written in two forms—bit notation and dotted decimal notation. Dotted decimal notation is generally the most common way to write a subnet mask in the Windows world. An example of a subnet mask expressed in dotted decimal form is 255.0.0.0. Bit notation defines the number of bits in the subnet mask, rather than writing all four octets of the subnet mask. The bit notation expression of the 255.0.0.0 subnet mask is written as /8 because all 8 bits are masked. Many internetworking devices, such as routers, express subnet masks in bit notation.

Network addresses are used by routers to route traffic throughout the internetwork. Routing tables only hold network addresses and use the concept of route summarization to simplify the routing tables. Route summarization refers to a group of networks by a portion of their network address. For example, if the organization uses 192.168.1.0 through 192.168.24.0 in its West Coast locations, and 172.16.0.0 through 172.16.24.0 in its East Coast locations, the router only has to look at the first few bits of each network address as it routes packets to determine whether the packet is destined to the East or West interface.

Broadcast addresses are used by hosts on networks to send messages to all hosts on a particular network. When a system is configured with an IP address, it automatically listens for broadcasts on the broadcast address of the network it's located on by default. A system must stop and analyze the broadcast packet to see if it must act on the result. Broadcasts are used to locate services or to send status messages to the network. Broadcasts can be used by an attacker to force all machines on a particular network to perform a specific task at the same time.

Internet Control Message Protocol (ICMP)

ICMP was defined in RFC 792 and is a network layer protocol that uses packets to report error conditions and other status information about the network. The following are some of the ICMP messages that can be generated:

- *Destination Unreachable*—Destination unreachable messages will send additional information to the host including the following messages:
  - *Network unreachable*—Indicating a routing or addressing failure
  - *Host unreachable*—Indicating a delivery failure, such as an incorrect subnet mask
  - *Protocol unreachable*—Indicting the host does not support the protocol specified in the packet
  - *Port unreachable*—Indicating that the host does not support that socket or port
- *Echo Request*—Echo requests are generated by the `ping` command and used to contact a host on a local or remote network to generate a response.
- *Echo Reply*—An echo reply is automatically sent to the source address when an echo request is received. This is used for legitimate purposes to see if a host is alive.
- *Redirect*—Redirects are sent to hosts by the router on the network to inform them if a more efficient route exists. Not all TCP/IP stacks support ICMP redirects. The Windows 2000 TCP/IP stack does support ICMP redirects, but only if the redirect comes from the default gateway or is an address on a directly connected network. If the redirect meets this criteria, a route is added to the host's route table with a 10-minute lifetime.
- *Time Exceeded*—Time exceeded messages are sent by a router to a host when the Time to Live (TTL) on a packet reached zero. The trace route (`tracert`) command is one command that used the TTL to its advantage. Trace route sends an echo request packet with a TTL of 1 to the default gateway and then sends subsequent echo request packets incrementing the TTL on the packet by 1. This gives a response from each hop in the path to the final destination address.
- *Router Advertisement*—This feature can be used to auto-configure a host's default gateway. The host will listen for periodic router advertisements and will select the router with the highest precedence field. The Windows 2000 TCP/IP stack supports auto-configuration of the default gateway through ICMP router advertisements.

- *Router Solicitation*—If a host does not hear router advertisements, the host can send a router solicitation message to try and locate a new default route. The Windows 2000 TCP/IP stack supports router solicitation messages.

Other ICMP message types include Timestamp, Address mask Request/Reply, Traceroute, and many others. For a complete list of ICMP message types, refer to `http://www.cotse.com/icmptypes.html`.

Transmission Control Protocol (TCP)

The TCP protocol is the TCP/IP stacks layer-4 protocol that provides reliable delivery of segments. TCP is used for one-to-one communications or unicast network conversations. TCP uses the concept of forward acknowledgements to provide streamlined data transfers. The source tells the destination the next packet it should receive. Packets that are not acknowledged within the timeout windows are requested to be retransmitted. This allows TCP to deal with changing conditions on the network that might delay or drop packets in transit.

TCP uses efficient flow control processes. The destination host notifies the sender of the largest sequence number it can handle without overflowing its buffer. The sending system can then adjust the data transfer to what the receiver can handle. TCP connections can also send and receive data at the same time; that also increases the throughput of the data transfer.

TCP packets include the following fields:

- *Source and Destination Port*—Identifies the application layer's process that should receive the request.
- *Sequence Number*—The number assigned to the segment to track the successful delivery of the segment.
- *Acknowledgement Number*—Contains the sequence number for the next byte the sender expects to receive.
- *Data Offset*—The number of 32-bit words that are in the TCP header. The Data Offset is used to identify the start of the data field and the end of the header information.
- *Reserved*—Not Used. 6-bit field and all bits must be set to 0.
- *Flags*—Includes the SYN, ACK, RST, Push, URG, and FIN bits.
- *Window*—The size of the sender's receive window in bytes.
- *Checksum*—Used to verify if the segment header was damaged in transit.
- *Urgent Pointer*—Used to point to the first urgent byte of data in the segment if the URG flag was set on the segment.
- *Options*—Used to specify TCP options, such as the end of the option list, no operation, and maximum segment size.
- *Data*—Information to be passed to the application layer.

Windows 2000 uses TCP for the logon process, file and print sharing, domain controller replication, distribution of browse lists, as well as many other functions. Windows 2000 TCP is compliant with RFC 793 and section 4.2 of RFC 1122.

TCP Connections

When a TCP connection is established, it uses what is known as the *three-way handshake*. The handshake synchronizes both ends of the connection, and both ends agree on the starting sequence numbers to use for the connection. Because TCP is a reliable protocol, the handshake process is done so that both sides of the connection are ready to send and receive data. The steps to establish connectivity through the three-way handshake is as follows:

1. The client sends a SYN request to the server with the initial sequence number (SEQ#).

2. The server receives the SYN, and records the sequence number (SEQ#), replies with a SYN/ACK that acknowledges the clients SYN with an ACK (SEQ# +1), and returns a SYN with the server's sequence number (SEQ#).

3. The client responds to the server's SYN with an ACK (SEQ# +1).

4. Connection established.

The process of returning an incremented sequence number is called *forward acknowledgement*. This increases the efficiency of the data transmission by minimizing the number of acknowledgements that are sent across the network.

TCP Sliding Window

The TCP sliding window increases the efficiency of data transmissions across the network. The sliding window allows multiple packets to be transmitted before an acknowledgement is sent. The receiving system sends its window size in every packet. This allows the sending system to send as many packets as the receiver's windows size will allow before waiting for an acknowledgement. The sliding window, combined with the forward acknowledgement, increases the efficiency of the data transfer, because a receiver can send one acknowledgement for many packets. If the receiver sends back a window size of zero, this indicates to the sender that the receiver's buffer is full and the sender must wait for another acknowledgement with a window size greater than zero before sending more data.

On Windows 2000 systems, the TCP window size defaults to 16KB (16,384 bytes) on the first connection request. On most Ethernet TCP connections, the window is adjusted automatically to 17,520 bytes. Windows NT 4.0 used a window size of 8760 bytes. Microsoft increased the windows size in Windows 2000 to support faster networking technologies, such as gigabit Ethernet.

Universal Datagram Protocol (UDP)

UDP is another layer-4 protocol in the TCP/IP stack. It differs from TCP in that it is a connectionless protocol and provides no flow control, reliability, or error recovery. UDP datagrams require less bandwidth, have less overhead, and are generally used for one to many network conversations, such as broadcasts or multicasts. Microsoft applications use UDP for browsing and NetBIOS name resolution. UDP can be used when the application-level protocols provide the flow control and error correction. UDP is also used by SNMP, TFTP, and DNS name queries. UDP datagrams contain the following fields:

- *Source Port*—Sender's port number
- *Destination Port*—Receiver's UDP port number to pass the request directly to the correct application level's process
- *Length*—Specifies the length of the UDP header and data
- *Checksum*—Optional integrity check on the header and data

Windows 2000 Clients, Protocols, and Services

This section of the chapter focuses specifically on Windows 2000 clients, protocols, and services. The Windows platform can be a confusing topic when discussing protocols. This section attempts to clarify some of the confusing terms and services that administrators come across when dealing with Windows 2000 networking.

Windows 2000 TCP/IP Stack Architecture

The following section discusses the Windows 2000 TCP/IP stack and networking architecture. It's important to understand the Microsoft terms and description of the stack and its upper-layer services. Most of the confusion about Windows networking comes from the upper-layer services, such as Netbios, RPC, and Mailslots. Microsoft describes the Windows 2000 network architecture as having the following levels:

- *NDIS Layer*—Allows the transport access to the physical layer. The NDIS layer acts as a buffer between network adapters and the network protocols. The NDIS layer manages the binding of the network protocol to network card.
- *Network Protocol Layer*—Provides the network transport. Services at this level include TCP/IP, IPX/SPX, DLC, IRDa, AppleTalk, NetBeui, and SNA.
- *Transport Driver Interface Layer*—Provides a standard interface between the network protocols and the clients that use their services, such as network applications or networking Application Programming Interfaces (APIs).

- *Network Application Programming Interface*—Provides standard programming interfaces from network applications and services. This includes the Messaging API (MAPI), Telephony API (TAPI), Netbios, Winsock, and Wnet.

- *Interprocess Communication (IPC)*—The IPC layer supports client/server computing and distributed computing, such as n-tier applications. At this level, services such as DCOM, RPC, named pipes, mailslots, and CIFS are supported.

- *Networking Services*—These include the standard Windows 2000 services that allow users to access information, such as the Workstation and Server service, as well as the Redirector.

The Windows 2000 network architecture is displayed in Figure 9.5.

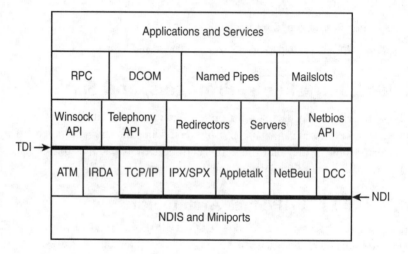

FIGURE 9.5
Windows 2000 network architecture.

The following sections describe the layers of the Windows 2000 network architecture in more detail. The NDIS level has been excluded from this discussion because it is at the lower layers, and most Windows 2000 administrators understand network cards and drivers.

Network Protocol Layer

The Windows 2000 network protocol layer supports many protocols, including TCP/IP, IPX/SPX, DLC, Infrared Data Associate (IRDa), AppleTalk, NetBeui, and ATM. By adding the services of Host Integration Server, Windows 2000 can also support SNA. This section focuses on the most often used protocols at this layer—TCP/IP and Netbios over TCP/IP.

TCP/IP

TCP/IP has become the standard networking protocol in Windows 2000 environments primarily due to the fact that it's fast, routable, and because of its use on the Internet. The details of TCP/IP were discussed in the previous section of this chapter. In this section of the chapter, the new features in the Windows 2000 TCP/IP stack are discussed. These are significant improvements in the TCP/IP stack that was used in Windows NT 4.0.

- *Large Window Support*—Large windows improve the data transmission efficiency, allowing more data to be transmitted across the network before an acknowledgement is required to be sent to the sender. Windows 2000 systems can use a window size of up to 64KB.

- *Selective Acknowledgement*—Normally, the TCP/IP stack retransmits all packets from the point of the retransmit request on. For example, if packets 5, 6, and 7 were sent and the receiver received 6 and 7 but not 5, all three segments would be resent. Selective acknowledgement allows for only the missing segments to be resent—in this case, 5. This allows the network to recover faster from periodic congestion.

- *RTT Estimation*—The Windows 2000 TCP/IP stack can estimate the roundtrip times. This is useful in setting the timeout value for how long to wait before the packet is assumed to be missing and a retransmission is requested. The RTT will adjust dynamically to changing network conditions. This is beneficial when sending data over international WAN links and satellite links that have additional latency.

- *IP Security*—IPSec allows for the encryption of network traffic at layer 3. This provides an increased level of security and confidentiality of network data. IPSec services are transparent to the upper layers and applications. IPSec can be configured through local Windows 2000 policies or through group policies configured in Active Directory. IPSec does increase the overhead of networking functions on the operating system because each packet must be encrypted and decrypted. For more information on IPSec, refer to Chapter 20, "IPSec."

- *Generic Quality of Service*—QOS is implemented within the Winsock Network Application Programming Interface and allows networking applications to request quality of service for certain types of traffic. This allows for developers to develop real-time applications that can use voice and video services without sacrificing quality.

Netbios over TCP/IP

Netbios over TCP/IP (NetBT) is the process of encapsulating Netbios information inside a TCP/IP packet so that it can be routed across the internetwork. NetBT is defined in RFC 1001 and 1002. Netbios is a software interface and not a protocol, and NetBT was developed to allow interoperability between operating systems using Netbios and to extend the reach of Netbios from the LAN.

NetBT was the only TCP/IP networking option for Windows NT 4.0 systems. NetBT systems require a Netbios name resolution system to locate services and function on the network. This can either be achieved by using a LMHOSTS file or by using the Windows Internet Naming Service (WINS) that translates Netbios names and services to IP addresses.

Windows 2000 provides the option of using NetBT or pure TCP/IP. Eliminating NetBT on the network will reduce the overhead of network communications, but it will also eliminate the ability to communicate with downlevel Windows NT and Windows 9.x systems.

Many older Windows applications were written using Netbios. These applications will not be able to function without NetBT. The Windows 2000 Alerter, Browser, Messenger, Netlogon, Server, and Workstation services are still Netbios-based. However, these services were rewritten to use the Transport Driver Interface Layer (TDI) that is more efficient and removes some of the limitations of legacy Netbios. See the following section in this chapter for more information on the Transport Driver Interface (TDI).

To support pure TCP/IP environments, the Windows 2000 Redirector and Server service support a new concept called direct hosting. This means they no longer require Netbios to function and will not send a Netbios header in their communications. When requests for services are made, the server will use Netbios calls and the direct hosting calls if NetBT is enabled. Both calls are made at the same time. The Windows 2000 operating system will use the connection from the first response returned. Direct hosting uses DNS for name resolution and uses TCP port 445.

Transport Driver Interface

The Transport Driver Interface (TDI) was developed to separate some of the Windows 2000 services, such as the Server service and the Redirector, from the network layer transport. In Windows NT 4.0, the services and protocols were linked through NetBT. In Windows 2000, the services are written to call the TDI that then talks to the network transport protocol. Using the TDI provides for modular development and allows services and protocols to act independently, provided they adhere to and use the TDI specification.

Microsoft has also provided a Netbios emulator. This is a mapping layer to allow legacy Netbios applications to have their calls mapped to functions within the TDI.

Network Application Programming Interfaces

An Application Programming Interface (API) is a "wrapper" for lower-level functions. The API can be called through a set of functions to allow the higher-level application to perform lower-level functions, such as locating machines on the network. Windows 2000 supports the following major Network APIs. A brief description of each of the major networking APIs follows:

- *Messaging API (MAPI)*—MAPI allows programmers to access messaging services, such as Exchange Server 2000, through a single programming interface. Establishing a session with a user's mailbox is one of the functions that uses networking capabilities.

- *Netbios*—Netbios is included in Windows 2000 to support legacy client/server applications. Netbios applications can communicate over various networking protocols, such as NetBEUI, NetBT, and NWLink (IPX/SPX).

- *Telephony API (TAPI)*—This API allows PCs to be integrated into telephone networks. TAPI is able to transmit both speech and data and supports call management, conference calling, and voice mail. Applications that can take advantage of TAPI include video conferencing services, voice-over IP applications, and other call center and PBX applications.

- *Windows Sockets (Winsock)*—This is the Windows version of the Sockets interface found on other operating systems that allows the application layer to access the transport protocols. Windows 2000 supports both Winsock 1.1 and 2.0 services. Winsock 2.0 provides access to name resolutions services, Quality of Service (QOS), and multicast capabilities.

- *Wnet API*—Wnet is also known as the Win32 APIs and it allows applications to take advantage of Windows networking functions. Wnet use the redirector for its network calls.

Interprocess Communication

Interprocess Communication (IPC) is a two-way communication mechanism that can run between clients and servers of an application and can occur within a single system's processes or in a distributed application over the network. Distributed applications divide up work among machines to allow optimization of the machine for faster processing. Classic distributed computing is the client/server model where multiple clients run a portion of the application on their local machines but access information and the information crunching functions from a single server.

Multi-layer applications, such as n-tier and Windows DNA applications, extend the client/server model to make it more modular and scalable by using a server tier and a middle tier called the business tier, as shown in Figure 9.6. The business tier handles the business rules and communicates with the servers in the server tier. Clients communicate only with the business tier.

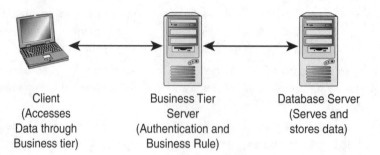

Client
(Accesses
Data through
Business tier)

Business Tier
Server
(Authentication and
Business Rule)

Database Server
(Serves and
stores data)

FIGURE 9.6
N-tier applications.

For most administrators, this stuff isn't very important, with the exception that something has to manage all the interactions between these application processes that can reside on single or multiple machines. This section is designed to give the Windows 2000 administrator an overview of the IPC mechanisms to understand how they fit into the Windows 2000 network architecture. The following IPC mechanisms handle the IPC communication within Windows 2000.

- *Remote Procedure Calls*—RPC is an industry standard IPC mechanism that allows client and server processes to communicate over the network. Windows is not the only platform that uses RPC. Windows is unique in that its RPC uses Winsock, named pipes, or Netbios for the client/server connections. RPC is implemented through DLLs. Clients have a stub version of the application's DLL that direct them to go to the RPC server. RPC clients must locate the RPC server to perform the work within the application so name resolution services are required. This is performed with Windows 2000 RPC locator service. RPC servers can now store information in Active Directory so clients have only one place to look to locate the RPC servers. RPC is also still supported through named pipes, mailslots, and Netbios broadcasts in Windows 2000.

- *DCOM*—DCOM is distributed COM. DCOM lets COM objects run across the network. COM objects normally are created on the local machine, but DCOM allows them to be created on another machine. For example, DCOM can allow a client to create a new session for an application and the session object could be created on the business tier server rather than the client machine. DCOM simplifies IPC between machines by the application only having to know what server the object is on, and then DCOM handles the network communication. DCOM also handles other functions, such as security permissions and authentication for remote objects.

- *Named Pipes*—Named Pipes is a high-level, connection-oriented service that configures a pipe or virtual circuit between two machines to transmit and receive information. Data transfer must be sequential and reliable for named pipes to function. Windows 2000 supports named pipes for backwards compatibility and has added an additional security feature called impersonation. *Impersonation* allows the server to impersonate the client to ensure the client permissions are applied when accessing data.

- *Mailslots*—Mailslots is a connectionless service used to locate and provide notifications about computers and services. Mailslots use a broadcast mechanism to deliver the notifications. An example of a Windows 2000 service that uses mailslots is the Computer Browser service. Mailslots are also included for backwards compatibility.

- *Common Internet File System (CIFS)*—CIFS is used to share files between machines and is an enhanced version of Microsoft's Server Message Blocks (SMB) protocol. CIFS is designed to share files over the Internet and replace legacy protocols, such as FTP. CIFS enhances HTTP, uses DNS for name resolution, and uses TCP port 445. CIFS can access files on a variety of systems and manages file locking and file integrity. CIFS is also optimized for slow links.

Networking Services and Clients

The networking services and clients section discusses some of the networking services within Windows 2000 and the functions they perform. Understanding what these services do is critical when securing systems and deciding if these services should be disabled in a particular configuration.

- *Redirector*—The Redirector is the component that permits computers to access one another over the network. The redirector resides above the TDI. The redirector determines what protocol and provider to use for the remote connection. Providers can be for Microsoft, Novell, or UNIX systems.

- *Server Service*—The Server Service is implemented within Windows 2000 as File and Printer Sharing for Microsoft Networks. File and Printer Sharing for Microsoft Networks is installed by default and can be disabled or uninstalled from the properties of the LAN adapter. The Server Service allows the Windows 2000 systems to permit connections to file shares and printers it's hosting. The Server Service is located above the TDI and is a file system driver—Srv.sys. The Server Service fulfills requests made by client-side redirectors.

- *Workstation Service*—The Workstation Service is implemented in Windows 2000 as Client for Microsoft Networks. Client for Microsoft Networks is installed by default and can be disabled or uninstalled from the properties of the LAN adapter. The Workstation Service allows the Windows 2000 system to access files and printers on other servers in the network. When requests are made to access resources, the Workstation Service passes the request to the redirector.

Additional information on other Windows 2000 services can be found in Chapter 7, "Windows 2000 Services."

Name Resolution Services

Name resolution services are required for computers to locate one another on the network. Name resolution services map machine names and network services to IP addresses. The name resolution service used will depend on the layer-4 protocol that is in use on the network. When using NetBT, organizations can use either WINS or DNS. When the network is using pure TCP/IP or Active Directory, DNS is required as the name resolution service. Active Directory also requires dynamic DNS allowing computers to register the services they provide so other clients can locate them. The following sections cover each name resolution service in more detail.

Windows Internet Name Service (WINS)

Windows Internet Name Service (WINS) is required in NetBT-based networks that do not use Active Directory. Netbios is a broadcast-based service and WINS must be enabled to enable Netbios-based communication in a TCP/IP internetwork. WINS allows computers to register in a central database that tracks the computer's Netbios name and its corresponding IP address. WINS also tracks the IP addresses of other required services in a Windows-based network, such as the Primary Domain Controller (PDC), Backup Domain Controllers (BDC), and the network browse lists. Each of these services is registered with a special code in the WINS database and maps to a machine or group of machines' IP address. All NetBT-based machines must point to a WINS server in their TCP/IP configuration for the client to look up the IP address or service in the WINS database.

Netbios over TCP/IP uses the following TCP/IP ports to communicate:

- *UDP 137*—Netbios Name Services
- *UDP 138*—Netbios Datagram Services
- *UDP 139*—Netbios Session Services

These ports must be open on the internetwork for name resolution and connectivity between machines to occur. For more information on planning WINS installations for Windows 2000 networks, refer to the Windows Internet Name Service (WINS) Architecture and Capacity Planning white paper available at http://www.microsoft.com/ntserver/techresources/commnet/WINS/WINSwp98/WINS02-12.asp.

Domain Naming System (DNS)

The Domain Name System (DNS) is the standard name resolution service on the Internet and on internal TCP/IP networks. Windows 2000 provides native support for DNS and dynamic registration of DNS records. It also provides the added advantage of being able to replicate

DNS records through Active Directory Replication. Windows 2000 DNS can be configured to support standard primary and standard secondary zones that are compatible with DNS servers running on other platforms.

DNS uses the following TCP/IP ports for communication:

- *TCP 53*—Zone Transfers
- *UDP 53*—Name Queries

For more information on planning DNS installations for Windows 2000 networks, refer to the Windows 2000 DNS Whitepaper available at `http://www.microsoft.com/windows2000/ techinfo/howitworks/communications/nameadrmgmt/w2kdns.asp`. Information on configuring secure Windows 2000 DNS servers is included in Chapter 15, "Protecting Other Internet Services."

Summary

This chapter has provided an overview of conceptual network connectivity and the TCP/IP protocol stack. It also provided some insight into the Windows 2000 network architecture and how the OSI model layer 3 and 4 protocols work together with some of the higher-level application layer mechanisms used in Windows 2000 networking. Lastly, the chapter provided a quick overview of the name resolution mechanisms that are commonly used in Windows 2000 internetworking.

Trojans and Backdoors

IN THIS CHAPTER

This chapter provides an overview of the challenges that network administrators face when trying to secure their company's Windows 2000 networks from code traditionally thought of as viruses. We chose the title for the chapter, "Trojans and Backdoors," because it is familiar to most network administrators. This chapter really addresses a much larger scope of security threats called Malicious Code Attacks. As the reader will see, it's difficult to classify a modern malicious code attack as only a virus, Trojan, worm, and so on because a single attack can have properties of each of several attacks.

Microsoft has designed the Windows environment with openness and ease of use in mind. While these design ideals are great for the end user, they pose significant challenges to network administrators and provide opportunities for those individuals who want to compromise systems or cause havoc. This chapter first examines the threats known as Malicious Code Attacks. The chapter then examines several of the recent high profile attacks and their resolutions. Understanding past attacks will help administrators understand the defenses that worked in the past. This can help reduce the impact of current attacks because many current attacks are variations of previous attacks.

The second section of this chapter provides a process that network administrators can follow to protect their networks from Malicious Code Attacks. Many Malicious Code Attacks are preventable when an organization follows a well thought out security plan, educates its users, and keeps its pattern files for its virus software updated.

The final section of the chapter provides network administrators with some additional sources of information to help them build and implement security policies that will secure their networks from Malicious Code Attacks. One such resource is the National Security Agency, which provides several extensive security recommendation guides for Windows 2000 and even provides Security Configuration Editor templates to implement the policies. Network administrators need to remember that securing their networks is an ongoing, continually evolving process and not a set-it-and-forget-it task. Hopefully, the resources in this section will continue to provide value throughout the life of your network.

Understanding Malicious Code Attacks

Malicious Code Attacks come in many different forms. A malicious code attack can be comprised of one or more different types of malicious code types defined in this section all working together in a single attack.

Terminology

Before reviewing the anatomy of a malicious code attack, let's review some of the terminology and definitions of the components used in the attack.

- *Virus*—The classic computer virus attaches itself to other programs and is executed whenever the infected program is run. Like human viruses, computer viruses need a human to help the virus spread. Viruses can be spread through e-mail, shared media, or shared files. Viruses come in the following forms: boot sector, macro, `.com` and `.exe` infectors, joke, and many others. The action the virus performs on a victim system is referred to as the *payload*.

- *Trojan*—This is any program that performs like a legitimate program but also performs unauthorized actions. The actions are most often unknown to the user. In some instances, the Trojan might provide the user clues that the program they ran is malicious. A Trojan requires that the user execute the program for the Trojan to activate. Trojans can perform any actions that the end user has permissions to execute. This can include deleting files, sending e-mail, or installing backdoor-type programs. This is one reason why administrators should never use an account with administrative rights for their daily office tasks. Many modern Trojans are received through e-mail attachments, but they can also be contracted from shared media or through social engineering leading to unauthorized access to systems.

- *Worms*—A worm is a virus that, when initiated, is capable of spreading to other computers without user intervention. Worms can propagate through e-mail, IRC chat clients, and unprotected Windows file shares.

- *Backdoor*—Backdoor programs, such as Back Orifice, Netbus, and SubSeven, allow others to remotely control the user's computer when they are installed.

- *Hacker*—The definition for this term depends on whom you ask. Some refer to hackers as "good guys" who push the bounds of systems for the sake of securing the systems. These types of hackers are usually system programmers or security consultants with an extremely high level of technical competency. Others, such as the media, make no distinctions between hackers and crackers. The Information Technology Association of America (ITAA) and CERT profiled a hacker as having any of the following motivations:

  - Explorers who turn the doorknobs of cyberspace just to see what opens.

  - Good Samaritans who cut information security corners to get the job done faster or better.

  - Hackers who break into systems to impress themselves and others.

  - Machiavellians who, not surprisingly, use computer hacking skills to advance a personal agenda.

  - Exceptions see themselves as candidates for special information security care and handling.

  - Avengers who are looking for revenge in response to perceived slights and setbacks.

- Career thieves who are computer-enabled, white-collar crooks, embezzlers, con artists, and others who view their employment as little more than a license to steal.

  - Moles steal too, but for governments or other companies.

- *Cracker*—A malicious individual or vandal seeking to compromise systems, prevent access to systems, steal information, destroy systems, or cause havoc. Crackers have been responsible for many modern malicious code attacks and denial of service attacks. Crackers usually exploit well-known defects and use simple tools to execute their attacks.

Malicious Code Attack Scenario

Malicious code attacks can be launched in various ways. Active X controls, Java applets, and JavaScript can all be used to exploit system weaknesses to install malicious code on Windows Systems with or without the user's knowledge. These technologies can all be exploited to install backdoor type programs, such as Back Orifice or SubSeven. They can also be used to install agents for denial of service attacks or scripts that can destroy the system integrity.

Other malicious code attack scenarios can involve receiving the malicious code through e-mail. Virus authors have been quite successful creating world-wide havoc over the past few years with viruses replicated through e-mail. CERT/CC, a major reporting center for Internet security problems, reported that more than 300 companies reported Melissa virus infections for a total count of more than 100,000 PCs when the virus was first released.

With either method, the user is lured to a Web site or sent an e-mail with the malicious code. The code is then installed either by the user launching a Trojan program or downloading the code. The code is then launched and attempts are made by the virus to replicate itself and cause destruction or collect information about the compromised system.

When a malicious code attack occurs, it's tough to control. End users can execute malicious code through Trojan programs without understanding the consequences and might not realize anything is wrong. After a malicious code attack strikes, the only option is to contain the strike and perform a cleanup. Virus protection software is essential, but when a malicious code attack hits, it might be hours until a pattern file is released to update the anti-virus installations. The ability to filter e-mail messages, Web sites, and network connections becomes essential to controlling the damage after an attack occurs. Organizations should also report the incident to organizations, such as CERT/CC, for assistance with the cleanup and for additional information of the severity and possible damage the attack is causing on the company network. Prevention of malicious code attacks should focus heavily on educating end users about the safe use of the organization's computer systems, as well as technical solutions.

Perpetrators

Several of the recent malicious code attacks have come from outside the United States. For example, the Love Letter virus and many other malicious code viruses were created in Asia and South America, which can make the attacks hard to trace. Because many of the authors of malicious code are overseas, prosecuting the offenders is difficult.

More powerful tools for attackers are arriving all the time. Many malicious code authors use Virus Creation Kits (VCKs) to build their viruses. For example, the Anna Kournikova virus was built through a VCK called the VB Script Worm Generator. The VCKs give less sophisticated attackers access to tools that can build some very powerful attacks.

Most of the modern malicious code authors seem to be young—between fourteen and twenty-five years of age. Many are motivated by the desire for attention through causing mischief. Some attackers are just curious, and others are looking to make a name for themselves.

> **NOTE**
>
> The Information Security industry is in the process of trying to prevent young people from becoming involved in computer crime and malicious computer-related activities. For information on preventing youth computer crime, see `http://www.trusecure.com/html/tspub/whitepapers/kids_criminal_hackers.pdf`.

Victims

The primary target of the malicious code attack is the general user population. In many of the recent attacks, the attack began as a Trojan that enticed the user to execute the file. From the experiences of Melissa and Love Letter, many users learned not to open files with `.vbs` extensions, unsolicited attachments, or believe offers that are too good to be true. However, variants of these viruses, such as Anna Kournikova, that used the same method of operation still struck thousands of users who opened the attachment included in the e-mail. This result shows organizations that if they are serious about information security, there can never be enough end user education.

The impact of the malicious code attack can depend on the user's industry. At a minimum, most malicious code attacks have the impact of a loss of trust in the computer system and the computer system support staff. There is also a loss of system access during the cleanup process after the malicious code attack. In the most severe cases, there can be monetary losses and loss in public confidence.

In many attacks, there are multiple victims. If a worm, such as Melissa or Love Letter, is transmitted by e-mail and replicates itself by using the user's address book, there can be countless secondary victims. If the secondary victims are the company's customers, the impact of the virus could be devastating to the company's reputation and bottom line. Refer to the "Protecting Windows 2000 Networks Against Malicious Code Attacks" section later in this chapter for information on how to reduce the impact of future attacks.

Recent Malicious Code Attacks

The following sections discuss some recent trends in malicious code attacks. As the reader will see, it's difficult to decipher if an attack is a Trojan, a worm, and so on because modern day attacks use pieces of each traditional attack type to increase the impact of the attack.

Melissa

On Friday March 26, 1999 the Melissa virus was released. Melissa was the first virus to spread using a user's e-mail address book. A message was received with the subject `Important Message from <User>`. The body of the message contained the text `Here is what you asked for ... don't shown anyone else ;-)`. The message also contained a Word document that, when opened, sent a copy of the message to the first fifty entries in the user's MAPI address book. Users using the Outlook 98 or Outlook 2000 client could spread the virus at an incredibly high rate of speed that was unheard of prior to the Melissa virus. The virus replicated fast enough that it shut down, or at least inhibited e-mail flow, in many organizations during the day it was released.

Melissa's remedy came in the form of virus definition *file updates* from anti-virus vendors that cleaned infected users. Virus definition file updates were also applied to the mail server to remove the virus as it entered the mail system. Some anti-virus vendors were faster at releasing new virus definition file updates than others. As a temporary fix, administrators who had content-filtering capabilities filtered for the subject line and body content to reduce the damage. Microsoft also released a tool to clean the virus from Exchange Server mail stores.

Melissa taught Windows administrators several key lessons about protecting against attacks:

- Disable Macro Execution in Microsoft Office Applications.
- Update the virus pattern files often.
- Desktop anti-virus protection is still a worthwhile investment.
- Messaging system virus protection is essential.
- Content Management products, such as MIME Sweeper, that can filter messages on subject, body, and attachments are a worthwhile investment.
- Train users to be wary of unsolicited attachments.

Security organizations, such as CERT/CC, state that Melissa was not a worm virus because its payload was really contained in the macro in a Word document. The virus could also be considered a Trojan because it had undesired effects and required the user to activate the virus. Melissa also showed that when a world-wide virus strikes, anti-virus vendor support could be taxed, and the company might need to suffer a system outage to contain the infection or prevent further infections.

Love Letter

The Love Letter virus began showing itself May 4, 2000. The Love Letter virus included the following characteristics:

- The message included an attachment named `LOVE-LETTER-FOR-YOU.TXT.VBS`.
- The subject contained `ILOVEYOU`.
- The body contained `kindly check the attached LOVELETTER coming from me`.

The Love Letter virus could be considered a Trojan and a worm. A Love Letter strike required users to run the attached `.vbs` file that contained many damaging consequences. It was also a worm because it would then replicate itself by e-mailing itself to everyone in the e-mail address book. Melissa only replicated to the first 50 addresses, so Love Letter shows the progression of damage from virus writers over time.

The payload of Love Letter overwrote many files types, such as `.vbs`, `.jpg`, and `.mp3`, with copies of itself that made recovery of the original files difficult. The virus could also be spread to network file shares the user might have been using.

The resolution for Love Letter again came from the anti-virus pattern file update. Temporary relief could be achieved through filtering e-mail content. Love Letter reinforced the idea that desktop and messaging virus-scanning systems are required, and that users can never get enough training regarding security and unsolicited attachments in e-mail.

Love Letter taught administrators that desktop configurations should not hide the extensions on known file types. This makes it more difficult for the user to decipher what type of attachment they are opening. See `http://www.irchelp.org/irchelp/security/trojanext.html` for information on un-hiding file types. Love Letter also taught administrators the dangers of allowing a system to have Windows Scripting Host (WSH) enabled, which enables automatic execution of any .VBS file. For information on how to disable WSH, refer to `http://www.sophos.com/support/faqs/wsh.html`. Love Letter was also the first world-wide virus that could be transmitted through IRC chat services.

The variants of Love Letter included Joke, Very Funny, and Mothers Day. Joke was relatively harmless, and Mothers Day carried a payload similar to Love Letter. Both of these variants were released within five days of Love Letter. It's amazing anyone contracted these viruses because they were released so close to Love Letter that received worldwide media attention—but they did! There can never be enough end user education.

Back Orifice

Back Orifice was released in its original form in 1998. Back Orifice provides the ability for a remote user to take control of a desktop or server system after it's installed. Back Orifice is distributed through a Trojan that silently installs the remote administration capabilities. The functionality is similar to that of PcAnywhere or Windows Terminal Services.

Back Orifice 2000 was released in mid 1999 and provided the source code for the "utility." The fact that the source code was distributed made the utility more powerful. Even if the original authors didn't intend for its misuse, another mischievous person could modify the source code and create a more devastating tool. By modifying the source code, malicious individuals can modify the signature of the file that anti-virus pattern files look for when scanning for the backdoor virus.

Part of the reason that Back Orifice and other backdoor malicious programs, such as SubSeven, have not been widely successful is that they listen on a specific TCP or UDP port. By default, Back Orifice listens for incoming calls on TCP port 54320 and UDP 54321, while SubSeven listens on port 27374. Both programs provide the attacker the ability to modify the default listening ports and variants, and versions of SubSeven have been reported to run on ports 1243, 2773, 6711, 6712, 6776, 7215, 16959, 27573, and 65283. Most ports on firewalls prohibit connections on these and most other ports that are initiated from outside the organizations network. However, these programs could be leveraged to attack systems from inside the organization's firewall unless virus scanning or other intrusion detection systems are in place.

> **NOTE**
>
> Additional information on Back Orifice and SubSeven is available at
> `http://www.sans.org/infosecFAQ/malicious/back_orifice.htm`.

Protecting Windows 2000 Networks Against Malicious Code Attacks

This section discusses what network administrators can do to reduce the likelihood that their Windows 2000 environment will be struck by a malicious code attack. Most malicious code attacks are preventable because many are re-infections of an existing attack. The key to prevention is preventing the initial execution of the malicious code. Following the steps included in this section can help network administrators reduce the risks and impacts of a malicious code attack.

Designing Windows 2000 Networks with Security in Mind

Security is expensive and time consuming to manage. Over the life of the network, security becomes more and more expensive to manage when it was not incorporated into the original design. Implementing changes to an existing network's security policy is also extremely difficult because of the complexity and biases that already exist in the environment. If your organization is moving from Windows NT to 2000 or to Windows .NET Server (Windows .NET Server is Microsoft's follow-up server product to Windows 2000 Server that is scheduled for release in 2002), now is the best opportunity you might have to change the organization's security policies.

Most network administrators in average size network environments have little time in their day to monitor the security logs on their systems. Think back to the last time you reviewed the security or virus scanning logs on your systems. Now think of how many e-mail messages, HTTP requests, file transfers, authentication requests, and so on occur every hour on the network. Administrators could literally spend every hour of the day monitoring the network for security-related events with no time left to service user requests or the rest of the systems of the network. Even large environments with dedicated information security departments can't manage it all.

Because security is both expensive and time consuming, it's critical to secure the areas of the network that leave the organization the most venerable to malicious code attacks. A few very simple design principles can be applied that can help reduce the likelihood of attack and reduce the amount of time involved in administering the solution.

Standardize

Standardization allows the network administration team to specialize in a particular technology and will reduce the number of hours spent administering the system security aspects. If the organization is a Windows NT 4.0, Windows 2000, or Windows .NET server shop, don't introduce another operating system into the environment, such as Linux. It's great to learn another operating system, but securing the Windows environment is tough enough by itself.

Standardization techniques should be applied to desktop, browser, e-mail, and server configurations. Remote Installation Services (RIS) or other imaging techniques can be used to deploy a consistent operating system and application images. Use the Office Resource Kit and Internet Explorer Administration Kit to standardize Internet Explorer, Outlook, and the other office applications. Items, such as disabling the preview pane in Outlook, disabling macros in Excel and Word, and disabling Active X controls and Java applets in Internet Explorer, can all be preset through the deployment tools. The Security Configuration Editor can be used to apply consistent security policies to desktop and server systems before they are placed in production.

10

Simplify

Simplification refers to items such as reducing the number of access points to the network, reducing the number of management systems, and reducing the number of inbound and outbound Internet services. It's much easier to determine if something is occurring on the network that is out of the ordinary when there are only a few services permitted on the network.

Examples of simplification include blocking outbound Internet traffic, such as chat or real audio, disabling analog phone lines not being used for desktop phone service to eliminate dial-up access to ISPs, and disallowing user access to company systems through modem pools to force them to come through a monitored VPN.

Automate

A network administrator's time is extremely valuable to the organization. Automation of simple tasks can save network administrator hours in a day. Items, such as log filtering and searching, virus and intrusion alerts, system failure notifications, virus definition updates, and security bulletins, can all be automated with a little effort.

Administrators should subscribe to list servers, newsgroups, e-mail notifications from user groups, vendors, and other communities on topics, such as security and product information about vendors and products they support.

When choosing new products, choose products that can be automated and have extensive support resources.

Educate

Administrators need to know the products that the organization uses. Critical security items include understanding the log entries, how to apply patches, how to rebuild the system in the event of failure, and what should be done if the system has been compromised. Administrators should also know the department security policies and continually educate the users on the department policies.

End users should be held accountable for compliance with security policies. To comply with the policies, users must be educated on the policy. Organizations can use quarterly or department meetings to distribute information. Posting a policy on the intranet and expecting the end users to read it is not an effective way to get end users to comply with the organizations security policy.

Designing and Implementing a Security Policy

Every organization should have a well thought out security policy. Security policies will differ among organizations based on their size and complexity. No matter the size or complexity of the organization, network administrators should know what is permitted and not permitted in the policy and what is required of them in a security emergency, such as a major malicious code attack. At a minimum, the organization's security policy should include the following items:

- *How to shut down e-mail servers and outside connection services*—The organization should be prepared to cut off e-mail to the Internet. The policy should define how to shut down Internet connectivity or the entire mail system. Disconnecting corporate e-mail services from the Internet will allow anti-virus vendors time to create a new virus definition file update for e-mail–transmitted attacks without continual infections from within or outside the company's network.

- *Preparing for and disconnecting from the Internet*—Can the organization afford to disconnect from the Internet? The security policy should state how the organization can disconnect if need be. Even if your organization's systems are prepared for an attack, the rest of the world might not be, and rather than becoming a secondary victim, it might be safer to temporarily disconnect from the Internet.

- *How to initialize backup systems for mission-critical systems, such as e-commerce, portals, and extranets*—Many organizations fail to consider redundancy when hosting their own mission-critical services. A collocation for mission-critical services or offline disaster recovery configuration might be necessary for the organization to shut down their primary connection in the event that a malicious code or denial of service attack is launched against the organization.

- *Adding filters to firewalls, routers, and mail servers*—Filtering policies should address who will make the changes and how the information for what to filter will be distributed to the team that needs to make the changes. Organizations should evaluate where placing filters will be most effective in limiting the damage from malicious code and denial of service attacks.

- *Plan for rolling out virus updates*—During most malicious code attacks, anti-virus vendor Web sites and phone lines are jammed. Organizations should evaluate their anti-virus vendor not only for speed in getting new pattern updates out, but also for their support capacity during an emergency. Also, the policy needs to state who will update the systems and when it is safe to reconnect to e-mail and Internet services.

- *Develop processes for containing and cleaning up infected systems*—Processes and procedures should be documented as to how to handle and clean up infected systems. The first priority should be to contain the spread of the infection. The second priority should be to analyze why the system became infected to prevent further infections. The last step should be to clean up or rebuild the infected system.

10

TROJANS AND BACKDOORS

Securing the Operating System

Securing the operating system for both desktop and server environments is key to protecting the organization from malicious code attacks from inside the organizations firewall. Operating system images should be standardized from simplicity and deployed through an imaging process. Windows 2000 allows even server configurations to be deployed through imaging processes. Directory services can be added after the image installed on the server if they are required.

Windows 2000 comes standard with a built in set of tools called the Security Configuration Tool Set. These tools can be used to analyze the security configuration of the server and can be used to create security configurations that can be saved as .inf files and deployed across multiple systems. By deploying the security policy to the master server and desktop image, a standard security configuration can be configured and deployed throughout the entire organization.

Securing the operating system should also include addressing items, such as network shares, that can be vulnerable to worm viruses. The organization's security policy should specifically address file sharing and the permissions that are set on file shares. Organizations might also want to consider using media, such as CD towers, for shared locations that contain applications that are installed across the network. This can avoid any tampering with the network installation points.

Microsoft Application Center 2000 can be used to standardize application server configurations for Web-based applications. Application Center 2000 can simplify the deployment of in-house, n-tier applications and other Web applications that take advantage of Network Load Balancing Services. Application Center 2000 will ensure that the application is deployed consistently throughout the entire server farm.

Virus Protection

Virus protection is one of the network administrator's primary defense mechanisms to protect the network against malicious code attacks. Virus protection is only as good as the last virus pattern file update. When choosing an anti-virus vendor, choose a vendor that is responsive when new viruses are discovered and has a proven track record. Don't implement the product just because it provides the best licensing deal. Organizations need to build a virus protection strategy that protects each component within the infrastructure. Organizations should plan on installing virus protection at the following levels.

Desktop

All virus vendors provide a component in their suite of products that protect the desktop. Many organizations debate whether to install virus protection at the desktop level when they have extensive protection at the server levels. Adding virus protection at the desktop level is an added expense, and many anti-virus applications do place a heavy load on the system's processor. Another argument against virus scanning at the desktop level was the overhead to manage the anti-virus application and virus definition files at the desktop level. Fortunately, most top-tier anti-virus software companies now provide a management console that can handle much of the administration for the desktop anti-virus application and the updating of the pattern files.

Server

File, print, and Web servers need to be protected from viruses too. For example, the Love Letter virus could spread to file server through mapped network drives just as easily as it affected the desktop machine. Web servers on both the internal and external networks are also subject to attack from denial of service attacks and worm viruses, such as Code Red.

Mail Server

Anti-virus software packages for messaging and collaboration systems, such as Microsoft Exchange and Lotus Notes, have been available for several years. Since the release of the Melissa virus, the frequency of viruses distributed through e-mail has skyrocketed. These packages include a real-time scan mode that will scan messages as they enter and exit the messaging system. A messaging server that is unprotected is a disaster waiting to happen. Plan on sizing mail servers to handle malicious code attacks. Remember that the anti-virus software will be working overtime when the server is suffering a malicious code attack, and a poorly-equipped server might allow an infected message to slip by or shut down due to the heavy load.

Internet Gateway Scanning

Most major anti-virus vendors provide a product that will scan FTP, HTTP, and SMTP traffic at the organization's Internet gateway. These products compliment the messaging scanning products by catching infected messages at the gateway before they reach the messaging server. During a large scale malicious code attack, virus scanning at the Internet gateway can prove invaluable.

The following are some best practice ideas for managing the anti-virus software on Windows 2000 networks:

- Use the vendor's management console to manage anti-virus clients and pattern file updates.
- Automate the virus warnings and alerts. Pass the alerts to a central network management system, such as HP OpenView or another enterprise management system, to handle items such as event correlation and paging.
- Automate pattern file updates to receive and distribute new pattern files nightly.
- Combine both the real-time and scheduled scan capabilities in the product for best results.
- Set scheduled and real-time scans to scan all files, including compressed files.

10

Refer to the planning information by TruSecure Anti-Virus Policy Guide for additional recommendations on deploying anti-virus software on your network. The guide can be found at `http://www.trusecure.com/html/tspub/whitepapers/av_policy_guide3_12.pdf`.

Firewalls

Firewalls are devices or servers that can restrict the sources and destinations for network traffic and the type of traffic between two or more networks. Most organizations have now installed a firewall at their corporate locations as a first line of defense. However, organizations are still vulnerable from telecommuters that might be using corporate systems and resources from their homes. Consider creating a security policy for telecommuters that requires that they have a home firewall device if they use broadband connections, such as DSL or cable modems, to access the corporate network. Organizations might also choose to enforce standards in remote communication by issuing company provided and configured firewalls, laptops, and workstations.

It's amazing how many network administrators do not understand the firewall system that is running on their network. Administrators need to understand the following aspects of their firewall system:

- What ports are allowed for inbound traffic?
- Is traffic limited to only certain hosts?
- What traffic is allowed to leave the inside network?
- How to read the firewall logs.
- How to upgrade or patch the firewall software.
- Who to call for support?
- How to assess its vulnerability?

Organizations should always have their firewall system under some type of support and maintenance contract. Discovering a major security hole in the company's firewall that requires an upgrade to the latest version on a Friday night is not the time to discover the firewall is off support and it won't be until Monday for purchasing approval to be granted.

Content Security

Content security solutions, such as the MIMESweeper family of products, can assist the organization in containing malicious code attacks that are initiated by e-mail–born viruses. Content security can be used to filter for subjects, attachments, and body text and eliminate the delivery of the message. For virus outbreaks, such as Melissa or Love Letter that have consistent subject, body, and attachment formats on the initial outbreak content, security products can reduce the damage the virus can cause even before an anti-virus vendor can release a pattern file. Content security products can also be used to police the messaging system for offensive or inappropriate content and add corporate standard messages to outgoing messages. The MIMESweeper family provides products for Microsoft Exchange, Lotus Notes, and SMTP gateways. For more information in the MIMESweeper family of products, refer to www.mimesweeper.com.

Intrusion Detection Software and Scanners

Intrusion detectionsoftware and scanners can be used to probe network for unauthorized activity. These software packages provide the benefit of automatic alerting when suspicious activity is occurring on the network. These packages can pick up activity on the network such as port scanning or the use of a backdoor utility, such as Back Orifice. Intrusion detection products will sniff the network and alert the administrator when they find something.

Scanners probe the network for possible vulnerabilities. Different scanners exist for different operating systems and network functions. Cisco provides a product called Secure Scanner that tests general network functions. An evaluation edition of Secure Scanner can be downloaded from http://www.cisco.com/warp/public/cc/pd/sqsw/nesn/index.shtml.

Microsoft also provides a scanner that can be used to analyze the security configuration of Windows 2000 systems through the Security Configuration Analysis MMC Snap-in. The Security Configuration Analysis MMC Snap-in uses a series of .inf files to analyze if the current security configuration matches the desired configuration. For more information on using the Security Configuration Analysis tool refer to http://www.sans.org/infosecFAQ/win2000/tools.htm.

There are a few issues that administrators should be aware of when using intrusion detection software and scanners. First is that these packages are built on information from previous security breaches. For the most part, they will provide information that will better secure the network, but there is no guarantee against a future attack. Second is that these products are only as good as the administrator who configured them. This specifically applies to the intrusion detection packages. If these packages are improperly configured, they can provide too much information and become useless. Consider hiring an expert consultant when implementing intrusion detection systems to avoid information overload.

Authentication and Encryption Services

Utilizing authentication and encryption services can reduce the ability for an attacker to compromise systems and launch denial of service or malicious code attacks by obtaining user information or passwords. Microsoft Certificate Services is central to providing tighter security by generating the keys needed to secure network resources and authentication. Web-based

10

TROJANS AND BACKDOORS

applications should require Secure Sockets Layer (SSL) for at least the authentication both inside and outside the corporate firewall. SSL will ensure that the username and password are encrypted when they cross the network.

Other Windows 2000 services, such as the Encrypting File System (EFS), can be used to encrypt files that contain sensitive information. EFS also requires the use of a certificate to encrypt and decrypt files.

Implementing IPSec is another component of Windows 2000 that requires certificates but can drastically raise the level of security on the network. IPSec is not recommended to be used in all situations, but it is highly recommended when connections are being initiated from a network of a lower security level to a network of a higher security level, such as from the Demilitarized Zone (DMZ) to the inside network behind the corporation's inside firewall. Refer to Chapter 20, "IPSec," and Chapter 21, " Virtual Private Networking," for information on IPSec and Virtual Private Networking (VPN).

Third-party options also exist for authentication through smart cards and SecureID. RSA labs pioneered the two-factor authentication that is used with their smart cards and SecureID products. The user must not only authenticate with their password, but they must also have a PIN or possess the smart card to log on to the network. Refer to http://www.sans.org/infosecFAQ/ authentic/twofactor.htm at the SANS Institute for an overview of two-factor authentication.

Additional Resources for Preventing Malicious Code Attacks

Security is an ongoing process and, unfortunately, there is not a set-it-and-forget-it approach to maintaining a secure network. Perpetrators and methods continually evolve and become more and more sophisticated. Network administrators must continually update their skills and systems to maintain an effective level of security on their networks. The following sections contain additional resources that can be used in the continual maintenance of an organization's systems and security policy and to review additional information about malicious code attacks.

CERT/CC

The CERT/CC is a major reporting center for Internet security problems. CERT/CC provides technical assistance when administrators are dealing with security compromises. CERT/CC also analyzes products for vulnerabilities and publishes and delivers training on information security topics. CERT/CC provides an extensive list of security related information on its Web site at http://www.cert.org.

The SANS Institute

The SANS (System Administration, Networking, and Security) Institute is a cooperative research and education organization made up of industry professionals. The SANS Institute provides extensive security articles and security information on Windows 2000, as well as other operating systems, at their Information Security Reading Room at `http://www.sans.org`.

ICSA Labs

ICSA Labs is the security industry's central authority for research, intelligence, and product certification. ICSA Labs sets standards for the performance of security products and certifies many of the firewall, anti-virus, cryptography, and IPSec products on the market. ICSA Labs provides an extensive list of white papers on security related topics available at `www.icsalabs.com`.

The National Security Agency (NSA)

The NSA coordinates, directs, and performs highly-specialized activities to protect U.S. information systems and produce foreign intelligence information. The NSA recently released several security configuration guides for Windows 2000. The NSA also provides the security configuration templates to be used with the Security Configuration Editor that support their recommendations. Security guides for Linux and Cisco routers are also available on their site. The resources from the NSA can be found at `www.nsa.gov`.

Information Security Magazine

Information Security magazine is an industry trade magazine that is dedicated to distributing information about security topics in the computer industry. Weekly e-mail notifications and paid subscriptions are available. *Information Security* magazine can be reached online at `http://www.infosecuritymag.com`.

2600

2600—The Hacker Quarterly is a great source of information regarding information security trends. *2600* provides information security professionals a view of security topics from the hacker's perspective. *2600* can be reached online at `www.2600.com`.

Anti-Virus Software Vendors

Most anti-virus vendors provide virus-related education and bulletins. It's usually best to stick with a top-tier anti-virus software vendor due to support capacity and research and development resources when selecting an anti-virus software package. Most vendors provide a comprehensive suite of products for desktops, servers, Web connections, and messaging servers.

Refer to the following product lines and vendors for more information:

- Trend Micro: `www.trendmicro.com`
- McAfee: `www.nai.com`
- Norton Anti Virus: `www.symantec.com`

NTBugtraq

NTBugtraq is a mailing list that discusses security related problems in the Windows platform. List enrollment is available at `http://ntbugtraq.ntadvice.com`.

Microsoft

Microsoft has been criticized in the past for not providing timely information and speedy fixes for security-related problems. Microsoft has set up a Web site at `www.microsft.com/security` dedicated to distributing security-related information about Microsoft products. The site provides information for administrators and developers on security operations and best practices. It also provides a link so that network administrators can sign up to receive security bulletins via e-mail.

Summary

Malicious code attacks can come in various forms and combine traditional virus methods such as Trojans, backdoors, and worms, to replicate themselves and initiate their payload. Network administrators need to realize that as attacker tools become more abundant and sophisticated, the malicious attacks will become more devastating.

Network administrators also need to understand that most malicious code attacks are preventable. Prevention of malicious code attacks requires a detailed security policy and a plan of action to take when the attack strikes. Technical components, such as virus protection, intrusion detection, and content filtering packages, can all assist the organization in combating the malicious code attacks when they occur.

The most important aspect of preventing malicious code attacks is user and administrator education. Users should be clear on the acceptable use of the network, how to determine if something appears suspicious, and what to do when they are victims of suspicious activities on the network. Administrators should know their systems inside and out and design their Windows 2000 networks with security in mind.

Active Directory

IN THIS CHAPTER

Windows 2000 introduced Active Directory to the Windows platform. Active Directory is the basis for Windows 2000 distributed networking. Administrators use Active Directory to store security policy information for overall domain management. Using Windows 2000 Server, you can define permissions all the way down to the level of an individual directory object attribute.

To understand Active Directory, it's important for you to understand some of the concepts used in Active Directory. The sections in this chapter cover the concepts of the Active Directory namespace, trees, forests, objects, containers, distributed security, and permissions.

Active Directory Namespace

Active Directory is a directory service. Every directory service has a namespace. A *namespace* is a circumscribed area in which names are resolved. What this means is that Active Directory forms a namespace in which the name of an Active Directory object can be resolved back to the object itself. This activity is referred to as *name resolution*. Name resolution is the process of translating a name into an object or into information that the object name represents.

In Active Directory, the namespace is the vertical or hierarchical structure of the domain name tree. A tree namespace is a single, contiguous namespace, with each name (or domain label) in the namespace directly descended from a single root name. Each domain label indicates a branch in the domain namespace tree. For example, domain labels, such as overseas and sales, that might be used in a fully qualified domain name such as overseas.sales.computers.com, indicate a branch in the domain namespace tree. The *root domain* of the tree is the first domain created in the tree of the forest. In the previous example, this would be computers.com.

A *forest* namespace is a collection of essentially equal trees with no single root to the namespace. A forest namespace consists of a peer group of trees, each tree having its own contiguous namespace. The groups of trees do not fit into an overall, contiguous namespace. You can't trace all of the trees back up to a single root. For example, perhaps due to a merger, an organization might have two trees within the forest overseas.sales.computers.com and retail.stores.com. As you can see from the two examples, the two forest namespaces do not have the same root. For further information about trees, forests, domains, and domain controllers, refer to Chapter 8, "Windows 2000 Network Security Architecture."

Active Directory Objects

An Active Directory object is a distinct set of attributes that represent a resource on the network, which can be manipulated by a program or a process. These resources can be something concrete that you can see through the user interface, such as computers, users, printers, registry keys, files, folders, and the Windows desktop. Objects also include resources that you cannot see, such as threads, processes, sessions, and access tokens.

An object that can hold other objects is referred to as a *container*. An object that cannot hold other objects is referred to as a *noncontainer*. Container objects can contain both noncontainer objects and other container objects. For example, a Folder object in the file system can contain other Folder objects (containers) as well as File objects (noncontainers). In an object hierarchy, a relationship is formed between the container and its contents. The container is referred to as the parent, and the object in the container is referred to as the child.

Objects in Active Directory with associated security attributes are called *securable objects*. A securable object is any object that can be shared. Examples of securable objects include registry keys, files, computers, and user objects.

Windows 2000 assigns each Active Directory securable object a unique security descriptor that defines the security attributes of that securable object. In other words, the security descriptor contains information about how access to that object is controlled. The security descriptor contains information about the object's owner and the object's primary group. It also contains two access control lists (ACLs). The *discretionary ACL (DACL)* describes who should have access to a particular object and the type of access to grant. The *system ACL (SACL)* defines the type of auditing to perform on an object.

Security Principals

Active Directory represents physical entities, such as computers and persons, as user accounts and computer accounts. Computer accounts, user accounts, and groups are Active Directory directory objects called *security principals*. On creation, Active Directory automatically assigns *security identifiers (SIDs)* to these objects for logon authentication and to enable access to domain resources. A Windows 2000 domain controller in the domain where the object resides authenticates the security principal object. You use the Active Directory Users and Computers console to add, disable, reset, and delete user accounts, computer accounts, and groups. You launch the console by clicking Start, pointing to Programs, pointing to Administrative Tools, and then clicking Active Directory Users And Computers. Figure 11.1 illustrates this console.

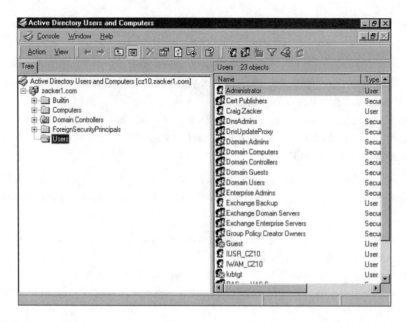

FIGURE 11.1

The Active Directory Users and Computers console.

Active Directory uses computer accounts and user accounts to perform the following functions:

- User and computer authentication
- Administer other security principals
- Deny or authorize access to domain resources
- Audit activity performed with user accounts and computer accounts

When an administrator establishes a trust between a Windows 2000 domain within his local forest and a Windows 2000 domain outside that forest, security principals from the external domain can be granted access to resources in the local forest. This is possible because each security principal from the trusted external domain is represented in the trusting (local) domain by a foreign security principal object that is created by the trusting domain's Active Directory.

NOTE

Directory objects for foreign security principals are created by Active Directory. You should never manually alter these objects because doing so would render them useless.

Foreign security principals can become members of domain local groups on the trusting domain. You can view security principal objects by enabling Advanced Features in the Active Directory Users and Computers console. To enable the Advanced Features option, perform the following steps:

1. Click Start, Programs, Administrative Tools, and then click Active Directory Users and Computers.

2. When the Active Directory Users and Computers console appears, expand the domain node in the console tree.

3. Click the View menu, and then click Advanced Features.

4. Click the ForeignSecurityPrincipals container in the console tree to view the current list of foreign security principals available in the domain (shown in Figure 11.2).

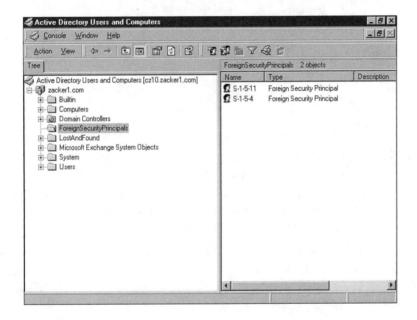

FIGURE 11.2
The ForeignSecurityPrincipals *container in the Active Directory Users and Computers console.*

User Accounts

Administrators should assign each user who logs on to the network a unique user account and password so that they and the network can identify who is logged on at any given time. The assigned user account enables a user to log on to computers and domains in your network with a unique identity that Windows 2000 can authenticate and authorize for domain resources access. Information such as a user's personal information, account information, and group membership are stored in the user account, as illustrated in Figure 11.3.

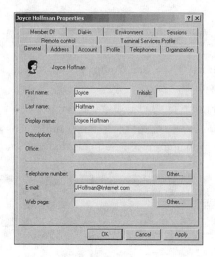

FIGURE 11.3
The User Properties dialog box.

Default User Accounts

When you install the Windows 2000 operation system, you are provided with two pre-defined, default user accounts that enable you to log on to your computer locally. You use these default accounts primarily for the initial logon and configuration of a local Windows 2000 computer and for access to resources on the local computer. These two accounts are

- *Local Administrator account*—The local Administrator account has extensive rights and permissions that permit you to do pretty much anything you want to on the local machine. Because the Administrator account is also used to log on to the domain, you should ensure that the local Administrator password and the domain Administrator password are different and are known only to the network administrators. This will ensure that users who might know the local Administrator password will not gain access to unauthorized network resources. The permissions for the local Administrator account include the following:

- Upgrades to the operating system
- Repairs to the operating system
- Installation and running of legacy Windows-based applications
- Installation of Service Packs, Hotfixes, and operating system components, such as drivers for hardware

- *Local Guest account*—The Guest account has very limited permissions and rights that restrict it to operating and saving documents to the local computer.

Computer Accounts

Windows 2000 uses a computer account to provide a means to authenticate the computer to the domain and to audit the computer's access to the domain's resources. A domain administrator creates a unique computer account for each computer that joins the Windows 2000 domain. By default, Windows 2000 adds each computer account that the administrator creates to the Domain Computers group. Information, such as a computer's role in the domain, the computer's operating system, membership, and location information, is stored in the computer account, as illustrated in Figure 11.4.

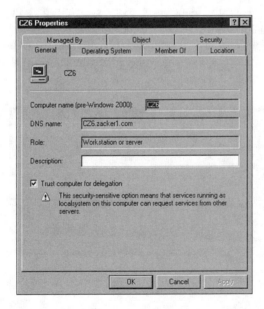

FIGURE 11.4
The Computer Properties dialog box.

When the administrator creates a new computer account, Active Directory automatically assigns a unique SID to it. The internal processes of Windows 2000 refers to the SID rather than to the computer account's name. This is because if a particular computer account is deleted and then, at a later date, a computer account is created using the same name, the new account will not inherit any of the rights or permissions previously granted to the old account. Windows 2000 will assign a new SID to the new computer account.

A domain administrator joins a computer to a domain when he or she creates the computer account name at the domain controller. After the domain administrator has named the computer account, the system takes over. A trailing dollar sign ($) is appended to the end of the computer account name. Windows 2000 assigns a default password to the new computer account that consists of the lowercase representation of the computer account name minus the dollar sign. The maximum length of this password is 14 characters. The password is truncated if the computer name exceeds 14 characters. After the computer account becomes active on the domain, the password provided at creation becomes invalid and a new random password takes its place.

Group Accounts

Group accounts arelocal computer or Active Directory objects that are collections of users, computers, contacts, and other miscellaneous entities. Typically, a group consists of all the resources necessary to run a specific service or application. You can use groups to create e-mail distribution lists, filter policy settings, and manage access to shared resources. You create groups by using the New Object-Group dialog box that you launch from the Active Directory Users and Computers console. This dialog box is shown in Figure 11.5.

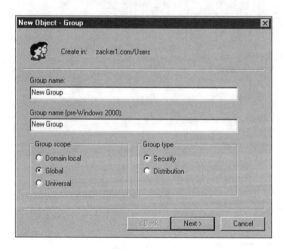

FIGURE 11.5

The New Object-Group dialog box.

There are two types of groups in Active Directory: security groups and e-mail distribution groups. You can use security groups to grant access to resources and objects in the domain and for e-mail lists. When you assign permissions for resources in a domain, you can simplify network administration and save time by assigning permissions to a security group rather than assigning permissions individually to users.

Security Group Scopes

Each security and distribution group is assigned a scope that identifies the extent to which the group participates in the domain tree or forest. Windows 2000 has four types of scopes:

- *Local Groups Based on Security Accounts Manager*—Windows 2000 Professional and servers that are not domain controllers store their Local Groups in the security accounts manager (SAM) of the local machine. Groups installed by default on these types of systems are stored in the SAM's built-in database. These default groups have inherent system privileges. For example, Backup Operators can override security restrictions for the sole purpose of backing up or restoring files on the local computer.

- *Domain Local Scope Groups*—Domain local groups include accounts from a Windows 2000 domain. These groups are the equivalent to the SAM-based local groups, but you can use them only to grant users permissions within a domain. Local groups are stored in Active Directory.

- *Global Scope Groups*—Global groups have no inherent system privileges. An administrator uses these groups to secure access to security objects in a Windows 2000 domain. You can only include user accounts and groups in a global scope group from the domain in which the group is defined. You can convert global scope groups to universal scope groups only in native domain groups, and only if the domain local group does not already have another domain local group as its member.

- *Universal Scope Groups*—By default, universal scope groups are disabled until the Windows 2000 domain is upgraded to a native mode domain. An administrator can include accounts and groups from any Windows 2000 domain in the domain tree or forest. When the Windows 2000 domain is in native mode, an administrator can group universal groups into other groups and he or she can assign permissions to them in any domain in the forest. Universal groups cannot be converted to any other type of group.

Default Group Accounts

When you install a Windows 2000 domain controller, Windows 2000 installs several default groups in the Built-in and Users folders of the Active Directory Users and Computers console. These groups are security groups that contain common sets of rights and permissions. You can use default security groups to grant certain rights, permissions, and roles to user accounts and groups.

Built-in Groups

The Built-in group folder in Active Directory Users and Computers contains default groups with domain local scope. Administrators use the groups included in this folder primarily to assign default sets of permissions to users who are assigned some administrative functions within the domain. The following lists all of the built-in groups for Windows 2000 domain controllers, member servers, standalone servers, and workstations.

- *Account Operators*—Members of the Account Operators group can create, modify, and delete user, group, and computer accounts in Active Directory, with the exception of the built-in groups themselves. By default, there are no members of this group.

- *Administrators*—Members of the Administrators group have full and unlimited access to the local computer and to the domain. Because of the unlimited power for members of this group, administrators should keep membership to this group to a bare minimum. Initially, the Administrator account is the only member of the Administrators group. However, as an administrator makes changes and additions to the domain, membership to this group changes. When a member of the Administrators group creates an object, the Administrators group becomes the default owner of that object. The Domain Admins group is automatically added to the Administrators group on each computer that joins the domain. When a server becomes a domain controller on the domain, the Enterprise Admins group is automatically added to the Administrators group of the joining domain controller.

- *Backup Operators*—Members of the Backup Operators group are granted permission to override security restrictions to back up and restore all files on a computer, regardless of any permissions that might protect those files. Members of this group are also granted permission to log on to a computer and shut it down. This group has no members by default.

- *Guests*—Members of the Guest group are granted the same access as members of the Users group. The Guest group is meant to provide occasional or one-time access to users with limited privileges. By default, the only member of this group is the Guest account.

- *Power Users*—Members of the Power Users group have more power than the average user and less power than members of the Administrators group. For example, Power Users can create user accounts but cannot alter or delete user accounts they did not create. Members can create local groups and can add, modify, and remove members from local groups that they have created. Power Users can modify certain system-wide settings, such as shares, printers, power configurations, and system time. This group has no members by default.

- *Pre-Windows 2000 Compatible Access*—This group is backward compatible and allows read access on all users and groups within the domain. By default, the only member of this group is the Everyone entity.

- *Print Operators*—Members of the Print Operators group are granted permissions to administer domain printers and the document queues. By default, the only member of this group is the Domain Users group.

- *Replicator*—Windows 2000 computers do not use this group. The File Replication service on Windows NT domain controllers uses it to support file replication in an NT domain.

- *Server Operators*—Members of this group are granted permission to administer domain servers. Permissions include logging on to a server interactively, shutting down the server, starting and stopping services, formatting the hard disk of the server, creating and deleting network shares, and backing up and restoring files. This group has no members by default.

- *Users*—Members of the Users group have restricted permissions that prevent them from making accidental or intentional system-wide changes, and that prevent them from running most legacy applications. Members of this group can perform tasks, such as locking the local computer, shutting down the local computer, using local and network printers, and running applications on the computer. By default, the only member of this group is the Authenticated Users group.

Predefined Groups

The Users folder in the Active Directory Users and Computers console contains predefined groups that possess global scope. These groups are installed on domain controllers during a clean installation and include the following:

- *Cert Publishers*—Members of this group include all computers that run an enterprise certificate authority. These members are authorized to publish certificates for User objects in Active Directory.

- *Domain Admins*—Members of this group are authorized to administer the domain. By default, the Domain Admins group is a member of the Administrators group on all computers that have joined the domain, as well as all of the domain controllers on the domain. Administrators add accounts to this group if they want an account to have broad administrative rights in one or more domains.

- *Domain Computers*—The Domain Computers group contains all of the computers that have joined a particular domain. This group does not include domain controllers.

- *Domain Controllers*—This group contains all of the domain controllers in the domain. When new domain controllers join the domain, they are automatically added to this group.

- *Domain Guests*—By default, this group is a member of the Built-in Guests group in the same domain. The default member of this group is the domain's Guest account.

- *Domain Users*—The Domain Users group includes all user accounts in the domain as its members. Each time an administrator creates a user account, the user account is automatically added to this group.

- *Enterprise Admins*—The Enterprise Admins group exists only in the root domain of an Active Directory forest of domains. The forest root domain is the first domain created in the forest. Members of this group are permitted to log on to any of the domain controllers in the forest and to make forest-wide changes in Active Directory, such as adding domains. By default, the only member of this group is the Administrators account for the forest root domain.

- *Group Policy Creator Owners*—Members of this group are authorized to create new Group Policy objects (GPOs) in Active Directory. By default, the Administrator account is the only member of this group.

- *Schema Admins*—This group exists only in the root domain of an Active Directory forest of domains. Members of this group are permitted to make changes to the schema in Active Directory. Simply put, the *schema* describes and defines each of the object classes and their attributes that are stored in Active Directory. By default, the only member of this group is the Administrators account for the forest root domain.

Special Identity Groups

The Windows 2000 operating system uses special identities to represent different users at different times, depending on the circumstances. The special identity groups are not viewable when you administer groups in the Active Directory Users and Computers console. Although you cannot see these groups and cannot place special identities into groups, you can assign rights and permissions to user accounts and to resources to these special identities. Special Identities include the following:

- *Authenticated Users*—Members of this group include users who are authenticated to one of the trusted domains.

- *Creator/Owner*—This special identity is replaced by the Owner's SID from the object's security descriptor. It permits the owner of the object to automatically have specific access to the object.

- *Everyone*—All current network users are included in the Everyone special identity group.

- *Interactive Users*—All users currently accessing a resource on the local computer are members of this group. A user becomes a member of this group when the user interactively logs on to a local computer.

- *Network Users*—All users currently accessing a given network resource are included in this group. A user becomes a member of this group when the user logs on to a network machine.

- *Principal Self*—This special identity is unique to each security principal and is replaced by the SID of the security principal object. It permits users and computers to have access to their own objects, and lets members of a group have permissions to the group.

- *Service*—Members of this group include service accounts used by the service controllers to start services under a specific account.

Active Directory Account Database

The Active Directory maintains an account database that the Key Distribution Center (KDC) uses to obtain information about security principals in the domain. The KDC is a Kerberos service that runs on a domain controller. Its purpose is to issue ticket-granting tickets (TGTs) and service tickets for network authentication in a domain. Read more about Kerberos in Chapter 8.

As we've discussed, security principals are represented as account objects in the Active Directory directory (or database). The encryption key that is used in communicating with a security principal (user, computer, or service) is stored in that security principal's account object as an attribute.

Each domain controller keeps a writable copy of the directory so that any domain controller can create accounts, modify group memberships, and modify passwords. Changes made at any domain controller are automatically replicated to all other domain controllers within the domain.

The Directory System Agent (DSA) manages the actual physical storage of account data in the database. The DSA is a protected process that Windows 2000 integrates with the Local Security Authority (LSA) on each domain controller. Clients in Active Directory are not ever given direct access to the database. Clients are given access to directory information through the Active Directory Service Interfaces (ADSI). The ADSI connects to the DSA and then searches for read and write directory objects and their attributes.

Even when a client requests information from the DSA, access might not be granted. Requests for access to an object in the directory are subject to validation by Active Directory. Access Control Lists (ACLs) protect Active Directory objects—actually, each of the Active Directory object's attributes has an ACL associated with it. The ACL specifies who is permitted access to a specific object and how it permits access.

Object Types, Managers, and Tools

An object manager controls each type of object in Active Directory and an authorized user manages each type of object with a specific tool. The following lists each type of object, its object manager, and its management tool.

Type of Object: Active Directory objects
Object Manager: Active Directory
Management Tool: Active Directory Users and Computers

Type of Object: Files and folders
Object Manager: NTFS
Management Tool: Windows Explorer

Type of Object: Printers
Object Manager: Print spooler
Management Tool: The Printers program in Control Panel

Type of Object: Registry Keys
Object Manager: The Registry
Management Tool: Regedt32.exe

Type of Object: Services
Object Manager: Service controllers
Management Tool: Security Templates, Security Configuration and Analysis

Type of Object: Shares
Object Manager: Server service
Management Tool: Windows Explorer

Distributed Security

Windows 2000 distributed security secures access to resources and to the network. It also ensures the integrity and privacy of communications and data within the network. This section covers a few important distributed security features: user authentication, impersonation, the access token, and access control. For information about Public Key Infrastructure (PKI), an additional distributed security feature, refer to Chapter 8.

User Authentication

Administrators provide access for legitimate users on their network by ensuring that Windows 2000 authenticates all authorized users for access to system resources. Domain users are authenticated through their Active Directory user accounts, which are stored in the Users folder of the Active Directory Users and Computers console.

Administrators create a single account for each user in the domain. The user needs only this one user account and password to log on to any client workstation or to access any network resources that they are authorized to access within the domain. Windows 2000 supports this single sign-on feature for all users within a domain forest. Because trust relationships in a Windows 2000 forest are bi-directional, authentication in one domain of the forest is sufficient for pass-through authentication to the resources of all other domains in that same forest.

When a user logs on to the network at a Windows 2000 computer, she is required to provide her account identification in the form of a user account name and password. She is also required to select the domain name to which she wants to log on. Winlogon collects and packages the proof of identity that she supplies into a data structure. Next, Winlogon passes this information to the Local Security Authority (LSA) to verify her identity. If the LSA determines that her account is a valid one and that she is the actual account holder, Winlogon sets up an interactive session on the computer. If the LSA cannot verify her account information, the operating system will deny her access to the computer and to the network.

Impersonation

Impersonation gives a *thread* (a piece of program code executing on a computer) the ability to operate in a security context other than the context of the process that actually owns the thread. To put it simply, impersonation is a thread's ability to use an access token that represents the client's credentials to obtain access to objects to which the client has access.

When a user is running an application that needs to access protected files, the application impersonates the user before it accesses the necessary file. In this way, the system ensures that the client obtains only authorized access to the information in the protected files. The purpose of impersonation is to allow application services to carry out an operation in a "least-privileged" mode when responding to a network request on behalf of client applications. The system either expands or restricts access to Impersonation network resources, depending on the permissions of the client.

Access Token

The access Impersonation token is an object that includes information about the identity and privileges of an account associated with a particular process or thread. A primary token is associated with each process that occurs on the system or network. The primary token includes information that describes the security context of the user account that is associated with the process.

The system creates and uses the token in the following manner. When a user logs on, the system compares the user's password against the one that is stored in a security database. If the system can authenticate the user's password, it creates an access token for the user account. Each process that executes during that session on behalf of the user receives a copy of the access token. When a user or a thread working on behalf of the user attempts to perform a task that requires privileges, the system uses the token to identify the user. Because a thread can impersonate a client account, the system permits the thread to interact with securable objects by using the security context of the client. The system assigns both a primary and an impersonation token to a thread that is impersonating a user. A thread uses an impersonation access token to temporarily adopt a different security context within a process. A primary access token represents the security context of a process.

Access Control

To understand access control, you need to understand the purpose of a thread. A *thread* is a sequential portion of program code executing on a computer. Windows 2000 coordinates the execution of threads by assigning each thread a scheduling priority for execution on the processor. A process can have several threads associated with it.

To gain access to an object, a thread must identify itself to the operating system's LSA. The thread must borrow a security identifier from a security principal (such as a user) because it does not have one of its own. As we've discussed, Winlogon encases a user's security identity in an access token when the user logs on for a session. When the user starts an application, the application runs as a process within the logon session. The application process and each of the application's threads of execution receives a copy of the user's access token. When the application's thread needs to open a file, the thread identifies itself as the user's agent by presenting the access token.

The operating system performs an access check on the thread to determine whether the security principal is permitted the level of access requested by the thread before it allows the thread's execution to proceed. The purpose of the access check is to compare the information contained in the thread's access token to the information contained within the object's security descriptor.

To determine whether a user is permitted access to an object, the security subsystem steps through each access control entry (ACE) in the object's DACL until it finds an ACE that either permits or denies access to the user. If the security subsystem reaches the end of the list and the ACE has not explicitly permitted or denied access, the security subsystem denies access to the object.

File and Folder Permissions

One of the most important things to remember about assigning permissions on your network is to keep it as simple as possible. Set as few restrictions as possible and assign permissions to groups, not individuals. If you don't follow this rule, you might find yourself spending most of your time managing permissions on your network.

There are two types of permissions—explicit and inherited permissions. *Explicit* permissions are the ones that you set on folders that you create. *Inherited* permissions are ones that flow from parent object to child object. By default, when you create a subfolder, it will inherit the permissions that you established for the parent folder.

It is possible to block inheritance at the parent or the child level. Just remember that when you block inheritance at the parent level, no subfolder will inherit permissions. When you block inheritance at the child level, some folders will inherit permissions, and others will not. You use Windows Explorer to set permissions or to block inherited permissions to any file or folder stored on an NTFS volume.

Windows 2000 contains a set of standard permissions that are actually combinations of specific kinds of access. You refer to the combination of permissions that make up the standard permissions as *special permissions*.

The standard permissions for folders are Full Control, Modify, Read & Execute, List Folder Contents, Read, and Write. Figure 11.6 shows the Properties dialog box that you use to set these standard permissions.

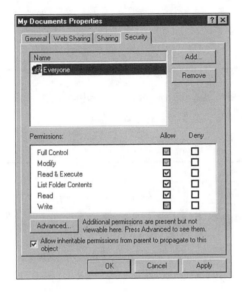

FIGURE 11.6

The Permissions Properties dialog box.

Table 11.1 shows the standard permissions for folders and lists the default special permissions that are associated with them.

TABLE 11.1   Standard and Special Permissions for Folders

Special Permissions	*FC*	*M*	*R&E*	*LFC*	*R*	*W*
Traverse Folder/Execute File	X	X	X	X		
List Folder/Read Data	X	X	X	X	X	
Read Attributes	X	X	X	X	X	
Read Extended Attributes	X	X	X	X	X	

TABLE 11.1   Continued

Special Permissions	FC	M	R&E	LFC	R	W
Create Files/Write Data	X	X				X
Create Folders/Append Data	X	X				X
Write Attributes	X	X				X
Write Extended Attributes	X	X				X
Delete Subfolders and Files	X					
Delete	X	X				
Read Permissions	X	X	X	X	X	
Change Permissions	X					
Take Ownership	X					

Table 11.2 shows the standard permissions for files and lists the default special permissions that are associated with them.

TABLE 11.2   Standard and Special Permissions for Files

Special Permissions	FC	M	R&E	R	W
Traverse Folder/Execute File	X	X	X		
List Folder/Read Data	X	X	X	X	
Read Attributes	X	X	X	X	
Read Extended Attributes	X	X	X	X	
Create Files/Write Data	X	X			X
Create Folders/Append Data	X	X			X
Write Attributes	X	X			X
Write Extended Attributes	X	X			X
Delete Subfolders and Files	X				
Delete	X	X			
Read Permissions	X	X	X	X	
Change Permissions	X				
Take Ownership	X				

Configuring Folder and File Permissions

Set all the permissions on the folder or file before you share a folder on an NTFS volume. In this way, you won't have to worry about users trying to access the folder or file before you've finished setting the permissions. To assign permissions to a folder (or file), perform the following steps:

1. Launch Windows Explorer.
2. Right-click the folder, and then click Properties.
3. When the Properties dialog box appears, click the Security tab.
4. If you need to add a user or group to the Name list box, click the Add button.
5. When the Select Users, Computers, Or Groups dialog box appears, in the Name list box, select the user or group to whom you want to grant permissions, click the Add button, and then click OK.
6. The user or group that you just selected should appear in the Name list box for the Security tab. Highlight that user or group in the Name list box, and then, in the Permissions list box, select the permissions that you want to allow or deny to that user or group.
7. When you are finished assigning permissions, click OK to close the Properties dialog box.
8. Close Windows Explorer.

Configuring Special Permissions

You might find it necessary sometimes to change the default special permissions that are associated with the standard permissions. To change special permissions, perform the following steps:

1. Launch Windows Explorer.
2. Right-click the folder or file and then click Properties.
3. Click the Security tab, and then click the Advanced button. The Access Control Settings dialog box appears, as shown in Figure 11.7.

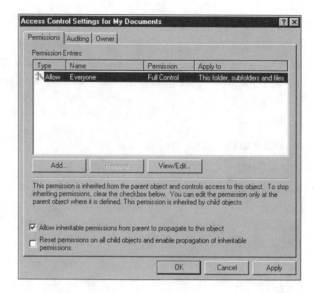

FIGURE 11.7
The Access Control Settings dialog box.

4. To add a user or group, click the Add button. When the Select User, Computer, Or Group dialog box appears, double-click the user or group name to display the Permissions Entry dialog box. Proceed to step 7.

5. To remove special permissions, highlight the user or group name and then click the Remove button. If the Remove button is grayed out, clear the Allow Inheritable Permissions from Parent to Propagate to This Object check box. A Security dialog box appears asking if you really want to remove this object. Click the Remove button if you really want to remove the object. Proceed to step 11.

6. If you want to view or modify the existing special permissions, highlight the name of the user or group and then click the View/Edit button to display the Permissions Entry dialog box, as shown in Figure 11.8. Proceed to step 7.

7. In the Apply Onto drop-down list, select where you want the permissions applied. For example, you can apply the permissions to the current folder, subfolders, and files.

8. In the Permission Entry dialog box, select the permissions that you want to allow or deny.

9. If you want to prevent subfolders and files from inheriting these permission, select the Apply These Permissions to Objects and/or Containers Within This Container Only check box.

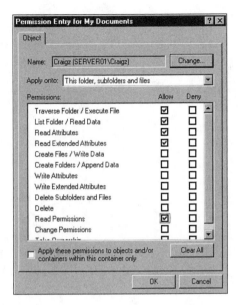

FIGURE 11.8
The Permission Entry dialog box.

10. Click OK to close the Permission Entry dialog box.

11. Click OK to close the Access Control Settings dialog box.

12. Click OK to close the Properties dialog box, and then close Windows Explorer.

Summary

This chapter explained some of the key Active Directory concepts. A good understanding of these principals is important to understanding Windows 2000 security because, to a large extent, security in Windows 2000 is built around Active Directory.

Security Policy and Configuration

IN THIS CHAPTER

This chapter covers the functions and uses of the Windows 2000 Security Configuration Tool Set. The Tool Set centralizes the management of configuration and analysis task from a common interface. The Security Configuration Tool Set enables you to configure such security areas as Account Policies, Local Policies, the Event Log, System services, the Registry, and access control for folders and files.

Security Configuration Tool Set

The Microsoft Security Configuration Tool Set includes the `secedit.exe` command-line tool and a set of Microsoft Management Console (MMC) snap-ins that are designed to centralize and integrate security configuration and analysis tasks for Windows 2000-based systems. The Tool Set components interact with Active Directory, Kerberos version 5 authentication protocol, and Windows 2000 Public Key Infrastructure (PKI). The Tool Set enables you to do the following:

- Define a number of configuration settings at the macro level.
- Group and automate configuration tasks.
- Perform security and security analysis on one or more Windows 2000-based computers.
- Perform the required operations automatically and in the background from an integrated and uniform framework.
- Perform security risk management and view information about system aspects that are related to security for your entire infrastructure.

What Is the Microsoft Management Console (MMC)?

The MMC hosts administrative tools, called snap-ins, that you use to administer such things as computers, system components, services, networks, and security policies. The MMC console consists of a window divided into two panes. The left pane is called the *console tree*, and the right pane is called the *details pane*. The console tree displays the snap-ins and items that are available for a particular console. The details pane displays functions and information about the snap-ins and other items. When you click a specific snap-in or item that is displayed in the console tree, the information in the details pane also changes to reflect functions and information available for that particular item. See Figure 12.1 for an example of an MMC.

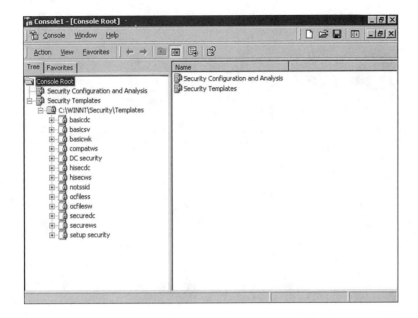

FIGURE 12.1
The Microsoft Management Console.

Security Areas

The Security Configuration Tool Set enables you to configure and analyze the security areas
covered in this section on machines throughout your network. Some of these tools are found in
the Microsoft Management Console, in the form of snap-ins. The Security Templates snap-in
provides a centralized method of defining security. The Security Configuration and Analysis
snap-in (see Figure 12.1) centralizes configuration and analysis tasks for individual machines.
You use the Group Policy snap-in to define security configurations as part of a group policy
object (GPO) that you then can assign to a specific computer, site, domain, or other organizational unit scope. You also can use the `secedit.exe` command-line tool to perform configuration and analysis functions.

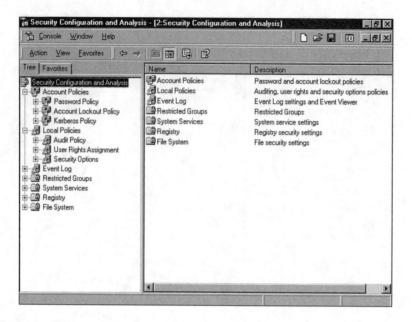

FIGURE 12.1
Security Configuration and Analysis areas for a domain controller.

Account Policies

On a domain controller, you can configure attributes for three security areas: Password Policy, Lockout Policy, and Domain Kerberos Policy. On a workstation, or on a standalone or member server, you can configure attributes for two security areas: Password Policy and Lockout Policy. These policies cover security areas related to user accounts.

Password Policy

You use this policy to configure domain or local user accounts. This policy enables you to set restrictions on reusing passwords, minimum and maximum password age, password complexity, and storing passwords using reversible encryption for all users in the domain.

Account Lockout Policy

You also can use this policy to configure domain or local user accounts. This policy enables you to define the rules for when an Account Lockout should occur. For example, account lockout duration (in minutes), and locking out an account after a specified number of failed logon attempts. By setting this configuration, would-be attackers will find that the account they are trying to access will lock up after a number of failed tries.

Kerberos Policy

This policy enables you to define the settings for Kerberos authentication, such as the Kerberos tickets lifetimes (in minutes, days, or hours) and the maximum tolerance (in minutes) for computer clock synchronization. Because Kerberos settings are domain-wide settings that are enforced by domain controllers, you use this policy to define Kerberos settings in the default domain controller to configure domain user accounts.

Local Policies

This policy is used to apply local policies to the local machine. When these local policy settings are imported to a Group Policy object in Active Directory directory services, the settings will affect the local security settings of any computer account in the site, domain, or organizational unit (OU) to which that Group Policy object is applied. Three security areas are included: Audit Policy, User-Rights Assignment, and Security Options.

Audit Policy

This policy enables you to determine which security events are logged into the Security log on the local computer. You use this policy to define successful and failed attempts for security events, such as logon attempts, object access, and policy changes. You use the Event Viewer in Windows 2000 to view the local computer's Security log.

User Rights Assignment

This security area enables you to specify which users or groups have logon rights and rights to perform a variety of tasks. These tasks can include such things as changing the system time, taking ownership of files or other objects, removing a computer from a docking station, loading and unloading device drivers, and backing up files and directories.

Security Options

The Security area allows you to enable or disable security settings for the computer. It provides you with many options that, in previous versions of Windows, you had to manipulate through the registry, such as restricting the use of the floppy disk or changing the message text for users attempting to log on.

Event Log

You use this security area to configure domain or local computer accounts. Consider implementing the Event Log settings at a site, domain, or organization unit level to match your organization's security requirements and to take advantage of GPO settings. This policy enables you to configure settings for the Event Log, such as values for the maximum application, security, and system log sizes restricting guest access to the Event Log, defining the number of days to retain logs, and shutting down the computer when the security audit log is full.

Restricted Groups

The Restricted Groups security area is a new security feature in Windows 2000, and it acts as a governor for group membership. It works in this manner. You add Windows 2000 groups that have predefined sensitive or privileged capabilities, such as Administrators, Powers Users, and DomainAdmins to the Restricted Groups security list. From there, you add this restricted group security list into the template you are using for the security configuration. You add user accounts and groups that should be assigned membership to each of the groups listed in Restricted Groups through the template or policy that defines the restricted group.

> **NOTE**
>
> You can add or remove groups to the Restricted Groups list at any time by deleting them from the template or policy where the Restricted Groups have been defined.

Let's look at an example of the restricted group security feature in action. When you need to assign temporary privileges to a user account, you add the user account with the temporary privileges to the specified group, such as Administrators, through the Active Directory Users and Computers snap-in. If no one remembers to remove the user account from the group, the user account will retain its privileges when it should no longer have those rights. Over time, these situations can add up, and you might be left with several user accounts that have too many rights not intended for them. This is where Restricted Groups comes in. When Group Policy settings are applied, user accounts (and groups) that are not listed in the groups contained in Restricted Groups are removed automatically from those groups in the system when their temporary privileges are removed from the Restricted Groups.

System Services

The System Services settings enables you to define the security parameters of all of the system services installed on the machine. These parameters include defining the startup mode (automatic, manual, or disabled), and access control on each of the services.

Registry

The Registry settings enable you to set security access on individual local registry keys. There are three security areas: Classes_Root, Machine, and Users. The Security Configuration Tool Set gives you three options for setting security access on each of the Registry keys. These options are set within the security template(s) that you configure for your network and your local machines. The three options are as follows:

- To propagate inheritable permissions to all subkeys for a specified Registry key.

- To replace all existing permissions on all subkeys with inheritable permissions for a specified Registry key.

- Do not allow permissions on a specified Registry key to be replaced.

File System

The File System settings enable you to configure security for the local system file volumes and directory trees. You configure security in the security template(s) you configure for your network and your local machines. The preconfigured security templates already include security for certain files and folders, which might include the folder where your operating system is stored. You can add or delete files and folders as necessary. As with the settings for security access for the Registry, you have three options for setting security access to files and folders:

- To propagate inheritable permissions to all subfolders and files for a specified folder or file.

- To replace all existing permissions on all subfolders and files with inheritable permissions for a specified folder or file.

- Do not allow permissions on a specified folder or file to be replaced.

Security Configuration Tool Set Components

The Security Configuration Tool Set consists of the following components. They will all be discussed in more detail later in this chapter. You can run these components on every Windows 2000-based system in your network, and they can be used for all security configuration and analysis functionality.

Security Templates Snap-In

The Security Templates snap-in enables you to create, edit, and save security configurations into a security template. You can import a security template into the Security Configuration and Analysis snap-in to configure and analyze security for a local machine. You import a security template into a Group Policy object with the Group Policy snap-in. After the template is in place, you can use it to configure security centrally in Active Directory for domain-wide security settings.

You can merge more than one security template into a composite template that you then can use for the configuration and analysis of a machine on your network. You also can save the composite template for future configuration and analysis on other machines in your network. If there are conflicting settings in a composite template, the last template you imported takes precedence.

Security Configuration and Analysis Snap-In

This snap-in enables you to import one or more security templates into a database. You can use the snap-in to analyze the current machine configuration against the security configuration that is stored in the database. You can apply a security configuration in the database to a local Windows 2000 domain controller, standalone or member server, or workstation.

Security Settings Extension to the Group Policy Snap-In

This snap-in extends the Windows 2000 Group Policy snap-in and enables you to define security configurations as part of a group policy object (GPO). You then can assign these group policy objects to a specific computer, or to a site, domain, or other organizational unit scope defined in Active Directory, so that any policy changes can be applied to all computers in that scope. The machines within the designated scope import the policy to the local computer-policy database. The security configuration from this database is then propagated periodically to ensure that the system adheres to your corporation's designated policy.

secedit.exe Command-Line Tool

`secedit.exe` is a command-line tool that enables you to perform security configuration and analysis functions using a graphical user interface (GUI). You can run `secedit.exe` from a batch file or a scheduler to automatically create and apply templates and to analyze system security. You also can run it directly from a command-line prompt. This tool is very helpful to administrators who need to configure or analyze security on multiple computers in their network during off-hours.

Security Templates

As mentioned in the "Security Configuration Tool Set Components" section of this chapter, you use the Security Templates snap-in (shown in Figure 12.2) to create, edit and save security configurations into a security template. You then can import the templates into the Security Configuration and Analysis snap-in or the Security Settings extension of the Group Policy snap-in.

A Group Policy object defines configuration, usage, and access settings for resources and accounts in your network. When you import a security template to a Group Policy object, any computer or user account included in the site, domain, or organizational unit (OU) to which the Group Policy object is applied will receive the security template settings. As a result, you can configure security for multiple computers and user accounts at once. Local Group Policy cannot override domain-based policy.

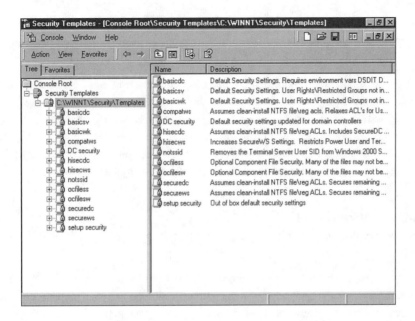

FIGURE 12.2
The Security Templates snap-in.

The security templates are stored in the `Systemroot\Security\Templates` folder as text-based files with an `.INF` file extension and you can read them with any text editor. However, Microsoft recommends that you do not alter the templates using a text editor, because you might unintentionally change the file's format and thus render the file useless.

Predefined Default and Incremental Security Templates

The Security Templates snap-in includes 11 predefined security templates, but you are not limited to using only them. You can create your own security templates (covered later in this section) that you then can apply to your local machine or to machines throughout the network.

> **NOTE**
>
> As with any changes you make to production systems, you should not apply security templates to them without first testing the templates to ensure that the proper level of functionality is maintained.

Predefined security templates consist of two categories: default and incremental. The default (or basic) templates are applied by the Windows operating system when you perform a clean install. You must apply them manually if you perform an upgrade installation.

Microsoft presumes that the predefined incremental security templates will be applied to Windows 2000 machines that are already using the default security settings. These Windows 2000 security templates incrementally modify default security settings, as long as the default security settings are already applied on the machine. They do not install the default security settings and then perform modifications on them. Therefore, you must ensure that the default security templates are applied to machines before you apply any incremental security templates.

Template Security Levels

The predefined security templates are comprised of five types, or levels, of security. These are as follows:

- *Basic*—These templates include the `basic*.inf` security templates. Microsoft provides the basic (or default) templates to reverse the application of other security configurations. All security areas (except for those that pertain to user rights) are reset to the original Windows 2000 default security settings. This default configuration adheres to strict security settings for members of the Users group. Members of the local Power Users group are assigned security settings that are less secure so they are able to run legacy applications that are not certified for the Windows 2000 operating system.

- *Compatible*—These templates include the `compat*.inf` security templates. If you are working in an environment where you don't want to assign any users to the local Power Users group, this template is for you, because it removes all members from the Power Users group. Microsoft presumes that administrators using this template will lower the security levels on necessary and specified files, folders, and registry keys that are accessed by applications not certified for use on the Windows 2000 operating system. This is so that members of the Users group will be enabled to run these legacy applications successfully.

- *Secure*—These templates include the `secure*.inf` security templates. They increase the level of security for all security areas except for files, folders, or registry keys. The Secure templates will not modify the file system or registry permissions because the Basic templates securely configure these security areas by default.

- *Highly Secure*—These templates include the `hisec*.inf` security templates. They define security settings for Windows 2000 network communications. IPSec is configured on these machines to set maximum protection for network traffic and for the protocols that are used between Windows 2000 machines. As a result, for all of the machines on your network to communicate properly, your network must be composed of only Windows 2000 machines, and you need to apply these templates to all Windows 2000 machines in your network. These computers will not be able to communicate with other machines that are running Windows 95, Windows 98, or Windows NT 4.0.

- *DC Security*—These templates include the DC*.inf templates. They optimize security for local users on domain controllers that do not run other server-based applications. If you do not run server-based applications on domain controllers, you can use this template to define the default file system and registry permissions for the local Users group in the same fashion as defined by default for Windows 2000 standalone servers and Windows 2000 Professional.

Predefined Default Security Templates

The predefined default security templates specify default Windows 2000 security settings for all of the security areas discussed earlier in this chapter, with the exception of user rights and groups. The default templates are meant to reset security system changes that have resulted in undesirable system behavior. Changes made to user rights and groups are not affected by applying the basic security templates. This is because administrators often modify these settings so that different levels of users can successfully execute applications.

The difference between the basic*.inf security templates and the ocf*.inf security templates is that the ocf*.inf security templates contain default security settings for all optional Windows 2000 component files that might or might not be installed during the installation process. When you apply the ocf*.inf security templates, you might notice a number of warning messages because not all of the files specified in the ocf*.inf security templates can exist on any given system. Receiving warning messages simply indicates that a component file doesn't exist on a particular machine because it hasn't been installed and, as a result, security can't be set on it.

The following are the predefined default (basic) security templates:

- Basicdc.inf   This template is the default configuration for domain controllers running Windows 2000 Server.
- Basicsv.inf   This template is the general default configuration for computers running Windows 2000 Server.
- Basicwk.inf   This template is the default configuration for computers running Windows 2000 Professional.
- Ocfiless.inf   This template is the default configuration for Windows 2000 standalone or member servers and is not meant for domain controllers.
- Ocfilesw.inf   This template is the default configuration for computers running Windows 2000 Professional.

Predefined Incremental Security Templates

Incremental security templates are meant to modify security settings on machines already running the default security settings. The following are the predefined incremental security templates:

- *Compatws.inf*   This template is used for both Windows 2000 Professional and Windows 2000 Server. It modifies default access permissions for the Users group so that users are able to execute legacy applications without being assigned membership in the Power Users group.

- *DC security.inf*   This template is used for Windows 2000 domain controllers only. It optimizes security for local users on domain controllers.

- *Hisecdc.inf*   This template is used for Windows 2000 domain controllers. The template includes increased security settings for parameters that affect network communication protocols. If you choose to use this security template, your network should be composed of only Windows 2000 machines, and this template should be applied to all Windows 2000 domain controllers in your network. (You also need to apply hisecws.inf to all Windows 2000 workstations and standalone and member servers in your network.) Access permissions to the Power User group are modified to be the equivalent of the Users group.

- *Hisecws.inf*   This template is used for Windows 2000 Professional and Windows 2000 Server. The template includes increased security settings for parameters that affect network communication protocols. If you choose to use this security template, your network should be composed of only Windows 2000 machines, and this template should be applied to all Windows 2000 workstations and standalone and member servers in your network. Access permissions to the Power User group are modified to be the equivalent of the Users group, essentially making end users either users or administrators.

- *Securedc.inf*   This template is used for Windows 2000 domain controllers. The template includes increased security settings for auditing, account policy, and security-relevant registry keys. The template removes all members of the Power Users group from the machine.

- *Securews.inf*   This template is used for Windows 2000 Professional and Windows 2000 Server. The template includes increased security settings for auditing, account policy, and security-relevant registry keys. The template removes all members of the Power Users group from the machine.

Loading the Security Templates Snap-In

You load the SecurityTemplates snap-in into an MMC by doing the following:

1. Click Start and then click Run.

2. In the Run dialog box, type **mmc /a** into the Open drop-down combo box and then click OK.

3. When the Console window appears, choose the Console menu and then choose Add/Remove Snap-In (see Figure 12.3).

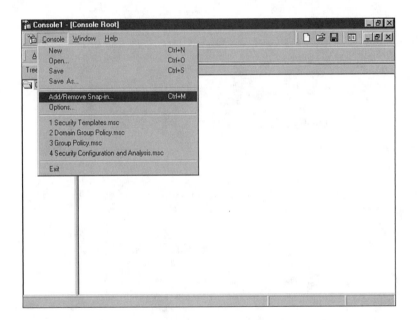

FIGURE 12.3
The MMC window.

4. When the Add/Remove Snap-In dialog box appears (see Figure 12.4), click the Add button.

FIGURE 12.4

The Add/Remove Snap-In dialog box.

5. When the Add Standalone Snap-In dialog box appears, choose Security Templates (see Figure 12.5), and then click the Add button.

FIGURE 12.5

The Add Standalone Snap-In dialog box.

6. Click Close to close the Add Standalone Snap-In dialog box.

7. Security Templates should now be listed in the Add/Remove Snap-In dialog box. Click OK to close the Add/Remove Snap-In dialog box.

8. The Security Templates Snap-In should now be listed in the console tree. Save this MMC by clicking the Console menu and then clicking Save As.

9. When the Save As dialog box appears, type `Security Templates` in the File Name text box (see Figure 12.6) and then click Save.

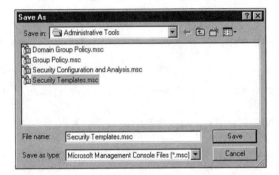

FIGURE 12.6
The MMC Save As dialog box.

Close the Console window. You now can access this console through the Administrative Tools program group.

Creating a New Security Template

You create a new template with the same security areas as the predefined security templates. However, none of the security areas' attributes have defined settings. After you create the template, you will have to define the attribute settings yourself. To create a new template, perform the following steps:

1. Run the Security Templates MMC that you created in the last section by choosing Start, Programs, Administrative Tools, `Security Templates.msc`.

2. Expand Security Templates, right-click Systemroot\Security\Templates, and then click New Template.

3. In the Text Name text box of the dialog box, type the name of the security template you are creating (see Figure 12.7).

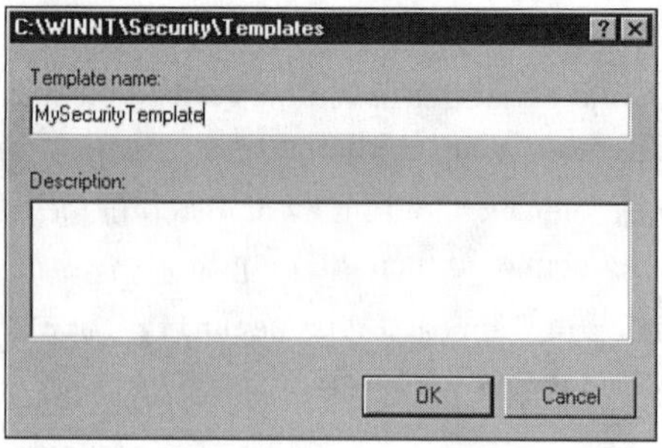

FIGURE 12.7
The dialog box for naming a new template.

4. In the Description text box, type a description for the security template you are creating.

5. Click OK. You should now see the new security template listed in the console tree.

Modifying an Existing Security Template

After you have created a new security template, you will have to define the security areas attributes. You also can modify settings in already existing security templates. If you modify settings in a predefined security template, you should save the modified security template with a different name so that you can keep the original security template in an unaltered state. As with all security templates, you can modify the Account Policies, Local Policies, Event Log, Restricted Groups, System Services, Registry, and File System security areas.

To define the settings in a new security template, or to modify settings in an already existing security template, perform the following steps:

1. The Security Templates MMC should still be opened from the last section. To modify the settings of the security template that you created, locate the setting(s) in the console tree that you want to define (see Figure 12.8).

2. Double-click the first setting you want to change.

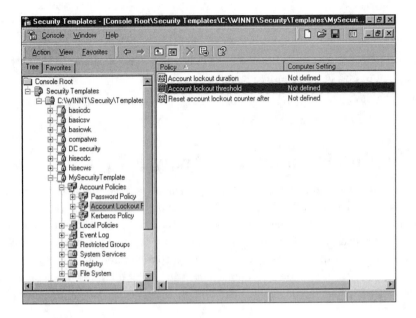

FIGURE 12.8
Modifying a setting in a security template.

3. A Template Security Policy Setting dialog box appears (see Figure 12.9). Select or clear the Define This Policy Setting In The Template check box to change the current setting.

FIGURE 12.9
A Template Security Policy Setting dialog box.

4. Click OK. The details pane should show the updated setting. Perform steps 1 through 4 for each security setting modification that you need to make.

5. After you have completed the security setting modifications, you need to save the new template to preserve the changes you have made. If the template is a newly created one, right-click the new security template name in the console tree, and then click Save.

6. If you are making modifications to a predefined template, right-click the predefined security template name in the console tree, and then click Save As.

7. In the File Name text box of the Save As dialog box that appears, type the new name that you want to give to the modified template.

8. Click the Save button.

9. Close the Security Templates MMC.

Security Configuration and Analysis Tool

The Security Configuration and Analysis Tool is a standalone snap-in that provides an interface to the Security Configuration Service. The Security Configuration Service is the core engine of the Security Configuration Tool Set. It is responsible for the security configuration and analysis functionality provided by the Security Configuration Tool Set, and it runs on every Windows 2000-based machine. Administrators use the Security Configuration and Analysis snap-in to configure and analyze security on a local machine. You cannot use it to analyze and test different configurations against the prevailing site, domain, or organizational unit's security configuration.

Security Configuration and Analysis uses a database, which is a computer-specific data store, to perform configuration and analysis functions. The database is considered to be the starting point for security analysis and configuration, because you can analyze and test different configurations by incrementally adding new security templates to the database, overwriting the current template(s) in the database, or by creating personal databases for storing customized security templates.

To use the Security Configuration and Analysis standalone snap-in, you must first add it to an MMC, and then you must create its database on a local machine.

Loading the Security Configuration and Analysis Snap-In

You load the Security Configuration and Analysis snap-in by doing the following:

1. Click Start and then choose Run.

2. In the Run dialog box, type `mmc /a` into the Open drop-down combo box and then click OK.

3. When the Console window appears, click the Console menu and then click Add/Remove Snap-In.

4. When the Add/Remove Snap-In dialog box appears, click the Add button.

5. When the Add Standalone Snap-In dialog box appears, click Security Configuration and Analysis (see Figure 12.10) and then click the Add button.

FIGURE 12.10
The Add Standalone Snap-In dialog box.

6. It is convenient to also load the Security Templates and the Group Policy snap-ins to this console. Click Security Templates, and then click Add.

7. Click Group Policy, and then click Add.

8. When the Select Group Policy Object appears, you must choose a Group Policy object type. The default type is Local Computer. If necessary, click the Browse button to select a different type of Group Policy object.

9. When you click the Browse button, the Browse For A Group Policy Object dialog box appears. This is where you select the Group Policy object type. After you've made your selection, click OK.

10. Click the Finish button to close the Select Group Policy Object dialog box.

11. Click the Close button to close the Add Standalone Snap-In dialog box.

12. The Security Configuration and Analysis, Security Templates, and Group Policy snap-ins now should be listed in the Add/Remove Snap-In dialog box (see Figure 12.11). Click OK to close the Add/Remove Snap-In dialog box.

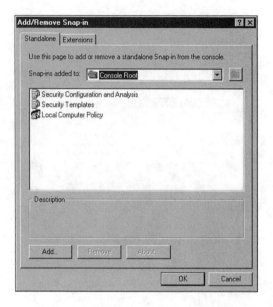

FIGURE 12.11
The Add/Remove Snap-In dialog box with the snap-ins added.

13. The Security Configuration and Analysis Snap-In should now be listed in the console tree. Save this MMC by clicking the Console menu and then clicking Save As.

14. When the Save As dialog box appears, type `Security Configuration and Analysis` in the File Name text box (see Figure 12.12) and then click the Save button.

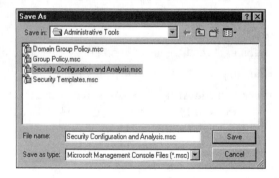

FIGURE 12.12
The MMC Save As dialog box.

15. Close the Console window. You now can access this console through the Administrative Tools program group.

Creating the Security Configuration and Analysis Database

You create a database for the snap-in by performing the following steps:

1. Choose Start, Programs, Administrative Tools, and then click Security Configuration and Analysis.msc (this is the MMC you created in the last section).

2. When the Security Configuration and Analysis console appears, maximize the console window and then, in the console tree, click Security Configuration and Analysis. In the details pane, notice that instructions are given for creating a new database (see Figure 12.13).

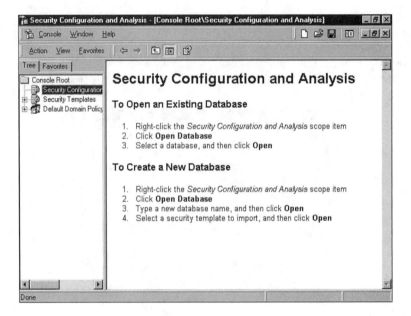

FIGURE 12.13
Instructions in the details pane for Security Configuration and Analysis.

3. In the console tree, right-click Security Configuration and Analysis and then choose Open Database. The Open Database dialog box appears (see Figure 12.14).

FIGURE 12.14
The Open Database dialog box.

4. In the File Name text box, type the name that you want to give to the database, and then click the Open button. The Import Template dialog box appears (see Figure 12.15).

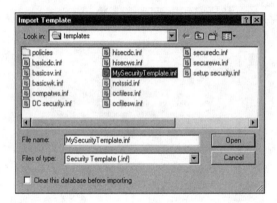

FIGURE 12.15
The Import Template dialog box.

5. In the Import Template dialog box, select the security template you want to import into the database. If you are creating a new database, step 6 will not be necessary.

6. If the database already exists, you have an additional choice to make. You can decide to merge the entries from the security template with those that already exist in the current database by ensuring that the Clear This Database Before Importing check box is cleared. Alternately, you can decide to select the Clear This Database Before Importing check box to clear the entries in the current database before you import the new entries.

7. Click the Open button in the Import Template dialog box. Notice that new information appears in the details pane of the Security Configuration and Analysis console (see Figure 12.16).

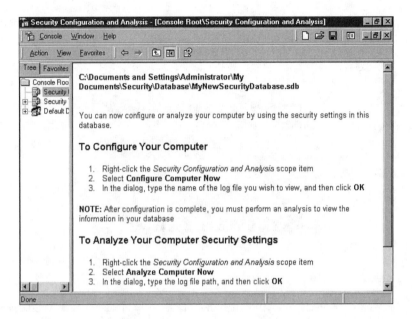

Figure 12.16
The Security Configuration and Analysis details pane after the database is created.

8. Close the Security Configuration and Analysis console window.

Analyzing Security

Now that you've created a database for the Security Configuration and Analysis snap-in, you can perform an analysis by comparing the current state of the machine to the security template that you just imported. The imported template contains the recommended security settings for the machine and is used as a starting point, or base configuration. When you perform the analysis, the snap-in queries the current system security settings for all security areas covered in the base configuration. Any mismatching attributes between the two are flagged as potential problems.

Performing an Analysis and Reviewing the Results

You perform an analysis on the machine in the following manner:

1. Choose Start, Programs, Administrative Tools, and then click Security Configuration and Analysis.msc.

2. In the console tree of the Security Configuration and Analysis console, right-click Security Configuration and Analysis, and then click Analyze Computer Now.

3. When the Perform Analysis dialog box appears, either click OK to select the default name of the log file, or specify the name of the log file you want to use. An Analyzing System Security progress box appears to display the progress of the analysis (see Figure 12.17).

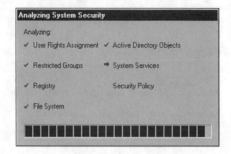

FIGURE 12.17
The Analyzing System Security progress box.

When the analysis is finished, you will notice that the security areas now are listed. Expand the security areas and examine some of the attributes. Notice that for each attribute, both the current system and the database configuration settings are displayed side-by-side (see Figure 12.18).

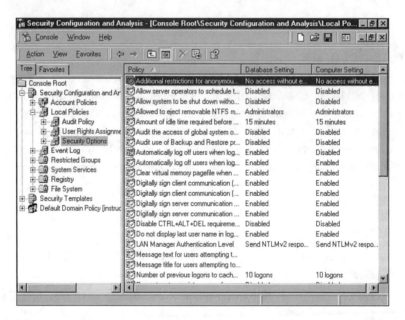

FIGURE 12.18
The analysis results.

Green flags (a green check mark enclosed in a white circle) highlight consistencies between the two configuration settings. Red flags (a white x enclosed in a red circle) highlight problem areas that signify discrepancies between the two configuration settings. If an attribute has neither a red nor a green flag, this means that the security setting is not configured in the template that you imported into the database. You can double-click any attribute listed in the details pane to display its current settings and to modify the database settings if you so desire.

Configuring Security

If, after reviewing the analysis results, you are comfortable with the security changes, you can configure the machine with the new security settings provided by the security template. To do this, you perform the following steps:

1. Choose Start, Programs, Administrative Tools, and then click Security Configuration and Analysis.msc (this is the MMC you created earlier in this chapter).

2. When the Security Configuration and Analysis console appears, maximize the console window. In the console tree, right-click Security Configuration and Analysis and then click Configure Computer Now.

3. A Configure System dialog box appears. Either click OK to accept the default log file path or enter the name of the log file you want to use, and then click OK. A Configuring Computer Security progress box appears to display the progress of the configuration (see Figure 12.19).

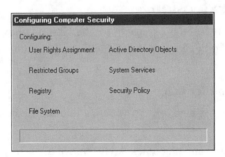

Figure 12.19
The Configuring Computer Security progress box.

4. The security template is now applied to your computer. Close the Security Configuration and Analysis MMC window.

5. Click Yes to save the console settings.

Security Settings Extension for the Group Policy Snap-In

You can configure the security structure of an entire site, domain, or organizational unit with the Security Settings Extension to the Group Policy snap-in. The settings are configured on the server and then automatically propagated to the clients. The Group Policy snap-in takes advantage of Active Directory scopes. A scope is a grouping of users and computers and consists of three levels—sites, domains, and organizational units.

When you expand the Security Settings container in the Group Policy snap-in, you will notice that, in addition to the security areas discussed previously in this chapter, there are two more security areas listed. They are

- *IP Security Policies on Active Directory*—This configures the IPSec policy object in Active Directory. In addition, it defines encryption and signature requirements for IP packets traveling between the source and destination computers.
- *Public Key Policies*—This configures policies used by Windows 2000 Public Key Infrastructure (PKI)-based technologies. These include the Encrypted Data Recovery Agents, automatic certificate request settings, trusted root Certification Authorities, and enterprise certificate trust lists.

Installing the Group Policy Snap-In and the Security Settings Extension

To be able to use the security settings extension for the Group Policy snap-in, you must first install the Group Policy snap-in and then install the Security Settings extension in the Group Policy snap-in.

1. Choose Start and then click Run.
2. When the Run dialog box appears, type `mmc /a` into the Open drop-down combo box and then click OK.
3. Click the Console menu and then click Add/Remove Snap-In.
4. When the Add/Remove Snap-In dialog box appears, click Add.
5. When the Add Standalone Snap-In dialog box appears, click Group Policy from the Available Standalone Snap-Ins list.
6. Click Add.
7. If you want to set default domain policy, click the Browse button in the Select Group Policy Object dialog box, and then select Default Domain Policy.
8. Click OK.

9. Click the Finish, Close.

10. In the Add/Remove Snap-In dialog box, choose the Extensions tab.

11. In the Available Extensions list, make sure that the Security Settings extension is selected to be installed and then click OK.

12. Save the Group Policy MMC you just created by clicking the Console menu and then clicking Save As.

13. When the Save As dialog box appears, type **Domain Group Policy** in the File Name text box and then click the Save button.

14. Close the Group Policy MMC window.

If you want to view the security areas for the Group Policy snap-in, expand the Default Domain Policy container, expand the Computer Configuration container, expand the Windows Settings container, and then expand the Security Settings container. You can edit security settings within the Security Settings Extension in the same manner as described earlier in this chapter. You double-click the security attribute you want to configure. When the Security Policy Setting dialog box appears, you configure the attribute as you want.

`secedit.exe` Command-Line Tool

As we've just discussed, the Group Policy snap-in can apply security configurations over a large number of machines within sites, domains, or organizational units. You can perform these same tasks, plus the configuration and analysis operations available from the Security Configuration and Analysis snap-in, with the `secedit.exe` command-line tool.

The `secedit.exe` command-line tool contains five primary switches: `/analyze`, `/configure`, `/export`, `/refreshpolicy`, and `/validate`.

- The `/analyze` and `/configure` switches perform the same analysis and configuration tasks available in the Security Configuration and Analysis snap-in.

- The `/export` feature is available through the Security Configuration and Analysis snap-in after a database has been created or opened. This switch dumps database configuration information into an `.INF` template file so that you can use the template at a later time.

- The `/refreshpolicy` switch propagates the system security policy after changes have been made. Otherwise, by default, a Group Policy propagation event occurs after certain events—every time the machine boots, every 60 to 90 minutes thereafter, and any time you make modifications to the local security policy using the Security Settings extension to Group Policy snap-in.

- You use the `/validate` switch to verify the syntax of a template that you create with the Security Templates snap-in.

Tables 12.1–12.5 list all of the switches for the `secedit.exe` command-line tool.

TABLE 12.1 Switches for Security Analysis

Switch	Description
`secedit /analyze`	You use this command switch to initiate a security analysis. Additional parameters include the following:
`/DB filename`	This is a required switch. It provides the database path and name that contains the existing configuration against which the analysis is performed. If the database is new, you also must specify the `/CFG filename` argument.
`/CFG filename`	This switch is required only when the database specified in the `/DB` parameter is new. It points to the path of the security template that will be imported into the database for analysis.
`/log logpath`	This switch specifies the path and filename of the log file that will be created during the analysis.
`/verbose`	Using this switch specifies that you want more detailed progress information during the analysis.
`/quiet`	When you use this switch, it provides very little screen or log output.

The syntax for this switch is as follows:

```
secedit /analyze [/DB filename ] [/CFG filename ] [/log logpath]
➥[/verbose] [/quiet]
```

TABLE 12.2 Switches for Configuring System Security

Switch	Description
`secedit /configure`	When you use this command switch, `secedit.exe` will configure system security by applying an existing template. Additional parameters include:
`/DB filename`	This is a required switch that provides the database path to the security template you want to apply to the machine.
`/CFG filename`	This switch is used in conjunction with the `/DB` switch. It provides the security template path that you want to import into the database and apply to the machine. If you don't use this switch, the template that is already stored in the database will be applied to the machine.

TABLE 12.2 Continued

Switch	Description
/overwrite	This switch only can be used in conjunction with the /CFG switch. It specifies whether the template specified in the /CFG switch should overwrite the template(s) stored in the database, or whether the template should be appended to the database to form a composite template. If this switch isn't specified with the /CFG switch, the template will be appended to the existing template.
/areas *area1 area2...*	This switch specifies the security areas from the template that you want to apply to the machine. The default is to apply the template to "all areas". Each area name should be separated by a space, rather than by a comma. The area names you can specify are: SECURITYPOLICY, GROUP_MGMT, USER_RIGHTS, REGKEYS, FILESTORE, and SERVICES.
/log *logpath*	This switch specifies the path to the log file for the configuration process. If you don't specify the path, the default path is used.
/verbose	This switch specifies that you want more detailed information about the configuration progress.
/quiet	When you use this switch, you suppress most screen and log output.

The syntax for this switch is as follows:

```
secedit /configure [/DB filename ] [/CFG filename ] [/overwrite]
➥[/areas area1 area2...] [/log logpath] [/verbose] [/quiet]
```

TABLE 12.3 Switches to Refresh Security Settings

secedit /refreshpolicy	This command switch refreshes domain system security by reapplying the domain security settings to the Group Policy object. Additional parameters include:
machine_policy	When you use this argument, you refresh the local computer security settings.
user_policy	This argument will refresh the security settings for the currently logged on local user account on the local machine.
/enforce	This switch will refresh security settings, regardless of whether any recent revisions have been made to the Group Policy object settings.

12

SECURITY POLICY AND CONFIGURATION

The syntax for this switch is as follows:

```
secedit /refreshpolicy {machine_policy | user_policy}[/enforce]
```

TABLE 12.4 Switches to Export Security Settings

`secedit /export`	This command switch will export an existing template from a security database to a template file. Additional parameters include:
`/MergedPolicy`	This switch will merge and then export local and domain policy security settings.
`/DB filename`	This switch provides the database name and path that contains the template that you want to export. The default is to use the system policy database.
`/CFG filename`	This switch provides the path and filename for the newly exported template.
`/areas area1 area2...`	This switch enables you to specify a specific security area to be configured. The default is `"all areas"`. You separate each area name by a space rather than by a comma. The area names you can specify are: SECURITYPOLICY, GROUP_MGMT, USER_RIGHTS, REGKEYS, FILESTORE, and SERVICES.
`/log logpath`	This switch specifies the location of the log file that will be created during the export process. If you don't specify a path, the default path will be used.
`/verbose`	This switch specifies that you want more detailed information about the configuration progress.
`/quiet`	When you use this switch, you specify that you want to suppress screen and log output.

The syntax for this switch is as follows:

```
secedit /export [/mergedpolicy] [/DB filename ] [/CFG filename ]
➥[/areas area1 area 2...] [/log logPath] [/verbose] [/quiet]
```

TABLE 12.5 Switches to Validate a Security Configuration File

`secedit /validate`	This command switch validates the syntax of a security template.

The syntax for this switch is as follows:

```
secedit /validate filename
```

Summary

This chapter introduced you to the concepts of security templates and the Security Configuration Tool Set. You learned that you can use the components from the Security Configuration Tool Set to configure and analyze individual machines by using the Security Configuration and Analysis snap-in. You analyze and configure multiple machines within a specified scope by using the Group Policy snap-in. You also discovered how to use the `secedit.exe` command-line tool to perform configuration and analysis tasks without the use of a GUI. Finally, you learned about numerous switches that can be used to enhance your work with the `secedit.exe` tool.

12

SECURITY POLICY
AND
CONFIGURATION

Exploiting Web Services

IN THIS CHAPTER

In this chapter, we will exploit the Web services—hack our way into a Windows 2000 Internet Information Services (IIS) Web server system. The goal of this chapter is to provide you, the reader, with a way to expose the various ways an IIS system can be compromised. In Chapter 14, "Protecting Web Services," we will focus on how to protect your IIS server from falling victim to the various holes and security attacks that can bring your Web server down.

Background of Web Services

With Windows 2000 Server, Advanced Server, and Datacenter, Internet Information Services (IIS) v5.0 is automatically installed on the system. The basic Web services provide World Wide Web (WWW) services to allow the server to host Web pages. Beyond just WWW services, the File Transfer Protocol (FTP) is also installed at the time of installation of Windows 2000. FTP provides the ability to host files that a client system attaching to the Web server can access to send or receive files.

Web services extends beyond just Web page hosting and file transfer and includes the option of setting up the server to provide Simple Message Transfer Protocol (SMTP) mail message routing (using the SMTP service). The SMTP component is not installed by default, but it can be easily added by choosing Control Panel, Add/Remove Programs, Add Components, Internet Information Services, and check marking SMTP. Enabling SMTP is necessary if you want the Web server to route Internet mail messages or to act as a mail host system.

Also part of Web services is the ability to enable the Network News Transport Protocol (NNTP). This too is an option that can be enabled on the Web server by choosing Control Panel, Add/Remove Programs, Add Components, Internet Information Services, and check marking NNTP. By enabling NNTP, the server can now participate as a NNTP discussion thread host system providing newsgroup information, either publicly external or exclusively internal to the networking environment.

The Need to Have Web Services Installed on Your Server

As Web services are enabled and accessible on a system, security holes are also introduced to the networking environment. An administrator of the network can choose to uninstall or disable Web services, but a thorough review of functions of the server should be considered before the Web services are eliminated from the system.

Beyond just traditional hosting of Web pages (WWW), file transfers (FTP), mail routing (SMTP), or newsgroup hosting (NNTP), many of the new Microsoft and tightly integrated third-party applications require Web services for basic application operation. As an example, Microsoft Exchange 2000 and SharePoint Portal Server 2001 use Web services to provide Web-based access to mail messages, documents, and other information stored on the system.

Other applications, such as SQL 2000 and IIS, provide remote administration using a Web-based client running on the server system. So simply disabling Web services can impact common default server operations.

Having Your Web Server Inside Versus Outside Your Firewall

The placement of your Web server either inside or outside of the firewall has a significant impact on how the server needs to be configured for security. If the Web server is inside the firewall on the organization's local area network with no planned access by remote (Internet-based) users, the need to harden the server against external attacks is not as crucial as the need to implement very strict security rules on a server being accessed regularly by the public.

However, even if a server is placed inside the firewall, every Windows 2000 server system needs to be reviewed for security protection because Web services are automatically installed on the system. A user of the local area network can compromise the Web component portion of a server and effectively access all files and data on the server system, or even gain administrative control to the entire domain.

The balance of this chapter is dedicated to providing an insight into how to compromise the security of a server to not only manipulate data on the system, but to also gain full control of the server and the network domain to which the server is connected.

Finding Vulnerable Pathways to Accessible Web Servers

The first thing a hacker needs to do to compromise a networking environment is to find a vulnerable pathway to the server or servers that are to be attacked. Servers go by various names and are frequently chained together in a front-end/back-end relationship where the first server you access is not the actual server that has the data or information you want to access. As a result, gathering information about the networking environment and then validating that the server(s) is the system(s) you want to access needs to be done to begin the server attack process.

Knowing Exactly Which Server to Attack

As noted, just knowing the name of the server you want to access is not enough information to successfully modify all of the Web pages or gain access to information stored on a Web-serviced environment. Web pages and data can be stored on several different systems, and gaining knowledge of the systems that have the information you want to access is crucial in your ability to manipulate or acquire the sensitive information.

Clustered Web Servers in a Server Farm

When resolving the IP address of a server that provides Web services to hundreds or thousands of users, you are most likely not accessing just one system; rather, you are accessing one of many servers that are clustered together to distribute access load across multiple systems, as shown in Figure 13.1. In many enterprise Web server environments, a single hostname or publicly-exposed IP address actually points to dozens of servers that all have the same information on them. There are many ways organizations accomplish this one-address-to-many-server configuration, including DNS name aliases (where the DNS resolution table points to several systems) or through software or hardware network load balancing that physically routes communication from one address to multiple systems.

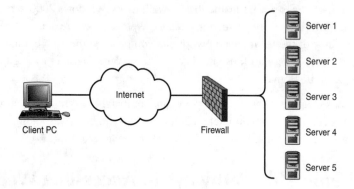

FIGURE 13.1
Distributed access load across multiple servers.

For systems that use the DNS table to provide a series of servers available to the client, also known as DNS Roundrobining, the list of servers typically shows up in the NSLookup response. When accessing a server name, the system resolves the first IP address of the server in the DNS table list and accesses that system. If that system is unavailable or busy, the request goes to the second server in the list, and so on. This not only provides the ability to cascade user access across multiple servers, it also provides a failover process where if a server is down, the request is automatically redirected to the next server in the list. After reaching the last server address in the DNS table list without successfully connecting to a server, a "Server Unavailable" error will be returned to the user.

The load balancing function is more active in its distribution of user load across multiple host systems. Instead of sequentially distributing the load across systems, load balancing analyzes the load of each server and distributes subsequent requests to servers with the least amount of traffic or server utilization.

When accessing servers for data manipulation, it is important to know that the modification of one system will not necessarily modify all systems, and the same process might need to be done several times to change all server instances of the data.

Front-End and Back-End Servers

Another Web services practice is to split information between a front-end system (or series of systems) and a back-end system (or series of systems), as shown in Figure 13.2. The front-end system might only have the basic Web pages to gain access to data stored on the back-end systems, so gaining access control to a front-end system might not provide you with access to the actual data or information you are trying to control.

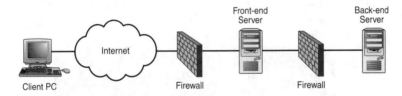

FIGURE 13.2
Front-end/back-end Web services configured environment.

Front-end/back-end server processes can have lateral server controls where a client is redirected from one system to another system when accessing information. The front-end/back-end processes can also be a linear controlled process where a back-end system is never exposed to the public, and only the front-end system can access data stored on the back-end server. An organization can minimize its exposure to unauthorized data access by preventing clients from ever accessing the actual data on the back-end server directly. By creating a two step process, an organization can protect the information stored on the back-end server.

However, this front-end/back-end relationship can also be used to your advantage when looking to compromise a system because many organizations harden their data servers that house their sensitive information, and they overlook hardening a supporting front-end system from attacks. In many cases, access to a front-end system can lead to the acquisition of an administrative password or a list of all of the back-end data servers that can then be used to easily compromise the core servers on the network.

Resolving the DNS Name of the Server

If you know the name of the server you want to access, you would want to resolve the common name to a physical IP address. All servers on a common TCP/IP network have an IP address that is the physical identification of the system on the network. Because IP addresses are not intuitive names (such as 10.1.1.32), a simpler common name (like "intranet") is given to the system. While the system will be better known by its common name, you need to know the IP address of the system to ensure that you are physically accessing the same system throughout your security infiltration process.

To resolve the name of a system, use the NSLookup utility that comes with Windows 2000. This is done by doing the following:

1. Drop to a command prompt (Start, Run, cmd.exe, OK).
2. Type **nslookup.exe**, and then press Enter.
3. Type the name of the server you want to resolve (for example, **intranet**) and press Enter.
4. Write down the IP address resolved by NSLookup.

In Figure 13.3, the server name "intranet" was resolved with the IP address 10.1.1.32.

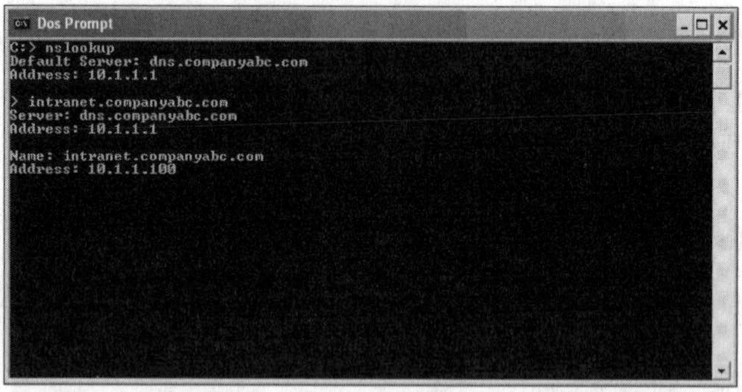

FIGURE 13.3
NSLookup name resolution to an IP address.

Using a Vulnerable Pathway to Search for Servers to Attack

For the hacker hobbyist, knowing which server to access might not be obvious, and the desire to access any server to modify or manipulate becomes the goal. In other cases, when an organization has several servers linked together, it might be challenging to find a specific server to access or acquire information, so having an automated program to search for available servers can be used to find a system accessible to crack. In many cases, an organization might have forgotten to harden a system after recovery or initial installation of the system, and finding a single vulnerable system can provide information, such as administrative passwords or even logon user accounts that can be used to break into other more secured systems on the network.

The key to hacking into a Web services environment does not solely depend on hacking into the primary destination server but effectively finding the most vulnerable system on the network. By exposing the most vulnerable system, you can gain valuable information, such as usernames, group names, or even administrative passwords. With this information, you can go back to the server you want to hack into and can most likely just log on to the system.

There are several tools readily available on the Internet that scan a network, firewall, router, or server to gather information about the system and network resources. These tools are the starting block for building an information base from which a Web services hack attack can be initiated.

Using Stealth HTTP Security Scanner to Find Security Vulnerabilities

A freely available security analyzing tool is the Stealth HTTP Security Scanner written by Felipe Moniz. It is a utility that can be used to validate the security strength of a networking environment. Very simply, it scans ports, connectivity, and access to a destination using a variety of tests and reports the broad number of openings to the destination. This utility does not provide specifics on which ports are open and whether the opening of the ports is good or bad, this utility more broadly notes if there are vulnerabilities that can be exploited.

Installing Stealth HTTP Security Scanner

Because URLs for downloading utilities change frequently, a version of the Stealth HTTP Security Scanner utility is available on the Sams Publishing Web site at `http://www.samspublishing.com`. The download is about 700KB in size and has the name `Stealth-1.0-b29.zip`. After downloading the utility, unzip the file that will expose a single file with the exact same name as the Zip file, but with an `.exe` extension. Run this executable and it will install the software on your system. You will need to specify if you want to install in English or Portuguese, your destination directory (such as `c:\Program Files\Stealth`), and whether you want an icon for the program added to your desktop. After it has been installed, the program will be ready to run.

Using Stealth HTTP Security Scanner to Map the Security of a Networking Environment

The Stealth HTTP Security Scanner utility is used to scan a network for system vulnerabilities. You will be prompted with a GUI interface with a handful of tabs and options. The key parameters to fill in are as follows:

- *On the Scanner Tab*—Enter in the Host Address of the destination server or device you want to scan. This will typically be the end server you want to access.

- *On the Hacking Techniques Tab*—You can choose to select all of the options listed (Include Internal DB, Include External DB, Loophole Test, Evade IDS, Common HTTP Exploit Test, and DoS (Denial of Service) Test).

- *On the Log Tab*—If you've run the scan before, you can choose to clear the log so that any subsequent scan will provide a clean table of results.

- *On the Preferences Tab*—If you use a Proxy Server between you and the Internet, you would have to enter it here. Most of these other options will provide variations on the results of the information requested.

After you enter in all of the information to the various tabs, click the Perform Scan button on the Scanner tab to launch the scan. You will see a results screen similar to the one shown in Figure 13.4 by clicking the Database button. In this example, 5677 ports were analyzed and 108 vulnerabilities were detected. This destination site can be deemed accessible for attack and the use of tools in the next several sections will exploit the vulnerabilities.

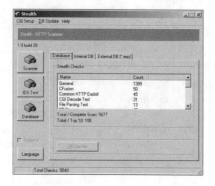

FIGURE 13.4
Using Stealth HTTP Security Scanner to determine Web services vulnerabilities.

Using NMapNT to Find Security Vulnerabilities

NMapNT by eEye Digital Security is one of many security vulnerability scanner utilities readily available to download off the Internet. NMapNT is a utility that can be used to validate the strength of security of a networking environment. For an organization that believes their firewall and security system has been hardened, a quick test by NMapNT will validate whether there are any security holes. To a less scrupulous individual, the NMapNT tool can be used to expose security holes in a network, effectively creating a framework for various ways and methods that can be used to attack a server system.

Installing NMapNT

Because URLs for downloading utilities change frequently, a version of the NMapNT utility is available on the Sams Publishing Web site at `http://www.samspublishing.com`. The download is about 1.2MB in size and has the name `nmapNTsp1.zip`. After downloading the utility, unzip the file that will expand an entire directory structure of files, including the `nmapnt.exe` program file plus a driver support directory and other source files for the program. When choosing your destination directory to unzip the files and directories, you might choose something like `C:\nmapnt` or simply your `c:\Program Files` directory to which to expand the files.

Using NMapNT to Map the Security of a Networking Environment

After installed, the NMapNT utility can be executed and used to scan a network for system vulnerabilities. The NMapNT utility is a DOS command-line type utility. There are several parameters that can be used when running the command line syntax, as shown in Table 13.1. A common command sequence would be as follows:

nmapnt –sT *x.x.x.x* –P0

where *x.x.x.x* is the destination IP address of the device you want to scan.

When you execute this sequence, you will see the open ports available, as shown in Figure 13.5. In this example, most of the more common ports are open (such as SMTP (Port 25), HTTP (Port 80), POP3 (Port 110), LDAP (Port 389), and so on). There are several other ports that are open that can be exploited, such as Port 445 (Microsoft Directory Services) or Port 139 (NetBIOS Services). Specific to this chapter on Exploiting Web Services, these open ports provide the pathways that will be used throughout the balance of this chapter to attack servers in the networking environment.

FIGURE 13.5
Response of the NMapNT utility showing open ports to a server.

TABLE 13.1   NmapNT Parameters

NMapNT Parameter	Effect
-sT	Uses TCP to do the port scan (default mode).
-sS	Uses TCP SYN to do the port scan (a more stealthy manner of scanning (preferred scanning if you want to minimize detection).
-sU	Uses UDP to dot the port scan (use this if the TCP port scan doesn't work, but the TCP SYN is still better).
-sP	This does a ping scan that lists all reachable machines.
-sR/-sI	Uses RPC (-sR) or Identd (-sI) port scan methods (again, the TCP SYN is still the better (stealthier) option.

TABLE 13.1   Continued

NMapNT Parameter	Effect

Note: One of these -s*X* parameters must be used. The following parameters are optional and can be combined to produce informative results.

-O	Uses TCP/IP fingerprinting to guess the remote operating system.
-p *<range>*	Specifies the range of ports to scan.
-F	Only scans the ports listed in the nmap-services settings.
-v	Displays information in verbose mode to give more details of the information provided (this is recommended when using NMapNT).
-P0	Specifies to not use the ping command to access the hosts.
-Ddecoy_host1	Allows the use of decoys when scanning.
-T <Paranoid, Sneaky, Polite, Normal, Aggressive, Insane>	Timing policy on how often a scan occurs. When a site or server with heavy security receives several scans, sometimes security shields or administrative notifications occur. If you feel your scanning might attract attention, use the -Tparanoid option that will take longer to scan but will not attract attention to the scanning.
-n/-R	-n never does DNS resolution; -R always does DNS resolution. The default is sometimes does resolution.
-oN/-oM *<logfile>*	Outputs information to a logfile (-oN is output normal; -oM is machine parsable).
-iL *<input file>*	Gets target file for devices to scan.
-S *<your_IP>* / -e	Specifies your source IP address (-S *<your IP>*) or your source network interface address (-e *<devicename>*).

Acquiring Administrative Access to a Web Server

After you have a clear pathway to a server or system environment, the next step is to attempt to gain administrative password or security information. By gaining administrative access information, an individual can easily make Web page modifications as well as enable permission controls typically to every server system in an environment.

There are several ways to gain administrative access to a Web server. Some of the methods are noted in the following sections.

Using the ShowPass Utility to Expose System Password Security

If you have physical access to a server system (where you can actually sit on the system and install a utility program), the ShowPass utility by MiSoSkiaN is a very simple and effective tool. This 150KB utility with a filename of ShowPassV1_0.zip, will display cached logon names and passwords as well as dial-up account logon and password information. In just seconds, an individual can view typically secured logon information. The only drawback to the ShowPass utility is that it must be installed and invoked right on a system, but with just a few minutes of server access (as described later in this chapter in the section "Physically Accessing an IIS Server"), an individual can gain very high level password rights that can then be used remotely for a variety of different needs and functions.

Installing the ShowPass Utility

After downloading the utility, simply unzipping the file will expose a single program executable with the name ShowPassV1_0.exe.

Using ShowPass to Gain Password Access Information

By running this ShowPass executable, a simple utility screen will be displayed, as shown in Figure 13.6. The three options to choose to uncover passwords are as follows:

- *Dialups*—This option will show any Dial-up account logon names and passwords known to this server system.
- *Cached*—This option will show any passwords stored on this system in cache memory.
- *Pick*—This option will show the password for a text box that might be displayed on screen showing ****** as the current password. This option is good at recovering passwords or determining passwords for any application or function that displays the password in ****** format onscreen.

By choosing one of the three options, the password will be displayed in the text box in the middle of the utility.

FIGURE 13.6
Default screen of the ShowPass utility.

Using L0phtCrack to Expose System Password Security

A very popular old time tool for exposing the password of a system is the L0phtCrack utility. In today's edition, the tool is now updated as LC3 and is available for purchase from organizations, such as @stake (http://www.atstake.com/research/lc3/download.html). This tool is just over 4MB in size and is named lc3setup01.exe. When the program is downloaded, it is in a fully-executable installation mode.

Installing the L3 Utility

To install the utility, run the lc3setup01.exe setup utility that will run through the installation process. As with all installation utilities, you will be prompted for a destination directory where you want the program installed. Specify the options you want and proceed with the installation.

Using L3 to Gain Password Access Information

After installation, the L3 utility can be executed typically out of your Start, Programs, LC3 Start button menu and can be used to display the passwords of key administrative accounts.

You will be prompted whether you want to retrieve passwords

- *From a local machine*—If the LC3 utility has been installed on the system in which you want to uncover passwords.

- *From a remote machine*—If you are running the LC3 utility on one machine but want to uncover the passwords on a remote system.

- *From an NT4 emergency repair disk*—If you have found an NT4 emergency repair disk lying around, you can shove it into a floppy drive and recover the passwords stored on the disk.

- *By sniffing a network*—If you don't have access to a machine but have a system running LC3 on the LAN or network segment where other systems are connected, you can sniff packets flowing across the network and capture encrypted hashes that can be analyzed and compiled into passwords.

Use whichever option is best for your environment. Most password analysis is done to a remote machine if you have access to analyze the machine itself or by doing a network sniff.

You will then be prompted for the auditing method you want to use. You can select:

- *Quick password audit*—This can crack simple passwords that you would normally find in a dictionary (typical words).

- *Common password audit*—This checks for simple dictionary words as well as common modifications to the dictionary words (where numbers are replaced for letters—1 instead of an l or i, or 0 instead of an o.

- *Strong password audit*—This uses the simple dictionary, common modifications to dictionary words, and performs a brute force attack on all combinations of standard letters and numbers in the analysis of the password.

When determining a password, you can start with the quick password audit and see if you can acquire the password (it's the fastest and simplest mode). If that doesn't work, you can jump right to the strong password audit to do a hardcore analysis.

The LC3 utility will begin the analysis immediately and will produce a report similar to the one shown in Figure 13.7. You will notice that the utility was able to crack the simple password assigned to this system's administrator account (PASSWORD) but was unable to extract a more complex password on an Exchange Store (EUSER_EXSTOREEVENT) account using the quick password audit. A more intense brute force analysis would need to be conducted to recover the password for a user account of this type. In this example, to uncover the complex password, the user would choose Brute Force Crack Enabled in the Session, the Session Options pulldown menu and then run Session, Begin Audit to scan the passwords again.

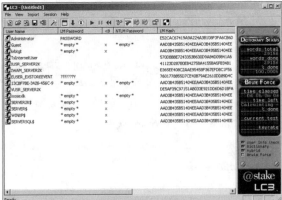

FIGURE 13.7
Output screen of the LC3 utility that uncovered system passwords.

Using a Keyboard Tracking Tool to Gather Logon Information

When a server cannot be physically accessed to load on a utility to expose the passwords on the system and when the brute force method does not reveal the desired information, one method of acquiring secured information is to scan the keyboard on a system and effectively capture keystrokes that can then be played back with full access by an individual.

One such utility that does keyboard tracking is a product called Desktop Surveillance by OmniQuad. The Desktop Surveillance tool loads on any system that is known to have someone with administrative privileges type in the logon and password information. The Desktop Surveillance tool captures keystroke-by-keystroke information that will eventually be used to decipher user logon passwords.

The Desktop Surveillance utility is available for download at `http://www.toolsthatwork.com/odse.shtml`. You can download the 1.2MB software for demonstration or trial basis by just entering in your name, address, phone#, and e-mail information.

Installing the Desktop Surveillance Utility

After downloading the utility, you run the `ODSEinstall.exe` program that will extract the files and install the program on your test server system. This creates the host system that all of the desktop clients will connect to for the installation of the client component or for remote administration or surveillance.

After the server component has been installed, `ODSHOST.EXE` needs to be run on each client system to which you want to have access. The utility can simply be placed in the system logon script of your network so that the tool is loaded up automatically on all systems on your network, or it can be installed from a RUN command on a specific systems autoexec boot installation process.

After the client component has been activated for the desktop systems to be accessed, a default administrative profile needs to be created. Run the `ODSCFG.EXE` program and select the following:

- Enable Desktop Surveillance in this Profile—ON
- Store Data Permanently—OFF (unless you want to record a trail of your surveillance)
- Forward Records by e-Mail—OFF
- Forward to FTP Server—OFF
- Generate Activity Logs—ON
    - Select Customize and enter for Activity Log Path to be any *server**share* path that the user's system will have access to write the keystrokes.
    - Capture Keystrokes—ON
- Enable Virtual Video—OFF

After entering these options, select SAVE.

Using Desktop Surveillance to Gain Password Access Information

After installed and configured, the Desktop Surveillance utility will capture the keystrokes of any system that is rebooted on the network running the ODS client software. System keystrokes can then be viewed, including password information to files, logon accounts, and any other locations accessed by the user.

Physically Accessing an IIS Server

Sometimes, an organization has implemented very stringent password logon authentication practices, making it difficult to acquire passwords remotely. Also, through properly configured firewall configurations, an organization can hide many of the critical systems from remote or public access.

However, because it is important to have the names and IP addresses of key servers as well as administrative access to the systems to successfully hack the systems, the acquisition of this information is very important.

There are some very low-tech methods of acquiring sensitive information that basically involves a simple physical visit to the organization's site or facility and acquire the information right at the data center facility.

Touring a Facility

A very quick and easy method of accessing server names, IP addresses, and even logon names and passwords is to take a tour of the facility of the organization you want to attack. IT organizations are very proud of their data centers and use them as showcases of the organization's use of technology. However, in making their data centers visible during public tours, they also make the mistake of displaying very critical and sensitive IT information, such as server names, IP address, and network maps.

By simply writing down server names and IP addresses that are typically very prominently displayed on the front of the servers (in many cases in very large printed labels), a hacker has the very critical information needed to find the end destination of servers to attack. In addition to simple server names and IP addresses, organizations frequently have their network diagrams posted on walls, cubicles, or throughout their data centers and IT department work areas. These network diagrams are typically printed documents that have every single device IP address, configuration setting, and frequently device passwords written right on the documents. Simply gaining access to one of these network diagrams is the full roadmap a hacker needs to begin the work of gaining unauthorized access to the organization's network remotely.

Touring a Facility As a Potential Customer

Most organizations will provide potential customers or business partners a tour of their facility. When requested, a potential customer is provided a complete tour of a data center or IT operations. Most marketing departments are unaware or naïve to the security threat they provide to competitors or participants on tours when they show people around the organization's facility. During these facilities tours, a hacker can gain access to data centers and view IP addresses, server names, or borrow a network diagram chart as they walk through the organizations facility.

Touring a Facility As a Potential Employee

Another common method of getting a tour of a facility is to apply as an employee of the organization. Employers are always willing to give potential employees a tour of the organization's facility. For IT positions, this always includes a tour of the data center, as well as even an online tour of the network management tools used by the organization. Not only can a simple tour provide a hacker with server names and IP addresses, but as the manager logs on to a system to demonstrate applications being used or network management tools in place, the hacker can acquire important logon name and password information by just peering over the shoulder of the demonstrator.

Visiting the Facility

While an organized tour, like one that involves posing as a potential client or employee, is one way to gain access to a facility, visiting a site during lunch hours, during staff meetings, early or late in the day, or during off hours is another way to gain access to critical information about an organizations network.

Most organizations that can spend upwards of $25,000 or $50,000 on a firewall and sophisticated network security tools spend no time and pay no attention to the very low-tech methods of acquiring sensitive information. By simply walking into a facility during lunch hours or at a time when the department has their regular staff meeting, a person can walk from cubicle to cubicle grabbing network diagrams off walls, flip through disaster recovery documentation sitting right on the shelves of employees offices, walk right into a data center and look at server configurations, or even open a cabinet door and gain access to a server that is already logged in as the network administrator.

Just 15–30 minutes roaming around a facility is all a person needs to gain access to enough information to complete all hacking remotely thereafter. The most successful facility breach is when a hacker can gain access to a server or workstation that is already logged in with administrative privileges and add themselves in as an administrator to the network. Administrative access, along with a quick glance on a network diagram to find VPN addresses or dial-up phone numbers, is all that is needed to gain full control of the network remotely.

Defacing (Tagging) a Server

With administrative control to a server, an individual can make modifications to Web pages on a server or replace Web pages one-by-one on the system with compromised access. Depending on the pages being manipulated, an organization might simply be embarrassed that another company gained unauthorized access to a server to having significant financial consequences if the information modified causes the loss of customers or revenues.

The ability to deface a server is the first step at validating the ability to compromise the security of an organization. If you can make modifications to Web pages on the server, you can typically take further action by accessing files or other information on the system.

What's Required to Deface a Server

To deface a server, all that is required is access to write information to the server. This can be through a Web page editor, such as Microsoft FrontPage or Microsoft Visual InterDev. Another way to write information to a server would be to actually be able to save files to the server using FTP (File Transfer Protocol) or WebDAV (Web distributed authoring and versioning).

Typically, Web servers are set to read-only, so that information can be accessed only by users. However, to update Web pages on a system, an administrator would loosen the security of a system so that they can post information to the Web server remotely. The sheer fact that an administrator or authorized user can remotely post information to the Web server means that anyone with an administrative password or authorized user logon and password information can also write information to the server.

Consequently, in addition to the Web editor software, an administrative or authorized editor logon and password is required. With these resources, anyone can make changes to Web servers.

Using FrontPage to Modify WWW Information

Microsoft FrontPage that comes with the Microsoft Office suite of products is a common tool used by organizations to update their Web pages remotely. FrontPage allows a Web administrator to create the Web pages on a laptop or remote system and then update the pages to the Web server without ever having to actually be directly on the Web server itself. The FrontPage Web Extensions are loaded on the Web server and allow an authorized Web administrator to update the pages.

To use Microsoft FrontPage to modify the WWW information on a Web server, do the following:

1. Launch a copy of Microsoft FrontPage on a client system.
2. Create a blank FrontPage Web where you can create blank Web pages (File, New, Empty Web).
3. Create a blank Web page that can be posted to the server
   a. File, New, Blank Page
   b. Type a few words on the page.
   c. File, Save As, `default.htm`
4. Post the new blank Web up to the Web site you want to access (File, Publish Web).

13

EXPLOITING WEB SERVICES

5. Enter in the administrator name and password for the Web. (Use either the guesswork method for updating the Web information to the server or use one of the logon names and passwords you acquired earlier in this chapter in the "Acquiring Administrative Access to a Web Server" section.)

If the server has the Microsoft FrontPage server extensions installed, you should be able to successfully post the information onto the Web server with a valid administrators password.

Using FTP to Modify WWW Information

Another way of modifying the pages of a Web server is to copy files directly to the system using the File Transfer Protocol (FTP). To post information to a Web server using Microsoft FrontPage noted in the previous section, the server must have the FrontPage Extensions loaded for remote posting of FrontPage data. However, organizations that do not use FrontPage extensions typically use FTP as the method of updating Web sites remotely.

FTP updates require that the FTP Web service is installed on the host system. An FTP client system can update information by simply logging in to the server and transferring files to the system.

To use FTP to modify the WWW information on a Web server, do the following:

1. Launch FTP on a client system (typically you can do this right from your browser, such as Internet Explorer or Netscape Navigator). Instead of typing `http://www.companyabc.com`, you can type **`ftp://www.companyabc.com`** (using `ftp://` instead of `http://`). Do note that the actual URL of the server (in this case, `www.companyabc.com`) might not be the actual FTP URL name. See the "Knowing Exactly Which Server to Attack" section earlier in this chapter to identify a valid server name.

2. Enter in a valid logon name and password (see the "Acquiring Administrative Access to a Web Server" section earlier in this chapter).

3. Move around the tree structure of the server to find the location of the HTM or HTML files and other Web documents that are publicly available on the system.

4. Drag and drop files over the files stored on the system to overwrite key Web server files.

Using WebDAV to Modify WWW Information

In the past year, Microsoft has begun to leverage WebDAV (Web Distributed Authoring and Versioning) on its servers as a method of remotely posting and accessing files on Web servers. WebDAV is similar to FrontPage Extensions in that it provides a built-in series of remote access protocols to access documents on a server.

Most of the new Windows .NET application server products, such as SharePoint Portal, recent service pack updated versions of Microsoft Exchange 2000, and so on, have the WebDAV extensions automatically loaded and running on the Windows 2000 server systems.

To access a WebDAV server, a user needs to run Internet Explorer v5.5 or later (the most recent version of the Internet Explorer is preferred because the WebDAV extensions have been updated several times over the past several months). The step-by-step access method to connecting to a WebDAV server is as follows:

1. Launch a copy of Internet Explorer v5.5 or later.
2. Click File, Open and type in the URL of the destination server.

> **NOTE**
>
> Unlike the FTP service that is typically independent of the WWW service where the URL for a FTP server destination is frequently different from a WWW server destination, WebDAV is integrated into the WWW service, and the URL for a WebDAV destination is typically the same as the site's WWW address. This simplifies the need to guess the WebDAV destination URL because it is typically the same as the WWW address of the destination server.

3. Click the Open as Web Folder check box as shown in Figure 13.8.

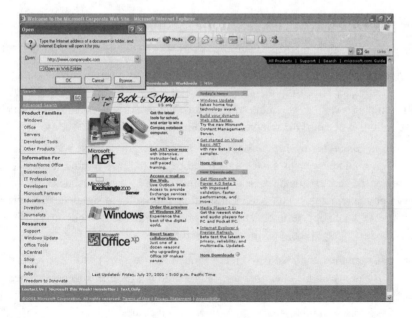

FIGURE 13.8
Accessing a Web server that has WebDAV extensions enabled.

4. Enter in a valid administrator logon name and password when prompted (see the "Acquiring Administrative Access to a Web Server" section earlier in this chapter).

5. Move around the tree structure of the server to find the location of the HTM or HTML files and other Web documents that are publicly available on the system.

6. Drag and drop files over the files stored on the system to overwrite key Web server files.

Causing Server Congestion

For e-commerce businesses that generate their revenues from their presence on the Internet, many of these organizations have implemented very secure password and remote access restrictions that limit a hacker's ability to modify Web pages or gain access to the system remotely. For these sites, rather than logging on to the sites and gaining control, a hacker could cause severe enough congestion on the site to prevent others from being able to do business on the site. Effectively, the hacker overloads the site with transaction requests that prevent real customers from gaining access to the system.

For informational Web sites, congestion to a site might be as harmless as preventing users from viewing information about the company and its services, but the congestion could be significant enough on an e-commerce site to cause significant financial impact by preventing serious business transactions from occurring.

What's Required to Cause Server Congestion

To cause server congestion, there are several ways to create communication traffic:

- *Sending spurious data to the remote server*—A hacker can send spurious data to a remote server, such as using the ping command, repeatedly accessing specific/known URLs on the server, or even requesting unknown/non-existent URLs on the server. All of these actions will cause the remote server to respond to the query.

- *Conducting simulated transactions on the remote server*—Because spurious data requests to a server could be seen as a hack attack and be filtered by a remote servers security system, or the spurious data request can be fulfilled by a cache response that has no impact on the remote systems server utilization, it is better to simulate a real server transaction. This would appear to be a user accessing Web pages or other information and would be less likely filtered by the remote server.

In both of these scenarios, the goal is to create enough real-looking traffic to overload a server system. In most cases, a single client hack session would not be able to generate enough traffic to bring down a server. What is required is the simultaneous access by dozens, hundreds, if not thousands of systems doing the same type of queries and requests.

One way of initiating queries from multiple systems is to physically go to multiple systems and invoke the query commands on the client systems. This could be done at a library or university lab that has several systems that can be accessed by the public, but you would still be limited to the number of systems you could access at the same time without drawing too much attention to yourself by physically logging on to several systems.

The better way to invoke several systems simultaneously is to create a script that can be invoked on hundreds or thousands of systems remotely. This scripted method of creating traffic is noted in the next section.

Scripting Continuous Client Sessions

Both Windows and Unix systems have remote session utilities that allow an administrator or user to initiate client sessions or commands remotely. This remote shell function is intended to allow organizations to leverage the CPU power of a distributed networking environment by having idle processor time across hundreds and thousands of systems to be used to calculate large sets of statistical data or process and render large graphics files. Like having a multi-processor system that enables a single server to aggregate the CPUs of several processors for transacting services, having multiple systems with multiple processors all transacting services creates huge data processing server clusters.

By tapping into those clusters, a hacker can easily simulate hundreds, thousands, or even tens of thousands of independent sessions that will effectively bring any server system to its knees for processing requests.

Invoking a Session on a Remote Windows System

Windows 2000 comes with a couple remote Windows system session utilities—Windows Terminal Services (run on Windows 2000 servers) and Telnet Server (run on either Windows 2000 servers or desktop systems). These programs allow a remote user to launch a session on the system just as if the user was sitting at the keyboard on the system.

To run a remote session for Windows Terminal Services, a user would install and run the Remote Desktop Client program that comes with Windows 2000 server and select the destination server IP address of the system the user intends to access. By using a logon name and password acquired from one of the methods noted previously in this chapter, a user will connect to the server and have the ability to launch a browser session, an executable program, or other tool that can leverage the CPU and connectivity power of this remote server to create congestion to other systems on the network or across the Internet.

To run a remote session for Telnet, a user would run the `telnet.exe` program that comes with the Windows 2000 operating system and gain access to a desktop system or server that has the Telnet Server service running on the system. By default, the Telnet service is installed on all Windows 2000 desktops and servers and only needs to be started to be activated for remote access. The service can be started remotely by running the Windows 2000 administrative tool called services (Start, Programs, Administrative Tools, Services), right-click the services and

13

EXPLOITING WEB
SERVICES

choose to Connect to Another Computer. Enter the name of the remote computer and enter in an administrative password you acquired from one of the password cracking utilities noted earlier in this chapter. Go down to the Telnet service and start the service. After started, use the `telnet.exe` program on your remote desktop and establish connection to your destination server. From that destination server session, you can invoke programs, utilities, or other functions to keep this server or other servers busy without ever having the remote system detected.

Crashing a Web Server

Crashing a Web server can take on several different expectations of the end result really based on the definition of a server crash. Some people would assume that a server crash would indicate that the system is temporarily not available. Others might think that a server crash indicates that the server system has been corrupted to the point where the system cannot be recovered. Because we have addressed simple server Web page modifications (also known as Web tagging) as well as server slowdown earlier in this chapter, we are focusing the balance of this section on more severe server events, such as server crashes and theft of information.

These server events can cause something as simple as the temporary loss of access to a system all the way to something that has significant financial impact caused by irrecoverable loss of data or permanent damage to a server system.

What's Required to Cause a Server Crash

In some of the more simple server crash scenarios, a server that has very heavy congestion (as noted in the previous section on server congestion) could be a system that locks-up or reboots due to over activity on the system. More complex methods, such as using any one of several Windows 2000 server vulnerabilities, can be enabled to cause system failure.

Stealing Information off a Server

While all of the previous sections have addressed security breaches that are pretty intrusive and would most likely result in relatively immediate awareness by an IT department that a hack has occurred (or is in progress), a more severe security threat is when information is stolen off a Web server without detection. In the cases of stolen information, the unauthorized access, acquisition of sensitive information, and the use of the information can be more damaging to organizations than simply defacing a Web site.

The compromise of secured information can have a financial impact when personnel data is distributed to competitors/head hunters to something as damaging as the distribution of regulated data, such as healthcare information or human resources information that can invoke lawsuits or fines.

What's Required to Steal Information off a Server

If organizations take note of the information summarized in Chapter 14 that sensitive or legally restricted information should not be placed on externally accessible servers, an organization would be relatively protected from external access to this sensitive information. However, many organizations have taken remote access for employee convenience too far by making virtually all of a company's information readily available from remote sessions.

In the cases where organizations have placed sensitive information on publicly accessible servers, all that is required to access this information is authorized password logon access to the server. The "Acquiring Administrative Access to a Web Server" section earlier in this chapter discusses how an administrative password can be acquired. However, in the case of data access, sometimes it's not necessary to get the administrator's password because many users in an organization have full access to key or sensitive organizational data. In those cases, simple access to just one user's system can gain access to a lot of company inside information.

Summary

Every organization is vulnerable to attack, and even organizations that have invested very heavily in the area of firewalls or VPNs but haven't implemented a complete security strategy can have their security systems easily compromised. The security breach of a Web services environment, which can be as simple as defacing a Web server, can minimally cause embarrassment to an organization all the way to the theft of data on a system or access to confidential information that can be financially devastating to an organization.

The methods to gain unauthorized access to a Web services system can come in the form of very sophisticated tools and utilities publicly available on the Internet to very low-tech methods of just walking into a company's data center during lunch time. The tools and methods to gain access to an organization's Web services system are readily available, as outlined throughout this chapter's step-by-step instructions.

Protecting Web Services

IN THIS CHAPTER

In this chapter, we will focus on how you can protect the Web services of a Windows 2000 Internet Information Services (IIS) Web server system. In Chapter 13, "Exploiting Web Services," we invoked a variety of attack methods, procedures, and tools to exploit the Web services of an IIS system. By following the steps in this chapter, you can maximize the security for your Web server and minimize the risk of downtime and loss of data from attacks like the ones highlighted in the previous chapter.

How Secure Can You Make Your Web Services

The first thing to realize when setting up a protection system for your Web services is that there is no single thing that can be done to provide you 100% security of your environment. As the title of this book describes, the best you can do is maximize your security systems to limit your exposure to security attacks.

Many people say that Microsoft Windows products are not very secure compared to Unix-based products, however each environment has its strengths and weaknesses. The people who think that any operating system environment is more secure than another are at most risk, because they might not follow the steps necessary to secure their environments. All operating system environments need to be hardened to limit exposure, whether it's Windows-based, Unix-based, or something else.

It takes several protection methods to maximize your security with the final security step of enabling logging to look for and track unauthorized access. If you are unsuccessful at completely blocking an attacker, at least if you are properly monitoring your system, you will know when a breach has occurred and can take steps to react to the security intrusion.

This chapter is written with sequential steps to walk you through procedures to strengthen the security systems for your Microsoft Windows Web services.

Step 1: Security Updates for IIS

The first step to secure a Microsoft Windows 2000 Web services environment is to apply security update patches to all Windows systems on the network. Security updates come in the form of periodic security update patches and formal service pack updates. It is extremely important to apply the patches and updates when they become available by following the instructions that come with the patch or update. When security vulnerabilities are found in the Windows 2000 operating system and a patch or update is announced, there are several notices that are published that not only explain what the patch or update does to protect a server system, but several notices are typically published that explain exactly how to compromise a system that has not had the patch or update applied. Effectively, a hackers guide is published every time a security vulnerability is exposed, and from the time the vulnerability is discovered until the time a server has been patched, the system is prone to attack.

It is also important that when a patch or update is applied, that it be applied on all systems on a network. Many of the security vulnerabilities expose administrative logon information or open holes in a system for a Trojan or other stealth attacks to be enacted. Even if a primary Web server is protected, if a less used FTP server or remote access server is not patched and is compromised, logon administrative access information can be acquired from one of those systems that can be used to access a system that has been patched. As noted in Chapter 13, hacking into a Web services environment is typically not done by accessing a primary, high-visibility server, but rather by compromising a less-used server on the network and gaining key bits of information that can be used to openly access the primary system.

Service Pack Updates

Every 3–6 months, Microsoft produces a formal Service Pack for the Windows operating system that includes patches and updates for the product. These service packs can be downloaded off the Internet at `http://www.microsoft.com/windows2000/downloads`.

A service pack can range from a small 5 to 6MB update to some fairly substantial services packs released in the past that have been in excess of 50MB in size. The larger service packs have included new product features, utilities, and other product enhancements. With the release of Windows 2000, Microsoft has stated that service packs will be strictly patches and product updates, leaving new feature enhancements to actual product upgrades.

While this new policy of keeping the services packs to just product updates and patches makes it less of a risk for an organization to apply a service pack soon after its release than with previous versions of Microsoft's products, thorough testing should be done on test servers before applying any update in a production environment.

With Windows 2000, it is suggested that you apply the service packs when they become available, but—like with any product installation or update—conduct a thorough backup of the server, including backing up the system state (Registry, security files, and so on) before conducting the update.

NOTE

Service packs do not necessarily include ALL security and product updates through the time of the service pack release. Just like core product releases, service packs go through beta and release candidate testing processes and are typically locked from any updates 30–45 days prior to the release of the service pack. Therefore, several security updates might be available on the Internet that are not included in the service pack. See the next section ("Security Bulletins") that notes how to check the available security bulletins for the various revisions and service pack levels for your systems.

Security Bulletins

In addition to major service packs that are released once or twice a year, Microsoft publishes security updates for all of their products on a more regular basis. These updates, known as Security Bulletins, are posted on the Internet for download. These bulletins can be accessed by going to the `http://www.microsoft.com/technet/itsolutions/security/current.asp` Web site.

By entering in the product (such as Internet Information Services 5.0) for all service packs and clicking GO, all security notices for the product are listed, as shown in Figure 14.1. If you have applied a specific service pack, when you specify the product and the service pack level, all security bulletins that apply to your system will be listed. As noted in the last section, just because a service pack was released in, say, May of a given year, service bulletins as far back as April or even March might need to be applied because service packs need to go through a beta and release candidate testing cycle before being released to the public, and the service packs are locked for the addition of security bulletin updates several weeks before the service pack release.

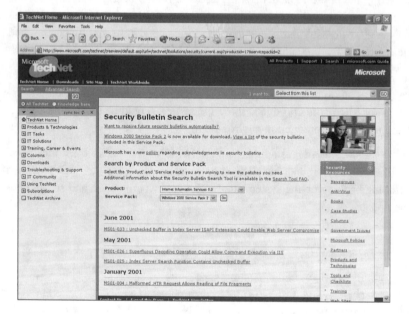

FIGURE 14.1

Finding security bulletins for IIS v5.0.

Many security bulletins are required, whereas several are frequently noted as optional for installation. Review the documentation notes on the service bulletins for the advisory of installing the update. Part of the documentation on the update will also include instructions on installation and any notes for configuration parameters or settings that would need to be applied relative to the update.

Using the Windows 2000 IIS 5.0 Hotfix Checking Tool

Another method to check for the availability of updates for the Windows 2000 Web services components is to run the Windows 2000 IIS hotfix checking tool, or HFCheck.exe. This tool can be downloaded from the Microsoft Web site at `http://www.microsoft.com/technet/security/tools.asp`.

The hotfix check tool can be run automatically on a server or run manually by an administrator of the network and, when run, the tool can check the status of the local system from which the tool is run, or against any remote system on the network.

When the tool finds an update that has not been installed on the target service, a notice can be displayed on the system or a warning can be written to the event log that can be flagged to notify an administrator that an update is available for the system.

Step 2: Who Needs Access to Your Web Server?

After routinely installing updates and patches to a Web services system, the next step in securing a server is to determine who needs to access the server. Many Web services systems only need to be accessed by employees within an organization. Just because a system is Web-enabled and users access the system from a browser doesn't mean that the server should automatically be set up for both internal and external Web-based access. If a system can be set up for internal access only, it minimizes the risk of unauthorized external access. Or if a system is set to be an internal server that requires access by employees remotely, if the organization has a Virtual Private Network (VPN) for remote user access to other internal server systems, establishing a secured VPN and leaving the Web services system access only from within the network or over the VPN shifts the security to the VPN and away from Web services functions.

Putting Your Web Server Inside Your Firewall

There are many servers that typically do not require primary remote access functions, such as intranet servers, SharePoint Portal servers, or WebStore systems. These servers are typically employee-only systems that can reside within the firewall of the organization. Organizations that want their employees to access the systems remotely can implement a strict VPN security access system and still leave their Web servers inside the firewall because the organization's VPN will provide secured access into the LAN for default secured access to any network service.

Many organizations configure Web services systems to have both internal and external access, requiring employees to use a VPN to get into the secured network to access the server, plus provide users access directly to the server without going through a VPN. While this provides flexibility to users on how to get access to the same server, it creates multiple access methods that need to be secured. If direct external access is unnecessary and secured, VPN access will fit the needs of the remote users. The organization can minimize its administration of two remote access methods to their server, and further decrease the organization's security risk by focusing attention to a single secured access method.

Planning for a Secured Internal Web Server

When a Web services system is installed inside a secured internal network, the two things a security administrator needs to focus on are ensuring that the VPN or other physical access method to the server is secured, and that the standard permission level security for user access has been applied to the system.

If no users need access to the system remotely, the implementation of a VPN system is unnecessary for access to the server. If remote security is needed, a thorough check of the VPN configuration should be conducted. See Chapter 20, "IPSec," and Chapter 21, "Virtual Private Networking," for information about creating secured access through a firewall into the organization's local network environment.

After access has been secured, the only other component to secure on an internal server is to limit permissions for access to the server and server services. This involves configuring service accounts and permission access to the system, determining the use of NTFS file system security permissions and enabling Active Directory permission access to the system and the system's services or resources.

Configuring Administrative Access for a Secured Internal Web Server

The best way to simplify the security of an internal Web server system is to add the system to the domain and set permissions by using Active Directory permission access. This single sign-on to the network and all applicable network resources allows the security administrator to focus on applying security at the domain level, thus centralizing access control to authenticated user access. This integrated security model is managed by globally unique identification (GUIDs), so that even if a user account is deleted and a new account with the same name is created, any previous security permissions are not applied to the new user.

To secure the access of an internal Web server to a specific administrator or group of administrators, do the following:

1. Make sure the administrator(s) are members of the Windows 2000 Active Directory domain.

2. Launch the Internet Service Manager MMC utility (Start, Programs, Administrative Tools, Internet Services Manager).

3. Right-click the Web site directory to which you want to assign administrative access and select Properties.

4. Select the Operators tab.

5. Add the administrators whom you want to administer the Web site from your domain list.

NOTE

While it is tempting to add the Domain Admins group to the Web operators, it is advised that you individually select users you want to administer the Web server. A group as broad as the Domain Admins group creates a security risk when the logon and password information for any Domain administrator will provide full unauthorized access to the system. By limiting the administration of the Web server to specific domain users, the risk of a security breach is limited.

Configuring User Access for a Secured Internal Web Server

Just as limiting administrative access to a Web server through the use of domain privileges minimizes the risk of exposure to unauthorized server access, limiting user access through the use of domain permissions also provides system controls.

To secure the access of an internal Web server to a specific user or group of users, do the following:

1. Make sure that the user(s) are members of the Windows 2000 Active Directory domain.

2. Launch the Internet Service Manager MMC utility (Start, Programs, Administrative Tools, Internet Services Manager).

3. Right-click the Web site directory to which you want to assign user access and select Properties.

4. Click the Directory Security tab.

5. Make sure that the only authentication method that is allowed is the Integrated Security option.

Putting Externally Accessed Web Servers Inside the Firewall

Web servers that require direct external access by employees of an organization should be placed inside the firewall with Active Directory user authentication enabled, and ports on the firewall should be opened to allow Web access by remote users to access the server.

14

PROTECTING WEB
SERVICES

Many organizations place intranet or secured information servers outside their firewall and, while remote users do not penetrate the firewall to gain access to these servers remotely, the servers themselves are exposed to access by unauthorized uses. An unauthorized user accessing a server could gain control of the server and extract data, files, or other information from the server. Additionally, an authorized user could gain control of the external server and enable the server to acquire confidential domain information, such as logon account information and passwords.

By placing the server inside the firewall, the security administrator only needs to open up ports on the firewall for the simple transfer of data and specifically block all other accesses to the system. Because the server physically resides within the firewall, as long as firewall security has been maximized (see Chapter 16, "TCP Filtering and Firewalls"), all services other than those opened by the firewall to the server are protected.

Configuring User Access for an Externally Accessed Web Server

To secure the access of an externally accessible Web server to a specific user or group of users, do the following:

1. Make sure that the user(s) are members of the Windows 2000 Active Directory domain.
2. Launch the Internet Service Manager MMC utility (Start, Programs, Administrative Tools, Internet Services Manager).
3. Right-click the Web site directory to which you want to assign user access and select Properties.
4. Select the Home Page tab.
5. Choose Read and Log Access for the minimal amount of Web services access.

NOTE

The default access rights are Read, Log Access, and FrontPage Web. FrontPage Web provides a Web page update and remote administration function for Web pages on the servers. If this function is not needed, it is best left disabled to reduce the risk of unauthorized modification of Web pages on the system. The other access privileges, including Write, Directory Browsing, and Index the Directory, should be enabled only if users specifically need these services when remotely accessing the system. Each of these access privileges compromises the security of the system when enabled.

Putting Your Web Server in a DMZ

Web servers that require public access by non-employees for acquisition of information residing on Web servers should be placed in an untrusted, or DMZ network segment. The DMZ is protected by a firewall or border router that provides limited access controls to the servers sitting in the DMZ. This network segment is considered untrusted because users that access servers on this segment do not necessarily need to log on to any specific server or domain to gain access to the servers.

Typical servers that are placed in the DMZ are WWW Web servers or FTP file transfer servers. These servers typically allow unlimited access to the contents of the server, and the security administrator of the organization wants to limit unauthorized modification of the information stored on the system.

Planning for a Secured DMZ Web Server

While the servers placed in the DMZ are typically open access servers with the expectation that information is easily accessible to Internet users, the security administrator of the server would want to ensure that only the information that is supposed to be accessed is available and that all other services are locked down.

The planning process to secure a DMZ Web server involves researching what services and functions need to be enabled, determine any specific user logon accounts and permission access required, and determine the true extent of external access to internal server services. By understanding the requirements for access, the appropriate security for the server can be configured.

The steps outlined later in this chapter in the "General Windows 2000 Server Hardening Practices" section describes the steps to take to secure a Web server.

Hosting Your Web Services at a Different Location

A popular strategy for organizations that have high volume access to Web Services that require no connectivity to the organizations internal LAN servers or services is one where the organization physically places their external Web servers at a different geographical site location. In many cases, these offsite locations are at co-location hosting facilities where an outsourced organization manages the day-to-day maintenance of the servers, provides firewall security, backs up battery or generator power, and provides physical security.

Because the organization's external client Web services are completely separate from internal Web services, there is no concern where an external security breach will impact internal network operations security. Additionally, if the outsource provider contracts their service level agreement for services and security, a known limit is set for operations and maintenance.

Planning for a Secured Externally Managed Web Server

The planning for a secured external server involves researching what services the external hosting provider offers, such as service level agreements, physical security services, firewall access security services, testing procedures, and monitoring and alerting services. The key to validating the external host provider's abilities is to ensure that the provider has a level of security, management, and administration that meets or exceeds your organizations standards. The first line of security defense for an outsourced arrangement lies not on the strength of the security *on* the server, but on the strength of security *of* the provider.

Step 3: From Whom Are You Trying to Protect Your Server?

A critical component of securing a server is determining who you perceive to be a threat to your system. Some organizations that work in fields that are frequently criticized by special interest groups or public awareness organizations are bigger targets than other organizations. Identifying the level of risk the organization poses determines the time, effort, and cost of securing the Web services system(s).

If you have extremely sensitive information on the server that would be financially disastrous if lost or if downtime of the system can be financially costly, implementing a very secure system is a necessity. Unfortunately, higher security means three things:

- It means that more time, effort, and cost must be expended to set up, secure, and validate/test the security of the system.
- It means more training would be needed for the system and network administrators.
- It means that users of your system might have to go through very rigorous logon procedures to remotely gain access to information on the system.

It is important for the implementer of the server to determine the level of the risk to enable an appropriate level of security for the organization.

Hobbyist Hacker

A hobbyist hacker is a person who reads articles off the Internet or books (like this one) and tries out what he or she has learned on Web sites. Typically, the intent of hobbyist hackers is just to prove they have mastered the ability to hack a site and they themselves tend to be minimal risk to an organization because they are rarely criminals that take advantage of unauthorized use of information (such as logon information, security passwords, credit information, and so on).

The end result of the work of a hobbyist hacker is usually a modified Web page that causes embarrassment to an organization that they've been hacked. However, the hobbyist hacker does pose a more serious risk when his or her seemingly innocent activities involve changing emergency access phone numbers that provide crucial information to the general public, or, as part of the hobbyist's activities, logon names and access information is posted that is then used by someone who does maliciously use the information to cause significant financial or operational harm to an organization or individuals.

The best way to minimize the risk from the activities of a hobbyist hacker is to implement the security measures that are outlined throughout this book and by putting in a monitoring system to detect unauthorized activities or access with the ability to track any changes made to the system and shut down services and systems where security has been compromised.

Disgruntled Employee or Customer

A common hacker to an organization is a disgruntled employee or customer whose intent is to cause significant interruption in services or to create a financial burden to the organization.

The activities of a disgruntled employee or customer typically go beyond just defacing a Web site and can include distributing access information, credit card information, or other sensitive information acquired off a Web server. This information can then be used by others to cause significant downtime or even a greater financial loss to the organization.

The disgruntled employee or customer typically is not the individual who uses the information for illegal or unauthorized purposes, but their actions create an environment where many others can use the information to create problems.

The best way to minimize the risk from activities of a disgruntled employee or customer is to ensure that, if the individual had access to the system, that the individual's security access to the system is deleted when the individual leaves the organization. If the person had access to all logon and password tables or lists, another thing to do is to ensure that the passwords are changed for specific access accounts or even all access accounts. Lastly, administrators should monitor suspicious activities and take immediate action to minimize the extent of damage that an unauthorized user can take against the organization.

Competitor

Another group of individuals that take an interest in hacking a site is a competitor to the organization. A competitor typically has two goals

- To deface their competitor's Web site to cause confusion and embarrassment to their competitor.
- To acquire sensitive or proprietary information about their competitor.

14

PROTECTING WEB SERVICES

As with any defacing of a Web site, the initial impact is the embarrassment caused by the activities of the hacker. However, a more damaging effect is the modification of key information that can direct customers to a wrong business location, provide incorrect product information or pricing, or provide the wrong phone number to contact the organization. Any incorrect information can cause confusion to customers that might make the customer do business elsewhere, cause orders not to be placed properly, or cause the public to lose confidence in the organization.

When a competitor actually acquires customer information, credit card information, or proprietary announcement or pre-product release information, the impact can be significant. In business, the timing of product announcements or other competitive information is frequently critical to the competitiveness of the organization. If the information is acquired through hacking activities and is then announced to the general public ahead of schedule or used by a competitor in their business activities, the breach of security can have significant impact on an organization.

The best way to protect against unauthorized access of critical or sensitive information is to keep critical information off publicly accessible servers until the timing is appropriate for the information to be available. If the information will be stored on publicly accessible servers, setting complex security for information access, such as smartcard or cardkey access, encrypted and encapsulated communications, and detailed file and resource access controls, is recommended.

Professional Thief

The most dangerous of hackers is someone who is purposely trying to cause financial damage or theft of information for financial gain. These individuals can be considered the bank robbers of the 21st century because they perform crimes electronically rather than with guns and pistols. Professional thieves are not that prevalent, but their activities can cause significant disruption of service for an organization as well as cause tens of thousands, hundreds of thousands, or even millions of dollars in damage and financial loss.

The professional thief would typically access server information to gain control of access account information or credit card information. Credit card information can be used to illegally purchase goods or acquire cash advances, both for financial gain. Access account information can be leveraged with other services for additional financial resource acquisition.

The best way to protect against a professional thief is to follow all of the hardening techniques outlined throughout this book, including enabling controls at the firewall and infrastructure level, authentication and validation information for user verification, and encryption and encapsulation for data integrity. Lastly, activities should be monitored so that when an excessive volume of downloads or transaction events occur, an alert is issued to administrators to take action to minimize the exposure of any breach of security.

Step 4: What Are You Trying to Protect

Web services on an IIS server are not limited to just the WWW Web service but also to FTP file transfer and SMTP mail routing. If a server is only a WWW server, it is very easy to uninstall or disable other Web services. By uninstalling these Web services, the organization maximizes the scope of protection.

There are several other steps to hardening a Windows 2000 Web services system that need to be followed to limit the exposure a system has to unwanted attacks on the security and integrity of the system.

General Windows 2000 Server Hardening Practices

When securing a Windows 2000 Web services system, there are two things that need to be hardened. First is the Windows 2000 operating system, and the second is the Web services subsystem. This first section focuses on hardening the Windows 2000 operating system, which includes securing the Windows kernel through disabling unnecessary Windows services and protocols.

Each step in hardening the operating system builds on the implementation of the other hardening steps to maximize the protection of server. If all but one area for hardening is implemented, the test tools to identify security holes described in the "How to Test for Vulnerabilities" section later in this chapter will potentially expose the weakness and create an unsecured server.

Set Up System-Level Security

The lowest level for security enhancement starts with the core operating system kernel and server filesystem. The Windows 2000 server disk subsystem must be formatted using the NTFS filesystem. NTFS provides an integrated security with the Windows 2000 operating system that allows disk and file level security permissions to be applied to the server.

To check that a system is formatted with NTFS, do the following:

1. Double-click My Computer on the desktop of the server.
2. Right-click the C> server drive and select Properties.
3. The File System should display as NTFS, as shown in Figure 14.2.
4. Repeat this for each hard drive process if you have more than one hard drive for the server.

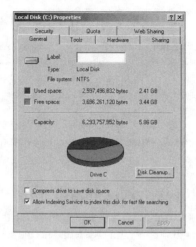

FIGURE 14.2
Confirming that the file system is set to NTFS.

If a server is not running NTFS, the system disk needs to be converted to NTFS. To convert a FAT or FAT-32 partitioned drive to be configured with the NTFS filesystem, do the following:

1. Choose Start, Run, cmd, OK.

2. Type `convert c: /fs:ntfs`.

3. Reboot the server when prompted.

After a reboot, the system will run through a boot process that will convert the filesystem to NTFS. After a complete reboot, recheck that the system is configured as NTFS.

Removing Unnecessary File Systems

By default, Windows 2000 installs several operating system subsystems for cross compatibility with OS/2, as well as POSIX. These subsystems, if not used, create additional security holes that are typically unnecessary for almost all Windows Web servers.

To remove the OS/2 subsystem, do the following:

1. Run Registry Editor by choosing Start, Run, Regedt32.exe, OK.

2. Select HKEY_LOCAL_MACHINE, Software, Microsoft, OS/2 Subsystem for NT.

3. Click each of the sub-keys in this branch of the Registry and press the Delete (DEL) key to remove all of them.

4. Select HKEY_LOCAL_MACHINE, System, CurrentControlSet, Control, Session Manager, Environment, Os2LibPath.

5. Delete the Os2LibPath sub-key.

6. Select HKEY_LOCAL_MACHINE, System, CurrentControlSet, Control, Session Manager, SubSystems.

7. Click all entries for OS/2 and POSIX and press the Delete (DEL) key to delete all of them.

Turn Off the 8.3 Name Generator

By default, the 8.3 name generator is enabled, allowing long filenames to be automatically converted to a standard DOS 8.3 filename. This dual namesystem creates a security hole by enabling a cache version of the filesystem to reside in memory to allow for the conversion of filenames on the system.

To disable the 8.3 Name Generator, do the following:

1. Run Registry Editor by choosing Start, Run, Regedt32.exe, OK.

2. Select HKEY_LOCAL_MACHINE, System, CurrentControlSet, Control, FileSystem.

3. Double-click NtfsDisable8dot3NameCreation.

4. Change the REG_DWORD from 0 to **1** and then click OK, as shown in Figure 14.3.

FIGURE 14.3
Changing the Registry setting to disable the 8.3 Name Generator.

Renaming the Administrator Account

A simple way of decreasing the risk of Web site intrusion from a hacker guessing at logon names and passwords is to rename the administrator account on the system. Because all Windows servers come standard with a user called Administrator, a hacker will already know a typical user for whom he or she can begin guessing passwords. By renaming the administrator account, in addition to guessing the password for the new administrator account, the hacker would actually have to guess the actual name of the administrator account in the first place. This can ward off the most novice of security intruders.

To rename the administrator account, do the following:

1. Choose Start, Programs, Administrative Tools, Computer Management.

2. Double-click Local Users and Groups to expand the tree.

3. Click Users.

4. Right-click the Administrator user account and select Rename.

5. Rename the administrator account to something abstract or unique (not your name and not something as simple as Admin).

Create a Strong Administrator Password

The uniqueness and complexity of the administrator password can either simplify or strengthen the security access to a Windows 2000 server. A simple password consisting of just a few letters can be guessed or someone can easily watch an administrator type in the simple password for future reference.

Creating a complex password that includes letters as well as numbers and punctuation and is at least nine (9) characters in length makes password guessing, as well as looking over an administrator's shoulder to identify the password, less likely. Also, the way Windows handles password creation, a password with nine or more characters uses two bytes for password entry and storage. Many of the password decryption utilities regularly available on the Internet can decrypt passwords of eight or fewer characters, but do not properly decrypt passwords nine or more characters in length.

Another tip on creating a strong password is to choose a password that is not used for other systems, functions, or services. Quite frequently, an administrator chooses the same password for public Web servers as well as to administer the network domain. While there might be an occasion to share an administrator password for the domain, that then provides someone with the password to the public Web servers. A compromise of one password creates a security hole on other systems.

Lastly, the password for the Web server should not be the same password used to log on to other public sites. Quite frequently, an administrator uses the same password for the Web server to set up secured communications when the person places an order on favorite Web sites for books, CD-ROMs, and guitar strings. A breach of security at a commerce site for a vendor can expose an administrator's e-mail address and password. The e-mail address will lead a hacker to the organization's Web onramps, such as VPN connections, Web servers, or remote administration tools. With a valid password from a vendor e-commerce site that is the same as the logon password to the organization's network domain, a hacker now has the ability to log on to the network of the organization as a full administrator.

Disabling Unnecessary Protocols and Communications Services

By default, many protocols, client drivers, and communication services are installed on a Windows 2000 server that are unnecessary for a standard Web services system. Because Windows 2000 is a multi-function server operating system where organizations use the server to provide access to shared files, shared printers, or for network logon access, many of these protocol, drivers, and services are not needed for simple Web services functions. In fact, an organization really does not want its Web server to have the ability to allow users to access the file system to store files or to log on to the server to access other server resources other than specific Web services resources. Some of the default services unnecessary for a Web server include the Client for Microsoft Networks, Network Load Balancing service, and File and Printer Sharing for Microsoft Networks.

In addition to these default services, there are several protocols and services that are frequently added after a server has been installed. Some of those protocols and services include the NetBEUI protocol, the DLC Protocol, the NWLink protocol, and Client Services for Netware. NetBEUI is commonly installed for compatibility with certain fax utility programs, monitoring or remote server administration utilities, or legacy management tools. DLC is commonly used for printing from Windows print servers to network printers or for access to mainframe systems using terminal emulation. NWLink and Client Services for Netware are used to allow a Windows server to communicate with a Novell network. All of these protocols and services do not need to be installed on a secured Web services system and should be removed.

To delete unnecessary protocols, do the following:

1. Choose Start, Settings, Network and Dial-up Connections.
2. Right-click the network connection icon and select Properties.
3. Deselect all protocols, client drivers, and communication services other than the Internet Protocol (TCP/IP), as shown in Figure 14.4.
4. Click OK.

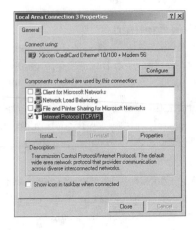

FIGURE 14.4
Disabling all but the Internet Protocol (TCP/IP) on a server.

Removing all Network Shares and Disabling AutoShare Services

Network shares for a server provide a user the ability to access the server remotely. For a secured Web Services system, you do not want someone to have remote access to your server. The two things that need to be done are to delete any network shares that have been created on the system and to delete the default shares automatically created on all Windows 2000 servers.

To delete all network shares created on the server, do the following:

1. Double-click My Computer icon on the Windows desktop.
2. Right-click any network share shown in the Explorer window (typically all drive letter shares beside the basic C> drive) and press the Delete (DEL) key.

Next, you should disable all default network shares on the server that will become a risk for a secured Web services system. This involves making the following registry modification:

1. Run Registry Editor by choosing Start, Run, Regedt32.exe, OK.
2. Select HKEY_LOCAL_MACHINE, System, CurrentControlSet, Services, LanManServer, Parameters, AutoShareServer.
3. For the AutoShareServer, change the REG_DWORD from 1 to 0.

General IIS Server Hardening Practices

After the core Windows 2000 server has been hardened, there are several Internet Information Services functions that also can be configured to strengthen the security of a server. Because a secured Web server is crucial to any and all organizations, there are several tools that assist with the hardening process for the Web server.

Setting the Authentication Method

The first thing to do on a Web server system is to set the authentication method appropriate for access to Web pages on the server. Microsoft Internet Information Services v5.0 allows for five Web authentication methods:

- *Anonymous*—When enabled, this authentication method does not require a user to provide any credentials to access a Web server. By definition, the user can be completely anonymous and will have access to Web pages or information in the default Web directory of the server.
- *Basic*—Basic authentication does require a logon name and a password to be entered, but the password is sent and received as clear text, meaning that if someone had a protocol analyzer ("sniffer") on the system, he or she would be able to see the person's logon name and password.

- *Digest*—The Digest method of authentication is similar to the Basic authentication, but passwords are sent as a hash value. A hashing process mathematically scrambles the password and transfers the password between the client and the server. Because the information is coded, a hacker cannot view the actual password, but the sending and receiving systems will be able to successfully validate authentication between each other. Digest authentication requires a Windows 2000 Active Directory Domain Controller to be on the network so that hash can be validated with a domain controller as part of the authentication process.

- *Integrated Windows Authentication*—The Integrated Windows Authentication method also uses a hash value, but, because the server is tightly integrated with a Windows 2000 Active Directory environment, the logon names and passwords are stored on the Active Directory domain controller. In this scenario, the actual password is not sent, but rather the hash value is sent between the client and the server, and the server hash is validated with the Active Directory to authenticate the remote client.

- *Client Certificate Mapping*—For client certificate mapping, client authentication certificates are issued to a remote client and, when the client uses the certificate to validate themselves against a secured server, the certificates are compared to allow access. One-to-One mapping requires that a remote client has a certificate that matches exactly with the credentials stored on the Web server system. This is a very strict mapping, and, while definitively authenticating each certificate, it does require significant administration to maintain all of the individual certificates on the server. A broader certificate mapping process is a Many-to-One mapping. This process allows certificates with a broad range of criteria to access the same server, so instead of looking for an exact match on the remote certificate to the server stored certificate, the Many-to-One mapping looks at a series of characteristics on the remote client and, if the individual matches the range of criteria, he or she will be authenticated to the system. One additional certificate mapping method is available called the Directory Service (DS) mapping. DS certificate mapping integrates with the Windows 2000 Active Directory authentication process to validate that a certificate issued by a Windows 2000 Active Directory authorized server matches the user logon account requesting authentication.

There is nothing wrong with a server that allows anonymous access if the information stored in the default Web directory of the server is information that is publicly accessible to users, such as a normal WWW Web server. However, if information stored on a Web server is confidential, a stronger security method, such as one using a One-to-One client certificate mapping, will significantly strengthen the access security to the information.

To set the authentication mode for a Web site, do the following:

1. Launch the Internet Service Manager MMC utility (Start, Programs, Administrative Tools, Internet Services Manager).

14

PROTECTING WEB
SERVICES

2. Right-click the Web site directory to which you want to assign user access and select Properties.

3. Select the Directory Security tab.

4. Choose the authentication method you want.

5. Click OK to set the authentication method.

Using Built-In Utilities to Configure Security

Internet Information Services v5.0 comes with a couple utilities that assist the administrator with lock down on a Web services system. Rather than starting from scratch and manually configuring all of the permission, authentication, and access methods to a server by starting with the supplied security utilities, an initial security baseline is established for the server.

The two utilities are the Permission Wizard and the Windows 2000 Internet Security Configuration Tool.

The Permissions Wizard

The Permissions Wizard automatically configures user access permissions based on a default set of criteria whether the server is going to be an open access public Web server or a secure limited access Web server. When the option for a secured Web site is selected, permissions are strengthened for user logon authentication to limit access to the server. However, if the public Web server option is selected, the server parameters are set to allow anonymous users to access to the server, but all other permissions specific to administering and updating server pages are limited.

The Public Web Site option sets up anonymous authentication and allows users to view all files and to access Active Server Pages on the server. It gives Web operators full control over the administration of the site.

The Secure Web Site option sets up Basic, Digest, or integrated Windows authentication and only allows authorized users to view Web pages and access files on the Web server. Web operator controls are limited to access only site administration tasks.

To launch the Permissions Wizard, do the following:

1. Launch the Internet Service Manager MMC utility (Start, Programs, Administrative Tools, Internet Services Manager).

2. Right-click the Web site directory on which you want to invoke and select All Tasks.

3. From the All Tasks option, choose Permission Wizard.

4. When prompted, choose either the Public Web Site or the Secured Web Site option to select the level of security you want enabled.

Using the Windows 2000 Internet Security Configuration Tool

The other utility available to simplify and enhance the security of a Windows 2000 server is the Windows 2000 Internet Security Configuration Tool. This tool also automatically configures server settings, but it goes beyond just Web services security, it also locks down Windows 2000 server security functions. This includes making Registry settings, setting security policies, and disabling unnecessary security configurations for the secured Web services system.

To download the tool, go to the Microsoft Windows 2000 download site at `http://www.microsoft.com/technet/treeview/default.asp?url=/TechNet/prodtechnol/windows2000serv/downloads/iislock.asp`.

After you download the tool, you run the `iislock.exe` program and it will expand the files into a directory you specify. Go to the directory to which you expanded the files and then run `tool\dataentry\default.htm`. This will bring up a screen similar to the one shown in Figure 14.5.

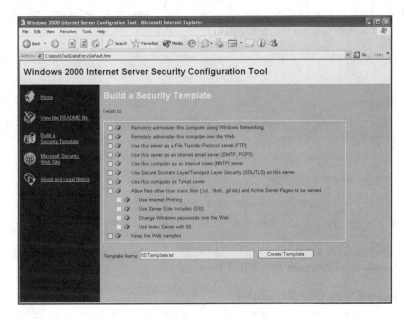

FIGURE 14.5
Building a security template with the Internet Server Security Configuration tool.

By choosing the configuration setting options you want to have enabled or disabled on your Web server, an `IISTemplate.txt` file is generated that can then be applied to the server to configure the system security.

To apply the template security, do the following:

1. Copy the IISTemplate.txt file to the server to which you want to apply the security template.

2. Run IISCONFIG -s (*servername*) -f IISTemplate.txt.

After the security template has been applied, the administrator should go back through each of the permission, access, and security settings to make any necessary minor modifications that are appropriate or applicable to the server.

Another Approach to Locking Down a Web Server

Another approach to locking down your Web server is to disable all services, completely lock the system down, and then enable components and services required for access. Most security methods start with a fully accessible server and then lock down components as the administrator remembers to disable services. By locking all services down to start, the security administrator is clearly aware of what functions are enabled for access and can assess the security impact when an access function is required.

To shut down all services and permissions as the starting baseline, the following procedure should be followed.

Stop All Services

Services that are commonly installed on a Windows 2000 Web services system include World Wide Web (WWW), File Transfer Protocol (FTP), Simple Message Transport Protocol (SMTP), and Index services. These can be stopped by doing the following:

1. Choose Start, Programs, Administrative Tools, Services.

2. Right-click World Wide Web and select Stop.

3. Right-click File Transfer Protocol and select Stop.

4. Right-click Simple Message Transport Protocol and select Stop.

5. Right-click Index Services and select Stop.

Restrict Web Operator Privileges

By default, the Web operator privilege is set to the administrator's group account of the Web server. It is recommended that you restrict the Web operator privileges to a single user account and specifically add individual user accounts to become Web operators. This will provide the security administrator with a very clear accounting of who has site access. To limit Web operator privileges, do the following:

1. Choose Start, Programs, Administrative Tools, Computer Management, Local Users and Groups, Users and select Action, New User.

2. Enter the name of a user account you want to create for Web operator administrator (for example, `weboperator`).

3. Enter a complex password (a password at least nine characters long, including both letters and numbers, and specifically do not use a password that is commonly used on other administrative accounts on the network).

4. Uncheck the User Must Change Password at Next Logon box.

5. Check the Password Never Expires option.

6. Click Create.

7. Choose Start, Programs, Administrative Tools, Internet Services Manager, right-click the server site, and choose Properties.

8. Select the Web Site Operators tab.

9. Add the new user you just created to be the Web operator for your site.

Restrict Access Permissions

To secure the access of Web site for specific access permission functions, do the following:

1. Launch the Internet Service Manager MMC utility (Start, Programs, Administrative Tools, Internet Services Manager).

2. Right-click the site named Default Web and select Properties.

3. Select the Home Page tab.

4. Deselect all access rights (including Read, Write, Log, Index, and so on).

Enable Only Desired Web Services

Now that all default Web services have been disabled, the next step is to enable only the Web services that are required for the function of the system. For a basic Web server, the following services can be enabled.

Start the World Wide Web Service

The basic Windows service that provides World Wide Web functionality is the World Wide Web service. This is started by doing the following:

1. Choose Start, Programs, Administrative Tools, Services.

2. Right-click World Wide Web and select Start.

Validate Web Operator Privileges

Validate that the Web operator privilege is set to an individual user whom you expect to be associated with this access. It is recommended that you use an individual user account rather than a group account, use a user account other than the common name administrator, use a complex password that combines letters and numbers, and use a password that is not used for any other account on the network. To validate the Web operator account, do the following:

1. Choose Start, Programs, Administrative Tools, Internet Services Manager, right-click the server site, and choose Properties.

2. Select the Web Site Operators tab.

3. Verify that the Web Operator account is a user you expect.

Enable Access Permissions

To secure the access of an externally accessible Web server to a specific user or group of users, do the following:

1. Launch the Internet Service Manager MMC utility (Start, Programs, Administrative Tools, Internet Services Manager).

2. Right-click the Web site directory on which you want to assign user access and select Properties.

3. Select the Home Page tab.

4. Choose Read and Log Access for the minimal amount of Web services access.

Step 5: Where Are Your Vulnerabilities

After you follow the steps to configure your server to meet the expected needs and security level of your organization, knowing where your vulnerabilities lie allows you to reassess your security model. Even after security permissions have been locked down for a server, there are other ways a server can be compromised. Most Web services systems are placed in the DMZ, or untrusted network, where an organization is aware that security attacks can occur. However, Web services systems are also placed inside firewalls and at offsite locations that create other challenges and require the security administrator to review the potential for security threats that extend beyond just the Web server itself.

Vulnerabilities When Your Web Server Is Inside Your Firewall

When the Web server is inside a firewall, any breach of the firewall security creates vulnerabilities to the Web server. Or more commonly, when a Web server is placed inside the firewall on a trusted network, administrators get a false sense of security that their servers are protected from external access and has secured controls.

Unfortunately, for any organization that wants users to access its servers from virtually anywhere on the Internet, the server needs to be made accessible and, thus, security controls need to be placed on the system. Because employees of the organization have access to the secured system, non-employees have the ability to violate the security of the system and gain unauthorized access to the server.

One common method for organizations to allow secured access to internal servers is to set up a Virtual Private Network (VPN) that establishes a secured tunnel between the server and the remote client. When properly configured, a VPN can allow access to the inside of a firewall by a remote user. After inside the firewall, a user (or a hacker) has access to more than just the initial server the user was attempting to access.

Ways to minimize this security hole are to ensure that the Web server security is maximized using all of the techniques noted throughout this chapter, and to then validate that the VPN has all security components installed and configured properly, as noted in Chapter 21.

Vulnerabilities When Your Web Server Is Hosted Elsewhere

Many organizations are choosing to outsource the hosting of their Web services systems to companies that specialize in the business of housing and managing secured server systems. These organizations are commonly called *co-location facilities* or *Web hosting providers*. The types of services each of these organizations provide is slightly different.

A co-location facility actually takes a server, frequently provided by the client itself, and provides rack space for the server to be mounted in, backup electrical power, environmental temperature controls, and connectivity to the Internet. In the scope of this chapter, it is the connectivity to the Internet, how the co-location facility provides security for the servers placed within their facility, and the monitoring of the facility for suspicious or unauthorized access to the systems that are of interest. Security is as good as the services provided by the co-location service provider.

In a Web hosting environment, the server is typically owned by the Web hosting organization and your Web page or Web services are run on its system, most commonly a system that is shared by several organizations. Because the server is shared, the cost for the hosting service in many cases is provided free of charge in many packaged monthly e-mail account costs; business accounts run under 25–75 U.S. dollars per month.

Key to evaluating the security provided and the risk of a security breach lies in the security policies and practices managed by the co-location operations staff or Web host provider. Review all security processes and ensure that they meet to the level and standards outlined throughout this book for maximizing the security of the network. Run tests to validate whether the provider is truly meeting your expectations by using the test tools outlined in the next section of this chapter ("Step 6: How to Test for Vulnerability") to ensure that the provider is successfully securing your server(s). No doubt, these organizations are in business to ensure that servers are secure, but don't assume that they have perfected the process, and take steps to validate that all security processes and practices meet your needs and expectations.

Step 6: How to Test for Vulnerability

Even after you have run your Web server through all of the security configuration practices, you should test the Web services system for vulnerabilities. One of the best ways is to attempt to hack your own site using the tools and utilities outlined in Chapter 13.

Some of the key tools noted in Chapter 13 that can help a security administrator test his or her own site for maximized security are as follows:

- Stealth HTTP Security Scanner
- ShowPass
- nMap NT

These tools attempt to violate Windows server security, so if these tools are successful at identifying vulnerabilities in a system, the security violation needs to be reviewed and steps should be implemented to further lock down the server.

Step 7: Monitoring and Logging Server Activities

Lastly, no process is 100 percent foolproof, and any belief that a Web server is completely secure is the first vulnerability an organization has that increases the risk the organization faces with regard to limiting security violations. Assume that, even with all of the steps followed at locking down and protecting a server, the risk remains that the Web services system can be attacked and security violated. It is then up to the security administrator to be aware of the problem as soon as possible, so that the organization can react by locking the system down, bringing the system offline until the security hole can be identified, and any modifications or changes to the system are traced so that the effort to undo any security breach can be rectified before the security violation creates significant downtime, interruption of service, or loss of data.

Monitoring will check to see if someone is attempting to breach the security of the system, and logging will report what a hacker is attempting to access. Chapter 22, "Log Monitoring and Analysis," outlines the steps necessary for logging and analyzing the logs of a server so that inappropriate access creates an immediate alert and that actions are implemented to minimize the impact of the attack.

Summary

Security for a system is not simply the installation of a utility and a couple key clicks to configure, but rather an ongoing process that spans from the server interface of the Web services system all the way down deep into the kernel of the Windows 2000 operating system. By following the seven steps outlined in this chapter, an organization can maximize the security of the Web services system and minimize the risk of embarrassment, downtime, or loss of data. Even after all the steps have been followed, the security of a Web services system must be tested by attempting to violate its security and ultimately monitoring and logging the activities of the server to catch any suspicious unauthorized access to the system.

Protecting Other Internet Services

IN THIS CHAPTER

Overview and Goals

Chapter 14, "Protecting Web Services," provided information on how to secure access to Web servers and services over HTTP and TCP port 80. This chapter focuses on securing some of the additional standard Internet services that most organizations have deployed. This chapter focuses the standard Internet services besides HTTP such as DNS, FTP, and SMTP. In general, these services have the same basic requirement in common—a hardened operating system.

This chapter is designed to get the reader started in the right direction when planning the implementation of these services. It begins with some general planning information and then covers information on hardening the operating system for supporting DNS, FTP, and SMTP. The chapter then covers some specifics on DNS, FTP, and SMTP services that will help administrators build secure Internet services. For more information on general security planning, refer to the SANS Institute at `http://www.sans.org/` and the National Security Agency's (NSA) Information Security home page at `http://www.nsa.gov/isso/index.html`.

General Planning for Secure Systems

To have secure systems, the organization must start with secure networks. This includes a solid firewall system with a well-planned and documented configuration. The border routers, firewall systems, and interconnections are the first systems that the organization must address and secure before attempting to secure the servers and services the internetworking systems protect. Securing these internetworking systems is beyond the scope of this chapter, but administrators should be aware how difficult it is to secure an existing unsecured network.

It's much easier to secure a new clean network than it is to try and secure an existing network. This doesn't mean that the organization has to throw all of their existing investments out the window to get an increased level of security. Parallel internetworking systems, including the firewall and DMZ network, can be built and tested while the organization continues to use the existing network. When the new internetworking systems are ready, the organization can switch over to the new network by moving a few connections on the firewall. New secured DMZ server systems, such as DNS, FTP, HTTP, and SMTP servers, can be installed at the same time as the new internetworking systems or shortly after. See Figure 15.1 for an example.

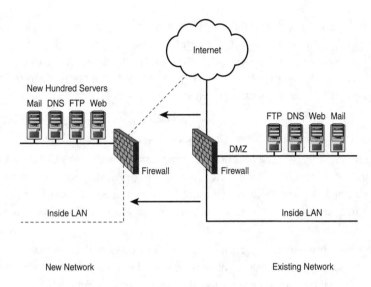

FIGURE 15.1
Using a parallel network to migrate to a secure system.

Building secure systems is a balancing act between risk, cost, and functionality. Architects, administrators, and managers should think through this concept when planning for the level of security to apply to their Windows 2000 systems. Highly secure systems have a lower risk, higher cost, and less functionality than low security systems. A low security system might have increased functionality, less cost, but more risk. The relationships between risk, cost, and functionality can be seen in Figure 15.2.

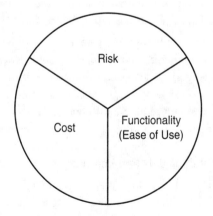

FIGURE 15.2
Secure system relationships.

15

It's important to keep risk, cost, and functionality in perspective when trying to secure the organization's systems and services. For most organizations, creating highly secure systems for every piece of the network is unrealistic, so organizations must be selective in where they focus their efforts in building secure systems. The following bullet points address some of the additional challenges of building secure systems:

- *Reduction of risk*—The goal of securing the system is to reduce the risk that the system will be attacked or compromised. The risk can be reduced but not eliminated.

- *Loss of functionality*—Tighter security also means a reduction in flexibility and functionality. Windows users and administrators are used to open, flexible systems and will need time to acclimate to new policies and procedures. Examples of loss of functionality might be frequent password changes or being forced to update Web sites from the server and not from a desktop.

- *Allocate time*—Implementing and maintaining secure systems takes time. Securing and maintaining systems is also labor intensive and is one of the tasks that fall off administrators' plates when they are overloaded or the organization is short staffed.

- *Budget for security*—It's easy to budget for the big items that include security reviews from outside firms, servers, and support contracts for Intrusion Detection Systems and virus protection software and updates. It's much more difficult to budget for the recurring items, such as the increased head count, to maintain secure systems or the costs of doing a post mortem on a breach of security.

- *Isolation and specialization*—Services should be isolated to reduce risk and increase the ease of maintenance for the secure systems. An example of isolation is to separate FTP and HTTP services onto separate servers. This increases the implementation, hardware, software, and general maintenance costs, but it creates a secure system that is easier to monitor with more consistent performance statistics and log events.

- *Some is better than none*—Applying some level of security is better than none at all— provided there is some planning involved. Applying some level of security haphazardly is a waste of resources. Categorize the systems in the organization and decide what level of security is required for each system category before starting the implementation. Domain controllers and databases might require a different level of security than desktop machines. Simple items, such as locking server rooms and racks and removing desktop floppy drives, can provide a sufficient level of security for internal systems, but these items need to be thought through before implementation.

- *Documentation*—Document the secure systems. Without documentation, no one understands what has been done to the system and, therefore, cannot trust the integrity of the system. An administrator might be forced to rebuild a perfectly solid system because they cannot find or do not trust the documentation. Also, keep the revision history of documentation so future readers can see how the system was adapted to new conditions.

- *Testing*—Secure systems should be tested as they are built. Test plans should be detailed, and the results should be documented. When was the system tested, what was it tested for, how was it tested, what tools and versions were used, what service pack and hotfixes were applied to the system at the time of the test are questions that the test results should answer. Secure systems should also be periodically tested after service packs are applied or on a quarterly basis. Organizations should also update the test plan to include new tests that check for newly-discovered vulnerabilities.

- *Monitoring*—Items to monitor include security logs, application logs, system logs, protocol logs, virus pattern file update logs, virus scanning logs, and so on. Build a monitoring system that is easy to manage and easy to review. Access to logs and monitoring systems should be protected to avoid tampering with the system's audit trail. Logs and monitoring are usually the only methods to piece together what occurred when a system was compromised or attacked.

Hardening the Windows 2000 Operating System

Administrators should plan on building at least two core builds of the Windows 2000 operating system. One build can be used as the base build for publicly accessible services, and the other build can be used on the internal network. After a core build configuration is determined, its best practice to use a disk imaging process, such as Ghost, to create an image of the operating system. Manually installing the operating system and then trying to set all the desired parameters usually leads to overlooked settings. Using the imaging process will avoid the possibility of human error when trying to build identical systems to the core server specification. Some organizations might choose to create additional builds, but most IT shops will find that trying to manage more than two system images becomes overwhelming. For more information on Symantec's disk imaging product, Ghost, visit `http://enterprisesecurity.symantec.com/products/products.cfm?ProductID=3&PID=8517281`.

Bindings, Network Adapters, and Protocols

One of the most basic things to consider when building a secure configuration to use for Internet services is the network adapter, binding, and protocol configuration. In most instances, a single network adapter per server is sufficient unless user demand is driving up the output queue length or bytes total/sec performance counters. Organizations should consider using multiple servers and Windows load balancing if the load on the server is the cause for multiple network adapters. Adding additional network adapters might help to alleviate the load, but if the service is receiving high levels of traffic, a load balanced cluster will remove many single points of failure and would be a better design decision. Using multiple network adapters will also remove a single point of failure in the system's network subsystem that could be a target of a denial of service attack.

A multi-homed server should not be used when multiple adapters are used for administrative convenience. In this situation, one adapter is placed in the internal network and the other is placed on an external network or DMZ. This allows the server's content to be accessed and updated from the inside network adapter and accessed by the public from the external network adapter. This is not a secure configuration because if this server is compromised, the attacker has access to the inside network. From this point, the attacker could configure the server to route packets and open up a route for backdoor programs, such as Back Orifice, to reach inside servers, such as domain controllers, mail systems, or databases. Multi-homed configurations used for administrative convenience should be avoided at all costs.

When building the network configuration for Internet services, such as DNS, FTP, and SMTP, administrators need to review the bindings on the network adapters. When building new Internet services servers, administrators should not select both Client for Microsoft Networks and File and Printer Sharing for Microsoft Networks during setup. When securing existing Internet services servers, administrators should uninstall or unbind both Client for Microsoft Networks and File and Printer Sharing for Microsoft Networks services.

By removing these services, the server will not be able to share files or printers or allow inbound and outbound network connections using the Server Message Blocks (SMB) protocol. For DNS, FTP, HTTP, and SMTP servers, these services are unnecessary. However, this configuration will not work for all Internet services. If the server provides Internet-based access to terminal servers and SQL servers, the Client for Microsoft Networks might be required on these servers, depending on the applications and data sources the terminal server and SQL server use.

To uninstall both Client for Microsoft Networks and File and Printer Sharing for Microsoft Networks on existing Internet services servers, do the following:

1. Select Start, Settings, Network and Dial-up Connections.
2. Right-click the LAN adapter and select Properties.
3. Select File and Printer Sharing for Microsoft Networks.
4. Click the Uninstall button, as shown in Figure 15.3.
5. Answer YES to the warning message.
6. Answer Cancel to the prompt to restart the computer.
7. Select Client for Microsoft Networks.
8. Click the Uninstall button as shown.
9. Answer YES to the warning message.
10. Answer OK to the prompt to restart the computer.

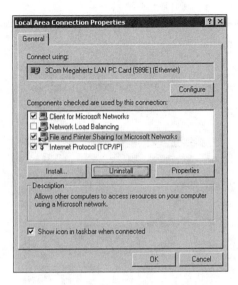

FIGURE 15.3
Uninstalling File and Printer Sharing for Microsoft Networks.

NOTE

Removing these services severely limits the functionality of the server. Remember that the idea in this chapter is build secure servers to host Internet services—not multi-use servers. If you are modifying an existing production server, experiment with this configuration on a test server to understand the impact of the loss in functionality before applying these settings to the production server.

Administrators should disable Netbios over TCP/IP when configuring the server for Internet services. Do not add other protocols, such as NetBeui, DLC, or IPX/SPX. The Windows 2000 TCP/IP stack provides two options for configuring TCP/IP on the server. Administrators can choose to enable or disable Netbios over TCP/IP. If the server is a dedicated Internet services server only supporting DNS, FTP, HTTP, and SMTP services or the server will only communicate with Windows 2000 servers configured with Netbios over TCP/IP disabled, disable Netbios over TCP/IP. If the server needs to communicate with down-level Windows NT servers, the administrator must enable Netbios over TCP/IP.

To disable Netbios over TCP/IP, do the following:

1. Select Start, Settings, Network and Dial-up Connections.

2. Right-click the LAN adapter and select Properties.

3. Select Internet Protocol (TCP/IP) and click the Properties button.

4. Click the Advanced button.

5. Select the WINS tab.

6. Click the Disable Netbios over TCP/IP radio button, as shown in Figure 15.4.

7. Click OK.

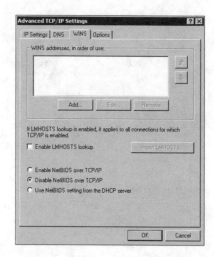

FIGURE 15.4

Disabling Netbios over TCP/IP.

Two additional TCP/IP settings administrators should disable are LMHOSTS lookup and dynamic DNS updates. Disabling the LMHOSTS lookup will prevent an attacker from modifying the LMHOSTS file and redirecting server traffic to a location where it can be recorded. The LMHOSTS lookup setting is located on the WINS tab of the TCP/IP protocol Advanced settings. To disable this setting, uncheck the Enable LMHOSTS Lookup radio button.

Allowing the server to attempt to register its services with a DNS server is less of a security concern than the LMHOSTS file, but it will prevent information about the server from leaving the server. To disable dynamic DNS updates, uncheck the Register This Connection's Addresses in DNS check box. The check box is located on the DNS tab of the TCP/IP protocols Advanced settings.

Filtering protocol port numbers is an additional way to secure the server's networking configuration. Filtering will prevent inbound connections on any port other than those listed in the filter list. Users at the console of the machine will still be able to establish outbound connections on ports outside of the filtered range. Using the operating system to filter the protocols does not replace a solid firewall, but it does provide another layer that an attacker must get through if he or she was to compromise the firewall.

To access the servers filtering settings, use the Options tab of the TCP/IP protocols Advanced settings, select TCP/IP filtering, and click the Properties button. Port filtering allows the administrator to filter the IP, TCP, and UDP protocols. If filtering will be enabled, administrators should filter IP protocol port 6 and then filter the necessary TCP ports, such as 21 (FTP), 25 (SMTP), 80 (HHTP), 443 (SSL), and 3389 (RDP). When configuring the filtering, also verify that the UDP filtering settings are configured as Permit Only with no ports listed as allowed (see Figure 15.5).

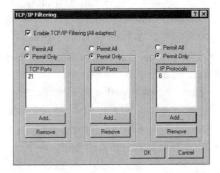

FIGURE 15.5
Enabling TCP/IP port filtering.

NOTE

This will not filter inbound ICMP traffic. To filter ICMP traffic from contacting the server, administrators should filter ICMP traffic at the border routers. Also note that the filtering settings apply to all network adapters in the server.

Tips for Securing the Operating System

This section provides an overview of the settings that should be configured to secure the operating system for servers providing Internet services. Many of these settings were discussed in other chapters, so references to locations where the full discussion and configuration procedures for the settings can be found are included. Readers should also refer to Chapter 12, "Security Policy and Configuration," for a detailed discussion on the security configuration tools set that provides information on using security templates from Microsoft that configure many of the settings listed here automatically.

Most of the group policy settings referenced in this section can be accessed through the Local Security Policies MMC Snap-in located under the Administrative Tools. The Local Policies folder within the Local Security Policies MMC Snap-in contains the Audit Policy, User Rights Assignment, and Security Options folders that contain most of the settings discussed in this section.

- *Physically secure the server*—The server needs to be behind locked doors or in a locked cabinet. The server case itself should also be locked to prevent floppy and CD-ROM access. Bios passwords can also be used to prevent the boot order from being modified on the server.

- *Format hard disks as NTFS*—NTFS allows administrators to set granular permission on files and should be used on all Windows 2000 server partitions. See Chapter 14 for information on converting partitions to NTFS.

- *Remove all unnecessary components during installation*—Items, such as accessories and Internet Information Server and its sub-components, such as the SMTP service, Index Server, and Script Debugger, are all installed by default. Any of these items that are not required for the specific server's configuration should be deselected during installation.

- *Place the Internet accessible servers in a workgroup*—Using a workgroup instead of a domain allows an administrator to create a self-contained configuration where a minimum number of services are enabled. Each server becomes a secured island. This configuration works for pure Internet servers such as DNS, FTP, HTTP, and SMTP servers. The downside to using a workgroup is the amount of administrative overhead involved. Each server has its own SAM database and policy configuration. Supporting other Internet services, such as Outlook Web Access for Exchange Server, Terminal Services, and SQL server, become difficult, if not impossible, to support in a workgroup. If the organization does choose to use a domain for its Internet servers, do not use the same domain as servers on the inside networks if at all possible. Create a new domain in a separate active directory forest for Internet servers.

- *Rename the administrator account*—Use a name other than admin and choose a name that doesn't stand out from the rest of the users accounts. The administrator account can be renamed either through Computer Management or through Local Security Settings under the Security Options folder.

- *Use strong passwords*—Use passwords that combine mixed case alphabet characters with numbers and special characters. Choose passwords that are at least eight characters. See chapter 14 for more information on passwords.

- *Install Service Packs*—Service packs need to be applied and so do the post service pack hotfixes if they patch a potential hole in the server's configuration.

- *Configure an audit policy*—At a minimum, the audit policy should include the following events for both success and failure: Audit account logon events, Audit account management, Audit logon events, Audit policy change, Audit privilege use, and Audit system events.

- *Configure a password and account lockout policy*—A password and lockout policy should use the following settings at a minimum:

  - Enforce password history—5 passwords.

  - Maximum password age—60 days.

  - Minimum password age—5 days.

  - Minimum password length—8.

  - Passwords must meet complexity requirements—Enable.

  - Store passwords using reversible encryption for all users in the domain—Disable.

  - Account lockout duration—30 minutes.

  - Account lockout threshold—5 bad passwords.

  - Reset account lockout after—Disabled. This will force an administrator to enable the account.

- *Allocate sufficient space for event logging*—Many administrators fail to allocate enough space to the event log. The proper size depends on the amount of activity on the server. After the proper size is determined, administrators should double or triple the size of the log. When errors occur, such as a runaway process or an attack, the log is going to fill faster than the normal rate. If the log is too small, events can get overwritten and the organization can lose the audit trail. The size of the event log and overwrite policy can be set by right-clicking the log name in the Event Viewer and selecting Properties.

- *Set the boot timeout to 0*—This forces the system to immediately boot the operating systems and not pause during boot to allow the administrator to select another reboot option from the boot.ini. To set the boot timeout, right-click My Computer and select Properties. Next, select the Advanced tab and then click the Startup and Recovery button. Set the Display List of Operating Systems For to 0.

- *Remove POSIX and OS2 subsystems*—Unnecessary subsystems create additional overhead and provide a potential security hole for an attacker to exploit. See Chapter 14 for information on disabling the POSIX and OS2 subsystems.

- *Disable all unnecessary services*—The minimum services required to run a Windows 2000 system are DNS Client, EventLog, Logical Disk Manager, Plug and Play, Protected Storage, and Security Accounts Manager. Any other services are optional.

- *Remove the 8.3 name generator*—Using the 8.3 file format can masquerade harmful files. See Chapter 14 for information on disabling the 8.3 name generator.

- *Remove default administrative shares and any other shares*—Windows 2000 creates a series of default network shares when it's installed. These should be disabled. See Chapter 14 for information on disabling the default shares. Publicly accessible servers should also not have any administrator created shares.

- *Hide the last logon name*—The winlogon dialog box displays the last account name that logged onto the server by default. To configure this setting, set Do Not Display Last User Name in Logon Screen to Enabled in the Security Options.

- *Use a logon message*—A logon message proves to the court system that ignorance is not an excuse for compromising the organization's systems in the event the organization prosecutes an attacker. Administrators can use the Message Text for Users Attempting to Log On and Message Title for Users Attempting to Log On Security Options settings to set the logon message. Administrators should have the text of the message and title reviewed by the organization's legal department before enabling these settings.

- *Set Permissions on executable files that could be used to assist an attacker*—Files that can be used against the organization include any network or IP related tools, such as `ping`, `arp`, `netstat`, `finger`, `FTP`, `NSLOOKUP`, `Telnet`, `regedt32`, `regedit`, and so on. Administrators can set permissions on these tools and create a specific group such as Net Admins to have read, execute, and take ownership access to these tools. The Administrators and LocalSystem accounts should be removed from the Access Control List (ACL) of these tools. If resource kits are installed on the server, the resource kit directories should have permissions similar to the networking tools. A better solution is not to install the resource kits on publicly accessible servers.

- *Additional Restrictions for Anonymous Connections*—This setting should be set to No Access Without Explicit Permissions. This forces an administrator to specifically designate directories for anonymous use only.

- *Deny Access to this Computer from the Network*—This setting prevents access to anyone listed in the policy setting from logging on remotely. This setting should be used on highly secure systems that require modification only from the system console.

- *Use a file integrity checker, such as Tripwire*—File integrity checking applications, such as Tripwire, can verify if a file was changed or added to the system. This can be invaluable when determining if a system was compromised. Refer to the following section ("Tools for Hardening the Operating System") for information on Tripwire.

Tools for Hardening the Operating System

The following sections cover several tools that can be used to help administrators test and maintain the hardened configuration of the Windows 2000 operating system. Most of the tools provide a limited trial download. Full product versions are relatively inexpensive when compared with potential costs and damage that is possible by not using the services that these tools provide.

ISS Security Scanner

System Scanner can be useful in closing some of the basic security holes in a base Windows 2000 installation. System Scanner is a simple way to check and baseline a Windows 2000 or Windows NT 4.0 system because the list of basic vulnerabilities are generated and checked automatically. What System Scanner can check in about five minutes would take a system administrator a few hours. The installation included in the resource kit can find about 270 known vulnerabilities. System Scanner can run different scans based on the potential use of the server or workstation in the following modes:

- Departmental Server
- Intranet Server
- DMZ Web Server
- DMZ FTP or Mail Server
- User Workstation
- User—Power User

A list of vulnerabilities is generated based on the type of server selected and the vulnerabilities are ranked as low, medium, and high in terms of risk. By right-clicking each vulnerability, the administrator will receive information on how he or she can correct the vulnerability.

Even though the version of System Scanner on the Resource Kit is a bit outdated, it's still a good tool to get administrators started on building secure systems. Internet Security Systems System Scanner 1.1 is included on the Windows 2000 Resource Kit in the APPS\ SystemScanner directory. System Scanner can be installed as a service or run manually. Current versions of System Scanner and full enterprise-wide intrusion detection systems are available for purchase at `http://www.iss.net/`.

Tripwire

Tripwire is a data integrity solution that allows administrators the ability to pinpoint a change on their system. Imagine the difficulty of locating a change on the system if the system was compromised. Which file or Registry key was changed, if any? Most administrators are forced to format and reinstall the system under these circumstances unless a baseline to compare the current configuration against is available. Tripwire provides the ability to create a baseline and allows an administrator to make comparisons between the system configurations at different points in time. Tripwire tracks information about files that are on the system, such as size, file flags, and access times. Tripwire also creates and stores a hash of the files. All the file information is then stored in a central database. Future checks then compare the current configuration and hashes against what is stored in the database. Tripwire also provides a centralized management console that can be used to centrally manage the Tripwire agents. Unfortunately, Tripwire is not a freeware utility for a Windows 2000 environment, but administrators can order an evaluation kit. Free versions of the utility are available for Unix and Linux systems. For more information on file integrity and Tripwire, visit `www.tripwire.com`.

LC3

LC3 is a password auditing and recovery tool that can be used to audit and recover user and administrator passwords. The tool can be used to check the passwords on hardened systems or for general auditing of end-user passwords. LC3 was formerly known as L0pht Crack. LC3 is available for download for a free 15-day trial at `www.atstake.com/research/lc3`.

The trial version of the utility will perform a dictionary attack and a brute/hybrid attack. The dictionary attack will crack passwords such as `password` while the brute/hybrid will crack passwords such as `password42` and `mypassword!`. A full version of the product is available for purchase and it can perform a brute force attack that can crack more sophisticated passwords that include combinations of upper- and lowercase letters, special characters, and numbers.

> **NOTE**
>
> Be forewarned that cracking strong passwords with LC3 can take up to 81 days for LC3 to cycle through all password combinations on a brute force attack using combinations of upper- and lowercase letters, special characters, and numbers when the utility is run on a single machine. Each password combination is tried against each account listed in the hash file LC3 is reading, and if no match is found, another combination is tried against all the accounts. This process continues until all combinations have been tried against all accounts. By distributing the workload to multiple machines, the passwords can be cracked faster. The full version supports distributing the workload.

LC3 provides the ability to audit/crack passwords from the following sources:

- The systems current database
- A remote server's Registry
- A SAM file
- Sniffer trace
- LC file—from previous versions of L0pht Crack
- PWDUMP file

Using LC3 requires administrative access to the workstation or server to install and run the utility. To run LC3 against another machine, the default ADMIN$ share must exist and the logged on user must have rights to the share. LC3 will crack both Windows NT with or without SYSKEY installed and Windows 2000 passwords.

PWDUMP3 is required to obtain the password hashes for installations using SYSKEY or Active Directory. PWDUMP3 also requires administrative access to run the utility and can be used to obtain the password hashes from a remote or local machine. PWDUMP3 will save the password hashes to a text file that can be imported into LC3 and then cracked. PWDUMP3 can be downloaded for free at http://www.ebiz-tech.com/html/pwdump.html.

Port Scanners and Other Utilities

Port scanning utilities can be used to verify that the server is not listening on ports that the administrator thinks are closed. SuperScan is a Windows-based port scanning utility that can be downloaded for free from www.foundstone.com. Administrators can use this utility on both workstations and servers to check open ports by providing an IP address and port range to scan.

Another free utility from Foundstone is Fport. Fport will display the open ports on the system, their process IDs, and the application that has the port open. This is a great tool for administrators to use to get more familiar with how the system functions under normal conditions. Foundstone also provides several other tools on their site that can scan UDP ports, stress test systems, and analyze file dates for intrusion detection.

Securing FTP Services

The File Transfer Protocol (FTP) was designed to move files between machines to increase collaboration and to shield users from the differences in the way operating systems handled files. By design, FTP is an unsecured protocol. The transfer and authentication processes are unencrypted. The only method to encrypt the FTP traffic would be to connect to a network through a VPN and then connect to the FTP server.

Several FTP vulnerabilities exist on many implementations of FTP servers. Some exploit the PORT command to establish Telnet connections to other servers on port 23 to launch further attacks. Others attempt to force buffer overflows by hitting the max number of connections and then launching malicious code when the server is impaired. Microsoft FTP server is not vulnerable to the PORT and buffer overflow attacks previously mentioned.

Many organizations have moved away from FTP as a way to transfer files—especially if the client is pulling a file down instead of uploading it. If files are read-only downloads, it's easier to download them through HTTP rather than configuring and managing a separate FTP server. Some organizations still use FTP servers to receive files, although most have switched to transferring files via e-mail. The secure shell protocol (SSH) is another way to securely move files and remotely administer servers, and is commonly used in Unix and Linux environments. For information on SSH server for Windows environments visit http://www.ssh.com/faq/index.cfm?id=709.

15

PROTECTING OTHER INTERNET SERVICES

The following section discusses how to install and configure an FTP server on Windows 2000. As stated before, building a secure FTP server is impossible because the protocol is unsecured. However, there are several configuration settings that are considered to be the best practices to use.

Installing the FTP Server

One of the enhancements to Windows 2000 and Internet Information Server is that the FTP Server does not automatically install itself during installation. The Windows NT 4.0 Option Pack installed the FTP service and enabled the service by default. The FTP service is still there, but it must be manually selected. To install the FTP Server, do the following:

1. Click Start, Settings, Control Panel.
2. Double-click Add/Remove Programs.
3. Click the button on the menu bar for Add/Remove Windows Components.
4. Click Internet Information Server.
5. Click the Details button.
6. Click the check box next to File Transfer Protocol (FTP) Server.
7. The installer is then prompted for the current service pack and operating system media.
8. Click Finish when setup completes.

After the FTP server is installed, the server is managed through the Internet Services Manager MMC Snap-in found under the Administrative Tools.

The default FTP site is quite simple. Unlike IIS, the FTP server only has five configuration tabs. Each FTP server can have a series of virtual directories that can reside on the FTP server or on remote servers. New virtual directories can be configured by right-clicking the default FTP server and selecting New, Virtual Directory.

Tips for Securing FTP Services

The following sections discuss the best practices to follow when configuring the FTP server.

- *Use anonymous connections and mark the check box to allow only anonymous connections*—Allowing connections other than anonymous will create situations where a username and password are passed over the network in clear text. If anonymous access is disabled, all accounts and passwords are passed over the network in clear text when users authenticate. Enabling the check box for Only Allowing Anonymous Connections, as shown in Figure 15.6, prevents the user's password from crossing the network.

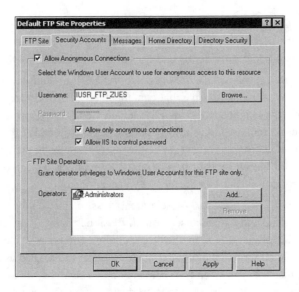

FIGURE 15.6
Forcing the FTP server to allowing only anonymous connections.

- *If combining Web and FTP servers, use separate accounts for the anonymous account*—Using separate accounts for each of the services allows for easier monitoring of the event logs. Create an account name **IUSR_SERVER_FTP** and configure the FTP server to use this account. The account setting is located on the Security Accounts tab of the FTP site.

- *Let IIS control the password*—This is one less password the administrator must manage. This is configured by selecting the Allow IIS to Control Password check box on the Security Accounts tab.

- *Create a separate group and accounts to manage the FTP site and add that group to the FTP site operators*—After the operator group is added, remove the Administrators group from the operator list.

- *Use local directories for secure configurations*—When the FTP server is configured for virtual directories on other servers, the FTP server's Workstation service must be enabled. If the FTP server was compromised, the attacker could use the Workstation service to attempt to connect to other systems and gain more information about the network.

- *Use directories on partitions other than the operating system partition to store files*—This will prevent the OS drive from getting cluttered with FTP files.

- *Enable write access on a few directories*—Administrators then only need to monitor one or two directories for abuse. Also consider disabling read access on the directories that have write access to prevent users from downloading files that were uploaded by other users.

- *Use the Unix directory listing style*—Unix-style directory lists are standard for FTP servers. Both the `dir` and `ls` commands can be used with either directory listing style. The `dir` command does provide the end user more information on the files.

- *Monitor disk space if allowing write access to the FTP site and directories*—Consider using disk quotas on the hard drive that contains the FTP directories to monitor the amount of data that is uploaded to the FTP server. Configure a low quota for the anonymous FTP user account and have it log events when the quota is exceeded or bypasses the warning level. This will prevent malicious users from using the FTP server as a distribution point for hacker tools or pornography. Remember to clean out the directories containing incoming files to not accidentally exceed the quota.

- *Use a virus scanning application*—Use a local virus scanner on the server and schedule a virus pattern update and a manual scan on all files once a day. Real-time scanning should be enabled and configured to scan all files, including compressed files such as zip files. There are additional virus scanning options for FTP services, such as Interscan from Trend Micro, that will proxy the FTP connection and scan the file as it is uploaded. Most anti-virus software vendors have similar products. Organizations might want to consider a virus proxy product if they plan on a high number of FTP transfers.

Securing SMTP Services

E-mail has become an essential tool for doing business. With the world's increasing dependency on e-mail services, organizations become more vulnerable that an attack will be launched against their mail service. Over the past few years, several attacks have been launched against corporate e-mail services with negative impacts to the business community increasing with each attack.

Simple Message Transfer Protocol (SMTP) is the interconnect that connects the world's e-mail services through the Internet. SMTP is also the transport that is used to distribute e-mail-based attacks across the Internet. If organizations can secure SMTP, they will reduce the likelihood of becoming a victim of an attack or being used as an intermediary system in an attack.

SMTP services have the following major vulnerabilities:

- E-mail–born viruses and trojans
- Unsolicited e-mail (SPAM)
- Abuse of content
- Denial of service

This section focuses on general SMTP security. With the quantity of mail systems that are in production, it's difficult to provide specific configurations. Hopefully, this section will provide the reader with a starting point that they can use to further determine the vulnerabilities in the systems in use on their networks.

E-mail–Born Viruses and Trojans

Over the past few years, administrators have had to deal with an increasing number of e-mail–born viruses. The list of viruses and trojans include Melissa, Love Letter, Back Orifice, and SubSeven, just to name a few. This section focuses specifically on SMTP virus protection. Refer to Chapter 10, "Trojans and Backdoors," for a full discussion of viruses and trojans.

The solution to e-mail–borne viruses is to implement an anti-virus product on the SMTP mail gateways receiving e-mail from the Internet. Vendors, such as Symantec, McAfee, and TrendMicro, all provide virus protection products that will scan SMTP messages as they enter the network. These products run as standalone SMTP gateways or as a service on an existing gateway server. For these products to be effective, organizations need to block or filter POP3, as well as disallow use of hotmail or similar free mail accounts, because these mail services and protocols will circumvent and undermine SMTP protections previously discussed. Blocking these mail services and protocols will force all e-mail through corporate system and the appropriate scanning and filtering software the administrator has installed to secure the organization.

For performance and redundancy, the organization should use multiple SMTP gateway servers capable of scanning for viruses in SMTP messages without delaying mail flow. The anti-virus servers should be configured to update their pattern files nightly.

For best results, anti-virus SMTP servers should be combined with content filtering servers to give administrators the option to filter messages with viruses by specific header or attachment information before the anti-virus vendor releases a new pattern update. See the "Abuse of Content" section later in this chapter for more information on content filtering.

Unsolicited E-mail (SPAM)

Advertisers use unsolicited e-mail to promote products and services. Unsolicited e-mail is also referred to as SPAM, Unsolicited Commercial E-mail (UCE), and Unsolicited Bulk E-mail (UBE), and senders of unsolicited e-mail are referred to as spammers or mailbombers. There are worse thing in life than getting unsolicited e-mail, and in most cases it's just an annoyance for end users and they delete the messages. Subscribing to public forums and enrolling on Web sites are ways the user's e-mail address is distributed. After a user has given out his or her e-mail address to the general public, he or she will start receiving unsolicited mail.

Most unsolicited mail is sent by unsecured SMTP mail relays. Many Exchange 5.0 and 5.5 servers were configured for relaying messages to support POP3 and IMAP clients. To send e-mail, POP3 and IMAP clients relay SMTP messages off a SMTP server. Many administrators left the relay function enabled for their POP3 and IMAP clients and were then exploited by spammers. Exchange 5.5 and Exchange 2000 have the ability to lock down an SMTP relay server to comply with RFC 2505, "Anti-Spam Recommendations for SMTP MTAs."

Another method of sending unsolicited e-mail is called reverse UCE. In this method, an SMTP relay server is configured not to relay, but it will send a non-delivery report to the sender when they attempt to relay a message. The spammer uses a bogus TO address and crafts the FROM address as the recipient to whom they want to send mail. The spammer then blasts the SMTP server with the crafted messages and then the SMTP server blasts the recipient with non-delivery reports. Because a non-delivery report is sent to the destination, reverse UCE is used as a method to harass a recipient or distribute malicious code—not to advertise products and services. RFC 2505 also defines that a mail server must be able to prevent reverse UCE.

To protect the organization from being a victim or UCE, administrators should disable SMTP relaying capabilities on SMTP servers receiving mail from the Internet. Administrators should also test their configurations by attempting to relay a message off the server to determine if their servers could be exploited by reverse UCE. If the administrator receives a non-delivery report, the SMTP server could be used to send reverse UCE. If the server is configured correctly, the administrator should receive a 550 Relaying Prohibited error.

If relaying is required to support POP3 and IMAP clients, the SMTP servers used for relaying should be located inside the company's internal network. The server should also force users to authenticate before relaying the message.

Abuse of Content

SMTP messages are subject to abuse of content either by internal users or from messages entering the organization from the Internet. Abuses of content include distributing inappropriate attachments, such as MP3 or AVI files, racial slurs, sexual content, profanity, and so on. There are several products on the market that scan e-mail content as it enters and exits the organization. Product names and vendors include MIMESweeper from Baltimore Technologies, eSafe from Aladdin Knowledge Systems, and Assentor from SRA International. Some of these products are pure content filters, while others provide content filtering and virus scanning.

Content filtering products can also be used to add standard company disclaimers and perform other modifications to e-mail messages before they leave the organization. They can scan messages based on subject, body, and attachment content and make filtering decisions whether to delete the message, quarantine the message, or deliver the message. These products can save the organization from new viruses as well by filtering on the subject and attachment and deleting the message before the end user has a chance to open it and propagate the virus.

Denial of Service

SMTP services are also vulnerable to denial of service attacks. A denial of service attack can come in the form of a mail bomb, virus plague, or a network-based attack against the router that links the SMTP servers to the Internet (see Chapter 17, "Denial of Service Attacks," for more information). Adding redundancy is the way to prevent the organization from being impacted from loss of SMTP service. Figure 15.7 shows a sample SMTP service design that incorporates redundancy to minimize the risk of losing SMTP services.

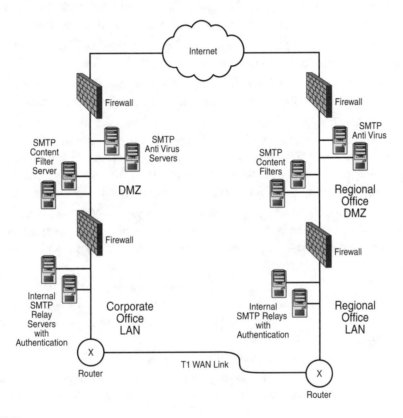

FIGURE 15.7
Redundant SMTP services design.

Consider the following bullet points that will help protect the organization from the loss of SMTP services:

- *Locate the SMTP mail servers behind a firewall*—Locating your organization's SMTP servers behind a stateful packet inspection firewall will hide the name of your organization's SMTP mailer. Try establishing a Telnet session on port 25 to your mail server from the Internet. Does it reveal the name of the mailer? If it does, spammers and intruders will know what e-mail software the organization is using for Internet mail and will have a head start on testing your SMTP server to see if they can use it as a SMTP relay to send SPAM messages.

- *Harden the operating system*—This makes the server harder to compromise in the event an attacker gets through the firewall.

- *Only allow TCP port 25 to contact the SMTP servers*—Locking the ports down makes the server more difficult to probe. The port should be restricted on the firewall and can also be restricted on the server through filtering on the TCP/IP configuration.

- *Enable logging on the SMTP servers and monitor the logs*—Logging allows the administrator to monitor successful connections and troubleshoot problems.

- *Distribute SMTP servers in different locations for redundancy*—In the event the organization is attacked, SMTP mail can still be delivered from the other location.

- *Lock down SMTP relay servers*—Organizations should lock down SMTP relay capabilities to prevent the propagation of SPAM. There are USENET groups that distribute information about open SMTP relays on the Internet. This is referred to as a blacklist, and many mail administrators will restrict their mail servers from accepting mail from blacklisted domains. Having an open relay can get an organization's domain on the blacklist.

- *Use redundant virus scanning and content filtering servers*—Virus and content filtering server should process the mail as it enters the company before it is accepted by the corporate mail system. These servers need to be engineered for failover and be able to handle any load they might receive.

- *Use SSL for Internet based interorganization connections*—If mail is sent between company locations over the Internet, the SMTP server-to-server communication sending the mail should be secured by SSL/TLS. Most messaging systems, including Exchange Server 2000, support this feature.

- *Use redundant Internet connections for interorganization connections*—Organizations that route internal mail over the Internet should have redundant Internet connections to allow internal mail to continue to flow during a denial of service attack or other outage.

Protecting Windows 2000 DNS Servers

There is a great deal of information on the Internet about how to secure Unix DNS servers. Unfortunately, there is not a great deal of information about securing Windows 2000 DNS servers. This section discusses how to secure Windows 2000 DNS servers that service requests from the Internet. The ideas expressed in this section do not apply to internal Active Directory integrated DNS designs that support internal clients and Active Directory replication.

DNS Designs

There are essentially two common designs for DNS installations that support external clients. The most secure implementation is a split DNS design. In a split DNS design, internal and external DNS records are hosted on completely separate servers, and there are no zone transfers taking place between the servers. The external DNS should only have the addresses of systems that are accessed from the Internet, such as those in the DMZ, and these should have a different TCP/IP network address than the systems within the organization. See Figure 15.8 for a diagram of a split DNS installation. This is the recommended way to implement DNS. Most medium and large organizations have already implemented this configuration.

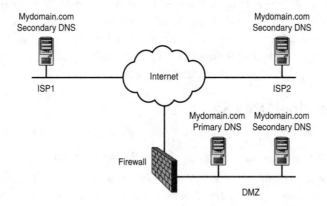

Figure 15.8
Split DNS installation.

The second DNS design is a non-split DNS design that combines internal and external DNS records and zones on the same servers. This design is primarily used as a cost-saving mechanism to reduce the number of servers in the environment and the cost of supporting the DNS infrastructure. This design is most commonly found in small and cost-conscious environments. The main problem with this design is that if a non-split DNS server is compromised, an attacker has a list of both internal and external IP addresses and hostnames. An attacker can then use this information to launch further attacks or use social engineering to further infiltrate the organization.

Organizations with a non-split DNS might have the DNS servers in the DMZ so that internal and external clients can access both servers. The worst of the worst DNS designs uses a multi-homed, non-split DNS server with one network adapter in the inside network and one in the DMZ. If this server is compromised, the attacker now has internal IP addresses, hostnames, and a direct connection to the internal network from which to launch attacks. Organizations that find themselves in this situation need to move to a split DNS design if they are concerned about security.

When installing Windows 2000 DNS servers to support Internet clients, administrators will choose to create standard primary and standard secondary DNS zones. At least two DNS servers should be used in any DNS server configuration to provide redundancy.

If the only DNS servers for the organization are hosted on the same network, the organization is open to a denial of service attack. Organizations should consider hosting additional secondary DNS servers for their domain offsite. Refer to Chapter 17 for a discussion of the denial of service attack launched against Microsoft's DNS servers.

If the organization is considering hosting additional DNS servers offsite, choose a security-conscious ISP for hosting the secondary DNS servers. Verify that the ISP has security policies regarding DNS and ask to review those policies. If they do not provide security policies, ask the ISP to adopt your security policy and sign a Service Level Agreement (SLA) for security. The SLA should be designed to compensate the organization in the event the secondary DNS server is compromised. If the ISP is not willing to adapt to the organization's security policy or is not willing to comply with an SLA, consider choosing another provider.

Tips for Securing DNS Servers

The following list includes some tips and best practices to follow when securing DNS servers.

- *Use split DNS design*—Any other design puts the organization at risk.
- *Host additional secondary servers offsite*—To avoid being a victim of a denial of service attack, host at least two secondary DNS servers on separate networks from the primary DNS server.
- *House the primary DNS server on your network*—Organizations should not trust their primary DNS server to another organization. Zone transfer configuration is configured on this server, and it should remain under the organization's control.
- *Harden the DNS server's operating system*—This provides another layer of security and will make it difficult for an attacker to compromise the DNS server to launch additional attacks.
- *Secure the DNS servers behind a* firewall—Many organizations used to choose to place DNS servers outside the organization's firewall. This is an outdated design and is not a recommended configuration. Placing the DNS server behind a stateful inspection firewall will make it easier to control the traffic that is directed to the server.
- *Only permit TCP and UDP port 53 through the firewall to the DNS servers*—Blocking additional traffic to the DNS server makes it difficult for the attacker to probe the server for vulnerabilities. The DNS server uses TCP for zone transfers and UDP for name queries. You might want to consider blocking TCP port 53 if the only DNS servers for the DNS domain reside on your organization's DMZ. However, before you do so, refer to the

"Microsoft Gets Attacked" section in Chapter 17 that discusses a DNS denial of service attack that exploited a DNS design that homed all DNS servers on the same DMZ network.

- *Only permit zone transfers for known secondary DNS servers*—Use the Notify option to only notify secondary DNS servers of zone changes. Add the secondary servers to the Name Servers tab on the zone Properties. On the Zone Transfers tab, mark the check box for Allow Zone Transfers and then mark the radio button for Only to Servers Listed on the Name Servers Tab. The Notify settings configuration defaults to servers listed on the Name Servers tab. This setting can be verified by using the Notify button on the Zone Transfers tab. The Zone Transfers tab is shown in Figure 15.9.

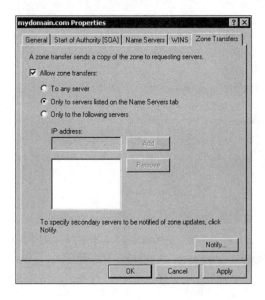

FIGURE 15.9
Only allow zone transfers to known secondary servers on the DNS server's Zone Transfers tab.

- *Enable logging and monitor the logs*—Use the Logging tab on the server's Properties in the DNS MMC Snap-in to enable logging. Logging will increase the overhead on the server, and Microsoft only recommends using the logging options when troubleshooting specific processes.
- *Block ping and trace route commands to the DNS servers*—ICMP traffic to the DNS servers should be blocked at the border router.
- *Avoid using HINFO records*—HINFO records are host information records that define the CPU type and operating system of a particular host. Because the HIFO record reveals information about the server, it's not recommended to use them. If the organization chooses to use these records, administrators should keep on top of security patches and fixes.

- *Prune stale records from the DNS database*—The records might reveal information to an attacker on the network design. Anyone can use NSLOOKUP to connect to a public DNS server, so stale records used for testing purposes can expose more information than necessary to the outside.

NOTE

For more information on properly configuring DNS services and common configuration errors to avoid, review RFC 1912, 2182, and 2219 available at `http://www.rfc-editor.org/`. Also refer to the following DNS configuration white papers from Microsoft:

- Windows 2000 DNS White Paper—
  `http://www.microsoft.com/windows2000/techinfo/howitworks/communications/nameadrmgmt/w2kdns.asp`

- DNS Best Practices—
  `http://www.microsoft.com/windows2000/en/server/help/default.asp?url=/windows2000/en/server/help/sag_DNS_imp_BestPractices.htm?id=1847`

- Windows 2000 DNS Issues (Chapter 6 Windows 2000 Resource Kit)—
  `http://www.microsoft.com/technet/treeview/default.asp?url=/TechNet/prodtechnol/windows2000serv/reskit/tcpip/part2/tcpch06.asp`

Summary

This chapter has provided some ideas on securing DNS, FTP, and SMTP services. The basic requirement for securing these services is to harden the Windows 2000 operating system before adding these services. Other common threads with these services are that they require the protection of a firewall and need redundant servers to function in a secure, highly-available design. Before deploying these services, be sure to review the RFCs that define many best practices for configuring these services, and review the latest security updates of these services from Microsoft.

TCP Filtering and Firewalls

IN THIS CHAPTER

When you connect your network to the outside world, you enter hostile territory. And, no more hostile territory exists than the Internet. There, thousands of nameless, faceless attackers can assault your network 24 hours a day, 7 days a week. To address this, you need a firewall or a reasonable facsimile. This chapter describes how to use firewalls and related technologies to protect your network.

What Is a Firewall?

A firewall is a device that prevents outsiders from accessing your network by enforcing security policies. Such devices are typically routers, standalone computers running packet filtering or proxy software, firewalls-in-a-box, or proprietary hardware devices that filter and proxy incoming and outgoing network traffic. The firewall can be a tool to help ensure that sensitive data or risky protocols (such as SNMP and NETBios) from within your network does not leak out, in addition to controlling what can come in.

A firewall should be a single entry point to your site (commonly called a *choke point*). As your network receives connection requests, the firewall evaluates them and will accept only connections from authorized hosts; it discards the remaining requests. No outside threat can undermine a site's policies as easily as, for example, a system that is connected to a network and also has a modem connection linking it to the Internet. All modem traffic will circumvent the firewall and the protection it provides. For this reason, secondary connections should be isolated from the remainder of the network or removed.

This offers you ample protection against outside attacks. However, sometimes, company policies, network architecture, or other factors require that you enforce a more stringent or complicated firewall scheme. In such cases, you might opt for nested firewall protection.

In a nested scenario, you specify a blanket security policy for the network at large and more defined and detailed policies for each subordinate department. Such scenarios are common in corporate environments.

So, at its most basic, a firewall is a device that applies and enforces network access policies. Hence, firewalls are to networks what permission-based access controls are to operating systems: They let authorized folks in and keep unauthorized folks out.

But this definition is too narrow. Many new firewalls perform diverse tasks including the following:

- *Packet filtering*—Firewalls can analyze incoming packets of multiple protocols and, based on that analysis, perform conditional evaluations ("If I encounter this packet type,

I'll do this.") Packet filtering firewalls perform static packet filtering. They examine packets based on the information found in the header and then decide how to handle those packets.

- *Stateful inspection firewalls*—This type of firewall is a type of packet filtering firewall. Stateful inspection firewalls go beyond merely examining a packet based on what it finds in its header, it also inspects the content of the packet to determine more about the packet than just its origin and destination. An added security measure of stateful inspection firewalls is that you can protect against port scanning by having the firewall close off specific ports until a connection to that specific port is requested.

- *Protocol or content blocking*—Firewalls can screen content, including Java, JavaScript, VBScript, ActiveX, and cookies. Moreover, you can use your firewall to block particular attack signatures.

NOTE

Attack signatures are patterns common to a particular attack. For example, when a user telnets to port 80 and issues commands, this activity "looks" a certain way to your machine. By teaching your firewall what these signatures "look" like, you can "train" it to block such attacks, even at the packet level. Indeed, some remote exploits rely on specially crafted packets that a firewall easily can distinguish from other, non-malicious packets.

- *User, connection, and session authentication and encryption*—Many firewalls use various algorithms and authentication schemes, including DES, Triple DES, SSL, IPSEC, SHA, MD5, BlowFish, and IDEA, to verify users' identities, ensure session integrity, and shield transmitting data from electronic eavesdropping.

So, firewalls—depending on their design—protect your network on at least two, and in some cases, all, of the following levels:

- *Who* can come in and send out information
- *What* can come in and be sent out
- *Where and how* users and data can come in and transmit out

In a more esoteric sense, a firewall is a *concept* rather than a product. It's the sum total of rules that you'll apply to your network. Generally, such rules mirror access policies already established (on a human level) in your organization.

Types of Firewalls

Many firewall types exist, but most fall into one of two categories:

- Network-level firewalls or packet filters
- Application Gateways

Let's examine each now.

Network-Level Firewalls: Packet Filters

Network-level firewalls are typically routers with packet filtering capabilities. Using a network-level firewall, you can grant or deny access to your site based on several variables, including the following:

- Content
- Port number
- Protocol
- Source address

Router-based firewalls consist of perimeter solutions and are often architecture-independent. Consequently, many companies use them as choke points as we previously discussed. Such choke points subject all outside traffic to *accept* or *deny* rules.

Router-based solutions offer a major advantage: they're generally operating system and application-neutral. That is, if you use them, you needn't fiddle with individual workstations behind the firewall, nor must you concern yourself with platforms or proxy support. Therefore, router-based firewalls offer quick, clean, sweeping solutions that eliminate or greatly reduce the "tinker" factor.

Also, advanced router-based firewalls can defeat spoofing and DOS attacks, and can even—in some cases—make your network effectively invisible to the outside world.

Finally, routers offer an integrated solution. If your network connection is dedicated, you'll probably need a router anyway, so why not kill two birds with one stone? These facts sum up router-based firewall advantages.

On the other hand, router-based firewalls do have deficiencies. One is that some remain vulnerable to spoofing attacks (though router vendors are now more diligent in this regard). Moreover, router performance can decline when you enforce excessively stringent filtering rules. This might or might not be an issue, depending on your network's traffic volume. And finally, router-based solutions can be expensive. Here, you get what you pay for, essentially. Low-end systems don't maintain state on incoming packets and often lack other key features.

Application-Proxy Firewalls/Application Gateways

16

The other major firewall type is the *application-proxy firewall* - often called an *application gateway*. Application gateways proxy connections between outside clients and your internal network. Throughout this exchange, the system never forwards IP packets. Instead, a translation of sorts occurs, in which the gateway acts as the conduit and interpreter.

In some ways, application gateways are more incisive than most other firewalls. They offer you more control over individual services and applications, and typically maintain packet state information.

However, application gateways also have deficiencies. One is that they demand substantial effort, because you generally must configure a proxy application for each networked service (FTP, Telnet, HTTP, mail, news, and so on). Additionally, inside users must use proxy-aware clients. If they don't, they'll have to adopt new policies and procedures.

The classic application-gateway firewall example is a package called the Trusted Information Systems (TIS) Firewall Tool Kit (FWTK). This package (which is free for non-commercial use) includes proxies for

- Telnet
- FTP
- rlogin
- sendmail
- HTTP
- The X Window system

The FWTK demands that you not only proxy each application, but that you also apply access rules for each one. This can get confusing. But, if you're interested in learning about firewalls and how to code them, I recommend downloading the FWTK and examining the source. The experience is well worth it and will give you an inside look at a firewall's construction. You can get the FWTK at `http://www.fwtk.org`.

IP Filtering

In conjunction with IPSec and tunneling, Windows 2000 offers substantial IP filtering capabilities. *Tunneling*, also referred to as *encapsulation*, is a technology that enables a network to send its data via connections on another network. These provide functionality that closely approximates traditional firewall functionality.

IP Security Policies Management (MMC)

To establish IP security policies, you must first open the IP Security Policies Management Console. To do so, choose Start, Programs, Administrative Tools, and then click Local Security Policy. The Local Security Settings console appears (see Figure 16.1).

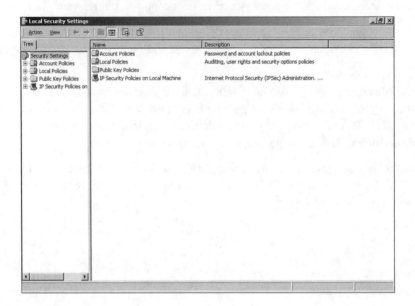

FIGURE 16.1
The Local Security Settings console.

Select IP Security Policies on Local Machine. You have three options (see Figure 16.2).

- *Client (Respond Only)*—This is for low-end, garden-variety connections from computers in environments that don't enforce security strictly. Intranets are good examples of such environments. Often, only some users and hosts in intranets strictly demand security, and therefore, in such environments, the majority of connection requests will be for non-encrypted, non-tunneled communication. The Client Respond Only settings specify how a host that exists in such a loose environment should respond when another host does request secure communications.

- *Server (Request Security)*—This setting is the next ramp up from Client (Respond Only); it is useful in environments where the majority of hosts do need or demand secure communication. Here, the server isn't passive anymore but, instead, always asks for secured communications. This policy specifies how the host conducts this exchange.

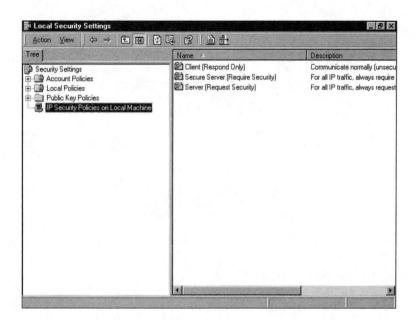

FIGURE 16.2
The IP Security Policies on Local Machine options.

- *Secure Server (Require Security)*—This setting governs the most restrictive state, the state in which your Windows 2000 host requires secure communications and rejects any connection request that fails to meet the requirements you set forth in this policy.

In each case, the setting options Windows 2000 provides are very similar. Here, we'll deal chiefly with the Client (Respond Only) settings, but these generally also apply to Server and Secure Server.

Client (Respond Only) Settings

To establish your Client settings, double-click the Client (Respond Only) entry in the IP Security Policies Management Console. In response, Windows 2000 will display the Client (Respond Only) Properties dialog box (see Figure 16.3).

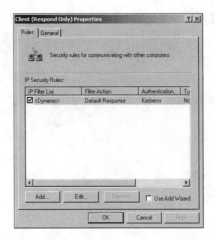

FIGURE 16.3
The Client (Respond Only) Properties dialog box.

The Client (Respond Only) Properties dialog box includes two tabs. These two tabs also are included in the Server (Request Security) and the Secure Server (Require Security) Property dialog boxes.

- *Rules*—This tab provides an interface from which to set security rules for communication with other computers.

- *General*—This tab provides an interface from which to set IP security policy general guidelines.

The Rules tab includes the Add, Edit, and Remove option buttons. These options pertain to rules. Let's run through these now.

Adding a New Rule
To add a new rule, clear the Use Add Wizard check box, and then click the Add button in the Rules tab.

NOTE

Note that by default in the Rules tab, Windows 2000 has the Use Add Wizard check box selected. This is suitable for casual users, perhaps, but, as an administrator, you should manually build your security policies. This way, you'll become intimately familiar with the process and what your rules do. Hence, before clicking the Add button, clear the Use Add Wizard check box.

The New Rule Properties dialog box appears. Note that this dialog box enumerates any IP security rules you specify. By default, this dialog box displays five tabs, shown in Figure 16.4, that are used to define values for each rule. (The New Rule Properties dialog box used by the Server (Request Security) and the Secure Server (Require Security) options include the same tabs).

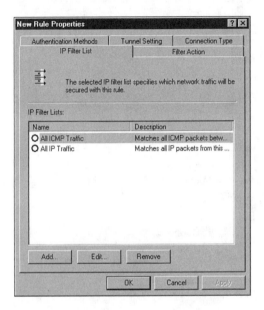

FIGURE 16.4
The New Rule Properties dialog box.

- *Authentication Methods*—You specify the means by which your host and remote hosts establish trust here. Kerberos is the default. Read more about Kerberos in Chapter 8, "Windows 2000 Network Security Architecture."

- *Connection Type*—You specify the connection type here—All, LAN, or Remote Access.

- *Filter Action*—This specifies the action your host will undertake with this rule when encountering a connection request. This could be Permit, Block, Request Security, Require Security, and so on.

- *IP Filter List*—This specifies what traffic to which your host will apply the instant rule.

- *Tunnel Setting*—On this tab, you specify if tunneling is required and, if so, what end point (by address) this rule will use.

For IP filtering, we're first concerned with the IP Filter List tab. To specify a new list here, click Add. In response, Windows 2000 will display the IP Filter List dialog box (see Figure 16.5).

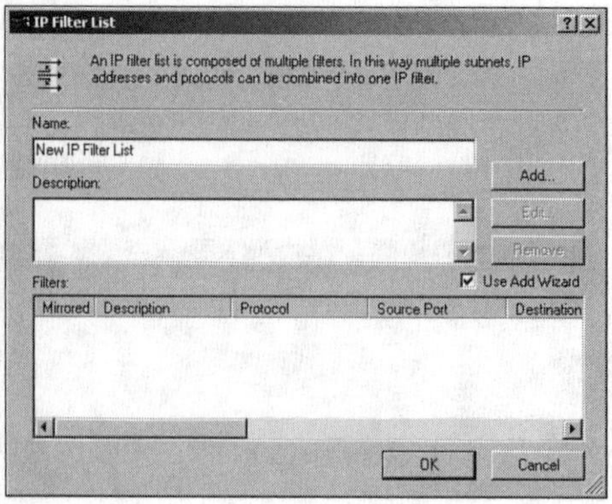

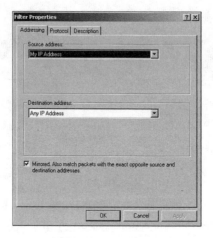

FIGURE 16.5

The IP Filter List dialog box.

At this point, clear the Use Add Wizard check box and then click Add. The Filter Properties dialog box appears (see Figure 16.6).

FIGURE 16.6

The Filter Properties dialog box.

The Filter Properties dialog box consists of three tabs:

- *Addressing*—Allows you to set the source and destination addresses, and offers several choices, including your address, any IP address, a specific IP address, a specific DNS name, or a specific subnet.

- *Protocol*—Allows you to specify what protocols and ports to filter, including EGP, HMP, ICMP, RAW, RDP, RVD, TCP, UDP, XNS-IDP, or OTHER (and of course, the source and destination ports).

- *Description*—Allows you to name the filter with a freeform textual description that carries some significance for you.

If you've had experience with Unix-based firewalls or filtering systems, this might seem like a protracted method—especially when compared to simple command-line directives. However, the result is the same. Using these options, you can use Windows 2000 to filter all TCP traffic to port 137 from all addresses except your own.

This is the essence of filtering, which works off simple assumptions. In TCP-based internetworks, compliant hosts run various network services on various ports. These ports listen for traffic from the outside world and consequently, invite mischief.

In `C:\WINNT\system32\drivers\etc\services`, you'll find a short list of commonly known and used ports and services. The file's structure unfolds in four columns that represent `service name`, `port number and protocol`, `aliases` (if any), and `comments`, respectively. For example,

```
name       port/proto   alias   comment
ms-sql-s   1433/tcp             #Microsoft-SQL-Server
ms-sql-s   1433/udp             #Microsoft-SQL-Server
ms-sql-m   1434/tcp             #Microsoft-SQL-Monitor
ms-sql-m   1434/udp             #Microsoft-SQL-Monitor
```

`C:\WINNT\system32\drivers\etc\services` is an abridged list, though. The official list, available at `http://www.isi.edu/in-notes/iana/assignments/port-numbers`, consists of some 9,280 lines as of this writing. Not every network supports all the protocols listed there, but many support several hundred.

IP filtering accounts for this, and lets you specify which protocols and ports remote hosts can access. Consequently, it makes it possible for you to deny, say, FTP services to all but a small list of trusted associates who hail from static IP addresses.

Because filtering rules—at their most basic—deal in accept/deny terms, they offer you incisive control. Indeed, you can make several seemingly disparate rules that together produce a specific and correct result. One such scenario is where you first establish a rule that denies all ports and protocols to all addresses. You then incisively backtrack, inserting rules that allow specific IP addresses.

> **NOTE**
>
> This is similar to the TCP wrappers approach in Unix where you initially place an ALL entry into hosts.deny and later insert approved addresses into hosts.allow. The result is that your system will reject connection requests from all but the approved addresses.

IP Filter List Options and Notes

Several IP Filter List options can make your work easier. One is the mirroring option. *Mirroring* proceeds on the assumption that you'll always want to establish the same rule bi-directionally. That is, it assumes that you'll want to flip access rules and thus match packet restrictions on the same ports and same designations on both source and destination addresses. This option is selected by default and I advise against disabling it. It shortens your overall work time because it alleviates the need to specifically articulate reverse rules.

Another issue to consider is whether to use DNS names (hostnames) rather than IP addresses. I advise against this. Neither method is reliable alone for authentication. Unless you run local DNS and hard-code known node addresses, it's hard to know if the results are accurate. Certainly, if you pull DNS entries from root servers (as you normally would when running local, non-cache-only DNS), you have better assurance than using, say, your local ISP's DNS. However, this doesn't account for bogus DNS entries at visited sites. Either way, of the two, hard IP addressing is slightly more reliable.

Table 16.1 addresses several other options that relate to your filtering system.

TABLE 16.1   Other Filtering Options

Option	Function
Authentication Method	Windows 2000 uses Kerberos by default for session authentication. Unless you have custom certificates that you implicitly trust (and therefore actually require another scheme), don't change this.
Key Settings	Windows 2000 key regeneration options allow you to specify regeneration either by byte size or time. The defaults are 100,000 bytes or 3600 seconds. You might want to reduce the key regeneration time if you feel that it will secure your network better, but it isn't really necessary.

TABLE 16.1   Continued

Option	Function
Perfect Forward Keys	Windows 2000's filtering system provides an option for Session Key Perfect Forward Secrecy. This option (disabled by default) specifies that subsequent keys will never derive themselves from preceding keys. That is, the system won't use material from any previous keys to generate new ones. This provides additional security and eats relatively nominal resources, so I recommend it.
Security Methods	You reach the Security Methods tab by clicking the Edit button on the Rules tab. Here, Windows 2000 displays the security methods used to check integrity, secure data transmissions, and so on. The defaults are SHA1 for session integrity and Triple DES for encryption. Carefully consider this option before changing it. SHA1 is more robust and more secure than MD5 and Triple DES is more secure than DES.

Differences in Server and Secure Server

The chief difference between Client (Respond Only) and Server/Secure Server configurations is that Server/Secure Server default settings are more stringent. If you alter settings, add new rules wherever possible rather than disabling the default rules to avoid weakening your security.

Firewalls for Windows 2000 Enterprises

Enterprise firewalls are firewalls designed to protect entire networks from attack. This section discusses some of the more popular ones.

Check Point FireWall-1

You can define and implement a centrally managed Security Policy with FireWall-1. You define the enterprise Security Policy centrally at a management console that downloads the Security Policy to key points throughout your network. FireWall-1 consists of three components:

- *Graphical User Interface (GUI)*—You use the GUI to define and manage your organization's enterprise-wide Security Policy. You define the Security Policy in terms of network objects (for example, gateways and hosts) and security rules. The FireWall-1 GUI also includes a Log Viewer and a System Status Viewer.

- *Management Server*—After you define your enterprise Security Policy, you save it on the Management Server. The purpose of the Management Server is to maintain the FireWall-1 databases, which include user definitions, network object definitions, the Security Policy that you defined with the GUI, and log files. You can deploy the GUI and the Management Server on the same machine.

- *FireWall-1 Firewall Module*—You deploy the Firewall Module on your Internet gateways and all other network access points throughout your network. The Management Server downloads the Security Policy to the Firewall Module, which in turn, protects your network. The Firewall Module contains a FireWall-1 Inspection Module whose purpose is to examine every packet passing through key locations, such as Internet gateways, routers, switches, servers, or workstations. If packets do not comply with the enterprise Security Policy, they are not permitted to enter the network.

  Check Point Software Technologies Inc.
  Three Lagoon Drive, Suite 400
  Redwood City, CA 94065
  (650) 628-2000
  E-mail: info@checkpoint.com
  URL: http://www.checkpoint.com/products/firewall-1/

Cisco Secure PIX Firewall

The Cisco Secure PIX Firewall is dedicated firewall hardware that delivers strong security without impacting network performance. All models have built-in IPSec encryption that permits both site-to-site and remove access VPN deployments. The Secure PIX Firewall consists of five models. Two of the models, the Secure PIX 535 and the Secure PIX 525, are meant for large enterprises and for service providers. The Secure PIX 520 delivers security to large-scale enterprises. The Secure PIX 515 is meant for small to medium businesses, and the Secure PIX 506 is meant for small or home offices.

    Cisco Systems, Inc.
    170 West Tasman Drive
    San Jose, CA 95134-1619
    (800) 553-6387
    E-mail: cs-support-us@cisco.com
    URL: http://www.cisco.com/warp/public/cc/pd/fw/sqfw500/index.shtml

Galea Secured Networks, Inc.

Galea has three firewall products that are designed for Internet service providers (ISPs), Web servers, e-commerce solutions, and mission-critical servers.

- *Server Protector-100*—A hardware-based solution that is designed to protect Web servers and servers that provide e-commerce security. The card provides combined firewall and Virtual Private Network (VPN) protection, encryption on the card, protection against Denial of Service (DoS) attacks, IP spoofing protection, and packet inspection, to name a few features.

- *SSL-100 Module*—Designed for ISPs, application service providers (ASPs), Web servers, collocation servers, e-commerce servers, and application servers. You have the option to use this card for a firewall or a VPN.

- *Web Protector-100*—Designed for network content providers, Web servers, managed services providers, application service providers, and ISP hosting or collocation servers. This card provides address translation (NAT), a high throughput firewall, protection against DoS, and protection against internal and external attacks against your network, to name a few features.

Galea Secured Networks, Inc.
602 Cure-Boivin
Boisbriand, Quebec, Canada J7G 2A7
(866) 979-8844
E-mail: pferron@galeasec.com
URL: http://galeasec.com/Welcome.html

Microsoft Internet Security and Acceleration (ISA) Server 2000

ISA has two editions— Server Standard Edition and Server Enterprise Edition. Microsoft recommends the Standard Edition for a stand-alone server supporting a maximum of four processors. The Enterprise Edition is for use with large-scale deployments, computers with more than four processors, server array support, and for multi-level policy.

ISA includes packet-level, circuit-level, and application-level screening. It also includes stateful inspection, integrated virtual private networking (VPN), integrated intrusion detection, and advanced authentication.

Microsoft Corporation
One Microsoft Way
Redmond, WA 98052
(800) 426-9400
URL: http://www.microsoft.com/isaserver/

SecureWay Firewall

SecureWay Firewall contains three firewall architectures—filtering, proxy, and application gateway. This product includes VPN support based on IPSec, disables unsafe applications running on your network, provides central management and configuration for multiple firewalls, and its Network Security Auditor scans the firewalls and other hosts on your network to find potential security exposures.

> International Business Machines Corporation
> New Orchard Road
> Armonk, NY 10504
> (888) SHOP-IBM
> E-mail: ibm_direct@vnet.ibm.com
> URL: http://www-4.ibm.com/software/security/firewall/

SonicWALL Pro-VX

The SonicWALL Pro-VX appliance firewall protects large geographically distributed networks, intranets, and single-site networks. SonicWall supports up to 1,000 branch offices or remote users. Its VPN is based on IPSec standards that make it compatible with other products, such as Check Point Firewall-1 and Cisco PIX.

> SonicWALL, Inc.
> 1160 Bordeaux Drive
> Sunnyvale, CA 94301
> (408) 745-9600
> E-mail: info@sonicwall.com
> URL: http://www.sonicwall.com

Personal Firewalls

Personal firewalls are firewalls designed largely for personal use or for protecting a single host from attack. This section discusses some of the more popular ones available.

LockDown Millennium

LockDown Millennium provides several features. You can use the Port Monitor to monitor specific ports or all 65,535 ports. The Connection Monitor shows every connection being made to your computer. The Process Monitor displays every program running on your computer, the complete program path, every DDL file and module used by a program, and identifies whether or not a program is capable of using the Internet. The Process Monitor also enables you to click a listed program to perform a clean kill of that program. The Trojan Scanner scans for Trojan files on your drives, automatically scans changes made to your folders, and scans for processes that start up on your computer.

LockDown Corp.
44P Dover Point Office Pk
Dover Point Rd.
Dover, NH 03820
603-740-4590
E-mail: support@lockdowncorp.com
URL: http://www.lockdown2000.com/

Norton Personal Firewall

Norton Personal Firewall monitors Internet connections to and from your computer. It alerts you to attempted intrusions, such as port scans, and automatically blocks any system that is trying to probe your machine. Personal Firewall also prevents personal data from being sent to Web sites without your knowledge.

Symantec Corporation
20330 Stevens Creek Blvd.
Cupertino, CA 95014
(408) 517-8000
E-mail: http://www.symantec.com/feedback/problem.html
URL: www.symantec.com

Sygate Personal Firewall

Sygate Personal Firewall is a bi-directional firewall, meaning that your computer is protected from malicious intruders, and it also prevents unauthorized access from your computer to a network. If an intruder attempts to gain access to your computer, Sygate Personal Firewall detects that attempt and blocks it, by default. A notification then is sent to you asking for your approval to adjust your Internet connection to prohibit further attacks. You also are notified when an unauthorized application running on your computer is trying to contact the Internet and it is blocked until you give your approval. The program is shut down if you don't give your approval for the application to access the Internet. This firewall is free for personal use. Businesses are required to purchase the software.

Sygate Technologies, Inc.
6595 Dumbarton Circle
Fremont, CA 94555
(510) 742-2600
E-mail: sales@sygate.com
URL: http://www.sygate.com/

Tiny Personal Firewall

Tiny Personal Firewall provides a number of features, including determining which applications are permitted or denied Internet access and reporting specific intrusion attempts and other types of suspicious activity. This firewall is free for personal use. Businesses are required to purchase the software.

> Tiny Software
> 3945 Freedom Circle, Suite 1020
> Santa Clara, CA 95054
> 888-994-TINY
> E-mail: sales@tinysoftware.com
> URL: http://www.tinysoftware.com/

ZoneAlarm 2.1

ZoneAlarm Pro provides home users and small businesses with firewall protection. ZoneAlarm includes a component called MailSafe. MailSafe is designed to protect you from malicious code such as the ILOVEYOU VBS script. When MailSafe detects a VBS script attempting to make a connection through Outlook, it alerts the user and prompts for acceptance or denial of the action. ZoneAlarm has a number of configurable features, such as setting how stringent you want your security settings to be, and configuring ZoneAlarm to determine which applications on your system are permitted or denied Internet or network access. Best of all, it's free for personal and non-profit use. Businesses must pay a small fee if they want to continue to use it after 60 days.

> Zone Labs Inc.
> U.S. Headquarters
> 1060 Howard Street
> San Francisco, CA 94103
> 415-341-8200
> E-mail: sales@zonelabs.com
> URL: www.zonelabs.com

Further Reading on Firewalls

Building Internet Firewalls (2nd Edition). Elizabeth D. Zwicky, Simon Cooper, D. Brent Chapman. O'Reilly & Associates. ISBN: 1565928717. 2000.

Firewalls and Internet Security. William R. Cheswick, Steven M. Bellovin. Addison-Wesley Pub Co. ISBN: 0201633574. 1994.

Hacking Exposed, 2nd Edition. Joel Scambray, Stuart McClure, George Kurtz. McGraw-Hill Professional Publishing. ISBN: 0072127481. 2000.

Firewalls 24seven. Matthew Strebe, Charles L. Perkin. Sybex, Inc. ISBN: 0782125298. 1999.

Practical Firewalls (Practical). Terry William Ogletree. Que. ISBN: 0789724162. 2000.

Firewalls and Internet Security : Repelling the Wily Hacker (Addison-Wesley Professional Computing Series). William R. Cheswick, Steven M. Bellovin. Addison-Wesley Pub Co. ISBN: 020163466X. 2001.

Microsoft ISA Configuration & Administration. Curt Simmons. Hungry Minds, Inc. ISBN: 0764548050. 2001.

Configuring ISA Server 2000: Building Firewalls for Windows 2000. Tom Shinder. Syngress Media Inc. ISBN: 1928994296. 2001.

Protecting Your Web Site With Firewalls. Marcus Goncalves, Vinicius A. Goncalves. Prentice Hall. ISBN: 0136282075. 1997.

Intrusion Detection: Network Security Beyond the Firewall. Terry Escamilla. John Wiley & Sons. ISBN: 0471290009. 1998.

Firewalls: A Complete Guide. Marcus Goncalves(Editor). Computing McGraw-Hill. ISBN: 0071356398. 1999.

Summary

A firewall can provide substantial security from external attack, but that doesn't make it a cure-all. You should guard against the temptation to rely on your firewall alone. Instead, choose your firewall carefully, learn it well, and try viewing it as just one major component in your overall security architecture. By taking these steps, you'll reap the maximum benefits that firewalls have to offer.

Denial of Service

IN THIS CHAPTER

Overview and Goals

The goal of this chapter is to distribute information about denial of service attacks and distributed denial of service attacks. The term DoS will be used in this chapter to refer to both denial of service attacks and distributed denial of service attacks from this point forward. As we become a more Internet-centric society, DoS attacks become more of a concern. Using voice and video over the Internet for live video conferences and telephone conversations is just in its infancy. Imagine the impact of a large denial of service attack on a backbone provider when large percentages of telephone conversations are routed through the Internet. Or worse yet, imagine the impact if a doctor is performing a complex surgery through a video conference over the Internet when a denial of service attack is launched.

Many readers have seen and read the security bulletins about how products that they own can be susceptible to denial of service attacks. However, the bulletins do not explain what a denial of service attack is and how it might be launched. This chapter attempts to define DoS attacks and will provide some examples of previous attacks and tips on how administrators can protect their networks from being victims of a denial of service or distributed denial of service attack.

Understanding Denial of Service Attacks

The following few sections provide some background information regarding denial of service attacks, such as their purpose, perpetrators, and victims. The most important concept in this section is that everyone is a victim when a denial of service attack occurs. Many organizations have taken a "not me" type of approach regarding DoS attacks and Internet security in general. The truth is that everyone has the potential of being exploited by a denial of service attack. This includes enterprises, universities, and even home users connected through broadband connections. When troubleshooting denial of service attacks, administrators need to remember that the source network of the traffic is another victim in the attack. The assistance of the administrators from the source networks will also be required to stop the attack.

What Is the Purpose of Denial of Service Attacks?

DoSattacks are used to disrupt access to any single network service, server, or the entire network. DoS attacks are initiated by an attacker manipulating the normal transfer of information on the network or by overloading the system's resources by exploiting known defects in operating systems. This can force routers to drop packets or force applications and operating systems to overrun buffers and shut down. The goal is to prevent legitimate users from using the system and its services or to take the victim's entire system offline. Examples of DoS attacks include the following:

- Flooding a network with traffic
- Disrupting service to a person or machine
- Disrupt communication between two machines
- Preventing individuals from accessing services

DoS attacks can also be used as a component in a larger attack. DoS attacks can be chained together to form distributed denial of service attacks, or they can be used as a diversion for another attack. For example, an attacker could use a denial of service attack to fill log files to cover his or her tracks after a system has been compromised.

Who and What Are Vulnerable to Denial of Service Attacks?

DoS attacks are not limited to the Windows platform. Every system and every service on the network is vulnerable to a denial of service attack—including the network itself. The most common denial of service attacks involve denying network services to users by generating TCP/IP traffic or by manipulating the source address of packets to redirect traffic to the victim of the attack. The most common targets are Internet routers, firewalls, and DNS servers. If the routers and DNS systems that support an enterprise are overloaded, users cannot access the services provided by other components, such as operating systems and applications.

This does not mean that the organization's servers are exempt from denial of service attacks. Operating systems and application servers such as FTP, HTTP, and SMTP servers can also be a target in a denial of service attack. An attacker could attempt to overload these application servers to exploit a known defect and cripple or shut down the server. Another common scenario would be to involve the application server as an agent in a denial of service attack to either generate traffic or redirect traffic to a victim network.

Internet Service Providers (ISPs) were a common target of early denial of service attacks, due to the quantity of ISPs and the lack of administration and security experience at lower-tier ISPs. Since early in 2000, many institutions of the Internet economy have found themselves the victims of denial of service attacks, including eBay and Yahoo.

In 1999 and 2000, many new potential victims of DoS attacks were introduced to the Internet. Cable modems and DSL connections have become commonplace. This is problematic and has increased the availability of machines to be used as distributed denial of service attack agents due to the lack of security knowledge of the average broadband user. Personal firewall applications and devices are available, but most home users either don't purchase them or don't configure them correctly. Most users throw their systems right out on the Internet where they can be probed and compromised 24/7.

NOTE

Average users are not the only ones with security problems. While writing this chapter, I met a few computer industry pros who were recent victims of sadmind. Sadmind first exploited the sadmind daemon on Solaris and then sought out IIS systems that it could infect. Sadmind is unique because it was the first cross-platform worm. The compromised IIS servers were un-patched and non-hardened installations of Windows NT 4.0 and Windows 2000 Web servers that were on the public Internet. Sadmind exploited a vulnerability in Internet Information Server (IIS) that allowed a file to be executed by the operating system. The security bulletin posted by Microsoft discussing the vulnerability can be found at `http://www.microsoft.com/technet/treeview/default.asp?url=/technet/security/bulletin/MS01-026.asp`. The batch file used in sadmind then manufactured HTML files and replaced the IIS server's default Web site's home page as well as other compromises. For more information on the sadmind attack, visit `http://www.antivirus.com/vinfo/virusencyclo/default5.asp?VName=PERL_SADMIND.A&VSect=T`.

Who Commits Denial of Service Attacks?

There has been some controversy on whether a perpetrator of a denial of service attack can really be considered a hacker. Many people feel denials of service are nuisances and are low-level or unintelligent attacks. Old school hackers refer to those who commit DoS attacks as "script kiddies" and "packet monkeys." Perpetrators of DoS attacks have fallen into the same category of the authors of e-mail–based viruses that exploit VBScript files. Preying on a weakness in a product or transport technology with tools that someone else has written is considered unsophisticated by older hackers.

For private businesses, this attitude is starting to change with the recent, well-orchestrated distributed DoS attacks launched the week of February 7, 2000 and, more recently, the Code Red worm (see `http://www.cert.org/advisories/CA-2001-19.html`) in July of 2001. These attacks prove that one attacker can posses thousands of DDOS agents under their control, and the results in lost productivity and revenue can be extremely costly. These agents can severely cripple many of the institutions of government and e-commerce within a few hours and make headline news.

NOTE

The Code Red worm exploited a defect Internet Information Server (IIS) that would replace the system's home page and launch a distributed denial of service attack against the Whitehouse's Web site. A second worm, using the same vulnerability as Code Red, named

Code Red II would also attempt to install a back door remote control program on Windows 2000 IIS servers. Code Red's activity changed depending on the date. At times, it propagated itself to other systems, and at other times, it launched a denial of service attack. Code Red became infamous because of the rate at which the virus would spread. For a full analysis of Code Red, see the following links at eEye Digital Security:

- Code Red—`http://www.eeye.com/html/Research/Advisories/AL20010717.html`

- *Code Red II*—`http://www.eeye.com/html/Research/Advisories/AL20010804. html`

There is no single answer why perpetrators want to deny service. They can be motivated by the desire for attention, notoriety, vengeance, grievances, curiosity, and political agendas, such as anti-globalization and human rights. The following link is to an article entitled "Why Do We Hack?" by Hex Edit that will give the reader an opportunity to develop their own opinions on hacking: `http://www.wiretrip.net/rfp/p/doc.asp?id=9&iface=2`. Spending some time at `www.wiretrip.net`, `www.2600.com`, `www.cultdeadcow.com`, and `www.phrack.org` is a worthwhile experience that can provide the reader some additional insight into hacker lifestyles.

Terminology

The terminology section is meant to be a quick overview of the concepts and terms that are used when discussing DoS attacks. Some of the terms have the same meaning, so this section will hopefully avoid some confusion for the reader.

- *Denial of service attack*—An attack on a system that prevents a legitimate user from using the system or the services it provides.

- *Distributed denial of service attack*—The coordinated use of multiple machines in different locations to generate a denial of service attack. By launching the attack from multiple locations, the magnitude of the attack is amplified and harder to trace. Victims will also have a harder time recovering from the attack. See Figure 17.1 for a sample DDOS communication scenario.

- *Handler*—Software components installed on a compromised system by an attacker that are used to locate and compromise additional machines and install DDOS agents (see next bullet) through automated processes. The attacker can use the handler to configure and launch a distributed denial of service attack on command. The handler is also known as the *master*.

- *Agent*—A software component installed on a compromised system by the handler that generates the traffic to attack the victim during a distributed denial of service attack. Agents are also known as *zombies* or *drones* and are usually installed through a Trojan.

- *IP Spoofing*—The process of manufacturing packets with a stolen IP address used to fool packet-filtering–based systems into passing unauthorized traffic. Some routers might route a packet if the source address is from a directly-connected interface. It's common for attackers to spoof addresses that are on the inside of the firewall or spoof the private address ranges described in RFC 1918 to conduct their attack. The TCP/IP address ranges defined in RFC 1918 are as follows:

  - 10.0.0.0
  - 172.16.0.0
  - 192.168.0.0

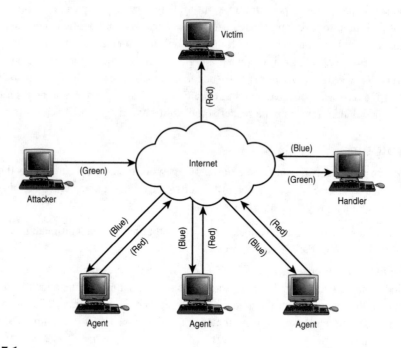

FIGURE 17.1
Distributed denial of service attack communication.

Modes of Attack

The modes of attack used by DoS attacks can be classified into three major categories as defined by CERT (www.cert.org):

- *Consumption of resources—either scarce, limited, or non-renewable*—These are the most common targets in denial of service attacks, and the target resources include network bandwidth, CPU, memory, disk space, data sources, and environmental factors, such as temperature and humidity.

- *Destruction or modification of configuration information*—Reconfiguring a router or modifying a server's Registry or configuration files would constitute this type of DOS attack. Strong passwords and administrative policies can help prevent these types of attacks.

- *Physical destruction or alterations of network components*—Unplugging components, recabling, or smashing components are examples of these types of DOS attacks. Physically securing network equipment can prevent these types of attacks.

The most commonly used method of attack is to deny service through the consumption of resources. CERT defines four additional subcategories to classify DoS attacks that use the consumption of resources mode of attack. The subcategories for the consumption of resources category are discussed in the following sections.

Network Connectivity

Some of the most common DoS attacks attempt to impair network connectivity. These attacks force a device to open a bogus TCP/IP connection. The system then must manage the connection until the connection times out. Because a system can only manage a finite number of connections at a given time, the bogus connections could consume the resources that would otherwise be available to legitimate users. Common attacks that exploit network connectivity are SYN Flooding and Land attacks. Both SYN and Land attacks are covered more in depth in the following section of this chapter.

Using Your Own Resources Against You

When attackers use your own resources against you, they can force two or more devices on your network to send bogus data to each other or to other servers on the network. The result is that the devices sending and receiving the traffic are impaired. A secondary result is that the devices on the same network are also impaired due to the increased traffic. UDP flood attacks are common attacks in this class. UDP flood attacks are discussed in more depth in the following sections of this chapter.

Bandwidth Consumption

Attackers can consume bandwidth by directing unwanted traffic to the victim network. This generally requires multiple agents to generate enough traffic to impair performance. SMURF attacks are common attacks used to consume bandwidth. See the following section for information on SMURF attacks and how to prevent them.

Consumption of Other Resources

Consumption of other resources includes malicious code programs that consume CPU cycles and disk space by creating copies of itself or launching multiple versions of itself into memory. These processes then compete with legitimate processes for CPU cycles and disk access. An example of this application would be anything that filled up the anonymous area of an FTP server, or an application that generates errors that continually fill up log files.

Attackers can also deny access to resources by triggering user account lockout controls by logging on with incorrect passwords. All a user needs to do is understand the company's naming convention for user accounts and have access to a list of employees. After an attacker has this information, a script can be created to log on with a bogus password to force the account lockout.

DOS Attacks and Prevention

The following sections of this chapter cover some well-known denial of service attack strategies. Administrators should investigate these DOS strategies to see if their networks are vulnerable to attack. Most of these strategies are aimed at networking devices, such as routers and firewalls. Many administrators that run an entire network might not have implemented the filters on their internetworking devices that are included in this section. Most large organizations with dedicated internetworking and information security groups have already implemented filters and alerts against these DOS attacks.

Ping of Death

The ping of death attack used the vulnerability of some TCP/IP implementations handling over oversize packets. The maximum TCP/IP packet size is 65536 bytes. During the mid 1990s, DoS attacks could be generated by sending `ping` packets greater than 65536 bytes to a destination host. The large packets could trigger unpredictable results, such as system lockups and reboots. Ping of Death is no longer a concern for administrators unless they have old or unpatched versions of operating systems still on their networks.

Teardrop

The teardrop attack was common as late as 1999. Both Windows NT 3.51 and Windows NT 4.0 service pack 3 could be susceptible to teardrop attacks and variations of the teardrop attack. The teardrop attack relies on a failure in the fragmentation and reassembly process in TCP/IP stacks. TCP/IP uses fragmentation and reassembly to transmit packets efficiently over different media types. When a packet is larger than the maximum transfer unit (MTU) of a particular media, it must be fragmented to be transmitted across the network.

Teardrop attacks manipulate the reassembly process of fragmented packets. Some attacks use overlapping offset fields that can cause systems to freeze when the packets are reassembled. Other attacks attempt to overwrite the header in the first packet to manipulate the TCP port number to get an unauthorized connection through the firewall. Most teardrop attack vulnerabilities have been corrected in recent operating system releases, but administrators should verify that an older operating system version on their network has been patched.

SYN Flooding and Land Attacks

SYN flooding attacks exploit the method that TCP/IP stacks use to establish a connection. TCP/IP stacks use what is known as the *three-way handshake* to establish connections. The steps to establish connectivity through the three-way handshake is as follows:

1. The client sends a SYN request to the server.
2. The server responds with a SYN/ACK that acknowledges the clients SYN with an ACK and returns a SYN.
3. The client responds with an ACK to the servers SYN.
4. Connection established.

During a SYN flooding attack, the client does not return the final ACK, as shown in Figure 17.2. The server will then wait for the client's ACK until the timeout value for the connection has expired. The server reserves the connection for the client until the session times out. This leaves one less connection available to legitimate clients and is known as a *half-open connection*.

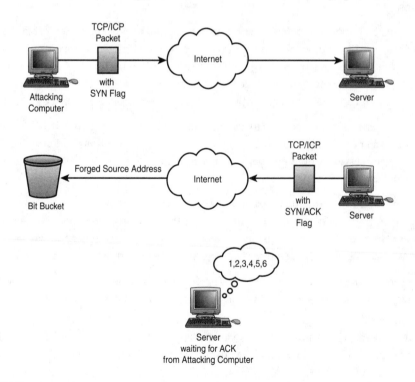

Figure 17.2
SYN attack communication.

When the server is continually hit with half-open connections, the maximum number of connections are filled, and the server begins rejecting new connections. To perform this attack, the attacker sends requests for new connections faster than the server can timeout the half-open connections. This leaves the server in a state where it is rejecting new connections until the server crashes or the attack is stopped.

Attackers almost always use a spoofed source address on the packet that initiates the connection. This prevents the attack from being traced to the original source. The spoofed address can be one of the private address ranges specified in RFC 1918 or a legitimate IP unused address.

Completely preventing these attacks is not possible. However, administrators can lessen the impact of the attack by filtering traffic at the border routers of the network. Filtering packets entering the network from private addresses (as defined by RFC 1918), broadcast addresses, and those that match internal network addresses is the first step. Additionally, internal routers should not let traffic leave the local networks if the source address in not known to the organization to prevent attacks from being launched against other companies from inside the company's firewall.

Many firewalls and routers now have a configuration option to prevent TCP SYN attacks. The router or firewall will validate the connection request by handling the request from the client and then merging the connections. This feature is called *TCP intercept* on Cisco products. Refer to `http://www.cisco.com/univercd/cc/td/doc/product/software/ios113ed/113ed_cr/secur_c/scprt3/scdenial.htm` for configuration information on TCP intercept.

Monitoring server connection states can also help determine when an attack is being launched. The `netstat -an` command can be used to view the current connections and open TCP and UDP ports on the server. A high number of connections with `SYN_RECEIVED` status might indicate a DOS attack is taking place against the server.

Other options for minimizing the impacts of SYN attacks include increasing the size of the connection queue and reducing the timeout value for the ACK from the client. To reduce the timeout values for ACKs, administrators can use the following Registry values in `HKEY_LOCAL_MACHINE MACHINE\System\CurrentControlSet\Services\Tcpip\Parameters`:

- *SynAttackProtect*—Set this value to 2. The default is 0. This will reduce the time the system waits for the ACK from the client that originates the SYN request.

- *TcpMaxHalfOpen*—Sets the number of connections in a half open state before the `SynAttackProtect` is initiated. This value is a `REG_DWORD` with a range of 100–0xFFFF. The default is 100 for Server and 500 for Advanced Server. Tune these values based on the number of connections you expect.

The Land attack is similar to a SYN attack with the exception that the attacker uses the target system address as both the destination and the source address. Most operating systems have been patched to not respond to Land attacks. To ensure they will not respond, use ingress filters on routers to prevent traffic entering the network with source addresses on the inside router interface. For more information on Land attacks, refer to the following article: `http://support.microsoft.com/support/kb/articles/Q177/5/39.ASP`.

SMURF Attacks

SMURF attacks use the ICMP protocol to direct traffic to the intended victim network to deny service. ICMP is the protocol that is used by TCP/IP to handle errors and exchange control messages. The ICMP protocol is used by the ping utility, as well as other networking functions. The ping utility sends an ICMP echo request to the target system, and the target system then responds with an echo reply. To initiate a SMURF attack, the attacker exploits the fact that the ICMP protocol is always expected to send an echo reply after an echo request. There is nothing in the specifications for ICMP that states a reply must have a request. So by "thinking out of the box" and looking at ICMP specifications, attackers were able to develop an effective denial of service attack in a new way.

The following are the steps that take place in launching a SMURF attack. A sample Smurf attack is also shown in Figure 17.3

1. The attacker selects a victim and spoofs the IP address of the device he or she will attack.

2. The attacker sends an ICMP echo request to an intermediary system's broadcast address. The source address for the ICMP echo request is the target victim's server or routers.

3. Because the request is sent to a broadcast address, all systems on the intermediary network receive the request.

4. All devices on the intermediary network then respond to the ICMP echo request with an echo reply.

5. The victim receives the unsolicited ICMP echo replies from every system on the intermediary host's subnet.

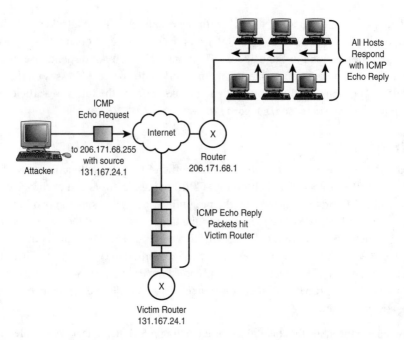

FIGURE 17.3
The SMURF attack.

To minimize the impact of SMURF attacks, organizations should disable IP-directed broadcasts on their border and internal routers. This will prevent a flood of ICMP echo request packets from reaching hosts that will then generate the flood of echo replies directed at the victim device. This doesn't mean that the attacker could not send the echo request to a single device to redirect the traffic at the victim. An attacker could send the echo request directly to the IP addresses of intermediary hosts. Blocking the directed broadcast will not prevent the SMURF attack, but it will make initiating the attack more time consuming for an attacker. Completely shutting down the possibility of SMURF attacks means closing off ICMP all together.

For more information on preventing SMURF attacks, securing Cisco routers, blocking ports, and shutting down ICMP, refer to the following links:

- *Blocking ports and shutting down ICMP on Cisco IOS 12 routers*
  `http://www.sans.org/infosecFAQ/firewall/blocking_cisco.htm`

- *Preventing SMURF attacks and securing Cisco routers*
  `http://www.cisco.com/warp/public/707/21.html`

UDP Flood

UDP flood attacks can come in various forms. The original variation of the attack exploited the Chargen UDP service that generates a series of characters to another server's echo service for diagnostic testing. Unix administrators should disable the daemon on public servers or filter access to the Chargen port from outside their networks. Windows systems do not have a Chargen service installed, so Windows 2000 administrators do not have to be concerned about an attack on this service.

Newer versions of UDP flood attacks leverage DNS servers. A DNS server response to a name query is much larger than the request. Attackers using the spoofed IP address of the victim can send bogus DNS name queries to unsuspecting DNS servers that will then flood the victim's network with the DNS responses. By distributing this attack against many name servers, the number of responses hitting the victims network is amplified. To avoid being the intermediary in the attack, DNS administrators can configure access restrictions on who can query the name server. Without access restrictions, the server might not log the bogus requests.

Many of the distributed denial of service attack tools can use UDP flooding to initiate their attacks. For example, the distributed denial of service attack tool Trinoo can send random UDP packets to its victim between the port ranges of 0–65534. Administrators should review the open UDP ports on their networks for the possibility of attacks on these ports. Refer to the "Distributed Denial of Service Attack Tools" section in the following section of this chapter for a discussion on the DDOS tools that can leverage UDP flooding techniques.

Infamous Denial of Service Attacks

The week of February 7, 2000, many major sites, such as Charles Schwab, eBay, and Yahoo were hit by extremely powerful denial of service attacks. Microsoft was also hit in January of 2001. This section provides a look at each of these attacks and the methods used in them. All of these attacks used distributed denial of service attack methods and tools. The public details of the attacks that are known have been included for each attack.

Distributed Denial of Service Attack Tools

The following list is a quick overview of the distributed denial of service attack tools that have been discovered in attacks over the past few years. Administrators can use the `netstat -an` command to check if their systems are listening on the known ports used by DDOS agents to discover if an attacker has compromised the system.

- *Trinoo*—Runs on multiple Unix flavors. Installs through a buffer overrun that gives the attacker root access. Floods victim networks with UDP packets. Trinoo communicates on TCP ports 27665, UDP 27444, and UDP 31335.

- *Wintrinoo*—The windows version of Trinoo. Installs an .exe called service.exe that is 23KB in size. Wintrinoo calls service.exe through the HKEY_LOCAL_MACHINE/ SOFTWARE/Microsoft/Windows/CurrentVersion/Run Registry key. Wintrinoo listens on port UDP 34555 and communicates on UDP port 35555. It is most often installed through a Trojan in e-mail and is found on systems also infected with Back Orifice.

- *The Tribe Flood Network (TFN)*—TFN can launch SYN, UDP flood, ICMP flood, and SMURF attacks. TFN communicates between the handler and agents through ICMP echo and reply packets that make detecting its presence difficult.

- *Stacheldraht*—Provides similar attack capabilities as Trinoo and TFN, but also allows for automated agent updates and encrypted attacks to master communication. Communicates over TCP 16660, TCP 65000, and ICMP Echo reply.

- *Trinity*—Similar attack methods as previous tools but adds additional attacks, such as RST and ACK floods. Trinity communications take place over IRC or ICQ. Trinity primarily uses TCP port 6667 but can also listen on TCP 33270.

- *Shaft*—Similar to Trinoo but assigns a unique sequence number to all TCP packets— 0x28374839. Communicates over TCP 20432, UDP 18753, and UDP 20433.

- *Tribe Flood Network 2K (TFN2K)*—Same attack modes as the original TFN and was also able to launch Land and teardrop attacks to exploit known vulnerabilities. Designed to be harder to locate the source of the attack by IP address spoofing. It can communicate over TCP, UDP, and ICMP. Visit the author of TFN at http://mixter.void.ru/.

The First-Known Distributed Denial of Service Attack

The first well-known distributed denial of service attack was launched against the University of Minnesota in 1999. The attack was executed by flooding servers with UDP packets for two days. The attack involved thousands of agents whose source addresses were not spoofed. Buffer over run bugs in the RPC services in Solaris 2.x machines were exploited to install Trinoo. As source networks were contacted to shut down traffic from their networks, that attacker was installing more agents.

Taking out the Internet Economy Institutions

The week of February 7, 2000 will remain fresh in the minds of information security professionals for a long time to come. On February 7, 2000, Yahoo's Internet portal was hit with a distributed denial service attack that took their Internet portal offline for at least three hours. This brief outage is estimated to have cost Yahoo about $500,000 in lost revenue in sales and advertising.

The following day, Amazon, Buy.com, CNN, and eBay were all attacked with a distributed denial of service attack. Amazon was down for approximately ten hours with a revenue loss of about $600,000. Buy.com and CNN were left with about 5–10 percent of normal network capacity.

On February 9, 2000 E*trade, Schwab.com, and ZDNet were hit with a distributed denial of service attack. Charles Schwab's losses from the attack were kept confidential. E*Trade and ZDNet were totally unavailable during the attack.

A 16-year-old Canadian boy, know by the handle Mafiaboy, was charged with the attacks and plead guilty in January, 2001. Articles at SANS claim Stacheldraht was used to launch the attacks during the week of February 7, 2000. A hacker from Germany who authored TFN, known as Mixter, stated in an interview that he believed that the attack was launched with a program based on Trinoo or TFN. Stacheldraht is a variant of TFN. Another German hacker, Randomizer, wrote the Stacheldraht DDOS attack utility, according to Mixter. For a full analysis of the internals of Stacheldraht and other DDOS issues, review the information maintained by David Dittrich available at `http://staff.washington.edu/dittrich/misc/ddos/`.

Microsoft Gets Attacked

Microsoft's Web servers were attacked January 25, 2001. The denial of service attack followed a 23-hour outage that prevented users from accessing Microsoft's Web sites. The Web site outage was caused by a mis-configuration by a Microsoft technician. The denial of service attack targeted Microsoft's Internet routers. It was made public several weeks prior to the denial of service attack that Microsoft had some mis-configurations in their DNS infrastructure. Microsoft had the same IP address listed as their primary and secondary DNS servers, which violates good DNS design practices. Microsoft's four DNS servers were all located on the same network segment behind a single router. Attackers targeted the Internet router in front of the DNS servers during the denial of service attack.

Very few details were released about the Microsoft outage and follow-up denial of service attack. Microsoft has outsourced and distributed portions of its DNS infrastructure since the attack. What has been learned from the attack is the importance of DNS to an organization's infrastructure. Refer to RFC 2182 on the configuration and selection of secondary DNS servers available at `http://www.dns.net/dnsrd/rfc/rfc2182.html#4.Unreachableservers`. The outage showed that even an organization with as many technically competent people as Microsoft can still make mistakes. Placing the only four DNS servers behind a single router in the same location left them with a single point of failure and a primary target for a denial of service attack.

Protecting Windows 2000 Networks Against Denial of Service Attacks

Protecting Windows 2000 networks from denial of service attacks is primarily done at the network level. Total elimination of DoS attacks is not possible, although there are many steps an administrator can take to limit the impact of a denial of service attack. Most organizations will never be the victim of a denial of service attack. However, the likelihood that attackers will attempt to use your organization's systems as an intermediary or an agent to conduct an attack on another network is quite high. The following sections discuss the areas administrators should focus on to protect their networks from being involved in a denial of service attack.

Use Firewalls

The first line of defense is to implement a firewall. This is true for both remote telecommuters with DSL or cable modems and corporate locations. Firewalls vary in functionality and price. There are also hardware-based firewalls and software-based firewalls. Firewall technologies can be defined through the following terms:

- *Packet filtering*—Monitors the source and destination addresses and source and destination ports of packets. Does not check the contents of the packet. Packet filtering can be bypassed by spoofing an IP address from the other side of the filter.
- *Application gateways*—Connections are made directly to the firewall, and the firewall proxies the communication to the destination host. This allows for inspection of packet contents, protocol filtering, and logging.
- *Circuit-level gateways*—The firewall application copies the bytes from one side to the other, but it does not proxy the communications. A circuit-level gateway is less seamless to the end user than an application gateway because it only monitors the traffic.
- *State-full inspection*—These firewalls check and validate content, translate addresses, authenticate connections, keep a connection state table, and monitor the state of the connections. Modern state-full inspection firewalls are hybrids that combine the best of packet filtering and application proxy technologies. For more information on state-full inspection firewalls, refer to
  `http://www.sans.org/infosecFAQ/firewall/anatomy.htm`.

For corporate firewalls, there are many choices on the market, with some of the more popular firewalls being Microsoft ISA Server, Cisco PIX, and CheckPoint Firewall 1. All three of these firewalls provide state-full packet inspection capabilities that can provide the highest level of security in a firewall.

For home users, software-based personal firewall packages exist from some of the major antivirus vendors, including Symantec and McAfee, as well as other utilities, such as BlackIce

Defender available at www.networkice.com and ZoneAlarm available at www.zonealarm.com. Many of the software-based personal firewalls come pre-configured with a list of open ports for ease of use. Personal firewalls are still new technology and are still maturing. They provide the lowest cost of entry but are more vulnerable than hardware-based solutions. The software-based personal firewall packages employ both packet filter technology and application gateway technology.

Hardware-based firewall solutions also exist from vendors such as LinkSys (www.linksys.com) and Netgear (www.netgear.com). The low-end firewalls just mentioned rely on packet filtering technology through Network Address Translation (NAT) to protect the home user. The hardware-based firewall physically separates the home users machine from the Internet and provides a bit higher security with a cost of about $150. In the $300–$500 range, solutions from 3Com and Netgear can provide protection from known DDOS attacks such as SYN, Land, Bonk, and so on, in addition to the NAT capabilities. The hardware-based personal firewall packages employ packet filter technology and address translation at the lower end with the higher-end products adding application gateway technology.

State-full packet inspection technologies can also be implemented to protect the home user through solutions from 3Com and Cisco but at a substantially higher cost—typically $2,000–$5000. These solutions are most often seen in small office or remote office environments. Solutions in this category are the Cisco 1700 series routers with Firewall IOS and 3Com's Super Stack III firewall.

The filtering on the firewall should not allow the private addresses (as defined in RFC 1918) to enter or leave the network.

Firewall filtering should also be configured so it will not pass an internal address from the outside interface to the inside network. Most firewalls will detect an IP spoof and drop packets that have a source address on the wrong interface, but administrators should test the firewall configuration before putting the firewall in production. Try passing traffic through the firewall from the outside to the inside with a source address from inside the network. Review the contents of the firewall log to determine how the firewall logs the attempt to spoof an inside IP address.

Also, plan on testing your firewall configuration. There are several sites that will provide a free port scan of your firewall. Shields Up (available at www.grc.com) will scan the basic ten ports, such as HTTP, FTP, and SMTP, and so on. DSLReports.com will provide a free port scan scanning 2086 ports, including the 1024 well-known ports. A full scan that performs additional vulnerability checks can be purchased at the site. DSLReports.com offers the service for a one-week license so administrators can use it to test their configurations as they are building their firewalls. Visit www.dslreports.com for more information.

17

DENIAL OF SERVICE

Harden Servers Accessible to the Public

Any server that is publicly accessible needs to be hardened to prevent intrusion. If a server is accessible to the public, it should be secured behind the firewall located on a DMZ network. Just because the server is behind the firewall doesn't mean that the operating system should not be hardened. Hardening the operating system will provide another layer of protection.

Some organizations choose to place the servers inside their networks instead of placing them on the DMZ. The choice in placement of the server depends on the organization's acceptance of risk, the additional services the server might provide, the resources the server needs to access, network complexity, and cost. When servers are on an inside network, it becomes more difficult to harden the operating system, because both inside users and outside users are generally accessing the system. One rule to follow is if the server does not need access to any internal services, it should be isolated on the DMZ. Some organizations also choose to place their servers directly on the Internet. With firewall technology being very affordable, there aren't many situations where this is a good idea.

If a server can be compromised, it can be used to house agents or handlers used in denial of service attacks. Microsoft has always developed their operating systems to be as open as possible when they're first installed. It only takes about four hours at most for the average administrator to configure a fully-functional Windows 2000 system for use on an internal network. On the other hand, Unix and Linux systems generally take much longer to configure. This is because a Unix and Linux system start with everything locked down, and the services are enabled as they are needed.

Windows administrators need to change their thought process when configuring publicly accessible servers. Reading this book is the first step in the right direction. Chapters 13, "Exploiting Web Services," 14, "Protecting Web Services," and 15, "Protecting Other Internet Services," explicitly address exploiting and protecting Web services. Administrators should plan on taking their time when installing a publicly accessible server. The sadmind virus recently showed how poorly configured Web sites could be exploited. If administrators had disabled the default Web site and explicitly used their own site within IIS, sadmind wouldn't have affected their servers.

Administrators should follow a plan when hardening their servers. Consider incorporating the concepts and best practice shown in the following list when hardening the organizations publicly accessible servers:

- Plan for isolation. Don't combine multiple services on the same server. See Chapter 14, "Protecting Web Services," and Chapter 15, "Protecting Other Internet Services," for information on isolating DNS, FTP, Web, and Mail services.

- List the minimum services that need to be provided and work toward that configuration. Refer to Chapter 7, "Windows 2000 Services," for information about Windows 2000 services.

- Disable all services and subsystems not required. Chapters 7, 14, and 15 all discuss disabling services to build secure Windows 2000 installations.

- Configure system policies and administrative access to allow the minimum access necessary. Chapter 12, "Security Policy and Configuration," discusses applying security policies to Windows 2000 systems.

- Plan how to handle logging. Plan how you will monitor and manage the logs.

- Build a test plan for testing the configuration.

- Test the configuration using the same tools an intruder would use. See Chapter 3, "The Hacker Toolkit," for information on tools you can use to secure your systems.

- Catalog the server's files by using an application, such as Tripwire, to perform future file integrity checks. Tripwire is discussed more in depth in Chapter 10, "Trojans and Backdoors."

- Use anti-virus and Trojan tools to protect the server. See Chapter 10 for information on anti-virus tools and strategies.

- Educate management on what you are doing and why you are doing it when you are hardening the server.

- Push back on schedules and mandates that do not provide adequate time to harden and test the server's configuration.

- Backups and contingency plans should also be planned out in advance so the members of the organization know exactly what to do in the event of an attack.

Keep Current on Security Bulletins

Subscribing to list servers and security notifications is a great way to stay up-to-date on the latest vulnerabilities and release patches. Microsoft provides enrollment for security notification services through e-mail at `www.microsoft.com/security`.

It is also important to receive notifications from sources other than the vendor of the product. The vendor has a reputation to maintain, and many of the concerns about security are brought to the vendor's attention through white hat hacking communities on the Internet before the vendor's customers are ever notified. Visit Steve Gibson at `www.grc.com` for breaking commentary on Windows 2000 and Windows XP security issues for an alternative viewpoint. The SANS Institute has an online library dedicated to Windows 2000 that can be found at `www.sans.org`.

Apply Patches

Apply patches and service packs to servers that contain security fixes as soon as possible. Many vulnerabilities are patched a month or two before the vulnerability is exploited in an attack. The sooner the patch can be applied, the safer the system is. Organizations that delay applying patches take the risk that attacks will mutate and get stronger. For example, the weekend after Code Red was discovered, a stronger variant, Code Red II, was created that installed a backdoor when it compromised a system. Those sites that didn't patch their systems early were subject to a stronger strain.

Always follow the vendor's instructions when applying patches. The Code Red patch was overwritten if administrators made configuration changes to the systems and added features or reapplied service packs. Many systems were re-infected with Code Red because administrators did not reapply the patch.

Monitor Resources

Using monitoring, such as CiscoWorks, HP Network Node Manager, and Windows 2000 System Monitor, can help to monitor activity on publicly accessible systems. Administrators should know what traffic levels are normal on their networks so that when abnormal activity occurs, such as a denial of service attack, it is easily spotted. Monitoring products can be used to build a baseline for performance and traffic comparisons. Also considering investing in a software- or hardware-based device that employs Intrusion Detection System (IDS) technology.

Use Redundant Systems

The attack on the Microsoft DNS servers was a good example of how administrators and network architects need to be thinking when they are designing the network. If Microsoft had redundant DNS servers in multiple locations, the effects of the attack would have been minimized. Multiple servers providing the same service behind the same firewall in the same location is not a good idea.

If the organization you are trying to secure lives by its Web presence and network connectivity, it makes sense to invest in redundant systems. Also consider redundancy if you are the administrator for an organization that is considered controversial or takes a hard stand on issues that are in the public eye. Organizations of this type are more likely to be the victims of a denial of service attack. Collocation services for Web and DNS services are worth the $200 a month if a brief outage will cost the organization thousands of dollars.

Summary

Unfortunately, DoS attacks are just another challenge with which administrators will have to deal. The ultimate solution for DoS and other attacks is to have networking equipment that can make intelligent decisions in real-time and adapt to changing conditions on the network as these and other attacks are mounted.

The products on the market today analyze information on the network based on previous attacks. This analysis information is only as good as the latest attack strategy. Unfortunately, this means one of the only defenses is to be reactive when the attack occurs. This means reporting the incident and working with organizations, such as CERT, upstream ISPs, and intermediary networks, to filter the attack traffic when an attack occurs.

The immediate proactive solution is to stay up-to-date on emerging trends and technologies, build a sound security policy, implement filters and configurations that minimize known attack effects, harden servers, utilize logging capabilities, stage attacks on our own systems, add redundancy, and count on the fact that the organization will be an intermediary or a victim at some point in time.

Spoofing

IN THIS CHAPTER

This chapter explains how hackers perform spoofing attacks and steps you can take to prevent them.

Spoofing is a sophisticated form of attack in which one machine authenticates to another by forging packets from a trusted source address. There are a number of different kinds of spoofs that hackers perform, some of which I discuss in this chapter.

General IP Spoofing Attack Concepts

Every packet on a TCP/IP network contains the source system and the destination system IP addresses. An intruder can use the IP address of another system and pretend to be that system to gain access to information that they are not authorized to access, or to launch a denial-of-service (DoS) attack against that system. You do not need to pass the username or the password of the victim machine during the attack. You call this type of attack *IP spoofing*.

Typically, in a communication session between a client and a server, the two machines establish a connection by using Transmission Control Protocol (TCP). They then exchange packets, each of which contains a sequence number. In a common IP spoofing attack, an intruder will impersonate one of the systems involved in the connection by

1. Capturing some of the packets
2. Using the IP address of one of the machines
3. Transmitting his own packets using the same range of sequence numbers

The intruder can, at the same time, initiate a denial-of-service attack against the machine he is impersonating, which results in preventing that machine from transmitting its own packets across the wire. The purpose of Denial of Service (DoS) attacks is to deny the use of the service, usually by crashing or hanging a particular program or the entire system. DoS attacks include:

- Crashing a TCP/IP stack by sending corrupt packets
- Flooding a victim or a service with more traffic than it can handle
- Interacting with a service in an unexpected way, thereby causing it to crash
- Making a system go into an infinite loop, causing it to crash

After the intruder has successfully taken over the role of the victim machine, he can then receive data originally meant for that machine, and can respond with messages of his own. This type of attack can be very damaging to your organization because it not only compromises the integrity of the data transmitted over the network, but it also allows the intruder to access files stored on drives to which he now has access.

Learn more about TCP/IP in Chapter 16, "TCP Filtering and Firewalls."

How Does an Intruder Capture Packets From the Network?

An intruder captures packets from your network by using a packet sniffer. You can think of a packet sniffer as a wire-tapping device that is plugged into your network for the purpose of eavesdropping on your network traffic. An intruder can use an underground packet sniffer to break into your machines. Hackers use a sniffer to

- Convert the data they capture to a readable format so that they can read your network traffic
- Sift clear-text (unencrypted) usernames and passwords from the network so that they can break into systems

Learn more about intrusion detection in Chapter 23, "Intrusion Detection."

TCP SYN Flooding and IP Spoofing Attacks

There are a number of ways that a hacker can perform an IP spoofing attack on your network. Let's take a closer look at one form of attack—using TCP SYN flooding and IP spoofing in conjuction.

A popular form of attack is to conduct denial-of-service attacks on systems connected to the Internet by creating TCP "half-open" connections. Systems at risk are those connected to the Internet that provide TCP-based network services, such as an FTP server, mail server, or Web server. In addition to attacks launched against these types of hosts, hackers can also launch attacks against your routers or other network server systems. This attack doesn't distinguish between hardware platforms, operating systems, or software version levels. All systems are vulnerable.

What Happens During This Type of Attack?

When a client attempts to establish a TCP connection to a server, the client and server exchange a sequence of messages. The client initiates the sequence of messages by sending a SYN (synchronize/start) message to the server. The server acknowledges the client's SYN message by replying with a SYN-ACK (synchronize acknowledge) message. When the client receives this message, it finishes establishing the connection by responding with an ACK (acknowledge) message. After the client and the server have established a connection, the two machines can begin to exchange data. You refer to this exchange of messages as a *TCP three-way handshake*. Figure 18.1 illustrates a TCP three-way handshake.

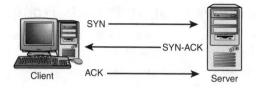

FIGURE 18.1

Sequence of messages sent to establish the client/server connection

The hacker takes advantage of this process at the point where the server has sent the (SYN-ACK) acknowledgement back to the client but has not yet received the final (ACK) message from the client. This is a half-open connection. The server contains a finite table, stored in memory, that describes all pending connections. A hacker can force this table to overflow by intentionally creating more partially open connections than the server can handle.

The hacker accomplishes the creation of half-open connections with IP spoofing. He uses his machine to send SYN messages (approximately 20 TCP SYN messages per second) that appear to be legitimate to the server. However, the SYN messages actually reference a client that is unable to respond to the SYN-ACK messages because

- The hacker has already disabled the client machine.
- The client is offline.
- The client doesn't exist (random IP source addresses might be used).
- The client is otherwise unavailable.

As a result, the client never sends the ACK message to the server. This means that the table on the server will eventually overflow and the server will then be unable to accept any new incoming connections until the server clears the table. The server normally has a timeout associated with a pending connection (approximately a minute), so that eventually the half-open connections will expire and the server will recover. However, in this attack, the hacker can use his machine to continuously send IP-spoofed packets to request new connections faster than the server can cause the pending ones to expire.

NOTE

This attack can also play havok on some stateful inspection firewalls that attempt to maintain the status of TCP/IP connections.

The result of this attack on the server, in most cases, is to render the server unable to accept new incoming network connections. The attack doesn't usually affect already existing incoming connections or the ability of the server to originate an outgoing network connection. Users with an existing connection to the attacked server might not notice anything unusual. Clients attempting to log on to the server, however, will notice the problem.

In some instances, the server might crash, exhaust all of its memory, or become otherwise inoperative. The hacker doesn't harm data residing on the server during the SYN flooding attack but he does impair the server's ability to provide service.

If the hacker's intent is to simply render the server useless for a period of time, the attack ends here. However, if the hacker's intent is to impersonate the server or to gather further information, the attack continues.

The hacker, at this point, spoofs his machine's IP address to be that of the victim server (which is still under a DoS attack) and sends a connection request (SYN) to a trusted target server on the network. The target server responds to the spoofed connection request with SYN/ACK. If the hacker has done his job, the SYN/ACK message makes its way to the victim server. The SYN/ACK message will drop off the victim server because it is unable to respond. The hacker waits for an appropriate amount of time after he has issued the SYN message to the target server and then sends an ACK to the target server, which includes a predicted sequence number. When the ACK packet is sent by either system, the thing that is being acknowledged is the sequence number.

We need to back up a bit here, and discuss how the hacker is able to predict the sequence number. This is the tricky part of the IP spoof. When the hacker attempts to spoof a TCP connection, he faces the problem of never seeing the responses from the target server. The reason that this is a problem is that the ACK message must contain a sequence number with which the victim machine would respond. This means that the hacker needs to predict what the sequence number should be. He can do this by connecting to a TCP port on the target machine (for example, SMTP) and sending a small series of SYN messages to the target server. Because the hacker connects to the TCP port of the target machine, he can use a sniffer to examine the packets for the sequence number that the target server has sent. He sends several SYN messages in a row to determine what the round-trip time from the target server to his machine is like. He needs this information to be able to predict what the next sequence number should be.

He waits for a bit before responding with an ACK message to make sure that he has given the target server ample time to respond. Depending on the accuracy of the hacker's prediction, a few things can happen when the spoofed segment arrives at the target server.

- If the value of the predicted sequence number is less than the target server expected, the ACK is considered to be a retransmission and is discarded by the target server.

18

SPOOFING

- If the value of the predicted sequence number is greater than the target server expected but is still within the bounds of what was expected, the message is considered to be a future segment and is held by TCP pending the arrival of the other missing parts.

- If the value of the predicted sequence number is greater than the target server expected and is not within the bounds of what was expected, the segment is dropped and the target server sends a broadcast back with the expected sequence number.

- If the hacker has predicted the sequence number exactly, the target server will accept the ACK. The hacker has now compromised the target server and he can begin to transfer data, using the IP address of the spoofed server to gain further information about the network.

It is difficult to identify the hacker, because he might use a random IP source address for each connection request during SYN flooding. It's possible to trace the source of the attack, but it takes tremendous effort, time, and the cooperation of all the networks involved between the source and the destination to do so.

Reducing IP Spoofed Packets by Filtering

Unfortunately, it's impossible to eliminate IP-spoofed packets, but you can take action to reduce the number of IP-spoofed packets from entering and exiting your network. The best method is to install a filtering router that restricts the input to your external interface (input filter). You shouldn't allow an external packet to pass through the router if its source address is one that is from your internal network. Conversely, you should filter out outgoing packets that have a source address different from your internal network so that you can try to prevent a source IP spoofing attack from originating from your network.

You should also take steps to block packets with the following addresses from coming through your filtering router from the Internet.

- Your local network addresses.

- The all zeros broadcast address 0.0.0.0 and the 255.255.255.255 broadcast address.

- You should never receive from or transmit to reserved private networks through a router. The private network numbers are

  10.0.0.0—10.255.255.255

  172.16.0.0—172.31.255.255

  192.168.0.0—192.168.255.255

  127.0.0.0—127.255.255.255 (loopback)

Vendors that Support Filtering Routers

The following vendors have reported support for this type of filtering:

Cisco
170 West Tasman Drive
San Jose, CA 95134-1619
Phone: (800) 553-NETS
Email: `cs-support-us@cisco.com`
URL: `http://www.cisco.com/`

3Com
Santa Clara Site
5400 Bayfront Plaza
Santa Clara, CA 95052
Phone: 800 NET-3COM
URL: `http://www.3com.com/`

Berkeley Software Design, Inc.
4945 North 30th Street, Suite 300
Colorado Springs, CO 80919
Phone: 800 800-4BSD
Email: `info@bsdi.com`
URL: `http://www.bsdi.com/`

IBM Corporation
New Orchard Road
Armonk, NY 10504
Phone: 800 IBM-4YOU
URL: `http://www.ibm.com/`

Livingston Enterprises, Inc.
(Recently acquired by Lucent Technologies)
600 Mountain Ave.
Murray Hill, NJ 07974
Phone: 800 621-9578
Email: `infoinssales@lucent.com`
URL: `http://www.lucent.com/`

18

SPOOFING

Other Types of Spoofing Attacks

IP spoofing is probably the most popular spoofing technique, but it is only one form of spoofing. Other spoofing techniques exist, some of which are listed in the following sections.

ARP Spoofing

ARP stands for Address Resolution Protocol. It is a protocol in the TCP/IP suite that provides IP address-to-Message Authentication Code (MAC) address resolution for IP packets. ARP is different from IP in that it works with Ethernet to move data between local machines. When a machine needs to send an IP packet to a nearby machine, it broadcasts the IP address across the local Ethernet asking for the corresponding Ethernet address. The machine that owns the address responds and then receives the IP packet.

This process makes ARP spoofing possible only on a local network. If an intruder breaks into one of your machines on a subnet, he can use ARP spoofing to compromise the rest of it.

You might wonder why the intruder doesn't just change the IP address to the one that the machine he wants to spoof owns. This doesn't work for a variety of reasons.

- Both his machine and the victim machine will answer ARP requests.
- A pop-up error message will display at each machine, shown in Figure 18.2.

FIGURE 18.2
Windows TCP/IP error message.

- An event is added to the Event Viewer log declaring that there is an IP conflict, shown in Figure 18.3.

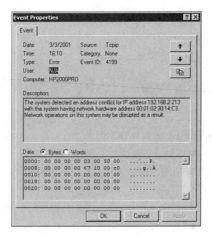

FIGURE 18.3
IP conflict reported in the Event Viewer log.

Any of these events could potentially alert the administrator that there is a problem.

There are a number of spoofing tools, such as send_arp.c, that an intruder can use to send an ARP message (ARP reply or ARP request) to the network. Basically, what the intruder wants is the ability to specify source and target IP and hardware addresses.

Consider the hypothetical network machine configuration for the machines in Figure 18.4.

IP Address	192.168.0.0	192.168.0.1	192.168.0.2
Hardware Address	AA:AA:AA	BB:BB:BB	CC:CC:CC
Machine Name	Machine A	Machine B	Intruder Machine

FIGURE 18.4
Hypothetical machine configuration.

The intruder targets two machines on the network that trust each other. He knows that Machine A trusts Machine B and that he wants to break into Machine A to gather information. This means he needs to spoof Machine B. To spoof Machine B, the intruder sends an ARP reply using the IP address of Machine B as the source address and his machine's MAC address as the source hardware address. For the destination address, he uses the correct IP and MAC address of Machine A. Machine A now thinks that the intruder's machine is Machine B. The intruder uses his ARP spoofing tool to continually send ARP messages to Machine A. He does this so that Machine A continues to think that the intruder's machine is Machine B. He also sends ARP messages to Machine B using the correct IP and MAC addresses for both machines

18

SPOOFING

A and B. He does this so that Machine B doesn't send a unicast ARP request. If this is done, it could change Machine B's ARP entry that the intruder is spoofing. The intruder can now begin information gathering.

Preventative Measures Against ARP Spoofing

There are a few things you can do to detect and protect against an ARP spoof attack.

- If you are experiencing unusual network problems and suspect that a machine might be under an ARP spoof attack, you can check the contents of the ARP cache by using the ARP command. The command for displaying the current ARP entries on a machine running Windows 2000 is arp -a.

- Your organization should consider investing in switched networks or smart hubs. These devices make ARP attacks unsuccessful or, at least, more visible.

- You can configure the ARP table manually to create static ARP entries, but this is hard work. Static ARP entries in Windows 2000 are valid only until you restart Windows 2000. To make static ARP cache entries persistent, you would have to create a batch file made up of ARP command that is run at system startup time.

DNS Spoofing

DNS stands for Domain Name Service. It is a static, hierarchical Internet and TCP/IP standard name service. This service enables client machines on your network to register and resolve DNS domain names, such as microsoft.com. The client machines use these names to find and access resources offered by other machines on your network or on other networks, such as the Internet.

DNS spoofing occurs when a DNS server accepts and uses incorrect (forged) information. The result is that the domain name server resolves the domain name to a different and wrong IP address, thus misdirecting traffic. Administrators refer to DNS spoofing as *malicious cache poisoning* because the DNS server puts the false information into its cache. This attack can potentially cause serious security problems. By providing false hostname and IP address information, the hacker can misdirect name resolution mapping—resulting in exposing network data to capture inspection and potential corruption. A hacker can, for example, direct users to wrong Internet sites, or he might misdirect email to non-authorized mail servers.

Preventative Measures Against DNS Spoofing

There are a few things you can generally do to reduce DNS spoofing.

- Run the newest version of your DNS server to help minimize the possibility of an attack. Make sure that you install any service packs or fixes that Microsoft has issued that relate to the DNS server. Among other operating system problems, Service Pack 1 fixes a number of bugs found in the Windows 2000 DNS server. Download SP1 at `http://support.microsoft.com/support/servicepacks/Windows/2000/SP1.asp`.

- Consider turning off recursion. When you allow your DNS servers to accept recursive queries from the Internet, it could make your DNS server vulnerable to DNS spoofing attacks. Hackers might be able to query your DNS server for information in the zones that are under their control. Recursion can also force your DNS server to query the hacker's server, which might then return false information. You can turn off recursion in the Registry by adding the value `NoRecursion` to the `HKEY_LOCAL_MACHINE\SYSTEM\CurrentControlSet\Services\DNS\Parameters` key. The data type is `REG_DWORD`, and the data value is `1` (`true`) to disable recursion.

- Restrict zone transfers for all DNS servers. Zone transfers replicate the resource records between DNS servers. Resource records are contained in a database on the DNS servers and are comprised of hostnames and their IP addresses. Hackers can use sniffers to capture information being replicated by your DNS servers and then list the contents of your zones to identify targets on your network, such as mail servers and other DNS servers. They also might be able to determine how many hosts you have on your network, plus their makes and models.

You restrict zone transfers in the Windows 2000 DNS server by doing the following:

1. Select Start, Programs, Administrative Tools, and then click DNS. The DNS console appears, shown in Figure 18.5.

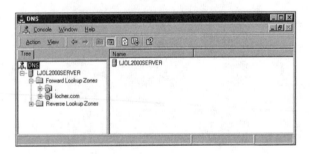

FIGURE 18.5
The DNS console.

2. Expand the domain controller's name, expand Forward Lookup Zones, right-click the DNS server, and then click Properties. The Properties dialog box appears, as shown in Figure 18.6.

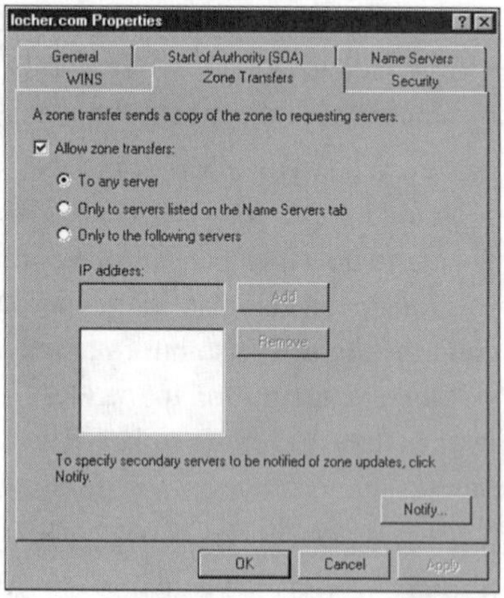

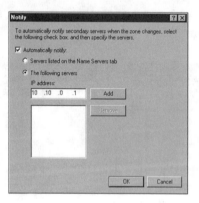

FIGURE 18.6

The DNS Properties dialog box.

3. Select the Zone Transfers tab.

4. Click the Notify button to select the option you want to use to notify secondary servers when the zone changes. The Notify dialog box appears, as shown in Figure 18.7.

FIGURE 18.7

The Notify dialog box.

5. You should restrict zone transfers by selecting The Following Servers radio button, and then listing the specific IP addresses.

Web Spoofing

Hackers use Web spoofing to create a convincing, but phony, copy of the entire Internet. To the victim, the mock Web looks and acts just like the real one in that he can still view any page or link on the Internet. The difference is that the hacker controls the mock Web so that the hacker filters all traffic between the victim's browser and the Internet through his own machine.

I'm sure you're wondering how this is possible. It's not at all that difficult, actually. No, the entire contents of the Internet are not stored on the hacker's machine. The hacker's machine simply grabs a page from the real Internet when it needs to provide a copy of the page on the mock Web.

The Attack

Hackers launch a "man in the middle attack" against the victim's computer. In this type of attack, the hacker's Web server sits between the victim's computer and the rest of the Internet.

This attack can begin in several different ways.

- The victim computer might visit a malicious or a hacked Web site.
- A hacker can add a fake link to a popular Web page that actually points to his Web server.
- A hacker can email a fake link to a victim.
- A hacker can do some DNS cache poisoning and redirect users to his computer and he can have a static entry pointing to the "real" site.

After the victim clicks the link, the hacker rewrites all the URLs on the Web page that the victim is visiting so that they point to the hacker's Web server rather than to a real Web server. For example, presume that the URL for the hacker's Web server is
`http://www.wearehackers.com`. The hacker will rewrite all of the URLs on the Web page by adding his URL to the front of every URL listed there. For example,
`http://www.microsoft.com` becomes
`http://www.wearehackers.org/http://microsoft.com`.

The rewritten URL causes the victim's browser to request the page from `http://www.wearehackers.com`. The remainder of the URL tells the hacker's Web server where on the Web to go to get the real page. When the hacker's Web server retrieves the real page from the Internet, all of the URLs in the page are re-written in the same form by adding the hacker's URL to the front. The hacker's Web server then provides the victim's browser with the rewritten page. If the victim continues to follow links on the rewritten pages, the hacker will continue to rewrite pages to include his URL. The attack can go on for some time, as long as the victim continues to follow links on rewritten pages. Figure 18.8 illustrates this attack.

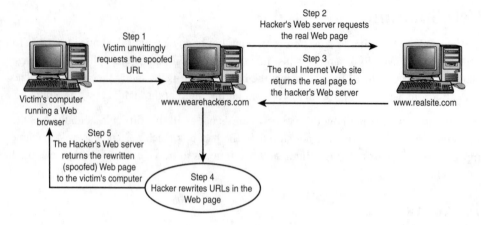

FIGURE 18.8
Illustration of a Web spoofing attack.

How the Hacker Hides the Attack from His Victim

You might be thinking that this attack certainly gives clues to the victim that he is under attack. For example, the status line displays the name of the server the victim's browser is contacting. Not so, if the hacker has done his job properly. It is possible for him to hide clues that an attack is in progress by using the following methods.

- When a browser retrieves a page from the Internet, the status line displays the server that it is contacting. A hacker can get around this by adding a JavaScript program to each Web page he rewrites. The script is meant to fool the victim into thinking that he is contacting a Web page in the real Internet by showing him what would have been on the status line in the real Internet.

- The browser uses the location line to display the URL of the Web page currently displayed. If the rewritten URL displays here, it could alert the victim to the attack. A hacker gets around this also by using a JavaScript program. The JavaScript program can hide the real location line by replacing it with a mock location line that looks accurate and that displays what the victim would expect to see in the location line. The fake location line can accept keyboard input, and it permits the victim to type URLs as he normally does. The JavaScript rewrites the URLs before the browser accesses them.

- If you were thinking that you would be able to examine the HTML source of the currently displayed page and would be able to see the rewritten URLs in the HTML source, you would be wrong. The hacker uses the JavaScript to hide the real browser's menu bar and to replace it with a mock menu bar that looks like the real thing. If the victim chooses to view the document source from the spoofed menu bar, the JavaScript opens a new window and displays the original HTML source code.

- The same thing happens when the victim tries to view the document information from the menu. The information displayed includes the page's URL. The hacker uses the JavaScript to hide this information also.

The Impact of Web Spoofing on the Victim

The impact of this attack on the victim can be severe. Because the hacker can observe and modify any data going from the victim's machine to the Web servers, and because he can also control all return traffic from a Web server to the victim's machine, the hacker has many possibilities for compromising the victim's machine.

- The hacker can use this attack as a surveillance tool, recording the contents of the pages that the victim visits. When the victim fills out a Web form, the victim's Web browser transmits the information to the hacker's Web server. The hacker can then observe such confidential information as Web server account numbers, passwords, or credit card numbers.
- This attack works even if the victim requests a page via a secure SSL (Secure Sockets Layer) connection. Everything appears normal on a fake Web page—the secure connection indicator (an image of a lock or key) will be turned on, and the page will be delivered. The victim's browser thinks it has a secure connection because it does—only the secure connection is with the hacker's Web server, and not with the one that the victim thinks it is.
- The hacker can modify any of the data traveling between the victim and the Web page in either direction. This includes form data submitted by the victim. For example, if the victim is placing an order through a Web site, the hacker can change the Ship To address.
- The hacker can modify the data that the legitimate Web server is returning. For example, he could insert misleading material to trick the victim further.

It might seem as though there is nothing you can do to fight this kind of attack, but there are a few protective measures you can take.

Preventative Measures Against Web Spoofing

The best defense known at this time is as follows:

1. Disable JavaScript, ActiveX, and Java in your browser so that the evidence of an attack cannot be hidden by the hacker. All three facilitate spoofing. Yes, some functionality will be lost, but when you know you are on a trusted site, you can enable them for the duration of the session.

18

SPOOFING

2. After you disable JavaScript, ActiveX and Java, make sure that your browser's location line is visible so that you will be able to see out of the ordinary URLs displayed there.

3. Finally, make sure that the URL displayed on your browser's location line is pointing to the server to which you think you are connected.

Lower the Vulnerability of Your Web Site

There are a number of steps that you can take to lower the vulnerability of a Web site to network attacks.

- Monitor your network boundaries for attacks. Many third-party companies have intrusion detection tools. One of the more popular ones is called ISS RealSecure by Internet Security Systems (ISS), Inc. ISS RealSecure is considered to be the market leader in intrusion detection. ISS RealSecure comes packaged with over 400 attack signatures with the ability for customers in both the network- and host-based solution to add or modify their own signatures. You can download an evaluation copy at `https://www.iss.net/cgi-bin/download/evaluation/evaluation-select.cgi`.

- Restrict routers to permit only the use of ports that are necessary for the site to function.

- Enable TCP/IP filtering, restricting access to only the ports that are necessary for the server to function.

- Disable unnecessary services on the server.

- Configure static IP address and parameters for both local and public network interfaces.

- Many third-party companies have tools that can detect your network's vulnerability to network attacks. One that you might want to consider using is called Internet Scanner. Internet Scanner performs a vulnerability assessment and audit analysis on your network. This software searches for vulnerabilities used by hackers to probe, examine, and attack your network. You can download an evaluation copy at `http://www.iss.net/securing_e-business/security_products/security_assessment/internet_scanner/`.

Registry Settings to Help Protect Your Network

The Registry settings listed in this section will help you increase the resistance of the Windows 2000 (or Windows NT 4.0) network stack to network attacks.

SynAttackProtect

Key: `HKEY_LOCAL_MACHINE\SYSTEM\CurrentControlSet\Services\`

`Tcpip\Parameters\SynAttackProtect`

Data Type: `REG_DWORD`

Valid Data Range (in decimal): 0, 1, 2

Default Value: 0

Recommended Value: 2

Description: You have three options available for the value of this Registry setting:

0   No synattack protection.

1   This value sets reduced transmission retries and delayed route cache entry (RCE) creation when the `TcpMaxHalfOpen` and `TcpMaxHalfOpenRetried` settings are satisfied.

2   In addition to the protection offered with 1, a delayed indication to Winsock is made.

Setting synattack protection involves reducing the amount of transmissions for the SYN-ACKs, which in turn will reduce the time it takes to clear the table that stores pending transactions. When you set this value to 2, the connection indication to the ancillary function driver (`AFD.sys`) is delayed until the three-way handshake is completed. This value setting acts only when the values of `TcpMaxHalfOpen` and `TcpMaxHalfOpenRetried` settings are exceeded.

TcpMaxHalfOpen

Key: `HKEY_LOCAL_MACHINE\SYSTEM\CurrentControlSet\Services\`

`Tcpip\Parameters\TcpMaxHalfOpen`

Data Type: `REG_DWORD`—Number

Valid Data Range: 100—0xFFFF

Default Value: The default value for Windows 2000 Professional and Server is 100. The default value for Windows 2000 Advanced Server is 500.

Recommended Value: The default value.

Description: Using this parameter, you can control the number of connections in the SYN-RCVD state permitted before synattack protection begins to operate.

TcpMaxHalfOpenRetried

Key: `HKEY_LOCAL_MACHINE\SYSTEM\CurrentControlSet\Services\`

`Tcpip\Parameters\TcpMaxHalfOpenRetried`

Data Type: `REG_DWORD`—Number

Valid Data Range: 80—0xFFFF

Default Value: The default value for Windows 2000 Professional and Server is 80. The default value for Windows 2000 Advanced Server is 400.

Recommended Value: The default value.

18

SPOOFING

Description: When you use this parameter, you can control the number of connections in the SYN-RCVD state for which there has been at least one retransmission of the SYN sent before the `synattack` protection begins to operate.

EnableICMPRedirects

Key: `HKEY_LOCAL_MACHINE\SYSTEM\CurrentControlSet\Services\`

`Tcpip\Parameters\EnableICMPRedirects`

Data Type: `REG_DWORD`

Valid Data Range: 0 (True), 1 (False)

Default Value: 1 (True)

Recommended Value: 0 (False)

Description: With this parameter, you control whether Windows 2000 will alter its route table in response to ICMP redirect messages sent to it by network devices, such as routers.

Further Reading on Spoofing

The following are Web pages for additional reading on spoofing.

RFC 2267—*Network Ingress Filtering: Defeating Denial of Service Attacks which Employ IP Source Address Spoofing*. P. Ferguson and D. Senie. `ftp://ftp.isi.edu/in-notes/` `rfc2267.txt`.

The Latest In Denial Of Service Attacks: "Smurfing" Description And Information To Minimize Effects. Craig A. Huegen. `http://www.pentics.net/denial-of-service/white-papers/` `smurf.cgi`.

TCP SYN Denial of Service Attack. Silicon Graphics Inc. Security Advisory, 1996. `ftp://patches.sgi.com/support/free/security/ advisories/19960901-01-A`.

DNS Spoof. Cyrus W. Young. `http://miavx1.muohio.edu/~youngcw/dnsspoof.html`. 1999.

Plug Common Internet Security Holes. ZDNet. `http://home.zdnet.com/devhead/stories/articles/0,4413,2257407,00.html`. 1999.

DNS Attack Scenario. Princeton University. Secure Internet Programming. `http://www.cs.princeton.edu/sip/news/dns-scenario.html`. 1996.

J-063: Domain Name System (DNS) Denial of Service (DoS) Attacks. U.S. Department of Energy Computer Incident Advisory Capability. `http://www.ciac.org/ciac/bulletins/` `j-063.shtml`. 1999.

RFC 1948—*Defending Against Sequence Number Attacks*. S. Bellovin.
`http://rfc.net/rfc1948.html`. 1996.

ARP problem in Windows9X/NT. Joel Jacobson. Rootshell.
`http://www.rootshell.com/archive-j457nxiqi3gq59dv/ 199906/winarp.c.html`. 1999.

Summary

Spoofing is a popular activity with hackers, and it leaves relatively little evidence behind. You can take preventative measures by following some of the advice given in this chapter, such as filtering IP addresses and using intrusion detection tools from third-party software vendors. In addition, try to keep up with the latest advisories and with the fixes issued by Microsoft for Windows 2000. New spoofing attacks are being discovered every few months.

Privacy and Encryption in a Windows 2000 Environment

Privacy and Encryption in a
Windows 2000 Environment

IN THIS CHAPTER

This chapter covers the concepts of basic privacy, cryptography and the public key infrastructure (PKI). You will learn about basic security functions and components of cryptography and about public and private key encryption. We will also cover some of the components of the Windows 2000 operating system PKI, such as the role of the Certification Authority (CA), smart card authentication, CryptoAPI, and the Encrypted File System (EFS). Finally, we discuss risk factors to consider for Windows 2000 cryptography features. But, first, we will look at basic privacy protection concepts that deal with protecting your privacy.

Basic Privacy Protection Concepts

Let's begin our discussion of privacy and cryptography with some basic concepts dealing with protecting your privacy. In doing this, we will take a look at steps you can take to secure your privacy while surfing online. Unfortunately, even though security vendors do hype personal privacy concerns to increase sales revenue, online privacy threats are real. If you use the Internet at all, unless you take steps to prevent it, your personal data, your identity, and perhaps other information will eventually fall into hostile (or at least, unauthorized) hands.

This exposure can manifest in many ways, degrees, and stages. Much depends on technical factors, including the following:

- Your network connection
- Your software
- Your public traffic
- Your networking habits

The two chief privacy concerns are Human Intelligence and Network intelligence. Let's examine each.

Human Intelligence

In human intelligence, human beings spy on you. Through such spying, they discover your identity, track your movements, and snoop your communications. Of all forms of intelligence, human intelligence is the oldest. In fact, spies often muse that human intelligence (and not prostitution) is the world's oldest profession.

Human intelligence comes in two flavors, *collective* and *penetrative:*

- *Collective Intelligence* is where the chief objective is to collect information without necessarily establishing direct contact. A good example is where agents photograph license plates at a political gathering; this is a collective operation.

- *Penetrative Intelligence* is where the chief objective is to establish direct contact, gain your trust, and obtain information on an on-going basis. Carol Elizabeth Howe, who infiltrated militia groups for the FBI and BATF, and who later testified in the Oklahoma bombing case, was a penetrative source or confidential informant.

The Internet favors both forms of intelligence, but is a natural for collective intelligence. Consider USENET posts. These are publicly available to anyone, 24 hours a day, via systems such as `http://www.dejanews.com`. Users can track your messages and, by doing so, learn a great deal about you, including your core interests, your political views and affiliations, and with whom you discuss these issues. Law enforcement agencies exploit this to analyze human networks online.

This represents a monumental shift from 25 years ago. To understand why, rewind to the early 1970s. In America, the '70s brought violent political turmoil. Many of the radical organizations that emerged advocated violent government overthrow. Our domestic and foreign intelligence operatives responded by conducting wide-scale collective and penetrative operations.

For example, to identify Students for a Democratic Society (SDS) members and supporters, police sent agents on foot. These agents were typically police officers, FBI agents, or civilian informants. Such agents mixed with crowds, recorded license plate numbers, gathered names at rallies, and so on. Later, police used the collective intelligence to match faces, fingerprints, and addresses to the gathered names, retrieved criminal records, and questioned other informants. Through these techniques—cornerstones of human intelligence—the FBI, BATF, and other agencies built profiles of suspected conspirators.

Historically, law enforcement agencies needed some lawful mandate, approval by department heads, or warrants from magistrates to conduct such activity. True, the process of obtaining these lawful mandates was often perfunctory, not difficult, and done chiefly to satisfy constitutional requirements, the absence of which could later threaten a conviction at appellate levels. But nevertheless, police were required by law to obtain them.

Today, police still conduct such operations, but these techniques are becoming less necessary. Instead, the Net permits government agents to monitor public sentiment from the comfort of cushy offices.

If you harbor radical political views and espouse them online, know that others are watching and archiving your statements. But USENET is just the beginning; everything you do online creates a record of some sort, both on your end and elsewhere. Some records are more difficult to acquire than others, but nearly all are obtainable at some level. And, as you'll learn in the next section, which focuses on network intelligence, spies needn't necessarily capture your statements or discussions to ascertain valuable information.

Network Intelligence

Network intelligenceis intelligence gathered by machines that watch machines. This type of intelligence has been around for decades and, until recently, involved chiefly electronic signal analysis or signal intelligence (SIGINT). SIGINT has long been a staple in military intelligence, but became more closely regulated after May 12, 1982, with the introduction of Director of Central Intelligence Directive 6/1. Directive 6/1 (a sister document to Executive Order 12333) established our Signals Intelligence (SIGINT) Committee, which was to

> "...advise the DCI on the establishment of SIGINT requirements, priorities, and objectives...and develop statements, based on the DCI's objectives and priorities, of collection and exploitation requirements for Communications Intelligence (COMINT), Electronics Intelligence (ELINT), foreign instrumentation signals, non-imagery infrared, coherent light, and non-nuclear electromagnetic pulse (EMP) sources.

The Ninth Circuit Court of Appeals in Bernstein v. U.S. Department of Commerce delivered a concise lay description of signal intelligence, what it does, and why it's important:

> "The national security of the United States depends in part on the ability of the government to obtain timely information about the activities and plans of potentially hostile foreign governments, organizations, and individuals abroad. The government's foreign intelligence-gathering activities include signals intelligence (SIGINT), the collection and analysis of information from foreign electromagnetic signals.

The USNI Military Database defines SIGINT as:

> "Intelligence information comprising either individually or in combination all communications intelligence, electronics intelligence, and foreign instrumentation signals intelligence, however transmitted. http://www.periscope.ucg.com/terms/t0000267.html."

Most Americans conceptualize SIGINT as something exclusively used in military and intelligence operations aimed at foreign enemies, like the VENONA Project. The National Security Agency (NSA) Web site now offers near full disclosure on VENONA, proudly (and rightfully) hailing it as responsible for our success in the Cuban Missile Crisis. As NSA personnel explain:

> "In July 1995 the Intelligence Community ended a 50-year silence regarding one of cryptology's most splendid successes—the VENONA Project. VENONA was the codename used for the U.S. Signals Intelligence effort to collect and decrypt the text of Soviet KGB and GRU messages from the 1940's. These messages provided extraordinary insight into Soviet attempts to infiltrate the highest levels of the United States Government. http://www.nsa.gov/docs/venona/index.html."

Traditional signal intelligence aims to obtain and decipher private communications but, as I earlier related, watchers needn't decipher your communications to learn more about you. Within signal and electronic intelligence is a more arcane field that deals strictly with *traffic analysis*.

In traffic analysis, which spies opt for if your encryption poses a serious obstacle, watchers watch *with whom* you're communicating rather than *what* you communicate. This is similar to how police who do not yet have the probable cause to satisfy a magistrate's requirements for a wiretap request your telephone bills.

For example, suppose you join a private discussion group ala Egroups or some similar organization. Members proceed under the assumption that their discussions are reasonably private. However, the mere centralized massing of their email addresses constitutes an assembly that represents a human network, a network of people who share similar views. If one or more participants are under investigation, your name will likely end up on a list somewhere.

Traffic analysis is particularly bothersome, too, because it's more difficult to defeat. After all, data passed by Internet Protocol (IP) must take deducible routes, right? Not necessarily. Next, we will briefly cover some basic privacy issues, progressing from minor issues that concern average users all the way to major issues that concern businesses and owners of proprietary information.

IP Address and Cache Snooping

Each time you visit a Web server, you leave behind a trail. Different server types record this trail in different ways, but nearly all capture at least basic information and some, if properly configured, record a lot.

A typical Web server log entry looks like the following:

```
153.35.38.245 [01/May/1998:18:12:10 -0700] "GET / HTTP/1.1" 401 362
```

Note the first entry (the IP address). All Web servers record (or can record) visitor IP addresses, and most Web servers can record other information as well, including your hostname, your username, your client software, and so on. To see what a Web server can tell about you, visit `http://www.easystreet.com/cgi-bin/test.cgi` or `http://www.privacy.net/analyze`.

The following is some typical output that the Web servers can capture:

```
The host SERVER_NAME, DNS alias, or IP address is: "www.ixd.com"
The name and revision of the SERVER_SOFTWARE is:
➥"Netscape-Enterprise/2.0a"
The name and revision of the SERVER_PROTOCOL is: "HTTP/1.0"
The SERVER_PORT number for this server is: "80"
The SERVER_ADMINistrator e-mail address is: ""
The name and revision of cgi GATEWAY_INTERFACE is: "CGI/1.1"
The extra PATH_INFO included on the URL is: ""
The actual extra PATH_TRANSLATED is: ""
The server DOCUMENT_ROOT directory is: ""
```

```
The cgi SCRIPT_NAME is: "/cgi-bin/cgi-test.cgi"
The query REQUEST_METHOD is: "GET"
The QUERY_STRING from Form GET is: ""
The CONTENT_TYPE of the Form POST data is: ""
The CONTENT_LENGTH of the Form POST data is: ""
The name of the REMOTE_HOST making the request is: "ppp-208-19-49-
➥216.isdn.jetlink.net"
The IP REMOTE_ADDRress of the remote host is: "208.19.49.216"
The authentication (AUTH_TYPE) method is: ""
The authenticated REMOTE_USER is: ""
The remote user (REMOTE_IDENT) for (rfc 931) is: ""
The MIME types that the client will (HTTP_ACCEPT):
➥"image/gif, image/x-xbitmap,
➥image/jpeg, image/pjpeg, image/png, */*"
The client's browser type (HTTP_USER_AGENT) is:
➥"Mozilla/4.04   (Win95; U)"
The page (HTTP_REFERER) that client came from:
"http://altavista.digital.com/cgi-
bin/query?pg=q&text=yes&q=%22test%2ecgi%22&stq=10"
The e-mail address (HTTP_FROM) of the client is: ""
```

In addition to grabbing the IP address, the server also grabbed the dial-up line:

```
The name of the REMOTE_HOST making the request is: "ppp-208-19-49-
➥216.isdn.jetlink.net"
```

However, more importantly, the server identified the last visited site:

```
The page (HTTP_REFERER) that client came from:
"http://altavista.digital.com/cgi-
bin/query?pg=q&text=yes&q=%22test%2ecgi%22&stq=10"
```

The script that captured this information is test-cgi, a common, freely available script that developers use to check HTTP environment variables on the server and client sides. Table 19.1 lists some common HTTP environment variables and what they represent.

TABLE 19.1   Some Common HTTP Environment Variables

Variable	Function
ALL_HTTP	Provides a list of all variables set when the Web server process first loads. This variable is IIS-specific and is not available in other popular http servers, such as Netscape or Apache.
ALL_RAW	Provides a list of all currently loaded variables. This variable is IIS-specific and is not available in other popular http servers, such as Netscape or Apache.

TABLE 19.1   Continued

Variable	Function
APPL_MD_PATH	Provides the current directory's Metabase key. This is IIS-specific and is not available in other popular http servers, such as Netscape or Apache.
APPL_PHYSICAL_PATH	Provides the application's root; IIS specific.
AUTH_PASSWORD	Stores passwords sent via HTTP basic authentication; IIS specific.
AUTH_TYPE	Stores the authentication method, which could be basic, digest (MD5), or NTLM (in the case of IIS).
AUTH_USER	Stores the username sent via basic HTTP authentication or, if NTLM is used, the domain, workgroup, and username.
CERT_KEYSIZE	Stores the security certificate's key size.
CERT_SERIALNUMBER	Stores the security certificate's serial number.
CERT_SERVER_ISSUER	Stores the security certificate's issuing entity.
CONTENT_LENGTH	Stores the length of any POST-submitted input string (such as the length of a user's search string).
CONTENT_TYPE	Stores the content type or what kind of data the server will return, such as html, text, and so on.
GATEWAY_INTERFACE	Stores the current Common Gateway Interface version.
HTTP_ACCEPT	Stores the MIME types that the server accepts.
HTTP_ACCEPT_LANGUAGE	Stores the languages that the server supports.
HTTP_COOKIE	Stores cookies that the server sends the client.
HTTP_HOST	Stores the server's hostname.
HTTP_REFERER	Stores the URL from which the client made the current request.
HTTP_USER_AGENT	Stores the client software's name (Netscape, Internet Explorer, and so on).
HTTPS	Stores the state of HTTPS (the secure HTTP protocol) and whether it's currently enabled.
HTTPS_CIPHER	Stores the cipher that the server is currently using.
HTTPS_KEYSIZE	Stores the HTTPS current session key's size.
HTTPS_SECRETKEYSIZE	Stores the HTTPS current private key's size.
LOGON_USER	Stores the username sent via basic HTTP authentication or, if NTLM is used, the domain, workgroup, and username.
PATH_INFO	Stores a CGI's virtual path.
PATH_TRANSLATED	Stores a CGI's absolute path.
QUERY_STRING	Stores a user's query string or the input to a CGI program.

19

PRIVACY AND
ENCRYPTION

TABLE 19.1 Continued

Variable	Function
REMOTE_ADDR	Stores the client's IP address.
REMOTE_HOST	Stores the client's hostname, if available.
REMOTE_USER	Stores the username sent via basic HTTP authentication or, if NTLM is used, the domain, workgroup, and username.
REQUEST_METHOD	Stores the method that the client is using to retrieve data. This is generally POST or GET.
SCRIPT_NAME	Stores a CGI script's name.
SERVER_NAME	Stores the server's address or hostname.
SERVER_PORT	Stores the port number on which the server accepted the current request.
SERVER_PORT_SECURE	Stores the port number on which the server serves HTTPS.
SERVER_PROTOCOL	Stores the current HTTP version.
SERVER_SOFTWARE	Stores the Web server software's name.
URL	Stores the client's requested URL.

Exploiting scripts that retrieve these values, Webmasters can pinpoint where you are, what your network address is, and where you've been. The remainder of this chapter deals with cryptography and the Windows 2000 public key infrastructure (PKI). These are tools within a Windows 2000 environment that are used to help you secure your privacy and content.

Cryptography Primer

To put it simply, *cryptography* is the science of information security. It is the cornerstone of modern security technologies that are used to protect data and resources on networks. Cryptography provides four basic information security functions:

- *Authentication*—Authentication verifies the identity of clients that communicate across the network. Without this function, anyone with network access would be able to forge originating IP addresses to impersonate other clients on the network. When your systems and network employ cryptography, however, the cryptography uses techniques to verify both the originators and recipients of data being transmitted across the network.

- *Confidentiality*—Confidentiality ensures that only authorized users and clients can read or use confidential information. Without this function, anyone with network access could eavesdrop on network traffic, and intruders would be able to gain stolen network rights and permissions to steal proprietary information. When your systems and your network employ cryptography, however, unauthorized users might be able to intercept information but, without a decoding key that is known only to authorized users, that information would be useless.

- *Integrity*—Integrity verifies that the original contents of data have not been corrupted or altered in transit across the network. Without this function, a malicious intruder might alter information being transmitted over the network, or information might become corrupted without being detected. When cryptography is employed on your network, an intruder might be able to alter data in transit, but the client would detect the modification because when data is altered, the unique digital thumbprint for the file is also changed.

- *Nonrepudiation*—Nonrepudiation assures that a client involved in a communication across the network cannot falsely deny that a part of the communication occurred, or even when that communication occurred. When cryptography is employed on your network, systems must provide evidence of communications and transactions. For example, when an e-mail message is sent, the messaging system adds a timestamp and then digitally signs the message with the sender's digital signature.

Components of Cryptography

Now that you have explored some cryptography fundamentals, let's take a look at the cryptography components found in Windows 2000. Windows 2000 can employ the following mathematical algorithms and techniques to provide network and information security, based on industry-standard technologies:

- Message Digest Functions
- Digital Signatures
- Encryption Algorithms
- Secret Key Exchange

You will learn about each of these technologies in the following sections.

Message Digest Functions

Message digest (also called hash functions) are used to produce message digests, which are digital summaries of information. Message digest (or hash) functions are mathematical algorithms that produce a different message digest for each unique document on your network. If any of the bits in the document changes, the message digest also changes.

Commonly, message digests are used along with public key technology to create digital signatures (also called digital thumbprints) that are used to provide integrity for the data on your network. Because the message digest is digitally signed with the originator's private key, it is not possible for a malicious intruder to intercept the message, make changes to it, and then create a new valid encrypted message digest to send to the recipient.

19

PRIVACY AND
ENCRYPTION

The two most commonly used message digest algorithms are MD5, developed by RSA Data Security, Inc., and the SHA-algorithm, developed by the National Security Agency. Generally, the SHA-algorithm is considered to provide stronger cryptographic security because it is not vulnerable to certain attacks that are launched again MD5.

Digital Signatures

Digital signatures are used to identify the originator of network transactions and to ensure the integrity of the signed data against tampering or corruption. Commonly, the system creates digital signatures by signing message digests with the originator's private key. Because only the message digest is digitally signed, the signature is relatively compact, which places a low load on computer processors during the signing process and consumes insignificant amounts of bandwidth. The two most commonly used digital signature algorithms in use today are the Rivest-Shamir-Addleman (RSA) digital signature and the Digital Signature Algorithm (DSA).

Only the originating private key can properly decrypt and validate a digital signature. If a different private key is used to try to decrypt the digital signature, or if the digitally signed data or the digital signature itself have been tampered with or are corrupt, the validity check will fail. Valid digital signatures are used to perform the following functions:

- Authenticate network clients
- Certify the origin of digitally signed data being transmitted across the network
- Ensure the integrity of digitally signed data against malicious tampering

Microsoft employs digital signing with Microsoft Authenticode, which is used to digitally sign software programs to help prevent the spreading of malicious code and software tampering. Digital signing is also employed by the Secure/Multipurpose Internet Mail Extensions (S/MIME) protocol to digitally sign e-mail messages. This is done to ensure the integrity of e-mail communications across the network and the Internet.

Encryption Algorithms

There are two types of encryption: *symmetric key* (or secret key) encryption and *public key* (or asymmetric key) encryption. Often, these two types of encryption are used in conjunction to provide stronger encryption for system and network security.

Symmetric Key Encryption

Symmetric key algorithms use the same key for both encrypting and decrypting data. A symmetric key is often referred to as a secret key because it is kept as a shared secret between the originator and the receiver. Symmetric key encryption is 100 to 1,000 times faster than public key encryption.

Security protocols commonly use symmetric keys as their session keys to provide confidential network communications. The Transport Layer Security (TLS) and Internet Protocol security (IPSec) protocols use symmetric session keys along with other encryption algorithms to encrypt and decrypt confidential communications being transmitted across the network. Other technologies that often use symmetric keys are S/MIME, used to encrypt confidential mail messages, and the Encrypting File System (EFS) that is used to encrypt confidential files.

Public Key Encryption

Public key algorithms (also called asymmetric key algorithms) use different keys for encrypting and decrypting data. Public key encryption is comprised of a private key, known only to its owner, and a public key, a key that is published and available in the Active Directory. The set of keys works in conjunction with one another. Data that is encrypted with the public key can only be decrypted with the corresponding private key.

Windows 2000 can use public keys to perform the following functions:

- Create digital signatures for authentication and no repudiation for network clients
- Create digital signatures for data integrity
- Encrypt symmetric secret keys to protect them during network exchanges, or while being cached, used, or stored by computer operating systems on the network

RSA uses private keys to encrypt data to create digital signatures. Only the public key for the RSA digital signature can decrypt data encrypted by its corresponding private key.

Secret Key Exchange

For public key encryption to work, the secret key must be securely shared with other clients on the network. At the same time, you must protect the secret key from use by malicious users. Public key encryption uses secret key exchange to provide highly secure key exchange between communicating clients. The two most common key exchange algorithms are the Diffie-Hellman Key Agreement algorithm and the RSA key exchange process. The Diffie-Hellman Key Agreement algorithm provides better security and performance than the RSA key exchange algorithm.

Diffie-Hellman Key Agreement Algorithm

The Diffie-Hellman key agreement algorithm was first proposed in 1975 by Stanford University researchers Whitfield Diffie and Martin Hellman. The algorithm is based on mathematical functions rather than encryption and decryption. Its formula is

$$G^{xy}\bmod^p = G^{yx}\bmod^p$$

Two authenticated users generate a shared secret key between them to exchange confidential data on the network. The algorithm works in this way: Both parties use the same public value

G and the same large prime number p in their formula. User1 assigns a secret value to exponent x, and User2 assigns a secret value to exponent y. User1 uses the secret value of x to derive the public value of $G^x mod^p$. User2 uses the secret value of y to derive the public value of $G^y mod^p$. When both clients finish their calculations, they exchange their public values. Each user then uses the other party's public value to calculate the shared secret key that they use between them to exchange confidential information. An intruder will never be able to intercept the secret key values for x and y because they are never visible on the network.

Internet security technologies, such as IPSec, use the Diffie-Hellman key exchange to secure the confidential exchange of data on the network.

RSA Key Exchange Algorithm

RSA Data Security, Inc. developed the Rivest-Shamir-Addleman (RSA) key exchange algorithm. The RSA algorithm works in this way: RSA encrypts the secret key with the intended recipient's public key. The intended recipient is the only client who can decrypt the key combination by using his or her private key. Any third party that might intercept the encrypted combined key cannot decrypt it.

The Windows 2000 Encrypted File System (EFS) uses RSA to protect the symmetric keys that are used to encrypt and decrypt confidential files stored on disks that use the NTFS version 5.0 file system.

Introduction to Public Key Infrastructure (PKI)

Because malicious software tools—readily available on the Internet—make it possible for intruders to access IP network information, administrators need to protect their network's data from both internal and external attacks. Using these software tools, intruders can exploit your IP network in any number of ways, including

- Impersonating authorized clients on your network
- Intercepting information transmitting over your network
- Altering intercepted information before it reaches its destination
- Redirecting intercepted information to other destinations
- Exploiting weaknesses in your network to cause denial-of-service attacks

How can a network administrator confirm the identity of and manage identification credentials of a user accessing information, and how can he or she control what information that user has access to across the entire organization's network? The administrator addresses these issues within a PKI.

Because today's networks allow security breaches, the software industry has attempted to develop new standards and technologies to improve the privacy and security of data and networks. One of the solutions for Windows 2000 is to provide strong, cryptography-based security via PKI. Windows 2000 employs distributed technologies that utilize public key technology to help provide security for your network. A few of the Windows 2000 network solutions that employ PKI include Certification Authorities (CAs), CryptoAPI, digitally signed software, smart card authentication, and the Encrypted File System (EFS).

Certification Authorities (CAs)

A Certification Authority (CA) runs on a domain controller to manage the Windows 2000 public key infrastructure (PKI). It issues certificates to verify identities of the certified users and entities to resources and other entities on the network. It can provide certificates for such things as Basic EFS encryption and EFS recovery agents. The certificates serve as public encryption keys for users in your domain. In the Windows 2000 PKI, you can use both enterprise CAs as well as external CAs, such as those provided by commercial service providers. This section deals with enterprise CAs.

The Windows 2000 PKI assumes a hierarchical CA model for scalability, administrative ease, and consistency with commercial and third-party CA products. A CA hierarchy consists of at least one CA, although a hierarchy can contain multiple CAs with defined parent-child relationships. CAs are not required to share a common top-level CA parent, or root.

The CA at the top of the hierarchy is referred to as a *root CA*. Subordinate CAs are referred to as intermediate or issuing CAs. Specifically, a CA that issues certificates is referred to as an issuing CA. A CA that is not a root CA, but only certifies other CAs, is referred to as an intermediate CA.

When you decide to deploy a CA, there are some key elements that you need to be aware of and that some that you should consider beforehand:

- *Decide which server will be the host server*—You can install the root CA on any Windows 2000 Server, including a domain controller. In making your decision, you need to consider such factors as security requirements and the expected processing load.
- *Select the CA name carefully*—Because the CA name is bound into its certificates, its name cannot be changed. Therefore, you should consider your organization's naming conventions carefully to distinguish between different issuing CAs in your network.
- *Active Directory integration*—During the CA installation, information concerning the CA is written into a CA object in Active Directory.
- *Enterprise Policy module*—The Enterprise Policy Module for the CA is automatically installed and configured during the installation. An authorized administrator can modify the policy, although in most cases it is not necessary.
- *The CA's certificate*—When you are installing a root CA, a self-signed CA certificate is automatically generated. For a subordinate (child) CA, you have the option to generate a certificate request that can be submitted to an intermediate or to a root CA.

19

PRIVACY AND
ENCRYPTION

- *Physical protection of the CA server*—It is always a good idea to physically protect your domain's servers. It is especially important to physically isolate and secure your CA server. This will protect them from malicious users who want to tamper with them and possibly compromise your network.

- *CA Restoration*—If you should lose your CA, due to a hardware failure for example, it can create operational problems, such as preventing the revocation of existing certificates. Therefore, it is good practice to perform regular backups of your CA so that, if the need arises, you will be able to restore the CA at a later time.

Enterprise CA Certificate Templates

Windows 2000 installs a set of default certificate templates for the enterprise CA that are published in Active Directory and that are used to control the contents of the certificates that the CA issues. There are two types of default templates:

- *Single-purpose templates*—These templates are used to generate certificates that can only be used for a single application, such as the Smart Card Logon Certificate template.

- *Multi-purpose templates*—These templates are used to generate certificates that can be used for a number of applications, such as EFS and SSL.

Refer to Chapter 8, "Windows 2000 Network Security Architecture," for a list of the certificate templates and the CA Roles.

Managing Certificates

The Windows 2000 PKI provides the features and components necessary to manage the domain's certificates and private keys through the certificate's lifecycle. The lifecycle of a certificate includes issuing and distributing the certificate, revoking the certificate, and the expiration and renewal of the certificate.

Issuing and Distributing Certificates

When a computer or a user requests a certificate, the CA verifies whether the requester is qualified to receive the certificate and either approves or denies the request. The certificate issuing policies for CAs varies, depending on the level of verification the CA needs to do to verify the requester's identity. Some certificate requests might be approved or denied relatively quickly because the CA might only check to make sure that the requester has a valid user account in Active Directory. Windows 2000 gives you the option to automate issuing certain types of certificates by configuring Public Key Group Policy to, for example, automatically enroll Windows 2000 computers for computer certificates.

After the CA has issued the certificate, it needs to distribute it to the requester as well as to distribution points (servers) where other users can access them as necessary. You can configure Windows 2000 to automatically distribute certificates through directories, public folders, and e-mail.

Revoking the Certificate

CA certificate revocation lists (CRLs) are used to identify certificates that have been revoked (for example, when a private key is compromised). During the user's certificate validation process, the system checks the CRL to determine whether the certificate is still valid. Any certificate listed in the CRL is considered to be invalid and so is not trusted (rejected). The CA's private key is used to digitally sign certificates in the CRLs to prevent malicious tampering with them.

The Expiration and Renewal of the Certificate

Certificates are all issued expiration dates. When the expiration date for the certificate is reached, the certificate is considered to be invalid and can no longer be used. However, Windows 2000 can renew the certificate by assigning new, valid dates to it so that the user can continue to use the certificate.

CryptoAPI

In Windows 2000, cryptographic keys and associated certificates are stored and managed by the CryptoAPI subsystem. A Cryptographic Service Provider (CSP) manages cryptographic keys. A CSP is a program you install on your local machine or a device that is accessible to your computer, such as a smart card, that performs cryptographic operations, such as secret key exchange, digital signing, and public key authentication. The default CSP on both an enterprise root CA and a standalone root CA is the Microsoft Base Cryptographic Provider.

The CryptoAPI certificate stores manage certificates. The CryptoAPI certificate stores are depositories for certificates and their properties. The PKI defines the following five standard certificate stores.

- *CA*—The CA certificate store contains issuer or intermediate CA certificates that are used to build certificate chains.
- *Enterprise Trust*—This certificate store contains the Certificate Trust Lists. These lists enable an administrator to specify a collection of trusted Certificate Authorities that must verify themselves to a self-signed Certificate Authority certificate in the Trusted Root certificate store.
- *Personal*—The Personal certificate store contains a user's or a computer's personal certificates for their private keys.
- *Trusted Root*—The Trusted Root certificate store contains only self-signed CA certificates for the trusted Certificate Authorities in the domain.
- *UserDS*—This certificate store provides a logical view of an Active Directory certificate repository.

19

PRIVACY AND
ENCRYPTION

Smart Card Authentication

In Microsoft Windows 2000, the operating system integrates smart card authentication with public key technologies, such as CryptoAPI, for strong network authentication and as an alternative to using passwords. They provide portability of credentials, such as certificates, tamper-resistant storage, and isolation for protecting private keys. The smart card itself is a portable credit card-sized plastic device that is essentially a miniature computer with limited storage and processing ability. The smart card is inserted into a smart card reader to achieve data communication between itself and an application running on a computer. Data communication is performed over a half-duplex serial interface that is connected to a computer using a USB, RS-232, or PCMCIA interface.

How Does Smart Card Authentication Work?

You can use a smart card to authenticate to a Windows 2000 domain in three ways:

- Interactive logon
- Client authentication
- Remote logon

The following sections take a closer look at each of these.

Interactive Logon

This authentication involves Active Directory, Kerberos version 5 protocol, and public key certificates. A smart card interactive logon begins when a user inserts his or her smart card into a smart card reader. The smart card signals Windows 2000 to prompt the user to enter his or her Personal Identification Number (PIN) instead of the usual username, domain name, and password. Inserting the smart card into the card reader is the equivalent of pressing the familiar Ctrl+Alt+Del key combination used to initiate a password-based logon in NT 4.0 or Windows 2000. The PIN the user provides authenticates only to the smart card, and not to the domain itself. The public key certificate that is stored on the smart card is used to authenticate to the domain using the Kerberos 5 protocol and its associated PKINIT extension. The PKINIT extension to the Kerberos version 5 protocol allows for the use of a public key certificate instead of a password for authentication purposes.

After the user inputs his or her PIN, the Windows 2000 operating system attempts to determine whether the user can be identified and authenticated based on the two credentials the user has provided—his or her smart card and PIN. Windows 2000 does this by first sending the logon request to the Local Security Authority (LSA), which, in turn, forwards the request to the Kerberos authentication package that is running on the local machine. (The main purpose of the LSA is to authenticate and log users onto the local system.)

The Kerberos authentication package transmits an Authentication Service (AS) request (which includes the certificate retrieved from the smart card and a digitally signed authenticator that verifies the owner of the certificate) to the domain controller's Key Distribution Center (KDC) services. This is done to request authentication and a Ticket Granting Ticket (TGT). The AS issues TGTs to authenticate users, machines, and services for admission to the Ticket-Granting Service (TGS). The TGS is responsible for issuing tickets for admission to services in the authenticating domain or to a TGS in another trusted domain.

Before the KDC can satisfy the AS request, it must verify that the certification path to the user's certificate can be trusted and that the issuing CA is authorized to issue certificates as a basis for authentication within the domain. To be trusted for authentication in Windows 2000 and to prevent a rogue CA from issuing certificates, the issuing CA must be an enterprise CA that is published in Active Directory.

After the user and the user's certificate are verified, the KDC needs to verify the digital signature. The KDC verifies the digital signature by using the public key from the certificate to prove that the request did come from the owner of the public key. Finally, the KDC service queries the domain controller for the user's account information by retrieving user account information from Active Directory based on the User Principal Name (UPN) specified in the user's public key certificate. The KDC uses this account information to build a TGT, which includes information such as the user's Security ID (SID) and the SIDs for any domain groups to which the user belongs. The KDC then encrypts the TGT and sends it to the client. The client is granted the TGT for authorization to the local domain. The default lifetime for the TGT is 10 hours and is renewed throughout the user's session without requiring the user to authenticate to the domain controller again. This process is illustrated in Figure 19.1.

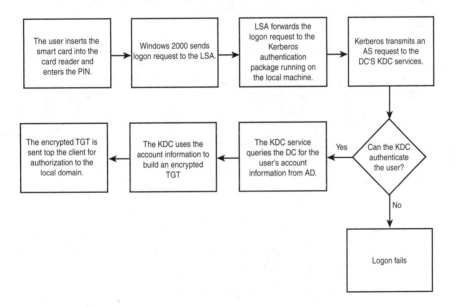

19

PRIVACY AND
ENCRYPTION

FIGURE 19.1

Interactive log on.

Client Authentication

Client authentication involves using a public key certificate to authenticate a user to an account stored in Active Directory. The role of the smart card in client authentication is to send a digital signature during the initial Secure Sockets Layer (SSL) session negotiation. This method of authentication is the strongest for a few reasons.

- The private key that corresponds to the user's public key certificate is stored on the user's smart card.
- The owner of the smart card is required to authenticate to both the card and to the domain.
- The private key operation performed during the initial SSL session negotiation is actually performed on the smart card, which means that the user's private key is never exposed to the network or to the host computer.

Windows 2000 public key authentication implements a security service that uses certificate information, based on the UPN stored in the user's certificate, to map to an account stored in Active Directory to determine access rights for the authenticated client. When the initial SSL session is established, the system will attempt to find the user account in Active Directory that is based on the UPN in the certificate. The UPN specifies the exact user account name and the domain name where the account is located. If the system cannot make a match with the UPN, or if the issuing CA has no authority to issue certificates for domain authentication, the system queries Active Directory to find an account that explicitly maps to that client certificate.

NOTE

An account can have multiple certificates associated with it, but a certificate cannot be mapped to multiple accounts that are stored in Active Directory. If a certificate is mapped to more than one account, authentication will fail.

Remote Logon

This authentication involves using a public key certificate with the Extensible Authentication Protocol (EAP) and Transport Layer Security (TLS) for remote logon user authentication. In Windows 2000, the remote access service (RAS) supports extensible authentication for remote users. The remote access server supports EAP to allow third-party vendor-supplied authentication modules (as well as a built-in module for smart card support), for authentication methods, such as smart card authentication, to enable strong authentication for remote users.

A remote logon is comprised of two separate authentications.

- The remote logon authenticates to the RAS server first. After the client authenticates to the RAS server, a connection is established between the client and the server. The server applies RAS-specific policies and account attributes to the client. The RAS policies are rules-based and usually specify how the server and the client should interact. The account attributes include properties, such as callback options and access rights.

- The remote logon then authenticates to the domain and, instead of using Kerberos or SSL as the authentication protocol, it uses EAP over TLS. This authentication to the domain is very similar to client authentication using SSL. The difference is that the public key certificate *must* contain a UPN that matches exactly to an account stored in Active Directory.

The Encrypted File System (EFS)

The Encrypted File System provides confidentiality for files by encrypting and decrypting Windows 2000 files that are stored on an NTFS version 5.0 hard disk. EFS accomplishes this confidentiality by issuing unique digital certificates that contain a private and public key pair to each end user in the network. Encryption and decryption take place automatically and transparently as information is read from or written to the hard disk. As long as the administrator has not disabled EFS when he configured the organization's EFS recovery policy, users can automatically begin using EFS with no effort on the administrator's part.

> **NOTE**
>
> If you are not the owner of an encrypted file but you have certain permissions for the file, such as the Take Ownership permission, you still cannot access or open the file without the owner's private key. However, certain other file permissions, such as the Delete permission, remain in effect. For example, if you have Delete permission to the encrypted file, you can still delete that file, even though you cannot open that file.

Examining How EFS Works

When someone uses EFS for the first time, it checks whether the user has a valid encryption key pair. If none exists for that user, EFS generates one that is composed of the user's public and private keys. The user's public key is stored in the form of a certificate. If the user is logged on to a domain and the CA is running, the generation for the key pair occurs on the domain controller. If the user is logged on to a workgroup or if the CA isn't available, the generation for the key pair takes place on the user's local computer.

When EFS generates an encryption key pair, it uses both public key encryption and symmetric key (or secret key) encryption. The user's local computer system or the domain controller

19

requests that EFS generate a pseudo-random number that then becomes the file encryption key (FEK). Next, the expanded Data Encryption Standard (DESX) encryption algorithm uses the FEK to generate the encrypted file. The EFS then encrypts the FEK itself with the public key that is found in the user's certificate. The unique encrypted FEK that results is then stored with the encrypted file, so that only the user's private key can decrypt the FEK.

To understand EFS better, there are a few things that you should know about public key encryption and symmetric key encryption. Public key encryption uses a pair of separate keys:

- A private key that is known only to its owner.
- A public key that is published in Active Directory in the form of a certificate that the CA manages.

The public key is published in Active Directory because it makes it accessible to other users within the network. Public key encryption is the more secure process of the two but, because it takes longer to process than symmetric key encryption, it is used only to encrypt the FEK. Symmetric key encryption uses the same key to encrypt and decrypt the file. This means, therefore, that EFS symmetrically encrypts and decrypts the actual data in the file with the FEK. Finally, EFS asymmetrically encrypts the FEK with the user's public key and decrypts the FEK with the user's private key.

Designating Recovery Agents for Encrypted Files

When the file owner's private key becomes unavailable (for example, it becomes corrupted or the user has left your organization) a designated recovery agent can open the file and recover it. This is made possible because the recovery agent's private key is stored in the Data Recovery Field (DRF) within the encrypted file. When the recovery agent recovers the file with his or her key, it is essentially the same as decrypting the file with the file owner's private key.

The EFS protects against unauthorized recovery agents decrypting protected encrypted files. This is possible because the recovery agent's private key cannot decrypt the file owner's Data Decryption Field (DDF). This is where the file owner's public key resides in the encrypted file.

By default, the EFS designates the Administrator user account on the first domain controller installed in the domain as the recovery agent for that domain. Although it isn't necessary to create additional recovery agents, it is possible for you to do so through the domain's Certificate Authority (CA).

Examining the Encrypted File Structure

A random cryptographic generator creates a unique FEK for each encrypted file. The EFS then uses the FEK to encrypt the file in blocks. A header is added to the file that stores all the FEKs; this includes the public key of the file owner as well as the public key for one or more recovery agents. This is represented in Figure 19.2.

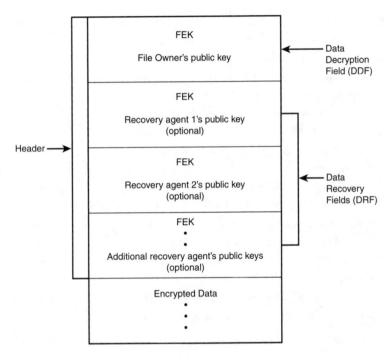

FIGURE 19.2
The encrypted data file structure.

The header is composed of two parts—the Data Decryption Field (DDF) and at least one Data Recovery Field (DRF). The DDF stores the file owner's FEK that is encrypted with the owner's public key. The DRF stores a recovery agent's FEK that is encrypted with the recovery agent's public key. Because more than one recovery agent can be designated within the domain, the header can contain more than one DRF.

Important Information Related to the EFS

The following lists important information that you need to know about EFS:

- You cannot share encrypted files, because the owner of the file is the only person who can decrypt the file with his or her private key.

- You can only encrypt files that are stored on a Windows 2000 NTFS hard disk. If you move or copy an encrypted file to a non-Windows 2000 NTFS disk, it will result in the decryption of the file at its new location.

- You cannot encrypt files that are compressed.

19

PRIVACY AND
ENCRYPTION

- Because some programs, such as Word, create temporary files on your computer, to ensure that an encrypted document remains encrypted during edits, you need make sure that the temporary files are encrypted in the folder in which the temporary files are created.

- EFS only encrypts and decrypts data at a workstation and does not encrypt and decrypt data transmitted over a network. This means that to keep confidential information encrypted as it is transmitted over the network, you need to use a security protocol, such as IPSec, to transmit the encrypted file.

- When you encrypt a folder, EFS asks if you want all files and subfolders within that folder to be encrypted also. If you answer yes, EFS encrypts all of the folder's current and subsequently created files and subfolders. If you answer no, none of the current files and subfolders are encrypted, but all subsequent files and subfolders will be encrypted.

- When you decrypt a folder, EFS asks if you want to decrypt the folder only and not its files and subfolders. If you answer yes, all of the current files and subfolders will remain encrypted, but automatic encryption will not occur with any subsequently created files and subfolders.

- EFS is especially helpful for the protection of confidential files stored on portable computers, due to the fact that portable computers can be lost or stolen.

The following lists the results of copying, moving, or renaming encrypted files:

- When you rename an encrypted file or folder, the file or folder remains encrypted.

- When you move or restore an encrypted file or folder to another computer, it remains encrypted as long as it is moved or restored to a computer that is running EFS on a Windows 2000 NTFS drive.

- If you use the Windows 2000 Backup program, the files and folders remain encrypted when you move or restore an encrypted file, regardless of where the target drive is located, as long as the drive is formatted using Windows 2000 NTFS. Because files and folders remain encrypted when you use the Windows 2000 Backup program, the file owner's private key is also restored, along with the files and folders.

- When you move or restore files to a different computer, the new computer must have your private key for you to open the file.

- When you move or copy encrypted file and folders across a network to a remote drive, the system transmits the data as plaintext. As long as the remote drive is a Windows 2000 NTFS drive that is running EFS, EFS will re-encrypt the data when it arrives on the remote drive. If the remote drive does not support EFS, the encrypted file will be stored as plaintext on the remote drive.

> **Note**
>
> There is a drawback to moving or copying encrypted files and folders across a network. By default, when a computer transmits data across the network, the data is transmitted as plaintext. To ensure that the data remains encrypted as it travels across the network, you need to use a secure network protocol, such as IPSec.

Encrypting a File or a Folder

You need Write permissionto a file or folder to encrypt that file or folder. However, there are some files and folders that you are not permitted to encrypt, even if you do have Write permission to them. You cannot encrypt system files and folders, and you cannot encrypt files and folders in the system root folder (for example, C:\Winnt). The system root folder is where the operating system files and folders are stored, which means that if you could encrypt system and system root files and folders, you would probably render your system useless. This is because there are certain files that are necessary during the system startup phase of your computer. During startup, the encryption keys are not available and so would not be able to decrypt these files. Fortunately, Windows 2000 has a built-in safety net. If you attempt to encrypt these files, the encryption attempt will fail, and you will receive an error message.

Windows 2000 gives you two ways to encrypt and decrypt files and folders:

- Encrypting or decrypting from Windows Explorer.
- Encrypting or decrypting using the Cipher command-prompt utility.

Windows Explorer

As long as you have Write permission to the file or folder, you encrypt it as follows:

1. Choose Start, Programs, Accessories, and then click Windows Explorer.
2. When Windows Explorer appears, right-click the file or folder you want to encrypt, and then click Properties.
3. When the Properties dialog box appears, click the Advanced button in the General tab.
4. When the Advanced Attributes dialog box appears, select the Encrypt contents to secure data check box and then click OK.
5. Click OK on the Properties dialog box.
6. If you are encrypting the contents of a folder and that folder contains subfolders, the Confirm Attribute Changes dialog box appears. You are presented with two choices: You can apply changes to the folder only, or you can apply changes to the folder, subfolders, and files. Select one of the choices, and then click OK.

7. If you are encrypting a single file, the Encryption Warning dialog box appears. You are presented with two choices: Encrypt the File and the Parent Folder or Encrypt the File Only. Select one of the choices, and then click OK.

NOTE

It is possible to encrypt a file that you don't own as long as you have Write, Create Files/Write Data, and List Folder/Read Data permission for the file. When you encrypt a file you don't own, it prevents the file owner from opening the file.

The Cipher Command-Prompt Utility

Files and folders can be encrypted and decrypted (by the user who encrypted them or by the recovery agent) with the Cipher command-prompt utility. In fact, the recovery agent cannot recover files by using Windows Explorer, but must recover files by using this utility.

The options available for the Cipher command are listed in Figure 19.3. When you use multiple options for the Cipher command, you must place a space between each of them. You can list the options in the Command-Prompt window by typing the following at the command-prompt:

```
cipher /?
```

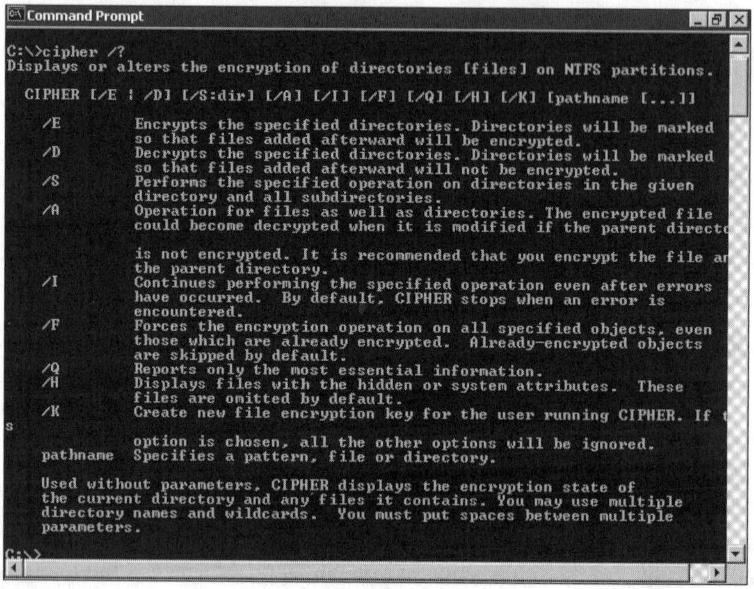

FIGURE 19.3

The Cipher utility options.

For example, to encrypt a folder named `Confidential`, you would type the following at a command-prompt:

```
cipher /e /a /f confidential
```

To decrypt a folder named `Confidential`, you would type the following at a command-prompt:

```
cipher /d /a /f confidential
```

To display the encryption state of the current folder and all of its file, you type the following command at a command-prompt:

```
cipher
```

Risk Factors to Consider for Windows 2000 Cryptography Features

The following are some of the factors that determine the risk of successful attacks against Windows 2000 cryptography:

- *Key lifetimes*—The longer a secret or private key is used, the greater the amount of information that is encrypted with the key and the more susceptible it is to attack. The rule of thumb you should use for the key lifetime is that the more valuable and confidential the information is, the shorter the key lifetime should be. A shorter lifespan limits the damage that can be done to your organization if a key is compromised after a successful key attack.

- *The public key length*—Public key cryptography is usually more susceptible to attack (especially factoring attacks) than the symmetric key cryptography. When an intruder to your network launches a factoring attack, the intruder tries all combinations of numbers that can be used with the algorithm to decrypt ciphertext. The length of the public key determines the effort that is required to compromise the key. A longer public key will require greater effort. The recommended minimum length of public keys is 512 bits. However, if you are protecting highly-confidential and valuable information stored on systems on your network, it is wise to use public keys greater than 512 bits, unless you find that it places a significantly higher performance load on the computer processors in your network.

- *The symmetric (or secret) key length*—Key search attacks (also known as brute-force attacks) can be launched against symmetric key encryption. During a key search attack, an intruder will try every possible key until the right key that will decrypt a file is discovered. This type of attack is often successful. To minimize the risk of key search attacks, you should choose longer key lengths and shorter key lifetimes. If you choose a 40-bit key, an intruder can try all possible keys in approximately 13 days (or less, depending on the speed of his or her computer's processor). If you choose a 128-bit key, it would take approximately 10 years (or less) to try every possible 128-bit key value. Symmetric key 128-bit or longer are considered unbreakable by key search attacks.

- *Private keys secure storage*—Because anyone who can manage to obtain a private key can impersonate the real owner during all communications and transactions on your network, the administrator must ensure that they are protected from unauthorized use. You can provide additional security for private keys by providing both physical and network security for computers and devices where private keys are generated and stored. You can also use hardware-based cryptography devices (such as smart cards) to store private keys. In this way, private keys are stored on tamper-resistant hardware so that the private keys are not revealed to the operating system or to cache memory.

Further Reading on PKI and Cryptography

Cryptography & Network Security: Principles & Practice. William Stallings. Prentice Hall. ISBN: 0138690170. 1998.

PKI : A Wiley Tech Brief. Thomas Austin. John Wiley & Sons. ISBN: 0471353809. 2000.

Understanding the Public-Key Infrastructure (Macmillan Technology Series). Carlisle Adams, Stephen Kent and Steve Lloyd. New Riders Publishing. ISBN: 157870166X. 1999.

RSA Security's Official Guide to Cryptography. Steve Burnett and Stephen Paine. McGraw-Hill Professional Publishing. ISBN: 007213139X. 2001.

Defending Your Digital Assets Against Hackers, Crackers, Spies, and Thieves. Randall K. Nichols, Daniel J. Ryan and Julie J. C. H. Ryan. McGraw-Hill Professional Publishing. ISBN: 0072122854. 1999.

Planning for PKI: Best Practices Guide for Deploying Public Key Infrastructure. Russ Housley and Tim Polk. John Wiley & Sons. ISBN: 0471397024. 2001.

Summary

This chapter introduced you to the concepts of basic privacy, cryptography, and the public key infrastructure. You learned about cryptography components, about how Certification Authorities issue certificates that serve as public encryption keys for users in your domain, about smart cards, and the Encrypted File System. Finally, you learned about some of the risk factors associated with cryptography.

IPSec

IN THIS CHAPTER

Some protocols you use on the Internet and within your internal networks have built-in safeguards to prevent hackers from snooping on your communications or from changing them along the way. For example, if you use a banking Web site or a stock trading Web site, you should notice a little padlock icon on the right side of the status bar on the bottom of your Internet Explorer browser window. This tells you that you have authenticated the Web site you are accessing to prevent spoofing, and that your Web session is protected from snooping. Spoofing is discussed at length in Chapter 18, "Spoofing." The protocol that protects your banking transactions over the Web is the Secure Sockets Layer protocol.

However, almost none of the communications in your internal network and most of what goes out on the Internet are not protected. When you access your company intranet site, access files on a corporate server, or download files from the Internet, the traffic is wide open to anyone who wants to take the trouble to look. Some protocols were designed long before security was a big concern (such as the File Transfer Protocol (FTP) and Telnet protocol), some protect only key portions of the communications (such as Kerberos password protection), and others require special configuration (such as the Secure Socket Layer (SSL) protocol). Having your internal communications wide open is particularly troubling because statistics show that you are far more likely to be attacked by an internal hacker.

Rather than worry about each protocol on a case-by-case basis, you would like to protect all your traffic in one fell swoop. You can do this for all TCP/IP traffic using the IP Secure (IPSec) protocol. IPSec can be configured to automatically make sure that your communications are coming from the right location (authentication) and are protected from snooping (encryption).

Peeping Tom or Protocol Snooping

A favorite game of hackers is to just watch the traffic that goes by and see what they can see—sort of like fishing. The crafty hacker will cast a net to see what fish he can catch. Hacking is frequently a crime of opportunity and, like criminals of the physical world, criminals of the digital world look for easy targets. Much of the traffic that wends its way around the Internet is wide open. Take, for example, an FTP session, very commonly used to transfer files across the Internet. This protocol has a very low overhead and is a useful way of transferring files, but it also has all the security of pup tent. Let us look at how easy it is to break into an FTP session.

The Scenario

Let's say that you have a couple computers that are communicating across the Internet using FTP, as shown in Figure 20.1. At the corporate office, you have set up an FTP site using a

Windows 2000 Advanced Server for traveling sales people to use, and you have made sure that each user has to use a password to get access to the files, making it "very" secure. Having read Chapter 6, "Password Security," you have even made sure to have users use complex passwords with a mix of letter cases and punctuation that will make it difficult for hackers to guess the passwords.

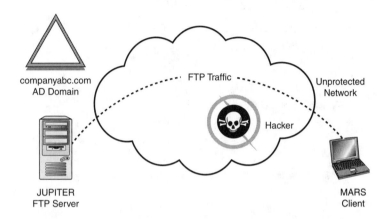

FIGURE 20.1
Corporate FTP server and client.

In our example, the server computer name is JUPITER and the client computer name is MARS. This is a typical setup, with the cloud in Figure 20.1 representing either the Internet or another untrusted network. You can see the hacker in the figure just waiting to tap into the FTP session.

Cast the Net

First, let's set up the hacker. Just using the basic tools that come with Windows 2000, we will see what we can do. In this case, we will use the Windows 2000 Network Monitor. This tool allows a computer to capture packets and analyze them. This is similar to taking a microscope to the information traveling over the wire between computers. It is important to note that you can find more sophisticated tools simply by doing a search on the Internet. However, for our nefarious purposes, this will be more than enough.

On the FTP server, we will launch the Network Monitor and start snooping:

1. Select Start, Programs, Administrative Tools, Network Monitor.
2. Press F10 to start the capture.

The Network Monitor tools will now capture any packets that come across the network inter-face card, as shown in Figure 20.2.

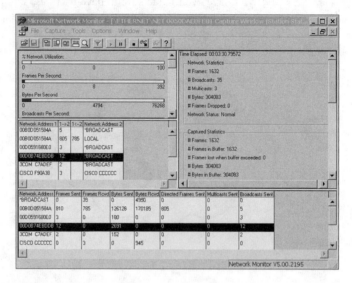

FIGURE 20.2
Network Monitor capturing frames.

NOTE

The Network Monitor tool that ships with Windows 2000 has some important limitations. The primary one is that it will only capture information that is destined for its own network card. You cannot use it to snoop on traffic between two other computers, which is why we are launching it on the FTP server. This would not be the normal modus operandi for a hacker, but is good enough for our demonstration. Microsoft ships a version of Network Monitor with their Systems Management Server that does not have this limitation.

Simple FTP Session

On FTP Client, we will start an FTP session in preparation for transferring some files.

1. Select Start, Run, and type **CMD**.

2. Type **FTP** at the command prompt.

3. Type **open JUPITER**.

4. Enter **administrator** for the user and press Enter.

5. Enter the password, which we will not show here.

We have launched a simple FTP session, as shown in Figure 20.3. This would be the normal actions of a user getting ready to transfer files.

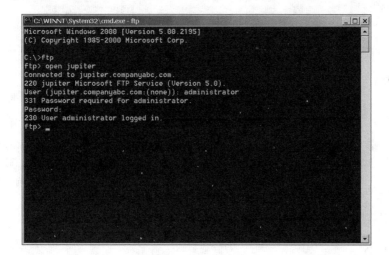

FIGURE 20.3
Simple FTP session.

Haul in the Net

Now we get to see what the hacker caught in his net.

On FTP Server

1. Press F11 to stop the capture.

2. Press F12 to display captured data.

You can see in Figure 20.4 that there is a lot of different traffic in the network; we captured over 1,800 different frames of data in this short session alone. However, in the center of the figure, you'll notice that there are a number of packets using the FTP protocol. Those are the ones that the hacker is going to zero in on.

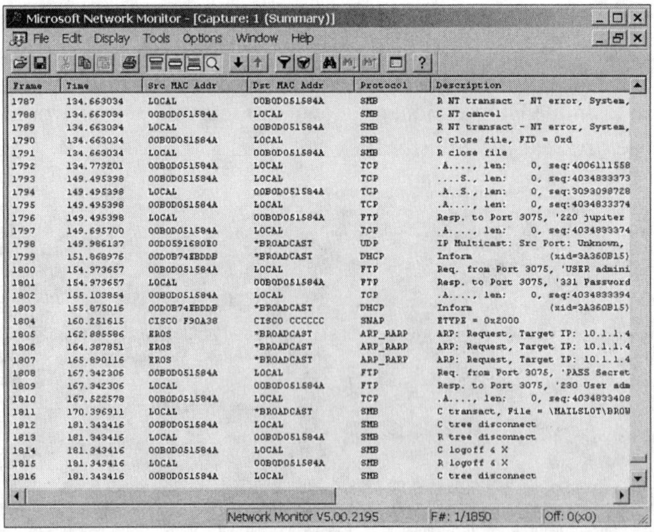

FIGURE 20.4
Captured packets.

The Catch

Rather than puzzle through all 1,800 frames to find the right ones and see what he has caught in his net, the hacker will use the filtering capability of Network Monitor to make his life easier.

1. Press F8 to edit the display filter.

2. Highlight Protocol == Any and click Edit Expression.

3. Click Disable All.

4. Highlight the FTP protocol in the Disabled Protocols and click Enable.

5. Click OK and then click OK again.

6. You should see a small set of FTP protocol packets.

7. Double-click the 4th frame, which should have the word PASS in the description field.

Right there in Figure 20.5 is the password Secret?, plain to see? Doesn't seem like that much of a secret, does it?

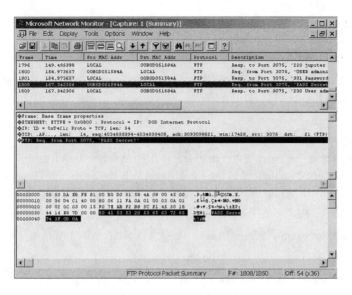

FIGURE 20.5
The catch—a password!

So, How Bad Can That Be?

In the case of this configuration, the FTP password is the same as the Active Directory domain password that the user would use to get access to resources within the domain. This is great for ease of use, but can lead to compromised security. Even if the password is complex, the hacker will still get it. In this case, the hacker captured the administrator password to the domain. This is about as bad as it can get, from a security perspective.

Privacy, Please!

It is obviously not acceptable to allow passwords to be sent unsecured across public networks, such as the Internet. However, it happens every single day. Some solutions to the problem in the previous section could be:

- *Don't Use FTP*—This would eliminate the problem with FTP at some inconvenience to the user, but many other protocols have the same problem.

- *Secure the FTP protocol*—This might be a useful solution, but FTP is a well-accepted and successful protocol. It would require a lot of effort to create an FTP II protocol and get it accepted by the industry. In addition, you would have to do this for every other protocol with the same problem.

20

IPSEC

- *Secure the base TCP/IP protocol*—Because most network traffic today travels over the TCP/IP protocol suite, protecting the underlying TCP/IP protocol would solve the problem at a root level.

In fact, the third solution is exactly what IP Secure (IPSec) does. Let's jump right in and see what it takes to set it up.

Setting up the Defenses

We will need to set up the defenses on both sides. Both systems are members of a Windows 2000 Active Directory domain within the same forest, which makes this process very easy. On the FTP Server, we will set up the Windows 2000 Advanced server to request a secure connection and end up with the result shown in Figure 20.6:

1. Select Start, Programs, Administrative Tools, Local Security Policy.
2. Highlight IP Security Policies in the left pane.
3. Right-click Server (Request Security) and select Assign.
4. Close.

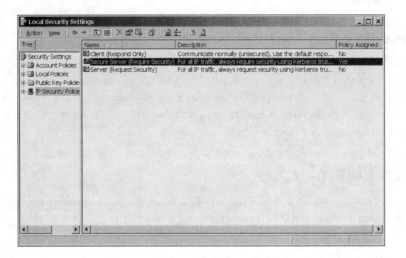

FIGURE 20.6
Server IPSec policy assignment.

On the FTP client side, we will set up the Windows 2000 Professional server to respond to security requests:

1. Select Start, Programs, Administrative Tools, Local Security Policy.

2. Highlight IP Security Policies in the left pane.

3. Right-click Client (Respond Only) and select Assign.

4. Close.

That's it! We are ready to defend against the hacker.

NOTE

If you do not see the Administrative Tools in the Windows 2000 Professional client, use the following commands to get it to appear in the menus:

1. Select Start, Settings, Taskbar & Start Menu.

2. Select the Advanced tab.

3. Check the Display Administrative Tools check box.

4. Click OK.

You should now see the Administrative Tools menu. Alternatively, you can also use the Control Panel to access the Administrative Tools.

Cast the Net, Again

On the FTP server, we will launch the Network Monitor and start snooping exactly as we did before:

1. Select Start, Programs, Administrative Tools, Network Monitor.

2. Press F10 to start the capture.

The Network Monitor tools will now capture any packets that come across the network interface card.

Simple FTP Session

On FTP Client, we'll start an FTP session again in preparation for transferring some files.

1. Select Start, Run, and type **CMD**.

2. Type **FTP** at the command prompt.

3. Type **open JUPITER**.

4. Enter **administrator** for the user and press Enter.

5. Enter the password, which we will not show here.

Figure 20.7 shows that nothing has changed from the user perspective.

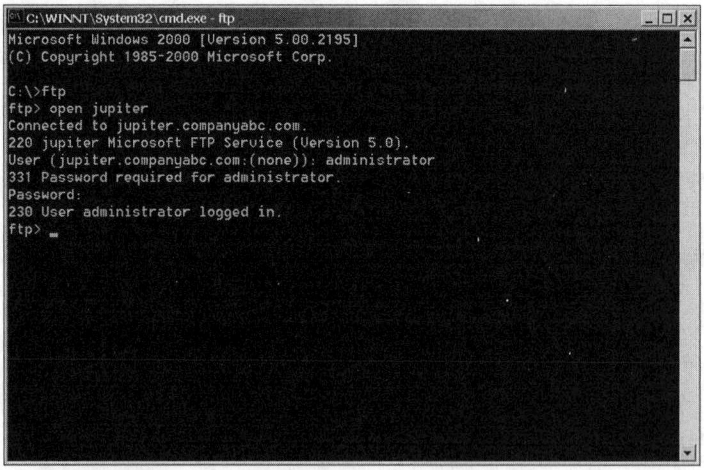

FIGURE 20.7
Simple FTP session.

Haul in the Net, Again

Now we get to see what the hacker caught in his net and if there are any differences from our unsecured session.

On FTP Server, stop the capture:

1. Press F11 to stop the capture.

2. Press F12 to display captured data.

There are a lot less frames shown in Figure 20.8 this time, simply due to the speed with which we accomplished our task, rather than any change in our process. Looking at the captured data, you will notice that we cannot see any FTP packets, and there are some new packets with the ISAKMP and ESP protocols.

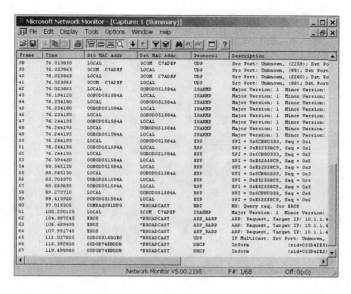

FIGURE 20.8
Captured packets with IPSec.

The Catch (Maybe Not!)

Again, the hacker will use a filter to find those FTP packets and grab the password.

1. Press F8 to edit the display filter.
2. Highlight Protocol == Any and click Edit Expression.
3. Click Disable All.
4. Highlight the FTP protocol in the Disabled Protocols and click Enable.
5. Click OK and then click again OK.

Right away, you can see there is something different. There is a warning in Figure 20.9 indicating that no frames matched our selection that was simply looking for FTP packets.

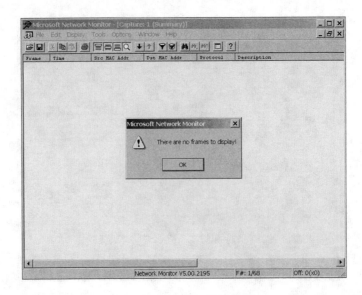

FIGURE 20.9

Where are the FTP packets?

We know that we captured an FTP session. Let's continue and look at it a little closer.

1. Click OK to clear the warning.

2. Press F7 to remove the filter and see all the frames.

3. Highlight one of the ESP protocol frames, say frame 56 in our Figure.

4. Double-click the frame to look at it in detail.

Rather than showing the password in plain text in Figure 20.10, all we see in the frame is a jumble of characters. The hacker was able to capture the packets; however, there is nothing that he can do with them. He cannot even figure out what protocol to which they belong. A victory for the good guys!

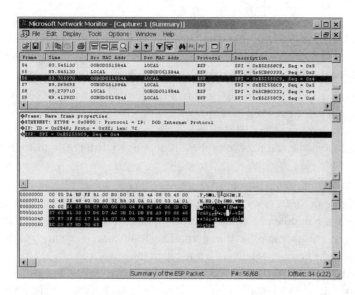

FIGURE 20.10
The catch: Nothing!

How Did We Do That?

It seems that we were able to protect the data traveling over the wire, but how exactly is this happening? Will it protect everything? How secure is it?

The scrambled text that the hacker saw is the original FTP protocol packets that have been encrypted by the IPSec protocol to protect them from just this sort of attack.

You might have noticed a couple things that were different about the two different capture sessions, one of which was that there were a lot more packets between the two computers in the secured session than there were in the unsecured session. Hold that thought because we will be exploring how IPSec impacts the flow of network traffic and participating systems later in this chapter.

Protecting IP Traffic

To understand how IPSec is protecting you, it helps to understand what you're being protected from. In other words, what are the threats facing the network communications?

- *Snooping*—As we demonstrated with FTP, most of the protocols used are unsecured. This is sometimes referred to as *cleartext* in that the text is clearly readable in the unsecured packets that traverse the network. This makes them susceptible to snooping with a protocol analyzer or sniffer by any hacker who has access to the network path.

- *Data modification*—Another threat to unsecured information traveling over the wire is that a hacker can modify the data in the packet. Even if confidentiality is not important, almost certainly you don't want the data changed in transit. If the packets are unsecured, this could be done without the knowledge of the sender or the receiver.

- *Password-based attacks*—Because much of the security in today's computing world is dependant on usernames and passwords, capturing these critical combinations—as the hacker did in our unsecured FTP session—can be devastating. After the hacker has obtained a username and password, there is nothing to distinguish them from an authentic user.

- *Man-in-the-Middle Attack*—Aside from having a cool name, Man-in-the-Middle attacks are very difficult threats to protect against. In this type of attack, a hacker inserts himself or herself in the middle of a communication stream. He or she receives packets from both sides by masquerading as the appropriate destination machine to each, and then can compromise the communication at a critical moment, such as key exchange or password change. At that point, the hacker can assume the identity of either system, depending on what he or she wants to attack. It is as if a hacker in your house picks up a second phone while you are calling your stockbroker and listens for a while until you give the broker your pass code and the hacker gets a good feel for your voice. Then, during a brief pause, the hacker disconnects your phone and continues the conversation with the stockbroker by imitating your voice. Your stockbroker will continue to have a conversation and follow whatever instructions the hacker gives because it still appears to be you.

These and many other threats face network communications after a packet of information leaves a system and travels across the wire. This rogue's gallery of threats illustrates the need for a solution that is both strong and broad.

A strong solution is needed to ensure that it is not compromised by would-be hackers. As new security technologies are developed, hackers race to compromise those technologies, and a strong solution will withstand those attempts longer.

A broad solution is needed to ensure that no protocol is left behind. As we saw earlier, there are existing protocols that protect some communications; SSL is an example of a strong solution that is narrowly focused on Web communication, but it did nothing to protect the FTP communications. A broad solution will ideally protect all traffic.

As we will see in the next section, IPSec provides a solution for securing IP traffic that is both strong and broad.

What Is IPSec?

The IPSec protocol uses authentication and encryption at a low level in the TCP/IP protocol stack, lower than other protocols such as SSL. Implementing the protection lower in the protocol stack makes it transparent to the upper layer protocols and applications. IPSec provides a very strong protection of packets because the encryption and authentication methods used are nearly impossible to break by today's standards. The IPSec solution is also very broad in scope because it can protect all traffic leaving the system.

As you can see in Figure 20.11, all communications are encrypted and authenticated starting at the network layer on down though the stack and over the wire when using IPSec.

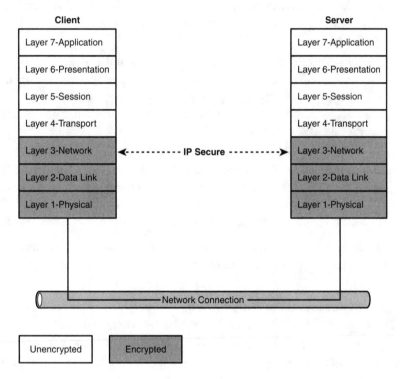

FIGURE 20.11
OSI protocol stack.

IPSec Features

The IPSec protocol addresses the threats previously outlined with the following security features:

- *Integrity*—The integrity of your data is protected by digitally signing each packet prior to it going over the wire. When it arrives at its destination, the signature is checked. If the packet has changed since being sent, the signature will not match, and the packet will be tossed.

- *Encryption*—As we saw when sniffing packets after turning on IPSec, the data in each packet is encrypted to be unreadable without the proper keys. Not only the data such as the password, but even key information such as what protocol is being used is encrypted for added security. This protects the packets from any hacker trying to read information traveling over the wire.

- *Authentication*—This feature assures that the originator of the packet is who you think he or she is by using credentials with each and every packet, rather than just when communications are set up. In our stockbroker example, the hacker waited until you had given your credentials to the stockbroker and then broke into the conversation. With IPSec, the stockbroker would have detected the hacker as soon as he or she spoke.

- *Anti-replay*—This prevents a hacker from capturing an entire stream of communication from end-to-end and then just playing it back. Each packet has a unique number that is incorporated into the authentication process and is not reused by either the sender or the receiver. If a hacker tries to replay a previously captured network session, the IPSec protocol will issue a unique number to the new session and the replay attack will fail.

While providing these security features, Windows 2000 IPSec also provides a number of management features. These features reduce the effort to use the technology and to get it out to the systems that need it.

- *Transparent*—The application did not have to know anything about the underlying security. This is because the IPSec operates at a lower level in the protocol stack.

- *Integrated security*—IPSec uses the Windows 2000 secure domain as a trust model. The default IPSec policies use the Windows 2000 Kerberos v5 authentication to identify and trust communicating computers. Computers that are members of a Windows 2000 domain in the same forest can easily establish IPSec secured communications.

- *Policy-based assignment*—IPSec is configured through security polices that are a collection of security settings. The use of policies makes it easy to create a specific set of security configurations and have the set assigned as a group, rather than have to set them individually. This ensures that all the settings needed to ensure the level of protection are applied consistently.

- *Ease of deployment*—IPSec policies can be assigned through the Group Policy features of Active Directory. This allows the IPSec policy to be assigned at the domain or organizational unit level, which eliminates the administrative overhead of configuring each computer individually.

Ease of management is critical to ensuring the widespread use of the protocol. If a particular system is left out of the secure communications, a hacker can easily identify that system and target it for attack. If it is easy to configure and enforce, it is less likely to be missed.

Pre-Configured IPSec Policies

Rather than have to create the IPSec policies from scratch, Microsoft Windows 2000 includes a set of pre-configured policies on every system. These policies match many of the most common situations and are useful as templates for creating new policies.

The default policies are as follows:

- *Secure Server (Require Security)*—This policy will force the computer to secure all traffic and will refuse connections with computers that do not respond to security requests.

- *Server (Request Security)*—This policy causes the computer to request security, but it will communicate unsecured if the other computer does not respond to the security request.

- *Client (Respond Only)*—This policy enables a computer to negotiate IPSec connections with any computer that requests or requires security. The computer will not initiate IPSec connections.

The default policies can be applied locally or by using group policy. These default policies can be modified, or additional policies can be added and then distributed and assigned via group policy.

You can easily protect an entire organization in the same Windows 2000 Active Directory domain with IPSec by creating the appropriate Organizational Units (OU) structure and applying the policies previously discussed. An example of a way you could do this is shown in Figure 20.12.

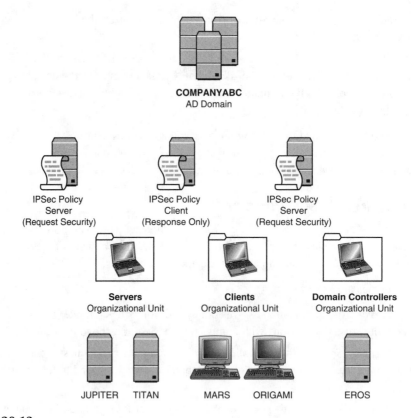

FIGURE 20.12
Protecting your domain with IPSec.

Figure 20.12 shows a Windows 2000 Active Directory domain (companyabc.com) with three OUs. The default Domain Controllers OU is where domain controllers are placed automatically. You have created two other OUs, one for servers and one for clients, making sure to place all computers in the domain in one of these three OUs. To secure the domain, you need to set up a group policy on each of the OUs to have them respond appropriately. On the Domain Controllers OU and on the Servers OU, configure a group policy to assign the Server (Request Security) IPSec policy. On the Clients OU, configure a group policy to assign the Client (Respond Only) IPSec policy.

You can either wait for the group policy to refresh or restart the systems to reapply the group policy, and then verify that the systems are communicating securely.

There's No Free Lunch!

So, what's the catch? There must be a downside to this cool technology. The downside is in additional processing time and traffic.

Going back to that protocol capture that we did, remember all the extra packets that we saw for the FTP session? Some of these are packets used to set up the IPSec SA. The encryption and authentication also add more bits to the packets, so more packets are needed to carry the same data. This is basically overhead on the network to secure the communications. For all but the most impacted networks, the additional traffic is not a significant concern. More critically, all that encryption and authentication add processing time to compute all the algorithms, both when a packet is sent and when a packet is received.

The performance impact of the IP Secure protocol can be significant and is proportional to the number of secure connections established. For a single connection, the overhead is approximately 1 percent of CPU processing time. For 10 simultaneous active connections, this can grow to 10–15 percent of the CPU processing time. This becomes a serious performance problem for servers that will need to establish a connection with each of its clients. The processing overhead to secure all those connections can degrade performance, causing problems for latency-sensitive applications, such as Voice over IP, or with high utilization servers.

In addition to the number of connections, the choice of the encryption algorithm can seriously affect the performance as well. The more secure the algorithm IPSec uses, the more processing time the algorithm requires. Selecting the triple DES option can increase the processing time by a factor of two, and even a single session might degrade the performance of latency-sensitive traffic, depending on the processing resources of the host system.

Mitigating the pain of this performance problem can be to limit the types of traffic that are secured or reduce the algorithm strength via policies. Higher performance systems can be procured with the necessary processing power to effectively handle the load. Alternatively, administrators and designers can take advantage of the offload capabilities of Windows 2000 by using offloading network cards, which are discussed in the next section.

Offloading IPSec Processing

The Windows 2000 TCP/IP protocol stack supports a feature called offloading that allows the operating system to hand off the processor expensive encryption and decryption to the specially designed network cards. Both Intel and 3Com have network cards that support this functionality, which are listed in Table 20.1.

TABLE 20.1 Offload Capable Network Interface Cards

Manufacturer/Network Card	Purpose
3Com 3CR990-TX-97	Workstation
3Com 3CR990SRV97	Server
Intel Pro/100 S	Server

When a packet needs to be encrypted, the operating system passes the unencrypted packet along with the encryption requirements to the network interface card. The card contains a special Application-Specific Integrated Circuit (ASIC) that will handle the encryption at much faster speeds than the operating system is capable of. This functionality is completely transparent to the other side of the connection. The result is an encrypted packet that is no different than if the Windows 2000 operating system had encrypted it.

These cards will not only offload the encryption processes from the CPU, they can also offload the TCP segmentation processing overhead. This further improves the performance of systems with the cards installed, even for traffic not secured by IPSec.

After installing the offload capable network card, ensure that it is configured properly to allow offloading. Verify that in the
`HKEY_LOCAL_MACHINE\SYSTEM\CURRENTCONTROLSET\SERVICES\TCPIP\PARAMETERS\` key there is the value `DISABLETASKOFFLOAD` of type `DWORD`. The value must be `0` to enable task offloading and `1` to disable task offloading. The default value is `0` to enable task offloading, which will be the value if the key does not exist.

Depending on the type of network adapter and the version of the driver, there might also be customizable options for what to offload. For example, the 3Com network interface card and driver allow eight different offloading options (see Table 20.2) to accommodate specific configurations. These can be found in the advanced properties of the driver under the Enable Offloads property. Normally, all options would be enabled, but disabling options is useful for troubleshooting or testing performance.

TABLE 20.2 Definitions of the Offload Functions under Advanced Tab

Parameter	Effect
All Offloads Disabled	No offload functions enabled
cksum	TCP Checksum function enabled
cksum-ipsec	TCP Checksum and IPSec function enabled
cksum-tcpseg	TCP Checksum and TCP Segmentation function enabled
cksum-tcpseg-ipsec	TCP Checksum, TCP Segmentation and IPSec function enabled

TABLE 20.2   Continued

Parameter	Effect
ipsec	IPSec function enabled
tcpseg	TCP Segmentation function enabled
tcpseg-ipsec	TCP Segmentation and IPSec function enabled

It is also useful to check the offload capabilities of the card through the Windows 2000 operating system. This ensures that the card has been properly detected by the operating system and that the offload functions are available. This will also allow administrators to verify the algorithms and functions supported, so that the IP Secure policies can be tailored to take advantage of the features of the network card. Obviously, it would not improve performance to create an IP secure policy that required an encryption algorithm that was not supported by the network card, because the operating system would be unable to offload that processing and no performance gains would be realized.

The following is the command to show offload capabilities:

NETSH INT IP SHOW OFFLOAD.

This will display a list of the offload features that the card offers, as is shown for the 3Com 3CR990SRV97 3XP network card in Figure 20.13.

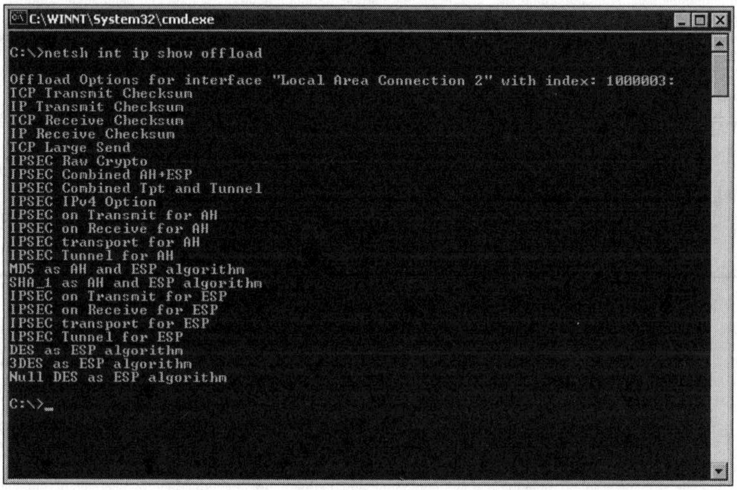

FIGURE 20.13
3COM NIC offload features.

We will see what all those parameters mean in the next section that covers the technical details of IPSec.

The Technical Details

IPSec uses a number of protocols and cryptography to secure the packets. Fundamentally, IPSec is composed of two major protocols that handle authentication and encryption—Authentication Header (AH) and Encapsulating Security Payload (ESP). They can be used independently or together.

Those protocols use a combination of secret key cryptography and public key cryptography that have been discussed earlier in the book. We will look at the specific algorithms used by the protocols later in this section.

IPSec is implemented using several components to allow flexibility in configuration and to avoid duplication:

- *IP Filter lists*—Combinations of IP addresses, protocols, ports, and direction. These specify the IP traffic and allow you to trigger IPSec protection.
- *Filter Actions*—These are the required response when IP traffic matches a filter in the list.
- *Rules*—This is where the filters and actions meet, and specific IPSec negotiation parameters are laid out.
- *Policies*—These are collections of rules. Only one policy can be assigned at a time to a specific computer.

The IP Filter Lists and Filter Actions are shared by all the policies on a computer.

We will number of protocols and cryptography to slook at all of these elements in detail within this section.

AH and ESP Protocols

The Authentication number of protocols and cryptography to sHeader (AH) provides authentication, integrity, and anti-replay for the entire packet (both the IP header and the data payload carried in the packet) through a signature process. AH does not provide confidentiality, which means the data is readable, but it is protected from modification though the signature process. The AH packets are IP type 500 (hex 1F4).

The Encapsulating Security Payload (ESP) provides confidentiality, in addition to authentication, integrity, and anti-replay. ESP encrypts the packet to prevent unauthorized viewing of the contents. These packets are IP type 50 (hex 34). ESP can be used alone or in combination with AH.

Figure 20.14 shows how AH and ESP modify the original IP packet, as well as what number of protocols and cryptography to portions of the packets are signed and/or encrypted.

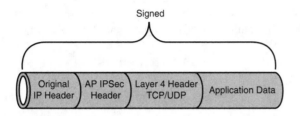

Authentication Header (AH) Packet

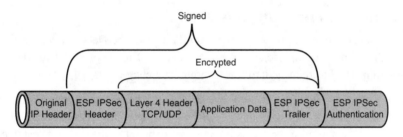

Encapsulating Security Payload (ESP) Packet

FIGURE 20.14
AH and ESP packets.

Because ESP does not sign the entire packet, only the IP data payload is protected and not the IP header. You need to use AH in conjunction with ESP to have the IP header authenticated, too.

Integrity: Hash Functions

The authentication, or integrity, in IPSec is obtained through a signature process known as a *Hash Message Authentication Code* (*HMAC*). IPSec uses the shared secret key, obtained from the authentication portion of the SA, to generate a cryptographic checksum using a hash function. These cryptographic checksums are also known as signatures.

An HMAC signature is generated for each packet by the sending computer with the shared secret key and attached to the packet prior to transmission. On receipt, the receiving computer generates the HMAC signature again and compares it to the one received with the packet. If they do not match, the packet is discarded.

20

IPSEC

Windows 2000 IPSec supports two HMAC algorithms:

- *HMAC-MD5*—Message Digest 5 (MD5) uses a 128-bit key to generate the cryptographic checksum.

- *HMAC-SHA*—Although very similar to MD5, the Secure Hash Algorithm (SHA) uses a 160-bit key to generate the cryptographic checksum, so it is a stronger hash function than MD5. However, it is also more mathematically complex and requires more processing resources to support.

NOTE

Purists would be careful to point out that the hash function is not a true digital signature because it uses a shared secret key to generate the cryptographic checksum. A true digital signature uses Public Key Encryption, generating the signature with public and private keys. However, the term signature for HMAC is almost universally used.

Confidentiality: Encryption Algorithms

To protect the data confidentiality, Windows 2000 IPSec uses the Data Encryption Standard (DES) algorithm to encrypt the packets. The U.S. National Bureau of Standards published the DES algorithm in 1977 as the standard for governmental encryption.

The basic DES algorithm has been widely characterized as being cryptographically weak due to the length of the key (56-bits) and the behavior of the algorithm when used with long strings of identical data. The length of the key is directly proportional to the time it takes to crack encrypted information, so longer keys are stronger. At the time DES was developed, computer-processing power was not as advanced as today, and the 56-bit key was deemed strong. There have also been rumors that the National Security Agency (NSA) might have forced the release of a weaker algorithm to be able to crack it, if necessary, with their superior computing power. The other concern is when encrypting long strings of identical data, which is typical of computer data, with the basic DES algorithm. The resulting encrypted text shows patterns that make it easy to crack the encryption.

To address these concerns, Windows 2000 IPSec uses Triple-DES (3DES) by default, changes the cipher key frequently, and uses Cipher Block Chaining (CBC).

Triple-DES uses a three-step DES process with three different keys, encrypting the plain text with the first key. The resulting cipher text is then decrypted with the second key, resulting in essentially incorrectly decrypted text. This incorrectly decrypted text is then encrypted again with DES, resulting in a encrypted text that has been run through the DES algorithm three times—both forwards and backwards. Very scrambled, which is good for encryption!

The cipher keys used in this process are changed frequently, specified by the IPSec rule (see Figure 20.15). Windows 2000 IPSec uses the Diffie-Hellman algorithm (DH) to exchange keys securely, although the actual key is never sent over the wire. After exchanging key generation information, both sides are able to compute a mutual key. This is done by using large prime numbers and modulo arithmetic that Windows 2000 protects with a hash function to prevent tampering.

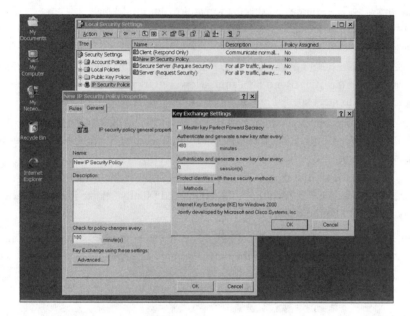

FIGURE 20.15
Key exchange settings in IPSec rule.

To address the problem of repeating characters in the plain text, CBC injects random blocks of data into the DES encryption process in such a way as to eliminate the repetition of the original text. In addition to eliminating the duplicating patterns from the encrypted text, the CBC process also prevents the data from expanding during the encryption process. This expansion of the resulting encrypted text is a side effect of the encryption algorithms, which results in more data if the same algorithm is applied to already encrypted text. The mathematical explanation of this is very complex and well beyond the scope of this chapter.

All these computations can be processor intensive, so Windows 2000 IPSec also allows the encryption algorithm DES to be chosen for situations where you are not as concerned with security or processing resources are constrained.

IP Filter Lists

Each computer has IP filters that specify traffic by IP source, destination, and type. This allows the rule to distinguish among different traffic. These filters are grouped into a list, appropriately called the IP Filter List.

Each filter contains the following parameters:

- *IP addresses*—The source and destination address of the IP packet. These can be configured from a very granular level, such as a single IP address, to a global level that encompasses an entire subnet or network.

- *Protocol*—The protocol over which the packet is being transferred. This defaults to cover all protocols in the TCP/IP protocol suite. However, it can be configured to an individual protocol level to meet special requirements, including custom protocol numbers.

- *Port*—The source and destination port of the protocol for TCP and UDP. This also defaults to cover all ports, but it can be configured to apply to only packets sent or received on a specific protocol port.

- *Mirror*—Mirror selection that matches the filter in the reverse direction. This just avoids having to create dual filters for both directions and usually selected because most filters apply equally in both directions.

The IP Filter List screen is shown in Figure 20.16 with a sample IP Filter defined. You can see that the protocol is defined as TCP and the port is defined as 21, which is a filter for the FTP protocol.

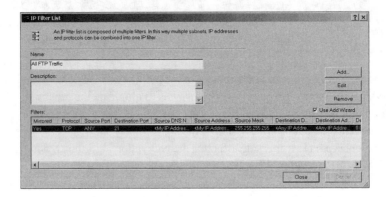

FIGURE 20.16
IP Filter List.

It is a best practice to create the IP filters you need before creating the rules into which they will be incorporated. Also, IP filters are not given any special order in the IP Filter List. Rather than applying the filters in a given order within the list, filters are applied to traffic by most specific to least specific. This can affect how rules are applied to traffic, so testing is critical to ensure the desired results.

Filter Actions

The filter actions set the security for the communication of the traffic that matches the filter. Security Methods define the security requirements, such as the algorithm and what protocols to apply to the packet. We looked at the different algorithms and protocols that can be used earlier in this section.

The actions that the filter actions specify are as follows:

- *Permit*—No security is used and the IPSec driver ignores the traffic, passing it straight through.
- *Block*—Rather than pass the traffic through, this action stops the traffic. This is useful for preventing either unwanted computers or protocols from being used.
- *Negotiate Security*—This is the action that results in secured traffic through negotiation. The action can also specify to fall back to clear, meaning unsecured.

If you select the Negotiate Security action, you can specify various Security Methods to determine the protocols and algorithms with which to attempt negotiation. The methods are different combinations of AH and ESP, as well as the different supported algorithms. One of these security methods has to match the opposite side of the IPSec connection, so that an SA can be agreed on.

Rules

IPSec rules determine what communications are protected by IPSec and how. They take the independent Filter Actions and apply them to packets that match one of the IP filters. The components of a rule include the following:

- Filters
- Filter actions
- Authentication methods
- IP tunnel settings
- Connection types

Rules are contained in the policies, and each policy might contain more than one rule. This is important because a computer can only have one policy assigned at a time. Multiple rules allow different types of traffic to be secured differently within the same policy. As an example, you might want to authenticate and encrypt FTP traffic from the corporate server, allow FTP traffic from Internet servers to travel unsecured, and simply authenticate all other traffic.

Authentication Methods

To establish an SA between two computers, they need to mutually authenticate—present a trusted credential. Windows 2000 IPSec supports several different authentication methods:

- *Kerberos*—This is the default authentication technology for Windows 2000 and is also the default in IPSec, as shown in Figure 20.17. Kerberos authentication requires that the Windows 2000 systems be members of a domain within the same Active Directory forest. This is the simplest option because it is completely transparent.

- *Certificates*—A public key certificate from a trusted CA can also be used. This method requires more configuration because you need to obtain and install an appropriate certificate.

- *Pre-shared key*—In this method, a secret key is shared between both sides of the IPSec connection prior to establishing communications. While easy to configure, there are security concerns with the pre-shared key because it is stored in plain text in the IPSec policy.

Kerberos is the authentication method of choice, especially among Windows 2000 systems. Kerberos is very secure and requires no additional administrative support. Kerberos can even be used with non-Windows 2000 systems if they support Kerberos v5 and are members of a trusted Kerberos domain.

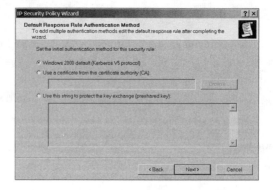

FIGURE 20.17
Default authentication method.

Certificates are natively supported by Windows 2000 and can be used between systems that are not members of the same forest, as long as a trusted CA, such as Microsoft or VeriSign, issues the certificates. You can even configure the Active Directory to automatically issue the computer account the appropriate certificate.

The least secure option is to use pre-shared keys. The main concern is that the pre-shared key is stored in plain text within the IPSec policy, making it easy to view. However, this method is very useful for testing and is required for compliance with the IETF RFCs.

> **NOTE**
>
> The key used in the pre-shared key method is only used for authentication, not for encrypting.

Pre-Shared Keys

IP Secure (IPSec) is a very effective way of protecting communications because it digitally signs and encrypts all IP traffic. It is also easy to set up within an Active Directory, simply by using the predefined policies. However, it is a little trickier to do if the two systems do not belong to the same Active Directory forest. Because the default method of negotiating security agreements is Kerberos, it does not work between peer systems.

To set up IPSec between standalone computers, you need to use either certificates or a shared secret. The simplest is to use a shared secret. To configure, run the following steps on both computers that will be communicating via IPSec.

1. Click Start, Settings, Control Panel, Administrative Tools, and select Local Security Policy.
2. Right-click IP Security Policies on Local Machine, click Create IP Security Policy, and then click Next.
3. In IP Security Policy Name, type **IP Secure Traffic**, and then click Next.
4. In Requests for Secure Communication, clear the Activate the Default Response Rule check box, click Next, and then click Finish.
5. On the Rules tab of the IP Secure Traffic Properties dialog box, click Add, and then click Next.
6. In Tunnel Endpoint, click Next to leave selected This Rule Does Not Specify a Tunnel.
7. In Network Type, click Next for All Network Connections.

8. In Authentication Method, change the initial authentication method from Windows 2000 default (Kerberos V5 protocol) to the selection Use This Key to Protect the Key Exchange (pre-shared key), and then type **0123456789ABCDEF** as the pre-shared key. This key must be the same on both systems. Also see the following Note on selecting a key to share.

9. Click Next.

10. In IP Filter List, click All IP Traffic, and then click Next.

11. In Filter Action, click Request Security (Optional), and then click Next.

12. Click Finish, and then click Close.

13. In the contents pane, right-click IP Secure Traffic policy, and then click Assign.

After completing these steps on both systems (or all systems participating in the peer IPSec), they should be communicating securely over IPSec. Check using IPSec Monitor (`ipsecmon.exe`) or a sniffer such as Network Monitor.

> **NOTE**
>
> You would normally pick a better shared secret key than **0123456789ABCDEF**, such as a particular passage from *Catcher in the Rye* or your favorite random number. It should be longer than 128-bits—at least 16 characters (128 bits divided by 8-bits per character).

Transport Versus Tunnel Modes

Up to now, we have been describing the IPSec Transport Mode, which is IPSec from computer to computer, protected the whole way. The other mode of operation is to use IPSec in Tunnel Mode, which is where unprotected traffic is tunneled between two networks secured but is transmitted unsecured within the individual networks.

You can think of this as bastion to bastion, where traffic is safe and only needs to be protected between bastions. This might be the case where not all clients are IPSec-aware or the overhead of all systems running IPSec is too high. Tunneling is also called *encapsulation* because the original packet is hidden or encapsulated inside a new packet, as you can see in Figure 20.18.

The only difference between mode and tunnel mode is where the original information appears. In tunnel mode, as with transport mode, the ESP protocol does not sign the entire packet. If you want complete authentication and integrity checking, you will need to use AH as well as ESP.

Authentication Header (AH) Tunnelling Packet

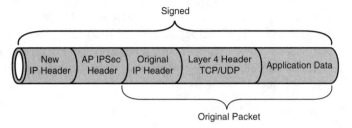

Signed

| New IP Header | AP IPSec Header | Original IP Header | Layer 4 Header TCP/UDP | Application Data |

Original Packet

Encapsulating Security Payload (ESP) Tunnelling Packet

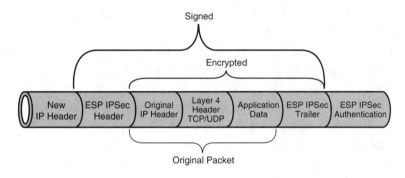

Signed

Encrypted

| New IP Header | ESP IPSec Header | Original IP Header | Layer 4 Header TCP/UDP | Application Data | ESP IPSec Trailer | ESP IPSec Authentication |

Original Packet

FIGURE 20.18
AH and ESP tunneling packets.

Connection Types

Connections can be either local area or dial-up. They are stored in the Control Panel applet Network and Dial-up Connections folder. The Connection Types setting allows you to broadly specify IPSec for traffic within the network (local area network) and outside of the network (remote access). You can configure the rule to apply to either type of connection or both.

Setting the connection type is useful when you do not want to incur the overhead of IPSec for traffic for a laptop that is connected to the corporate LAN. However, you do want to have the security that IPSec provides when the laptop user is traveling and using a local ISP dial-up connection to access corporate resources. For this situation, you would configure a rule with the connection set to Remote access.

20

IPSEC

Negotiating an IPSec Security Association

When two computers that are configured for security communicate for the first time, they need to negotiate security. Between each pair of computers, there needs to be a Security Association (SA). This SA specifies the IPSec protocol, authentication protocol, and the algorithms used on that specific connection, which are determined by the rule that the traffic matched in the IPSec policy.

The specific steps are as follows:

1. The client application sends a packet destined for the server that is passed down the client protocol stack.

2. The IPSec driver on the client intercepts the packet as it enters the IP layer and checks to see if security needs to be negotiated for that type of traffic.

3. The IPSec driver then passes the packet to the Internet Security Association Key Management Protocol (ISAKMP) to negotiate an SA between the client and the server if one does not exist already. This process is also referred to as the *ISAKMP process*.

4. The ISAKMP process negotiates the SA using UDP type 500 packets and passes the negotiated SA to the IPSec driver. These packets are not protected by the IPSec protocol because it is in the process of being negotiated.

5. The IPSec driver performs the appropriate actions specified by the SA, such as applying encryption and authentication algorithms.

6. The IPSec driver then passes the resulting encrypted and authenticated packet to the network card driver, where it intercepted it in the first place.

On the server-side, the reverse happens upon receiving the IPSec protected packet. The process should be much quicker because there will be an SA already negotiated and the IPSec driver simply needs to get the correct parameters of the existing SA.

Let's look at that capture from our secure session again, repeated here in Figure 20.19. We see that the packets are listed as protocol ESP, per the callout. We also see other packets listed as protocol ISAKMP, which are the negotiation packets.

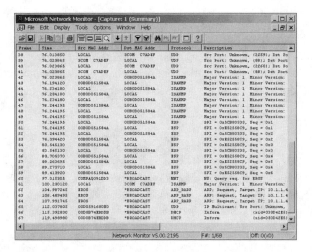

FIGURE 20.19
Negotiation and encrypted traffic.

Protocols Not Protected by IPSec

IPSec cannot protect all protocols, due to the nature of the technology. The IPSec SA negotiation process requires a one-to-one communication, so one-to-many communications cannot be secured using IPSec. In addition, the protocols used to set up the IPSec SA cannot be secured using IPSec either. These protocols are excluded by the IPSec driver.

* *Broadcast*—Traffic going from one sender to many receivers that are unknown to the sender. This type of packet cannot be classified by IPSec filters because it is not in contact with any particular station with which to negotiate security parameters.

* *Multicast*—As with Broadcast traffic, one sender sends an IP packet to many receivers that are unknown to the sender and cannot negotiate security parameters.

* *Internet Key Exchange (IKE)*—IKE is a protocol used by IPSec to negotiate security parameters, so it has to be exempt to be able to set up the secure traffic. It uses its own built-in security mechanisms.

* *Resource Reservation Protocol (RSVP)*—This traffic uses IP protocol 46 and is used to provide Quality of Service (QoS) in Windows 2000. Exemption of RSVP traffic was done in the original release to allow QOS markings for traffic that can be secured by IPSec. This was seen as a limitation for some applications and was changed as of Windows 2000 SP 1 to allow the protocol to be secured via IPSec if needed.

20

IPSEC

- *Kerberos*—Kerberos is the core Windows 2000 security protocol typically used by IKE for IPSec authentication. Kerberos is itself a security protocol that does not need to be secured by IPSec, or so the thinking went on the original release of Windows 2000. This was also considered to be a limitation and was changed as of Windows 2000 SP 1 to allow the protocol to be secured via IPSec under special circumstances.

NOTE

The securing of Kerberos and RSVP protocol has a relatively narrow application for domain controller to domain controller communications. This might be the case where you want all traffic to be encrypted between domain controllers for high security applications. Because Kerberos is exempted by default, special configuration is necessary to secure it with IPSec.

It also applies to cases where you are using IPSec across a firewall and do not permit any traffic that is not secured by IPSec to pass through the firewall. The two IPSec protocols are ESP (port 50) and IKE (port 500), which would be allowed to pass through the firewall. In this configuration, Kerberos and RSVP would be blocked. This is because the two protocols are exempted from IPSec by default and, thus, travel over the wire with their native protocol types.

As of the SP1, Kerberos and RSVP can be not exempted by adding the Registry key `HKLM\SYSTEM\CurrentControlSet\Services\IPSEC\NodefaultExempt` of type `REG_DWORD`. Setting the value to 1 will cause the IPSec driver to not exempt Kerberos and RSVP from encryption.

However, if IPSec is required and Kerberos is not exempted, IPSec has to be configured to use certificates to establish the Security Association (SA). This is not the authentication method of choice, due to its higher administrative overhead.

Directly related to the exemption of certain protocols from IPSec, you might have seen the following Event Viewer event on the original pre-SP1 release of Windows 2000:

Event ID: 4284

Source: IPSec

Received *<n>* packet(s) in the clear from *<IP address>* that should have been secured. This could be a temporary glitch; if it persists, please stop and restart the IPSec Policy Agent service on this machine.

The problem is that IPSec driver is receiving broadcast or other exempt packets from the TCP/IP driver. The broadcast traffic is not encrypted and causes the IPSec driver to log an event about the packet being in the clear instead of being secured, which is exactly what the driver is supposed to do. These false errors can be ignored and are resolved as of Windows 2000 SP1.

IPSec and Firewalls

For a security gateway, firewall, proxy server, router, or any server that is an access point from the intranet to the outside world, special filtering must be enabled on that computer to ensure that packets secured with IPSec are not rejected. The following protocols should be allowed to pass through the firewall in both directions:

- *Authentication Header*—IP Protocol ID of 51 (hex 33) for IPSec AH traffic
- *Encapsulating Security Protocol*—IP Protocol ID of 50 (0x32) for IPSec ESP traffic
- *Internet Key Exchange*—UDP port 500 (0x1F4) for IKE negotiation traffic

Because the packets are encrypted, if using ESP, the firewall and other network equipment will be unable to classify or filter the traffic based on content.

In addition, Network Address Translation (NAT) and IPSec do not work together. Network address translation relies on the translation of

- The IP addresses in the IP header
- The TCP port numbers in the TCP header
- The UDP port numbers in the UDP header

Because the translation changes these fields, the authentication and decryption for IPSec will fail. Any routers or switches in the data path between the communicating computers should simply forward the encrypted IP packets to their destination.

IPSec Tools

IP Security can be tricky to diagnose and monitor, but there are tools specific to IPSec included with Windows 2000 to simplify the task.

IP Security Monitor

You can use the IP Security Monitor (IPSECMON) to see secured and unsecured SAs that IPSec has established. The IPSec monitor can confirm whether your secured communications are successful by displaying the active security associations on local or remote computers. The IPSec monitor runs on the local computer, or it can be run remotely if you have a network connection to the remote computer and the appropriate rights.

To start the IPSec monitor, do the following:

1. Click Start, and then click Run.
2. Type **ipsecmon** *<computername>*, where *computername* is the optional name of a remote system you want to monitor.

A typical IPSECMON screen is shown in Figure 20.20.

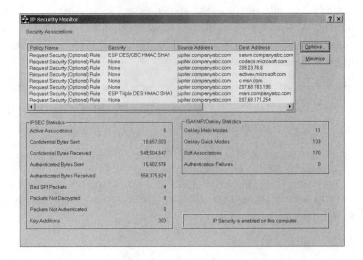

FIGURE 20.20
IP Security Monitor.

You can see in the screen a number of different SAs that have been negotiated, some secured and some not. Note at the top that the destination saturn.companyabc.com has ESP DES/CBC and HMAC SHA1 in the Security column, which indicate that ESP is using standard DES encryption and that AH is using SHA1 for signing. On the bottom of the screen, mars.companyabc.com shows ESP Triple DES in the security column, indicating that ESP is using the stronger encryption algorithm when communicating with MARS.

Network Connectivity Tester

Located in the Support tools on the Windows 2000 distribution CD-ROM, the Network Connectivity Tester (netdiag.exe) is a command line tool for testing network issues. It is used to test a variety of network-related elements, including IPSec. The command to test IPSec is netdiag /test:ipsec /debug /v, which results in the following output:

```
IP Security test . . . . . . . . . : Passed
    Local IPSec Policy Active: 'Server (Request Security)'
    IP Security Policy Path: SOFTWARE\Policies\Microsoft\Windows\IPSec\Policy
➥\Local\ipsecPolicy{72385230-70FA-11D1-864C-14A300000000}

    There are 4 filters
    ICMP
     Filter Id: {EDD665AA-000A-4D87-91AA-1955476170EC}
     Policy Id: {1B3321C8-8031-4C78-BBF3-0BF37198BBBA}
```

```
 Src Addr   : 10.1.0.2      Src Mask   : 255.255.255.255
 Dest Addr : 0.0.0.0        Dest Mask : 0.0.0.0
 Tunnel Addr : 0.0.0.0      Src Port : 0   Dest Port : 0
 Protocol : 1     TunnelFilter: No
 Flags : Outbound
ICMP - Mirror
 Filter Id: {EDD665AA-000A-4D87-91AA-1955476170EC}
 Policy Id: {1B3321C8-8031-4C78-BBF3-0BF37198BBBA}
 Src Addr   : 0.0.0.0        Src Mask   : 0.0.0.0
 Dest Addr : 10.1.0.2       Dest Mask : 255.255.255.255
 Tunnel Addr : 0.0.0.0      Src Port : 0   Dest Port : 0
 Protocol : 1      TunnelFilter: No
 Flags : Inbound
No Name
 Filter Id: {112D30BC-61AF-4B1A-B6F7-AA4B4E0BFD58}
 Policy Id: {77F1D04E-156E-4F05-A784-35642990F53D}
    IPSEC_POLICY PolicyId = {77F1D04E-156E-4F05-A784-35642990F53D}
          Flags: 0x1
          Tunnel Addr: 0.0.0.0
    PHASE 2 OFFERS Count = 4
          Offer #0:
    ESP[ 3DES SHA1 HMAC]
    Rekey: 900 seconds / 100000 bytes.
          Offer #1:
    ESP[ DES SHA1 HMAC]
    Rekey: 900 seconds / 100000 bytes.
          Offer #2:
    AH[ SHA1 HMAC]
    Rekey: 300 seconds / 100000 bytes.
          Offer #3:
    AH[ MD5 HMAC]
    Rekey: 300 seconds / 100000 bytes.
    AUTHENTICATION INFO Count = 1
          Method = Kerberos
 Src Addr   : 10.1.0.2      Src Mask   : 255.255.255.255
 Dest Addr : 0.0.0.0        Dest Mask : 0.0.0.0
 Tunnel Addr : 0.0.0.0      Src Port : 0   Dest Port : 0
 Protocol : 0      TunnelFilter: No
 Flags : Outbound
No Name - Mirror
 Filter Id: {112D30BC-61AF-4B1A-B6F7-AA4B4E0BFD58}
 Policy Id: {77F1D04E-156E-4F05-A784-35642990F53D}
 Src Addr   : 0.0.0.0        Src Mask   : 0.0.0.0
 Dest Addr : 10.1.0.2       Dest Mask : 255.255.255.255
 Tunnel Addr : 0.0.0.0      Src Port : 0   Dest Port : 0
```

```
              Protocol : 0       TunnelFilter: No
              Flags : Inbound
```

```
The command completed successfully
```

The output only shows the section relevant to the IPSec test. This command line tool is a good way of getting a summary of the IP policy that is active on a system and the detailed configuration of that policy.

Oakley Logging

The Oakley logs are detailed logs of the negotiation of SA through the ISAKMP process. They are not enabled by default and require an edit to the Registry to enable. The Registry key to create is HKLM\System\CurrentControlSet\Services\PolicyAgent\Oakley and the value is EnableLogging of REG_DWORD with a value of 1 to enable logging. You will need to reboot after making the change.

The resulting logs are stored in c:\winnt\debug\oakley.log and the following is a sample of a log:

```
<continued>
8-13: 15:33:42:12c Phase 2 SA accepted: proposal=1 transform=1
8-13: 15:33:42:12c GetSpi: src = 10.1.0.3.0000, dst = 10.1.0.2.0000,
➥ proto = 00, context = 00000000, srcMask = 255.255.255.255, destMask =
255.255.255.255, TunnelFilter 0
8-13: 15:33:42:12c Setting SPI 836407080
8-13: 15:33:42:12c Tunnelling: 0
8-13: 15:33:42:12c constructing ISAKMP Header
8-13: 15:33:42:12c constructing HASH (null)
8-13: 15:33:42:12c constructing SA (IPSEC)
8-13: 15:33:42:12c constructing NONCE (IPSEC)
8-13: 15:33:42:12c constructing ID (proxy)
8-13: 15:33:42:12c constructing ID (proxy)
8-13: 15:33:42:12c constructing NOTIFY 24576
8-13: 15:33:42:12c Copy messid e510ae59
8-13: 15:33:42:12c constructing HASH (QM)
8-13: 15:33:42:12c Construct QM Hash mess ID = 1504579813
8-13: 15:33:42:12c In state OAK_QM_AUTH_AWAIT
8-13: 15:33:42:12c Throw: State mask=34080
8-13: 15:33:42:12c Doing tripleDES
8-13: 15:33:42:12c Added Timeout f1308
8-13: 15:33:42:12c Setting Retransmit: sa 1310c90 centry 23dc30
➥handle f1308 context 130aab0
8-13: 15:33:42:12c
8-13: 15:33:42:12c Sending: SA = 0x01310C90 to 10.1.0.3
```

```
8-13: 15:33:42:12c ISAKMP Header: (V1.0), len = 188
8-13: 15:33:42:12c   I-COOKIE d77b5371e75d48b2
8-13: 15:33:42:12c   R-COOKIE 7fbefeb31e03c88f
8-13: 15:33:42:12c   exchange: Oakley Quick Mode
8-13: 15:33:42:12c   flags: 3 ( encrypted commit )
8-13: 15:33:42:12c   next payload: HASH
8-13: 15:33:42:12c   message ID: e510ae59
<continued>
```

Doing a brief analysis of the Oakley log, you can see on the second line from the top that the source (src) is 10.1.0.3 and the destination (dst) is 10.1.0.2. You can see that on the third line down from the top of the list, the Security Parameter Index (SPI) is being set to 836407080. This is the unique identifier for the SA negotiated between 10.1.0.2 and 10.1.0.3. The next line down shows tunneling set to 0, so the two systems are using the transport mode. Lastly, some 18 lines down from the top of the listing is the line Doing tripleDES, which indicates that the two system are communicating with the highest encryption.

To put the logs in perspective, the first output was produced within a 1-second time frame. The listing for the entire second output was three pages long, and the listing for a 1-day period was an over 2MB text file. Not for the faint of heart to analyze, but useful when things go wrong.

Request for Comments

For additional late night reading, some of the Request for Comments (RFCs) that pertain to IPSec are listed in Table 20.3. The Internet Engineering Task Force (IETF) manages the development of the RFCs. You can obtain these directly from the IETF Web site at http://www.ietf.org/rfc.html.

TABLE 20.3   IPSec Request for Comments

RFC	*Title*
RFC 2085	HMAC-MD5 IP Authentication with Replay Prevention
RFC 2104	HMAC: Keyed Hashing for Message Authentication
RFC 2401	Security Architecture for the Internet Protocol
RFC 2402	IP Authentication Header (AH)
RFC 2403	The Use of HMAC-MD5-96 within ESP and AH
RFC 2404	The Use of HMAC-SHA-1-96 within ESP and AH
RFC 2405	The ESP DES-CBC Cipher Algorithm with Explicit IV
RFC 2406	IP Encapsulating Security Payload (ESP)
RFC 2407	The Internet IP Security Domain of Interpretation for IKE

20

IPSec

TABLE 20.3   Continued

RFC	Title
RFC 2410	The NULL Encryption Algorithm and Its Use with IPSec
RFC 2411	IP Security Document Roadmap
RFC 2451	The ESP CBC-Mode Cipher Algorithms

Summary

The IP Secure protocol can protect all traffic extremely effectively, providing strong encryption and authentication at the packet level. This thwarts a wide variety of malicious threats, including snooping, data modification, replay of packets, and spoofing.

What's more, it provides this level of protection completely transparently to the upper layer applications and protocols. No application modification is required to implement it. Implementation of the IPSec policies is easy as well because they can be deployed using the groups policy.

Given these clear advantages, IP Secure is truly Maximum Windows 2000 Security for TCP/IP traffic!

Virtual Private Networking

IN THIS CHAPTER

Users are out in the field—at customer sites, at home, and in hotels. They want access to corporate data and applications as well as to corporate messaging systems. They need this to do their jobs and to maintain the competitive edge. For most organizations, that edge is in getting the best information quickly to the people who need it.

The challenge is to provide that access and still keep it secure. This was simple when users dialed into the corporate network, but it has become more complex as users become connected to the Internet and wanted to use it to connect to corporate resources. Windows 2000 Virtual Private Networks meets that challenge by providing secure access to corporate resources over unsecured networks.

Microsoft's original releases of the their VPN were roundly criticized by the security community. Windows 2000 locks down the previous problems and has been well received, particularly for the default VPN protocol Layer 2 Tunneling Protocol (L2TP).

Why Not Call In?

In the old days, users in the field would call long distance to their corporate office and connect directly to a bank of modems. Sometimes the number would be an 800 number to reduce toll costs to the user. Large organizations would contract with telecommunications companies to allow their users to dial local access numbers and be connected to the corporate network through a private network, typically by using X.25 technology.

Users on the Move

As users came to rely more on their corporate systems, such as messaging, enterprise applications, database, and even simple file systems, they needed access from hotels while on the road, from home when working after hours, and from customer sites during sales calls.

To meet this need, dial-up infrastructures were built to support these users. A typical dial-up model included a client, phone line, and modem bank, allowing the traveling or home user to connect to corporate servers, as shown in Figure 21.1.

Some of the options in this model included the following:

- *Direct dial*—Users essentially dial long distance calls to the corporate office. If a user happens to live close by, the toll charges are reasonable. If a user is a long distance from the office or traveling out of the country, these toll charges can be a huge expense.

- *800 numbers*—This accomplished two things for the users—not having them pay out of pocket for the toll charges and also allowing corporations to get volume discounts on toll charges.

- *Private networks*—In this development, corporations would sign up with major telecommunications carriers and reserve a section of their world-wide networks for private traffic. Users would get local dial-up access numbers, thus avoiding long distance toll charges. Only large organizations could contract with the major carriers at this level, and it was still very expensive. This was the precursor to VPNs.

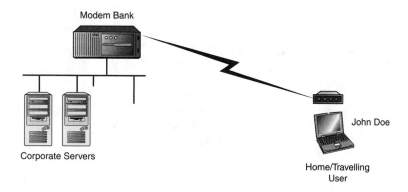

Modem Bank

Corporate Servers

John Doe

Home/Travelling
User

FIGURE 21.1
Dial-up model.

For a long time, these solutions met the needs of the majority of users. The main downside was cost and there were no good alternatives.

As time progressed, the limitations of the technology became more apparent. This included performance problems because the connection was slow compared to the normal user experience at the office. From an IT perspective, the model is very expensive to maintain and to scale. These costs included huge toll charges, especially when connected for long times and far away from home. Costs vary, but hotel long distance charges are typically at premium rates. A typical dial-in session of an hour at a major hotel can cost you upwards of $20 in the continental U.S. and hundreds of dollars in a country such as Japan.

Then more and more users started connecting to the Internet. Home users would dial into their Internet Service Provider (ISP) to access the Internet, but have to hang up and dial the corporate number to access corporate resources. Most organizations already had connections to the

Internet, so it just became a matter of connecting the dots between a home user and the corporate network through the Internet. Users started accessing resources over the Internet, but at great risk from hackers.

This led to the birth of the Virtual Private Network (VPN).

Virtual Private Network

Virtual Private Networks provided the answer to this three-headed problem of providing users access to corporate resources, maintaining strict security, and maintaining their Internet connections.

Virtual Private Networks are so named because they are virtual, not physical networks. They are private—secured from prying eyes. They are networks, because it connects the client computers with the corporate network.

As shown in Figure 21.2, the model is a little more complicated than just dialing up to the modem bank at the home office. Both the client and the corporate office have established Internet connections, and then established a secured VPN tunnel through the hacker-infested Internet. This tunnel protects the communications.

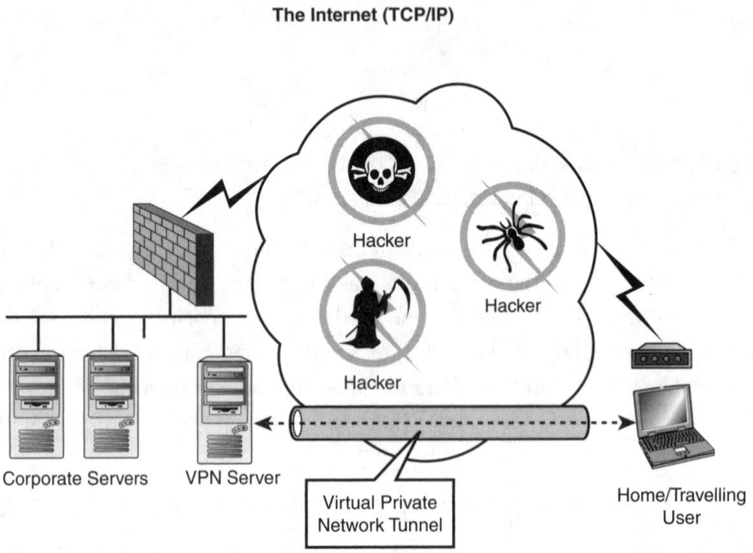

FIGURE 21.2
VPN model.

This solution is both fast and inexpensive. It leverages the infrastructure that both sides already have in place, namely the connection to the Internet. The typical cost for an Internet connection is less than $100 a month, compared to a single toll call that might be $20. Users are connecting to the Internet locally from a hotel or at locations that already have high-speed Internet access. The solution is fast because home users typically have high-speed dedicated DSL or cable modem connections.

Some of the different ways for users to connect using the VPN are as follows:

- *Home Internet DSL/Cable Modem*—As users become Internet enabled, they are perfect candidates to connect to the corporate office VPN. The connection is high-speed and there are usually no incremental charges.

- *Dial-up ISP*—Traveling users or home users without a permanent Internet connection can dial an Internet Service Provider (ISP). Because larger ISPs are building and maintaining their dial-up infrastructure and have locations nation/world-wide, the toll calls are local.

- *Customer Premise*—Another frequent use is to have employees that are at customer sites connect to the corporate VPN by using the customer facilities.

Setting Up the VPN

The best way to learn is by doing, so let's set up a VPN server, VPN client, and then connect them.

In Figure 21.3, we have a Windows 2000 Advanced Server named JUPITER, which is a member of the Active Directory domain companyabc.com. We also have a user John Doe with a Windows 2000 Professional client named MARS, which is a standalone system. John wants to access the Company ABC corporate network from home and while traveling after he has connected to the Internet.

The internal Company ABC corporate network is 11.x.x.x. John Doe's Windows 2000 Professional client system is in the 10.x.x.x network, assigned the IP address 10.1.1.115. The VPN server has a network card in each of the two networks; it has been assigned the IP address 11.2.0.1 for the internal network card and the IP address 10.1.0.2 for the external network card. As you can also see within the Internet cloud, there are quite a few nasty-looking hackers waiting to hack John's connection.

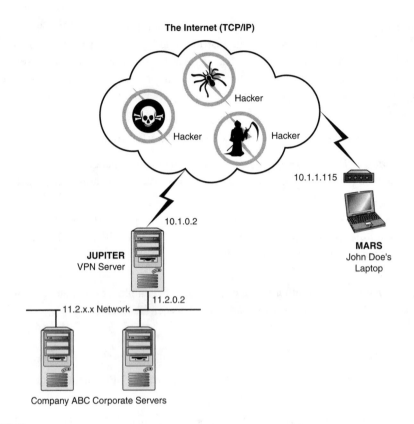

FIGURE 21.3
Typical client setup.

Setting Up the Server

To set up the server, do the following:

1. Select Start, Programs, Administrative Tools, Routing and Remote Access.

2. Select Action, Configure and Enable Routing and Remote Access to launch the wizard.

3. Click Next.

4. Select Manually Configured Server, click Next, and click Finish.

5. Click Yes to start service.

You should now have a configuration similar to the one shown in Figure 21.4, which has the Ports container highlighted. You can see that the wizard has automatically created 10 VPN ports, 5 each of PPTP ports and L2TP ports.

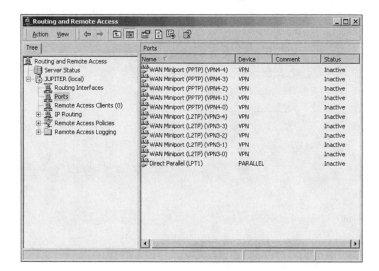

FIGURE 21.4
VPN ports in RRAS tool.

The system is ready to support PPTP as is, but it needs an additional step to support L2TP. The L2TP protocol uses IPSec, which needs a method of mutually authenticating both parties in a session. We'll run through the steps to get it working, and then breakdown what it is that we did and why in the "Technical Details" section later in this chapter.

To set up the Server computer with a Certificate, do the following:

1. Launch Internet Explorer.

2. Go to http://sectestca2.rte.microsoft.com/certsrv.

3. Click on Request a Certificate.

4. Click Advanced Certificate Request.

5. Click Create and Submit a Request to this CA.

6. Fill out the Identifying Information.

7. Select Type of Certificate Needed from the pull-down menu, which should be IPSec Certificate, as shown in Figure 21.5. Leave everything else as is (default).

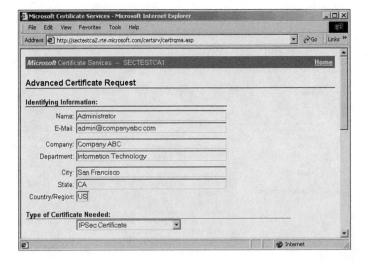

FIGURE 21.5
Server certificate identifying information and type.

8. Scroll down to Key Options and check Use Local Machine Store, as shown in Figure 21.6. Leave everything else as is (default).

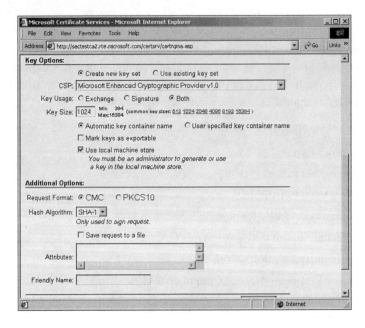

FIGURE 21.6
Certificate key options.

9. Scroll to the bottom of the form and click Submit.

10. This will generate the certificate and then give you the option to install the certificate, as shown in Figure 21.7. Click Install This Certificate to install.

11. After getting the Certificate Installed screen, close the browser.

12. You will need to reboot to have the certificate used by the Remote Access Server.

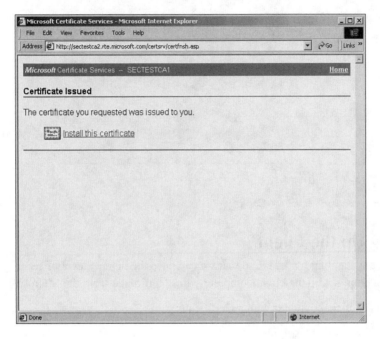

FIGURE 21.7
Install the Certificate.

You're now ready to accept VPN connection from clients using either PPTP or L2TP. We'll now set up a client for our Sales Representative John Doe. By default, all users are denied Remote Access for security reasons, so we'll allow access for John Doe using the Active Directory for Users and Computers tool on the domain controller. Figure 21.8 shows the John Doe object with the proper permissions.

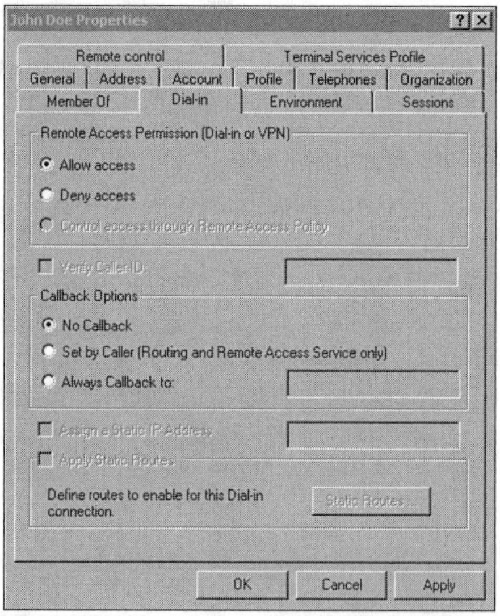

FIGURE 21.8
Allowing remote access in Active Directory.

Setting Up the Client

We'll set the client up for L2TP, so that we can have the highest level of security. Following the instructions, set up the client computer with a certificate from the Microsoft CA.

To set up the client computer with a Certificate:

1. Launch Internet Explorer.

2. Go to http://sectestca2.rte.mcirosoft.com/certsrv.

3. Click Request a Certificate.

4. Click Advanced Certificate Request.

5. Click Create and Submit a Request to this CA.

6. Fill out the Identifying Information, this time with the user information shown in Figure 21.9.

7. Select Type of Certificate Needed from the pull-down menu, which should be IPSec Certificate. Leave everything else as is (the default).

8. Scroll down to Key Options and check the Use Local Machine Store. Leave everything else as is (default).

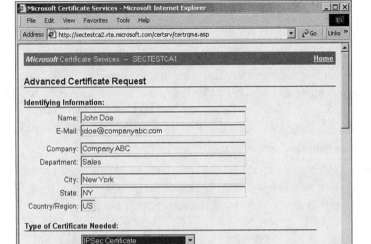

FIGURE 21.9
User certificate identifying information.

9. Scroll to the bottom of the form and click Submit.

10. This will generate the certificate and then give you the option to install the certificate. Click Install This Certificate to install.

11. After getting the Certificate Installed screen, close the browser.

Now we're ready to configure the connection to the server.

To set up the VPN connection, do the following:

1. Select Start, Settings, Network and Dial-up Connections, Make New Connection to launch wizard.

2. Click Next.

3. Select Connect to a Private Network Through the Internet and click Next to continue.

4. Enter the Destination Address, which is the IP address or fully-qualified domain name of the VPN server, and click Next.

5. Click Next to create the connection for all users.

6. Enter the name **Company ABC VPN** for the name and click Finish.

Connect!

Now we are ready to actually connect and start using the VPN. When connecting, we will establish the tunnel and authenticate the user to verify proper permissions.

1. The connection automatically launches after the previous steps. If the connection did not launch automatically or you are doing this part at a later time, launch the connection by selecting Start, Settings, Network and Dial-up Connections, Company ABC VPN.

2. Enter John Doe's login and password. We'll use the user principal name format, which is **jdoe@companyabc.com**, as is shown in Figure 21.10. Also, enter the password.

3. Click Connect to Setup the VPN Tunnel. After authentication and registration, you should see a message indicting that the connection was established. Figure 21.11 shows the message. You can now access internal resources.

FIGURE 21.10
Authenticating to a VPN session.

FIGURE 21.11
Successful VPN connection!

At this point, all the features of a VPN are present. The client system has established an encapsulated tunnel to the Windows 2000 server and has secured it from prying eyes with encryption. The user, John Doe, has been authenticated with his username and password combination. Lastly, John Doe's laptop has been integrated into the corporate network by being assigned an internal IP address and having the computer name registered with the corporate network.

Figure 21.12 shows the VPN connection that we established to the corporate office. Note that John Doe's laptop has been assigned an internal IP address (11.2.0.101) from the IP address space of the Company ABC corporate network. This address is used for communicating with the corporate network services, while the 10.1.1.115 address is used to route the VPN packets across the Internet.

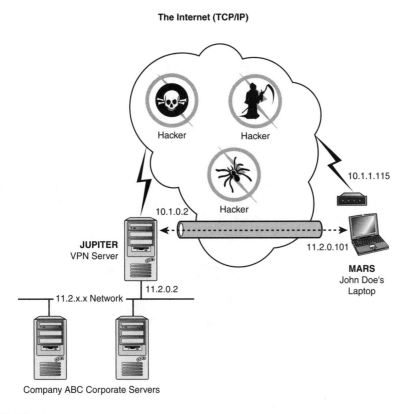

The Internet (TCP/IP)

Hacker   Hacker

10.1.1.115

Hacker

10.1.0.2

JUPITER
VPN Server

11.2.0.101

MARS
John Doe's
Laptop

— 11.2.x.x Network —   11.2.0.2

Company ABC Corporate Servers

FIGURE 21.12
After VPN connection.

All this ensures that the connection to the corporate network is private. Rather than just take the author or Microsoft's word for it, we will look at the connection in detail to verify the security.

Verifying the Connection

On the server, you should see that the port has switched from Inactive to Active in the RRAS Tool, as shown in Figure 21.13. You might need to refresh the screen because it does not refresh automatically by default.

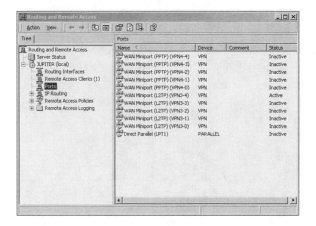

FIGURE 21.13
Active ports in RRAS tool.

If you double-click the active connection, you'll see Port Status information on the line speed, the user authenticated, statistics, communication errors, and other useful information. For the session we just established with John Doe, the Port Status is shown in Figure 21.14. You can also reset or disconnect the session if needed.

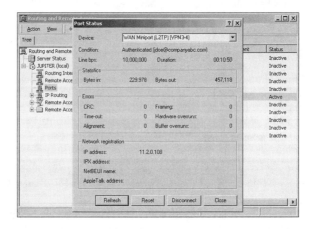

FIGURE 21.14
VPN port status.

We had saidthat we were going to set up the VPN for the highest level of security through L2TP. Let's make sure that the client is communicating securely. Going back to what we learned in Chapter 20, "IPSec," we will use IPSec Monitor to see if we have a secure connection. Use Start, Run to run the `ipsecmon.exe` program and you should see something similar to Figure 21.15. You can tell from the figure that there is an IPSec rule named L2TP Rule that it is using Triple-DES for ESP encryption and MD5 for AH signing. Very secure.

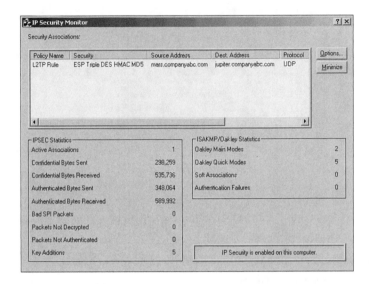

FIGURE 21.15
Verifying VPN encryption with IPSec monitor.

To verify that our packets are being encrypted, we've also used Network Monitor to capture the packet stream at the server. Figure 21.16 shows the familiar ISAKMP packets during the initial stages of the connection and then a series of ESP packets after the SA has been negotiated. In this capture, JUPITER is our server and 10.1.1.115 is John Doe's laptop.

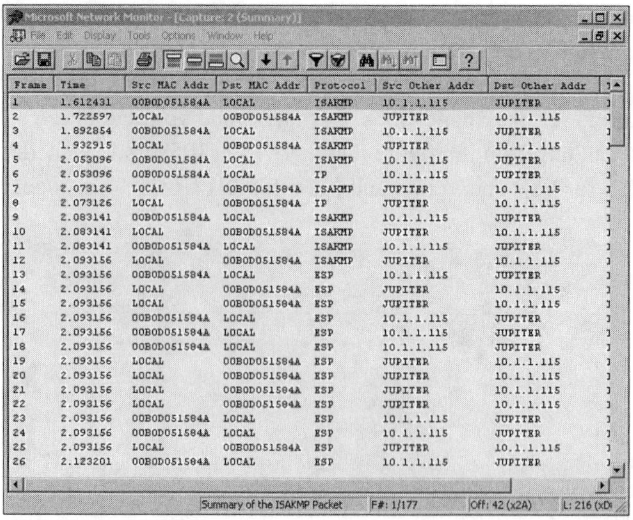

FIGURE 21.16

Sniffing VPN traffic.

Can we see the password that John Doe entered when authenticating? We can't, for two reasons:

- *Encryption*—The individual packets are encrypted by IPSec.
- *Password protection*—The actual password is never sent over the wire!

The latter point is one of the clever tricks that Microsoft Windows 2000 employs to keep the connection secure. This is accomplished through defense in depth, where there are multiple layers of protection. Even if one layer of protection is broken by a hacker, the next layer will continue to provide protection. In the case of the password, even if a hacker manages to break the IPSec encryption (highly unlikely), the packets that he or she captures would not reveal the password and, thus, would be useless.

We'll see how the system manages to authenticate John Doe without actually sending his password over the wire in the "Authentication" section later in this chapter.

Technical Details

Microsoft Windows 2000 VPN has evolved over many years and with a lot of candid (and usually harsh) feedback from industry experts and customers alike. The result is a mature and highly-secure remote access solution.

Unfortunately, this evolution results in different options and choices to be made. With Windows 2000 VPNs, the major choice is which VPN network protocol to use:

- Layer Two Tunneling Protocol
- Point-to-Point Tunneling Protocol

We will look at both protocols and compare them. To do that, we will first look at what features make a Virtual Private Network.

No security discussion would be complete without looking at some algorithms and comparing the relative security of each. Luckily, in the case of Windows 2000 VPNs, there is a clear winner.

VPN—Private!

There are some key features that make a VPN different from just a TCP/IP connection, a dial-up link, or any other method of connecting to the corporate network. These are as follows:

- Encapsulation
- Authentication
- Data encryption
- Internal address and name integration

Without all of these features, a connection does not qualify as a Virtual Private Network. Encapsulation provides the virtual aspects of the connection by creating a tunnel from the remote client to the corporate network. Authentication and data encryption provide the privacy. Lastly, the internal address and name integration ensure that the remote client becomes part of the corporate network logical address and namespace, as if it were physically attached to the corporate network.

Encapsulation

A virtual tunnel is established using encapsulation, similar to putting a letter in an envelope to be sent via the U.S. Postal Service. The letter is encapsulated in the envelope. Packets of data traveling to the corporate network are encapsulated in the tunneling protocol.

The benefit of encapsulation is that it allows the encapsulated protocol to travel through the tunnel completely unmodified, even if the tunnel imposes authentication and encryption. The encapsulated packet is treated simply as data, so the VPN does not need to have any knowledge of or treat the encapsulated packet in any special way. On the flip side, the protocol being tunneled does not have to be aware of the tunneling process and arrives at the other end of the tunnel completely unchanged.

Data Encryption

Encryption to protect the confidentiality of the data you are sending across the Internet is a critical component of the VPN. At minimum, the data payload is encrypted. At best, the entire packet is encrypted. This prevents unauthorized viewing of sensitive corporate traffic.

Microsoft Windows 2000 VPNs employ the following data encryption protocols:

- *Microsoft Point-to-Point Encryption (MPPE)*—This encryption protocol is a Microsoft modification of the PPE encryption protocol and uses the Rivest-Shamir-Adelman (RSA) RC4 algorithm. MPPE can use 40-bit, 56-bit, or 128-bit keys for higher security.
- *Data Encryption Standard (DES)*—Uses 56-bit keys to encrypt the data.
- *Triple DES (3DES)*—Also uses 56-bit keys, but it processes the text three times with three different keys. Very secure.

See Chapter 20 on IPSec for descriptions of the DES encryption algorithms.

There are two layers of encryption that you get with VPNs configured with the default level of protection, which is the encryption of the authentication negotiation and the encryption of the VPN tunnel. This is important to the defense in depth strategy to provide multiple independent layers of protection.

In addition, as we will see in the authentication discussion, some forms of authentication do not protect the password of the user at all.

> **NOTE**
>
> RC4 is a stream cipher symmetric key encryption algorithm. RC4 stands for Ron's Code #4. It was developed in 1987 by Ron Rivest and kept as a trade secret by RSA Data Security. However, the RC4 algorithm was anonymously posted on the Internet late in 1994.
>
> The RC4 key is often limited to 40 bits, because of export restrictions, but it can be used with keys as high as 2048-bits. The main concern with RC4 in MPPE is that the key is combined with the user's password for encryption. This makes the encryption susceptible to password dictionary attacks because the user password is usually quite short and often predictable.

The encryption protocol 3DES is widely considered to be extremely difficult, if not impossible, to crack with today's computing resources. If security is of paramount importance, the design of your VPN should require the options needed to support 3DES.

Authentication

Users are authenticated to both prove their identity and to ensure that they have the proper access rights. To prevent tampering, all packets are signed for integrity purposes.

The users account in the Windows 2000 domain is used to authenticate users, to both verify identities and to ensure they are authorized to use the remote access. You can use a RADIUS server for the authentication. Microsoft Windows 2000 provides a RADIUS server—Internet Authentication Service. The IAS can use a variety of data sources, such as its own database, an ODBC-compliant database, or a Microsoft PDC.

Windows 2000 VPN clients can authenticate using a variety of methods, not all of which are equal:

- *Extensible Authentication Protocol (EAP)*—This authentication protocol supports two-factor authentication, such as smart cards or retinal scan. This uses Transport Layer Security (TLS) to protect the authentication process, so it is sometimes referred to as EAP-TLS. This is the most secure authentication protocol because it requires two forms of identification from the user.

- *Microsoft Challenge Handshake Authentication Protocol (MS-CHAP)*—MS-CHAP is the most common authentication protocol for Windows 2000 VPNs. This is really two protocols—MS-CHAP and MS-CHAPv2. These protocols use the Message Digest 4 (MD4) hash to pass the authentication information between hosts. It further protects the transfer using Microsoft Point-to-Point Encryption (MPPE). In addition, MS-CHAPv2 has mutual authentication, longer encryption keys, and separate keys for sending and receiving. MS-CHAPv2 is very secure, whereas MS-CHAP offers medium-level security.

- *Challenge Handshake Authentication Protocol (CHAP)*—This protocol uses a hash function at the client to process the server challenge and user-supplied password. It then sends the result back to the server. The server performs the same process and compares the results. This requires that the user password be stored in plaintext on the domain controller, which is a security risk. This protocol provides medium-level security.

- *Shiva Password Authentication Protocol (SPAP)*—This is an authentication protocol supported by Shiva remote access servers, as well as Windows 2000. It uses reversible encryption to pass the password from the client to the server, making it susceptible to dictionary attacks. It provides no security against impersonation. This is a low-security protocol.

- *Password Authentication Protocol (PAP)*—This is supported by almost all remote access network services and sends the users password in clear text, making it completely susceptible to packet sniffing. This is a very low-security protocol, bordering on no security.

One of the more clever processes used by CHAP, MS-CHAP, and EAP is to not actually send the password over the wire when authenticating. The process of computing a one-way hash function and sending that over the wire instead of the password itself ensures that even if a hacker captures a packet with the authentication information, he or she will be unable to reverse the hash computation and discern the real password.

In contrast, SPAP sends the password over the wire with reversible encryption. If a hacker captures a packet that contains the password, he or she can then leisurely crack it and use the password later. Obviously, there's no cracking required with PAP because the password is sent in clear text. Nothing clever about that.

The default authentication methods are MS-CHAP and MS-CHAPv2, as is shown in Figure 21.17. Both these protocols protect the password by never sending it over the wire, but rather only sending the result of a hash function computation. From a security standpoint, the most secure authentication protocols are EAP and MS-CHAPv2.

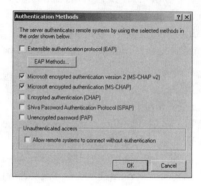

FIGURE 21.17
Default authentication methods.

Internal Address and Name Integration

Another key feature of VPNs is that the remote client has to integrate with the corporate network. The remote client has to operate as if it were a node plugged directly into a jack in the office. This is what gives the VPN its virtual network designation.

To accomplish this, the VPN server needs to have IP address assigned to client to integrate into the corporate network. This can come from an internal pool of addresses on the VPN server, but more often from the corporate Dynamic Host Configuration Protocol (DHCP) server. The IP address that gets assigned does not replace the IP address of the network interface card on the remote client, but rather it is assigned to the logical network adapter associated with the VPN tunnel. In effect, the remote client has a logical IP leg in the corporate network.

The assignment of the IP address brings several other changes as well, such as the assignment of DNS server assigned to resolve names using corporate namespace. If being used, a

Windows Internetwork Naming Server (WINS) can also be assigned. The default routing on the remote client is also changed for the duration of the session to default to corporate network, ensuring that packets travel through the protected tunnel.

After the client is assigned an IP address and a DNS server, Windows 2000 clients automatically register themselves with the corporate DNS and the corporate WINS if assigned. This integrates the remote client system into the corporate namespace and the corporate IP address space.

Point-to-Point Tunneling Protocol

Microsoft Windows 2000 supports two major VPN protocols, PPTP and L2TP. The earlier versions of the Windows operating system supported the PPTP VPN. The Point-to-Point Tunneling Protocol (PPTP) is a modification of an even older protocol, the ISO High Level Data Link Control (HDLC) protocol. The HDLC protocol was developed to handle communications over serial links, and PPP is a variation of it used for dial-up connections. To support remote access over networks rather than a dial-up line, PPTP was jointly developed by Microsoft and 3COM to tunnel PPP over IP networks.

PPTP uses IP packets to route PPP frames between the tunnel endpoints through the Internet. The protocol uses two different types packets to maintain the tunnel and to send data, as shown in Figure 21.18. PPTP uses a TCP connection for tunnel maintenance, using TCP port 1723. For data transmission, PPTP uses PPP encapsulation, further encapsulated in a Generic Routing Encapsulation (GRE) packet of IP type 47. Finally, the GRE encapsulated packet is encapsulated in an IP packet addressed to the tunnel endpoint. This can sometimes be a problem for Internet routers that do not always support the routing of GRE IP packets.

PPTP Tunnel Control Packet

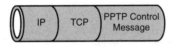

PPTP Tunneled Data Packet

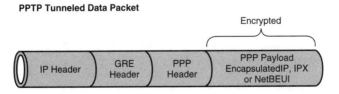

FIGURE 21.18

PPTP tunnel control and data packets.

As you can see from the previous paragraphs, PPTP has relatively high overhead to work the data through all the encapsulation layers.

PPTP uses Microsoft Point-to-Point Encryption (MPPE) for encryption, but only with the stronger authentication protocols, such as MS-CHAP, MS-CHAPv2, and EAP-TLS. One of the big security concerns with PPP was the use of the same key for multiple packets, which made it susceptible to cryptographic analysis. To avoid this, PPTP generates a new key with every packet. The trade off is that the encryption key change with every packet adds overhead.

An important point to understand is that PPTP only encrypts data between the tunnel ends. While in the tunnel, all traffic will be secured. However, after exiting the tunnel on either side, the traffic is no longer secured and will traverse the wire in its native form. If you want server to client encryption, use IPSec on both the client and the destination server. The IPSec traffic will be encapsulated between the client and server, while being encapsulated in the PPTP packets.

To conserve bandwidth, PPTP supports compression using the Microsoft Point-to-Point Compression Protocol (MPPC). Developed in 1997, the MPPC protocol uses an LZ algorithm for compressing sequential streams of data, maintaining an 8KB window of data for compression. The MPPC algorithm is designed to optimize processor utilization to support large numbers of simultaneous connections, which is a nice way of saying that it does not compress very well. Good compression can be very processor-intensive, so the protocol does not employ any really complex algorithms to be able to have more connections. Typical compression results are in the 30 percent range, but this can vary substantially, depending on the data being transmitted.

Authentication in PPTP supports all the authentication methods described in the authentication section, from EAP-TLS on down to PAP. This is important for supporting legacy and third-party clients that might not support the advanced protocols. However, choosing an authentication protocol such as PAP, SPAP, or CHAP requires special configurations, such as storing passwords in reversible encryption. Also, any VPN sessions established with these authentication methods will be unencrypted and extremely susceptible to hacking. Bottom line, do not choose an authentication other than MS-CHAP, MS-CHAPv2, or EAP-TLS if security is at all a concern. Computer authentication is not supported in PPTP.

The clients supported with PPTP include Windows 95, Windows 98, Windows NT 4.0, and Windows 2000. This makes it very flexible for supporting legacy clients.

The Point-to-Point Tunneling Protocol provides an effective VPN solution, providing it is configured properly.

Layer Two Tunneling Protocol

With the release of Windows 2000, Microsoft addressed many of the security concerns with its previous VPN technology by including L2TP. Layer Two Tunneling Protocol (L2TP) is a combination of two other protocols. One is the Point-to-Point Tunneling Protocol described earlier and the other is Layer 2 Forwarding (L2F) proposed by Cisco Systems and Shiva. IETF mixed the two to produce L2TP, based on a proposal by Microsoft and Cisco. L2TP combines the best features of both protocols.

More flexible than its predecessor PPTP, LT2P can encapsulate PPP frames to be sent over IP, X.25, Frame Relay, or even ATM networks. To date, only PPP encapsulation over IP has been defined. The simple reason for this is that IP is supported over all these networks, so there is no commercial reason to have L2TP run native on anything other than IP. The description of L2TP in this chapter is specific to the IP implementation of L2TP.

Tunneling and control of tunnel in L2TP uses the same type of packets, UDP port 1701 in both directions. The packet format for both tunnel control messages and for the tunneled data are the same, which is shown in Figure 21.19.

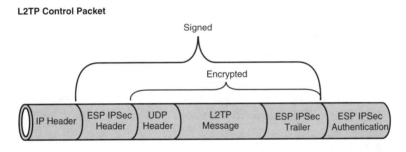

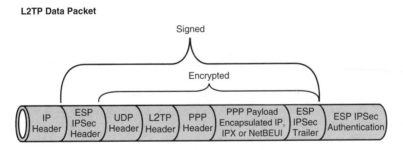

FIGURE 21.19

L2TP tunnel control and data packets.

Looking at the figure, you'll notice right away that the L2TP packets are IPSec packets. Unlike PPTP, which provides its own encryption and compression with MPPE and MPPC, L2TP only performs compression with MPPC. When encapsulating the data in PPP, L2TP does not negotiate encryption. Instead, L2TP security is provided though IPSec, with all the protection that brings. See Chapter 10 for a detailed description of the IPSec protocol.

One difference with L2TP is that the IPSec policy is created by the RAS manager service specifically for it, rather than using the default policy or a user-created one. The default security parameters for the IPSec policy is 3DES for encryption and HMAC-MD5 for the signature. New encryption and authentication keys are generated every hour or 2GB of data, whichever comes first.

When establishing a VPN connection using L2TP, an IPSec SA is negotiated first and then the VPN tunnel is negotiated. Establishing an IPSec tunnel first ensures that no VPN packets travel over the network unprotected.

Authentication with L2TP is provided for both user and for computers. The user-level authentication methods are the same as for PPTP, but L2TP doesn't need to use a specific authentication protocol to ensure the encryption of the tunnel because that service is provided by the IPSec tunneling. There are still advantages to using MS-CHAP, MS-CHAPv2, or EAP-TLS, such as mutual user authentication and not having to store passwords in reversible encryption.

Computer level authentication is provided by certificates or pre-shared keys through the IPSec negotiation. This requires an additional step of obtaining a computer certificate from some Public Key Infrastructure (PKI), either from a trusted third-party Certificate Authority (CA), such as VeriSign or Microsoft, or by creating a corporate CA. These certificates need to be distributed to each VPN server and each client, although the task can be automated through certificate enrollment.

In the demonstration at the beginning of the chapter, we manually obtained certificates from the Microsoft CA and installed them on both the server and the client.

The only client that supports L2TP today is Microsoft Windows 2000, all versions. There is no support for Windows NT or 9.x, which can be a limitation in mixed environments.

The Layer Two Tunneling Protocol provides a high security VPN solution that is generally recognized as being extremely difficult to compromise, mainly due to the use of IPSec as the security provider. It takes advantage of modern techniques but requires new operating systems, such as Windows 2000. It also requires additional configuration to distribute certificates to the client computers.

L2TP Versus PPTP

In selecting which VPN network protocol to use, there are several decision points to consider. This includes, first and foremost, which protocol will give you the most security in your environment. Other considerations are what clients you will be supporting, any deployment issues your organization faces, what your firewall constraints are, and what performance issues might come into play.

The highest level of security you'll get is with L2TP because it uses IPSec for security. IPSec is the gold standard for security and is also very customizable. When IPSec is configured for ESP 3DES and AH, the security is extremely difficult to crack. The ability to require computer authentication as well as user authentication is invaluable to protect against lost passwords or users that choose weak passwords.

In looking at what clients are supported, PPTP is the hands-down winner for supporting clients ranging from Windows 95 on through Windows 2000. In comparison, L2TP only supports Windows 2000. If your organization has a diverse mix of clients, you might have to choose PPTP. Deploying to clients is also a concern when using L2TP because computer certificates need to be installed on every machine. As we saw in the demonstration, this can be very easy but does require some extra work.

Another big difference between L2TP and PPTP is that L2TP combines the control and data and runs over UDP as opposed to TCP. UDP is a faster, more efficient protocol for sending packets. PPTP, by contrast, separates the control and data channels into a control stream that runs over TCP and a data stream that runs over GRE. Combining the channels and using UDP makes L2TP more firewall-friendly than PPTP. On the PPTP side, it supports operations through NAT firewalls, which L2TP does not.

In keeping with the "No Free Lunch" principle, L2TP has approximately 25 percent more overhead than PPTP, as measured in independent testing. This means that for a given server or WAN connection, you'll be able to support 25 percent more clients with PPTP. If you are resource or equipment constrained, this might make a difference.

For Windows 2000 clients, the default VPN network protocol selection is automatic, which means that the client tries L2TP first and then tries PPTP if the negotiation fails. You can set the client to either L2TP or PPTP, in which case it will only attempt the protocol selected.

VPN Versus Terminal Services

Virtual Private Networks and Windows 2000 Terminal Services share much in common for providing corporate remote access to users. They both allow users to access network services over the Internet, both are concerned with security, and both are concerned with performance. How do you choose one over the other?

Where the two technologies differ is in how they meet the challenges of providing secure, high-performance access. As we've seen, VPNs provide a remote link to the corporate network as if the remote client were directly attached via a long network cable. All the processing takes place locally at the client, and all the data the client needs has to come over the network link.

Windows 2000 Terminal Services provides a remote desktop, in effect providing a long key-board and monitor cable that reaches all the way back to the corporate office. It does this by running a virtual desktop on the Terminal Server. This virtual desktop sends screen scrapes to the remote client and receives key presses and mouse movements in return (shown in Figure 21.20) using the Remote Desktop Protocol (RDP). The entire processing takes place on the corporate server in the virtual session, and data only needs to travel to the corporate server, rather than across the network to the remote client.

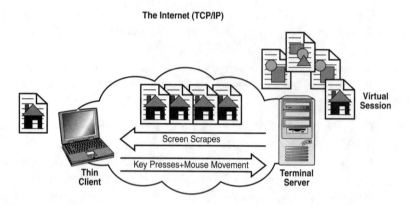

FIGURE 21.20
Terminal server and client.

This technology requires very little hardware at the client side, known as a *thin client*. Because no processing takes place locally, the client has only modest requirements for CPU and memory. Thin clients can be 32-bit applications run on 32-bit operating systems (such as Windows 2000 or Windows 9x), browser-based clients in browsers (such as Internet Explorer), 16-bit clients run on 16-bit operating systems (such as Windows for Workgroups), or even dedicated devices (such as Wyse Winterms).

Windows 2000 Terminal Services allow a small hardware footprint at the client side. Because the server is typically connected directly to the corporate network backbone, it allows high bandwidth access at the processing side of the session. In addition, because the server is local and virtual sessions on the same server share the installed application code, upgrades and software maintenance only need to be applied once to the server. Users establishing a session after that will all get the upgrade, regardless of the local client that they use.

While the client footprint is small, the server footprint is correspondingly larger to support multiple virtual sessions. In cost of ownership studies, there is usually no net savings in capital costs for hardware and software. Another big drawback of terminal services is that it requires you to be connected at all times. In other words, laptop users cannot work offline with this solution. Last, there is considerably less flexibility in how users configure their systems and what software to load. Because the users share the same system in effect, they are typically locked out of making any real changes for both security and flexibility reasons.

From a security standpoint, there are three levels of protocol security for the Windows Terminal Services sessions:

- *Low encryption*—Low encryption will encrypt only packets being sent from the client to the server running Terminal Server. This client-only encryption protects sensitive data, such as a user's password. This uses the RC4 algorithm with a 40-bit key.

- *Medium encryption*—Medium Low encryption will encrypt both outgoing packets from the client and also encrypt all packets being returned to the client from the server. This ensures that all data traveling over the wire is encrypted. This setting uses the RC4 algorithm with a 40-bit key.

- *High encryption*—High Low encryption will encrypt packets to and from the client, but will use the industry standard RC4 encryption algorithm—again with a 40-bit key—unless the 128-bit High Encryption Pack or Service Pack 2 is installed.

The low- and medium-security options are not acceptable if you are at all concerned about security because they transmit information in clear text form. With the high encryption option, the Windows 2000 Terminal Services connection is very secure. While not as secure as IPSec running 3DES would be, RC4 with a 128-bit key is a formidable challenge to a hacker.

From a security perspective, the best solution would be to run Terminal Services on top of a VPN solution. That is, have a VPN to provide secure access to the corporate network and run the appropriate applications through the tunnel that you create. This includes terminal services as an application.

Getting Through the Firewall

One of the tasks of a VPN is to operate through a firewall. A common configuration is to have the VPN server sit behind the firewall, which requires opening a hole through the firewall for the VPN to come through, as shown in Figure 21.21.

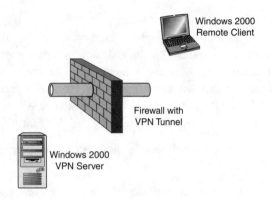

FIGURE 21.21
VPN tunnel through the firewall.

The two different VPN network protocols have different port requirements and restrictions.

For L2TP, the requirements are as follows:

- *ISAKMP (UDP Port 500)*—These are the IPSec negotiation packets.
- *ESP (IP Port 50)*—IPSec ESP Packets at IP port 50. After negotiation, all L2TP authentication and data packets travel through the firewall encapsulated in ESP packets.

For PPTP, the requirements are as follows:

- *PPTP Control (TCP Port 1723)*—These are the tunnel control packets used by PPTP.
- *GRE (IP Port 47)*—Generic Routing Encapsulation, used by PPTP for data transmission.

If the firewall is performing Network Address Translation (NAT), only PPTP can be used. Because L2TP is encapsulated in IPSec and IPSec can not operate through NAT, L2TP can not operate through NAT. The problem is that NAT changes the UDP header information, which causes IPSec to consider the packet to be corrupt and drop it.

If the firewall is Microsoft Internet Security & Acceleration (ISA) server, the ISA server can be configured as the end-point of an L2TP tunnel. The ISA server is a NAT-only firewall, for security reasons, so it cannot pass L2TP traffic through. However, you can still have the security benefits of L2TP with the ISA server by configuring the ISA server as your VPN server as well. The ISA server ships with wizards that step you through the process of configuring the server correctly for both L2TP and PPTP.

Request for Comments

For additional late night reading, some of the Request for Comments (RFCs) that pertain to Microsoft VPN technologies are listed below in Table 21.1. The Internet Engineering Task Force (IETF) manages the development of the RFCs. You can obtain these directly from the IETF Web site at `http://www.ietf.org/rfc.html`.

The two key ones to look at are the RFC2637 describing PPTP and RFC2661 describing L2TP. Other good ones are RFC3078 on MPPE, RFC2118 on MPPC, and the RFCs from Chapter 10.

TABLE 21.1 Microsoft VPN Request for Comments

RFC	Title
2637	Point-to-Point Tunneling Protocol—PPTP
2661	Layer Two Tunneling Protocol "L2TP"
2716	PPP EAP TLS Authentication Protocol
1549	PPP in HDLC Framing
1552	The PPP Internetwork Packet Exchange Control Protocol (IPXCP)
1334	PPP Authentication Protocols
1661	The Point-to-Point Protocol (PPP)
1990	The PPP Multilink Protocol (MP)
1877	PPP Internet Protocol Control Protocol Extensions for Name Server Addresses
1994	PPP Challenge Handshake Authentication Protocol (CHAP)
2097	The PPP NetBIOS Frames Control Protocol (NBFCP)
2118	Microsoft Point-to-Point Compression (MPPC) Protocol
2125	The PPP Bandwidth Allocation Protocol (BAP)/The PPP Bandwidth Allocation Control Protocol (BACP)
1570	PPP LCP Extensions
2138	Remote Authentication Dial-In User Service (RADIUS)
2139	RADIUS Accounting
2548	Microsoft Vendor-specific RADIUS Attributes
2284	PPP Extensible Authentication Protocol (EAP)
3078	Microsoft Point-To-Point Encryption (MPPE) Protocol
3079	Deriving Keys for use with Microsoft Point-to-Point Encryption (MPPE)

Summary

Microsoft Windows 2000 Virtual Private Networks provide an excellent way to allow users to access corporate resources while working from home, traveling out in the field, or working from customer site. The VPN technology ensures the privacy of these communications by using sophisticated encryption and authentication protocols, while also providing ease of configuration and maintenance.

Maintaining Windows 2000 Server Security

IN THIS PART

Log Monitoring and Analysis

IN THIS CHAPTER

One of the top advantages that Windows 2000 offers in terms of security is event logging. Logging is an essential component of any network operating system. This chapter focuses on logging tools and techniques that help you keep your finger on your system's daily pulse.

What Is Logging, Exactly?

If you're just now migrating to Windows 2000, you might not be familiar with logging. Most desktop-oriented operating systems—and in particular, Microsoft systems that preceded NT—offer minimal logging or, sometimes, no logging at all.

Logging is any procedure by which an operating system or application records system events and preserves these for later perusal.

It's difficult to say when logging first became a staple procedure in computing, but it hails from the discipline of programming. Even when you write a simple program, it's useful to have diagnostic information on hand. Some examples are

- Whether the program faulted and if so, when and why?
- The program's context information, such as the User ID (UID) the process is running under and the tracking number assigned to the process by the operating system called the Process ID (PID).
- Who has used the program, and when did they use it?
- Does the program perform tasks in the way you want it to?

Sometimes, you have other reasons to incorporate logging into your programs. For example, suppose you're hired to write a CGI program that creates and manages a contact database. It's not a bad idea to track changes (and deletions in particular) as follows:

```
open(DELETELOG, ">>deletelog");
    $date=`date /t`;
$linenumber = $.;
$linerecord = $_;
@fields=split('\!\:\!', $linerecord);
  select(DELETELOG);
  print "On $date, you deleted line $linenumber: ";
  print "$fields[0] : $fields[1] : $fields[2]\n";
  close(DELETELOG);
```

This way, if your client inadvertently deletes an irreplaceable record, they can later recover it from the log.

In a security context, logging serves a different purpose: *to preserve a record of an attacker's evil deeds.* Logs provide the only real evidence that a crime has occurred.

Default Logging Support in Windows 2000

Logging in Windows 2000 is pervasive and occurs at the system, application, and security levels. And, although there are exceptions (for example, third-party software that fails to conform to Windows 2000 's logging scheme), most Windows 2000 services output log information to centralized log files.

The following are default logging mechanisms we'll examine here:

- Event viewer
- The application log
- The security log
- The system log

The Event Viewer

The Windows 2000 main log destination (and equivalent of Unix's syslog and kernel messages files) is the Event Viewer. The Event Viewer is a snap-in to the Microsoft Management Console (MMC). The MMC is used to administer most components in Windows 2000 and should be familiar to most administrators. To start the Event Viewer, choose My Computer, Control Panel, Administrative Tools, Event Viewer. In response, Windows 2000 will display the Event View console (see Figure 22.1).

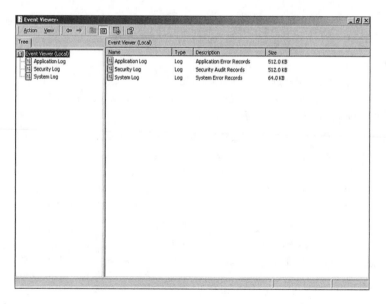

FIGURE 22.1

The Event Viewer main window.

Event Viewer catches messages in a way very similar to standard Unix kernel loggers, including audit events such as

- *Errors*—Errors indicate serious problems that require the administrator's attention. These could be instances of data loss, application faults, drivers that fail to load correctly, and so on.

- *Warnings*—These are the equivalent of kernel or system warnings in Unix. They need not necessarily signal a partial or fatal failure, but instead warn that the specified resource did not (or soon will not) behave as intended. The administrator should review these events to see if they require further action.

- *Information*—These are events that report successful loading of applications, drivers, or service. Rarely do informational events indicate anything wrong.

- *Success Audits*—These signal that this or that security access attempt succeeded (as in a successful login). For Success Audits to appear in the security log, the administrator must have configured auditing to log success events. The administrator configures the events to audit in the Security Log in the Domain Security Policy or Local Security Policy.

- *Failure Audits*—These signal that this or that security access attempt failed (as in a failed login). For Failure Audits to appear in the security log, the administrator must have configured auditing to log failure events. The administrator configures the events to audit in the Security Log in the Domain Security Policy or Local Security Policy.

Like most default Unix logging configurations, Event Viewer also breaks these records up into separate modules:

- *Application Log*—The Application Log records events from applications. Application developers generally define the event ID and detail information that the application will log to the Application Log. Many applications have the ability to configure the level of detail that is logged to the Application Log.

- *Security Log*—The Security Log logs security related events, such as logons (failed or otherwise), file access, and permission usage. Failure and Success audits are logged to the Security Log. By default, nothing is recorded in the Security Log. The administrator configures the events to audit in the Security Log in the Domain Security Policy or Local Security Policy. After auditing is configured, events will appear in the Security Log.

- *System Log*—The System Log logs events from within the operating system and system components, such as hardware and other services. The System Log tracks events, such as driver loads, service start-up, and system errors.

Let's look at each log now.

Application Log

Microsoft defines the Application Log in the Windows 2000 online help accessible from the Event Viewer application as follows:

> "…contains events logged by applications or programs. For example, a database program might record a file error in the application log. The developer decides which events to record."

Most modern commercial Windows applications write their events to the Application Log. Event types are `Error`, `Information`, and `Warning`, and each such event consists of several values. The values of the event are accessible by double-clicking a specific event in the Application Log. The event properties are as follows:

- *Date and time*—The precise time that the event occurred
- *The event type and category*—Error, informational, and so on
- *Identifying information*—The user, computer, and application source
- *Event ID*—A number that uniquely identifies the event
- *Description*—Generally, a textual representation of the message

A description, incidentally, can consist of and report many variables, including object types, related file names, the relevant domain and user, and so on (see Figure 22.2).

22

LOG
MONITORING AND
ANALYSIS

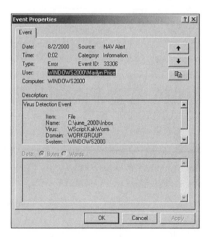

FIGURE 22.2
An Application Log event record.

Figure 22.2 is an Application Log event generated by Norton Antivirus. Note the values:

Description: Virus Detection Event

Item: File

Name: `C:\june_2000\Inbox`

Virus: `WScript.KakWorm`

Domain: `WORKGROUP`

System: WINDOWS2000

User: Marilyn Price

Action: Access to the file was denied.

Here, we see that Norton identified a virus in a Netscape Communicator mail file and, on this basis, Norton denied the user and system access to the file. This demonstrates the first point about logs, that they are tremendously valuable from a statistical and investigative standpoint. In this case, for example, it's clear that Application Log provides enough information that you could perform an exhaustive analysis of which users bring in viruses, how often, what type, and so on.

But you needn't use Event Viewer to examine such information. Event Viewer, in fact, is merely a front end. This same data exports to plain text for lexical analysis:

```
Error    10/20/2000    11:41:47 AM
➥NAV Alert    Information    33306
➥Marilyn Price    WINDOWS2000
```

NOTE

Event Viewer exports to either tab- or comma-delimited text in either ASCII or Unicode.

The tab-delimited values are Type, Date, Time, Source, Category, Event, User, and Computer. But you can manipulate which values Windows 2000 gives. Let's briefly look at log configuration and customization.

Configuring Logs

To configure log behavior, right-click your desired log (here, we'll use Application Log) and choose Properties. In response, Microsoft Management Console (MMC) will display the Application Log Properties window (see Figure 22.3).

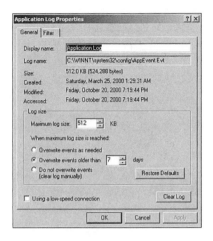

FIGURE 22.3

The Application Log Properties window.

The Properties window displays two tabs—General and Filter. The General tab offers an interface through which to view or manipulate the Application Log's general characteristics. Table 22.1 enumerates those values and what they mean.

TABLE 22.1   Application Log General Configuration Values

Value	Meaning and Discussion
Accessed	A locked value that reports the date on which the log was last accessed.
Clear Log	This clears the log. Use this with care, and only after you're certain that you've preserved the logs.
Created	A locked value that reports the date on which the log was created.
Display Name	An editable value that refers to the Application Log (default: Application Log). Changing this has no objective affect and is largely a matter of personal preference.
Log Name	A value that points to the actual physical log's absolute path (default: `C:\WINNT\system32\config\AppEvent.Evt`). Depending on what you did here, this could have security implications. It's best to leave this in a system area to which the mere mortal user has no access. If you change this property, double-check the permissions on the resulting file.

TABLE 22.1   Continued

Value	Meaning and Discussion
Log Size Options	In the Log Size group box, the system offers several choices on what the Application Log should do when it reaches its maximum file size: Overwrite Events as Needed, Overwrite Events Older Than *N*, or Do Not Overwrite Events. These options aren't nearly as important as backing up the file. However, in relation to backups, the most suitable choice is to Overwrite Events Older Than *N*, where *N* is one day longer than the interval by which you perform backups. That is, if you backup every 2 days, make this value 3 days.
Maximum Log Size	Also in the Log Size group box, the administrator can specify the maximum allowable file size before the system starts over. The default is 512KB and the maximum allowable (altogether) is 9999999 bytes. However, in practice, you should limit these files to a manageable size. Better to backup smaller files (which are easier to process) than define an impossible large and bulky size. Do try to accurately ballpark your log volume, though. You should specify a size that, based on your traffic and usage, won't trigger overwriting before your backup intervals come due. Thus, when considering size, ensure that this value fits into both your backup scheme and your Overwrite Events option. The idea of this is to ensure that you have backups of *all* logs.
Modified	A locked value that reports the date on which the log was last modified.
Size	A locked value that reflects the log's current size.

But this is merely the beginning. Microsoft incorporated substantial intelligence into the logging system, including event, time, and type-sensitive filtering. You reach these controls by choosing the Filter tab (see Figure 22.4).

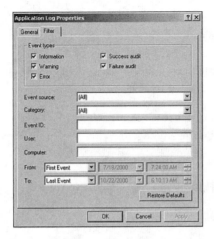

FIGURE 22.4
The Application Log Filter tab.

The Filter tab provides an interface by which to dice and slice your log output to a fairly granular degree, and filter by

- *Event types*—Informational, warnings, errors, and audit successes and failures.

- *Event Source*—Here, Windows 2000 offers a staggering array of choices, including ALL, Active Server Pages, Windows Management, COM+, most services, and all major registered applications. The Event Source filter is set to ALL events by default.

- *Category*—If you choose an event source, the log allows you to specify various categories of events and devices, such as disks, printers, and so on. The Category filter is set to ALL categories by default.

- *Event ID, User, or Computer*—Here, you can actually narrow your focus down to something as granular as a particular event, user, and host.

- *From and To*—These options let you specify a date range. By default, the From filter is set to the first event and the To filter is set to the last event.

You might be wondering the ultimate utility of all this. After all, isn't it sufficient to generate one massive log file that logs all events, categories, applications, users, computers, and so on? Actually, no, not really.

Here's why: By giving you such granular logging capabilities, Windows 2000 lets you apply refined control to your logs for custom scenarios. For example, suppose you want to watch each user separately or, you're trying to diagnose problems with a specific application.

Rather than lump these focused logs in with the rest (and subject them to overwrite intervals specified in the general Application Log view) you can add an entirely new log view. This new view will contain data relevant to the specified user or machine *only*. In this situation, you can specify different overwrite intervals, different logging depths, and logging for different values—custom logs. Let's treat that issue now.

Custom Logs in the Event Viewer

To create a custom log, right-click any log, and click New Log View. In response, MMC will display a new log view (see Figure 22.5).

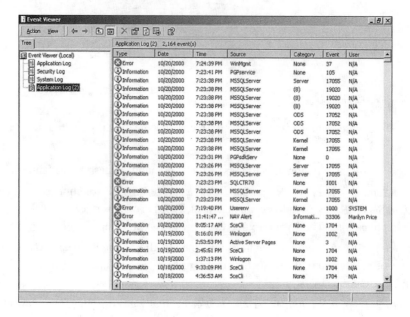

FIGURE 22.5
The second Application Log.

As depicted in Figure 22.5, MC adds a new Application Log, a virtual clone of the original. To give this new log view a new and unique name, right-click it and click Rename. Now, you have a fresh log view and you can specify custom settings (an issue we'll get to next).

Note that when creating custom logs, you should avoid duplicating work or resource utilization. That is, if you create a custom log view that captures ongoing data that is effectively redundant (because the general Application Log already collects such information, for example), you should adjust the general log to omit such information.

NOTE

Situations might arise where you would conceivably want redundant logs. Perhaps you're not big on scripting languages or lexical scanners. If so, you could use a partially redundant log to auto-create reports on this or that user, device, or computer.

The Security Log

The Security Log shares many characteristics with the Application Log, especially with regard to its options. However, it reports a slightly different format. The summary fields are the same: Type, Date, Time, Source, Category, Event, User, and Computer. However, the event descriptions can vary widely.

The Security Log primarily catches audit successes and failures, and summaries of such events appear (on initial examination) simple (see Figure 22.6).

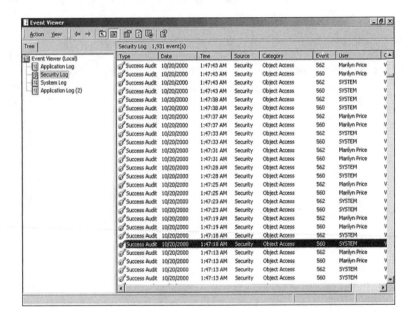

FIGURE 22.6
A sample Security Log summary list.

As you can see, the line items don't tell you much. They merely reflect the time and whether the audit was a success or failure. However, if you look at an event, a different picture emerges. To do so, right-click any event in the summary list and choose Properties. In response, QWindows 2000 will display that event's details (see Figure 22.7).

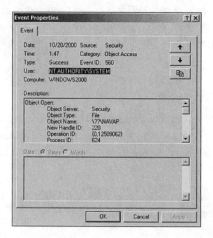

FIGURE 22.7

A sample Security Event's Properties.

As depicted in Figure 22.7, the security event is an object access. In the Description field, Windows 2000 logs some very detailed information. The following is the full record:

```
Object Open:
Object Server:    Security
Object Type:    File
Object Name:    \??\NAVAP
New Handle ID:    220
Operation ID:    {0,12509062}
Process ID:    624
Primary User Name:    WINDOWS2000$
Primary Domain:    WORKGROUP
Primary Logon ID:    (0x0,0x3E7)
Client User Name:    -
Client Domain:    -
Client Logon ID:    -
Accesses  READ_CONTROL
    SYNCHRONIZE
    ReadData (or ListDirectory)
    WriteData (or AddFile)
    AppendData (or AddSubdirectory or CreatePipeInstance)
    ReadEA
    WriteEA
```

```
    ReadAttributes
    WriteAttributes
Privileges           -
```

As illustrated by this record, Windows 2000 records detailed information on precisely who accessed what, when they did it, and how they did it. Through such logs, you can determine if users attempt to overreach their assigned permissions and privileges or access resources they have a right to access.

NOTE

All the configuration options previously enumerated for Application Log apply to Security Log, including granular customization.

System Log

The final default log in the Event Viewer is the System Log. Microsoft defines the System Log in the Windows 2000 online help accessible from the Event Viewer application as follows:

> "… contains events logged by the Windows 2000 system components. For example, the failure of a driver or other system component to load during startup is recorded in the system log. The event types logged by system components are predetermined."

The System Log shares characteristics with both the Application Log and Security Log (supporting identical configuration and customization options), and even the same line item output fields—Type, Date, Time, Source, Category, Event, User, and Computer. However, here, events are expressed differently, depending on the service or system resource.

In many cases, System Log output is more verbose and suggests possible solutions. For example

```
The system failed to register pointer (PTR) resource
records (RRs) for network adapter with settings:

    Adapter Name: {7A6AB2E3-1A30-4F16-80BC-147393177D33}
    Host Name: windows2000
    Adapter-specific Domain Suffix: samshacker.net
    DNS server list: x.xx.xx.220, x.xx.xx.220
    Sent update to server: None
    IP Address: x.x.xx.219


The reason that the system could not register these
RRs was because of DNS server failure. This may be
```

```
due to a zone transfer lock on the DNS server for
the zone that your computer needs to update.

You can manually retry DNS registration of the
network adapter and its settings by typing "ipconfig
/registerdns" at the command prompt. If problems
still persist, contact your DNS server or network
systems administrator. For specific error code
information, see the record data displayed below.
```

FTP Server Logs

If you've used any network operating system, you know that services like FTP invariably have integrated logging systems. Such systems gather data on access, transfers, and server usage. For example, in Unix, this log file is called `xferlog`.

`xferlog` records FTP file transfers. As explained in the `xferlog` manual page:

> "The xferlog file contains logging information from the FTP server daemon, ftpd(8). This file usually is found in `/usr/adm`, but can be located anywhere by using a option to ftpd(8). Each server entry is composed of a single line..."

`xferlog` output fields include:

- The current time
- The duration of the file transfer
- The remote host (hostname/IP)
- The size of the file transferred
- The transfer type (binary/ASCII)
- The direction of the transfer (incoming or outgoing)
- The access mode (anonymous, guest, or authenticated user)
- The username
- Authentication method
- The authenticated user ID

The following is some sample output:

```
[root@linux6 log]# more xferlog
Thu Jul  1 12:15:14 1999 1 172.16.0.1 694 /home/hapless/index.html
➥a _ i r hapless ftp 0 *
Thu Jul  1 13:20:17 1999 1 172.16.0.1 694 /home/hapless/index.html
➥a _ o r hapless ftp 0 *
[root@linux6 log]#
```

These entries show that user `hapless` (from `172,16.0.1`) conducted two transfers, one incoming (i), one outgoing (o), of `index.html` as an authenticated user (r) at the specified times.

IIS FTP supports a similar system that records not merely the values previously described, but also some Windows-specific variables (including, as we'll see next, Win32 status). By default, such logs are piped to `%WinDir%\System32\LogFiles` in files marked by their status and date. On my system, these files reside in `MSFTPSVC1/` and a typical filename would be `ex001016.log`.

By default, such files have the following format:

```
time c-ip cs-method cs-uri-stem sc-status
```

These values are

- `c-ip`   The client's IP address
- `cs-method`   The access method
- `cs-uri-stem`   The type of resource accessed (for example, HTML or CGI)
- `sc-status`   The protocol status or what protocol the client used to access the specified resource

For example

```
#Software: Microsoft Internet Information Services 5.0
#Version: 1.0
#Date: 2000-10-16 13:49:09
#Fields: time c-ip cs-method cs-uri-stem sc-status

13:49:09 207.171.0.111 [1]USER (none) 331
13:49:09 207.171.0.111 [1]PASS - 530
13:49:12 207.171.0.111 [1]QUIT - 530
```

This shows that a user from `207.171.0.111` tried an erroneous or unsupported command (hence the 501 return code). Now let's run through FTP log configuration and customization.

FTP Log Configuration and Customization

To configure your FTP services logs, choose Start, Run and issue the following command:

```
mmc
```

In response, Windows 2000 will load the Microsoft Management Console (see Figure 22.8).

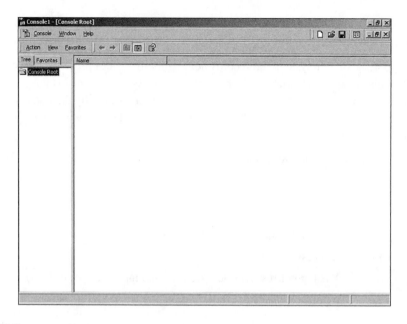

FIGURE 22.8

The Microsoft Management Console main screen.

Here, choose Console, Add/Remove Snap-in from the main menu, or press the key combination Ctrl+M. In response, MMC will display the Add/Remove Snap-in window (see Figure 22.9).

FIGURE 22.9

The Add/Remove Snap-in window.

Here, you'll be adding a new snap-in, so choose Add. In response, MMC will display the Add Standalone Snap-in window (see Figure 22.10).

FIGURE 22.10
The Add Standalone Snap-in window.

Here, scroll down and choose Internet Information Services and click Add, Close, and Okay. In response, MMC will load the IIS snap-in to the console (see Figure 22.11).

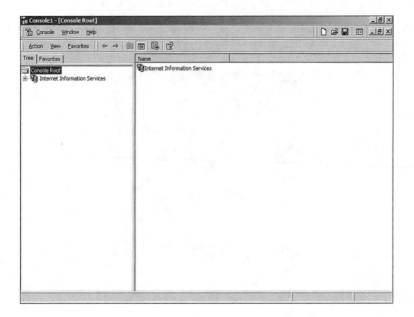

FIGURE 22.11
MMC with the IIS Snap-in loaded.

Finally, in the left pane, below Console Root, choose Internet Information Services, *hostname* (where *hostname* is your system's name), right-click Default FTP Site from the right pane and choose Properties. In response, MMC will display the Default FTP Site Properties window (see Figure 22.12).

FIGURE 22.12
The Default FTP Site Properties window.

Next, under the Enable Logging check box, click Properties. In response, MMC will display the Extended Logging Properties window (see Figure 22.13).

FIGURE 22.13
The Extended Logging Properties window.

The Extended Logging Properties window presents two tabs—General Properties and Extended Properties. The first provides an interface to manipulate the time period (or other trigger) that determines when the service creates new logs. The options are:

- *New Log Time Period*—This option offers you three choices, or rather, three scenarios in which the server will create a new file: after a certain time period (an hour, a day, a week, a month), after the file reaches a certain size, or never. (Never is achieved by assigning the file an unlimited size).
- *Use Local Time for File Naming and Rollover*—This is an On/Off proposition.
- *Log File Directory*—Here, you specify the log file location. Exercise care with this option. In general, you should ensure the directory you choose doesn't expose your log files to unauthorized access. True, their contents might not contain exceptionally sensitive information, but someone could use it to perform traffic analysis or determine the names of local and remote users.

On the other hand, the Extended Properties tab leads to the Extended Logging Options list, a scrolling list containing multiple variables you'll likely want to log (see Figure 22.14).

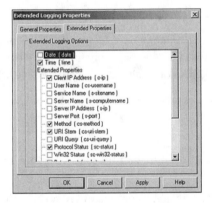

FIGURE 22.14
The Extended Logging Options list.

The choices are

- Bytes Received
- Bytes Sent
- Client IP Address
- Cookie
- Http Status

- Method
- Protocol Version
- Referrer
- Server IP
- Server Name
- Server Port
- Service Name
- Time Taken
- URI Query
- URI Stem
- User Agent
- User Name
- Win32 Status

IIS Web Server Logs

The IIS Web server works in a similar fashion, and you adjust log values in precisely the same way. However, in addition to the FTP log fields previously described, IIS' Web server also provides logging of processing accounting values, including the following:

- s-active-procs   The active processes or total number of CGI processes spawned when the log was created
- s-event   The process event
- s-kernel-time   The total kernel time or the total kernel time used during the specific interval
- s-page-faults   The total page faults or memory references that caused page faults
- s-process-type   The process type
- s-stopped-procs   The total terminated processes or the total number of CGI processes spawned and stopped due to process throttling
- s-total-procs   The total processes or the total number of CGI applications or processes spawned during a given interval
- s-user-time   The total user time or the accumulated processor time used during the current interval

Of these, the most interesting is the process type (s-process-type), which records a wide range of happenings. Table 22.2 summarizes these.

TABLE 22.2   Process Types and Their Characteristics

Type	*Characteristics*
Eventlog-Limit	The system started an Eventlog for the Web server because it reached its process limit.
Eventlog-Limit-Reset	You either manually changed the Eventlog limit or its interval was reached.
Periodic-Log	A log value that you (or the Webmaster) defined to occur at specific intervals.
Priority-Limit	The system assigned a low priority to a CGI process.
Priority-Limit-Reset	You either manually changed the Priority Limit or its interval was reached.
Process-Stop-Limit	A process reached a Process Limit you set and, therefore, it died.
Process-Stop-Limit-Reset	You either manually changed the Priority Stop Limit or its interval was reached.
Reset Interval-Change	You (or the Webmaster) amended the Reset Interval.
Reset Interval-End	The Reset Interval has expired (stopped) and restarted.
Reset Interval-Start	The Reset Interval has started because some condition you specified has arisen.
Site-Paused	Someone paused the Web server.
Site-Pause-Limit	The Web site paused because a process reached a Process Limit you set.
Site-Pause-Limit	You either manually changed The Site Pause Limit or its interval was reached.
Site-Start	Someone started or restarted the Web server.
Site-Stop	The Web server died or was stopped.
Update	The site stopped or started, or an interval started or stopped.

And naturally, the Web server records all HTTP status codes. Table 22.3 provides a quick status code reference.

TABLE 22.3   HTTP Status Codes

Code	*What it Means*
200	The 200 code indicates that everything went well; the transfer was successful and occurred without error.
201	The 201 code indicates that a POST command was issued and satisfied successfully without event.

22

LOG
MONITORING AND
ANALYSIS

TABLE 22.3   Continued

Code	What it Means
202	The 202 code indicates that the client's command was accepting by the server for processing.
203	The 203 code indicates that the server could only partially satisfy the client's request.
204	The 204 code indicates that the client's request was processed, but that the server couldn't return any data.
300	The 300 code indicates that the client requested data that has recently been moved.
301	The 301 code indicates that the server found the client's requested data at an alternate, temporarily redirected URL.
302	The 302 code indicates that the server suggested an alternate location for the client's requested data.
303	The 303 code indicates that there was a problem because the server could not modify the requested data.
400	The 400 code indicates that the client made a malformed request that could, therefore, not be processed.
401	The 401 code indicates that the client tried to access data that it is not authorized to have.
402	The 402 code indicates that a payment scheme has been negotiated.
403	The 403 code indicates that access is forbidden altogether.
404	The 404 code (the most often-seen code) indicates that the document was not found.
500	The 500 code indicates that an internal server error occurred from which the server could not recover. (This is a common error when a client calls a flawed CGI script).
501	The 501 code indicates that the client requested an action that the server cannot perform (or does not support).
502	The 502 code indicates that the server is overloaded.
503	The 503 code indicates that httpd was waiting for another gateway service to return data, but that the external service hung or died.

Let's look at a complete record, with all logging enabled. The following is a log entry:

```
2000-10-22 05:06:58 127.0.0.1 - W3SVC1 WINDOWS2000
➥127.0.0.1 80 GET /localstart.asp - 401 5 3871 552 41
➥HTTP/1.0 127.0.0.1 Mozilla/4.04+ +(WinNT;+U) - -
```

Let's break it down:

- `date   2000-10-22`
- `time   05:06:58`
- `c-ip   127.0.0.1`
- `cs-username   -`
- `s-sitename   W3SVC1`
- `s-computername   WINDOWS2000`
- `s-ip   127.0.0.1`
- `s-port   80`
- `cs-method   GET`
- `cs-uri-stem   /localstart.asp`
- `cs-uri-query   -`
- `sc-status   401`
- `sc-win32-status   5`
- `sc-bytes   3871`
- `cs-bytes   552`
- `time-taken   41`
- `cs-version   HTTP/1.0`
- `cs-host   127.0.0.1`
- `cs(User-Agent)   Mozilla/4.04+ +(WinNT;+U)`
- `cs(Cookie)   -`
- `cs(Referer)   -`

You'll notice that some fields have nothing but a dash symbol (-). This indicates that IIS could not determine a value for that particular log element.

The Performance Logs and Alerts Tool

The Performance Logs and Alerts Tool lets you watch system resources and log their performance (or examine earlier log files for an overview of system performance). Microsoft defines the Performance Logs and Alerts Tool in the Windows 2000 online help accessible from the Performance Logs and Alerts Tool application as follows:

"Performance Logs and Alerts contains features for logging counter and event trace data and for generating performance alerts. With counter logs, you can record data about hardware usage and the activity of system services from local or remote computers.

Logging can occur manually on demand, or automatically based on a user-defined schedule. Continuous logging, subject to file-size or duration limits, is also available. Logged data can be viewed using the System Monitor display or can be exported to spreadsheet programs or databases for analysis and report generation. Trace logs record data as certain activity, such as disk I/O or a page fault, occurs. When the event occurs, the provider sends the data to the log service."

To reach the Performance Logs and Alerts Tool, choose My Computer, Control Panel, Administrative Tools, Performance. In response, Windows 2000 will display the Performance Console (see Figure 22.15).

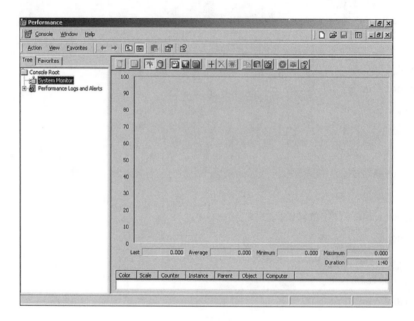

FIGURE 22.15

The Performance console.

Next, choose Performance Logs and Alerts. In response, Windows 2000 presents three log types:

- *Counter Logs*—Counters watch hardware and system utilization from the local computer.

- *Trace Logs*—Trace logs record internal system events such as I/O failures, page faults, and so on.

- *Alerts*—Alerts are used to trigger a reaction, such as a message being sent, a program being run, or a log being started when a selected counter's value falls below or exceeds a setting that the administrator has specified.

To fully exploit Performance Logs and Alerts, you need some familiarity with counters. Let's cover those now.

Setting Counters

To set your counters, right-click the main screen of the Performance Logs and Alerts window and choose Add Counters. In response, Windows 2000 will display the Add Counters dialog box (see Figure 22.16).

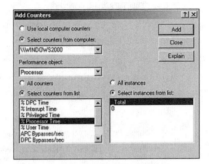

FIGURE 22.16
The Performance Console's Add Counter dialog box.

Listed are the performance object types you can watch with counters. Each object class is discussed in more detail in the following sections. The performance object types you can watch with counters are as follows:

- Processor
- RAS Port and RAS Total
- Redirector
- Server and Server Work Queries
- System
- TCP
- Telephony
- Thread
- UDP
- Web Service

Let's run through what you're likely to use and see what counters typically do.

Processor Counters

Processor counters watch CPU performance. Table 22.4 summarizes various processor counters that you can manipulate in the Performance Logs and Alerts console.

TABLE 22.4   Processor Counters

Counter	What It Records
%DPC Time	Watches the percentage of time the processor spent processing deferred procedure calls
%Interrupt Time	Watches the percentage of time the processor spent processing hardware interrupts
%Privileged Time	Watches the non-idle processor time spent with system processes (or processes that run in privileged mode)
%Processor Time	Watches the time during which the system executes non-idle threads
%User Mode	Watches the percentage of non-idle time during which the system ran applications, environmental tasks, or other processes related to users
APC Bypasses Per Sec	Watches the rate at which the system avoids kernel APC interrupts
DPC Bypasses Per Sec	Watches the rate at which the system avoids deferred procedure calls
Interrupts	An average of the number of hardware interrupts the system processes each second

RAS Port and RAS Total

RAS Port and RAS Total counters watch Remote Access Service performance. Table 22.5 summarizes various RAS counters that you can manipulate in the Performance Logs and Alerts console.

TABLE 22.5   RAS Counters

Counter	What It Records
Alignment Errors	Watches byte alignment errors in RAS transmissions
Buffer Overrun Errors	Watches buffer overruns (where the buffer chokes on incoming data)
Bytes Received	Watches the bytes received in the specified RAS transmission

TABLE 22.5 Continued

Counter	What It Records
Bytes Received/SEC	Watches the bytes received in the specified RAS transmission by second
Bytes Transmitted	Watches the bytes transmitted in the specified RAS transmission
Bytes Transmitted/SEC	Watches the bytes transmitted in the specified RAS transmission by second
CRC Errors	Watches cyclical redundancy check errors
Frames Received	Watches the frames received in the specified RAS transmission
Frames Received/SEC	Watches the frames received in the specified RAS transmission by second
Frames Transmitted	Watches the frames transmitted in the specified RAS transmission
Frames Transmitted	Watches the frames transmitted in the specified RAS transmission by second
Percentage Compression (in)	Watches the compression ratio for incoming transmissions (bytes)
Percentage Compression (out)	Watches the compression ratio for outgoing transmissions (bytes)

22

LOG
MONITORING AND
ANALYSIS

Redirector

Redirector counters watch Redirector performance. Table 22.6 summarizes various Redirector counters that you can manipulate in the Performance Logs and Alerts console.

TABLE 22.6 Redirector Counters

Counter	What It Records
Bytes Received/SEC	Watches the bytes received in the specified Redirector transmission by second
Bytes Total	Watches the rate by which Redirector is processing bytes (in either direction, or from whatever resource)
Bytes Transmitted/SEC	Watches the bytes transmitted in the specified Redirector transmission by second
Connects Core	Watches the number of connections via MS-NET SMB (Vax, XENIX, and so on)
Connects LM 2.0	Watches the number of connections via LAN Manager 2.0
Connects LM 2.1	Watches the number of connections via LAN Manager 2.1
Connects Windows NT	Watches the number of connections via Windows NT
Current Commands	Watches the number of commands in queue that Redirector processes

TABLE 22.6   Continued

Counter	What It Records
File Data Operations	Watches the rate at which Redirector processes bytes
File Read Operations	Watches the rate at which applications request data from Redirector
File Write Operations	Watches the rate at receives data from applications
Network Errors	Watches network errors between Redirector and other systems, nodes, services, and so on
Packets Received/SEC	Watches the packets received in the specified Redirector transmission by second
Packets SEC	Watches the number of packets total per second
Packets Transmitted/SEC	Watches the packets transmitted in the specified Redirector transmission by second
Read Bytes	Watches the rate at which applications access Redirector's cache
Read Packets	Watches the rate at which READ packets hit the network
Server Disconnects	Watches the number of times that this or that server disconnects from Redirector
Server Reconnects	Watches the number of times that this or that server reconnects to Redirector
Write Bytes	Watches the rate at which applications use the Redirector cache to write data
Write Packets	Watches the rate at which WRITE packets hit the network

System Counters

System counters watch system performance and events (such as system calls). Table 22.7 summarizes various system counters that you can manipulate in the Performance Logs and Alerts console.

TABLE 22.7   System Counters

Counter	What it Records
Alignment Fixups	Watches the rate at which the system repairs alignment faults
Context Switches	Watches the rate at which threads cut the processor loose because of priority, mode switching (privileged versus user)
Exception Dispatches	Watches the rate at which the system dispatches exceptions
File Control Bytes	Watches the rate of bytes transferred in file control operations

TABLE 22.7   Continued

Counter	What it Records
File Control Operations	Watches the rate of file control operations
File Data Operations	Watches the rate of read/write calls
File Read Operations	Watches the rate of read operations
File Write Operations	Watches the rate of write operations
Processes	Watches the total number of processes
System Calls	Watches NT system calls
Threads	Watches the number of threads

Watching Counters in Action

To set your counters, pick your categories and object types and choose Add, Close. The
Performance Logs and Alerts window will immediately fill with statistics (see Figure 22.17).

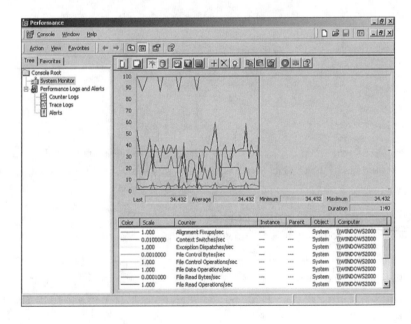

FIGURE 22.17
Counters in action.

The graph area is click-sensitive. You can navigate to any object type and its statistics merely
by clicking its rate (on the graph). Or, you can click the object type's listing in the list box
below the graph.

The Performance Logs and Alerts system lets you get some very detailed data. Essentially, Microsoft incorporated extremely low-level debugging into Windows 2000.

Configuring Counter and Trace Log Behavior and Output

To configure log behavior output, navigate to the specified log and double-click the desired log listed in the Details pane. In response, Windows 2000 will display the log's Properties window (see Figure 22.18).

FIGURE 22.18
The System Overview Properties window.

The log Properties window presents three tabs (General, Log Files, and Schedule) and each provides an interface to manipulate some aspect of your log's behavior or output. Let's run through them now.

General Performance Log Properties

The General tab lets you include the following properties:

- *Current Log File Name*—This points to the log file itself (the default is C:\PerfLogs\System_Overview.blg). The Log File name cannot be changed.

- *Counters*—This list box is where you add your desired counters (do so by choosing Add).

- *Sample Data Every*—This lets you specify the intervals (by minutes, seconds, hours, or days) by which to count.

Using these properties, you can segregate your performance logs (one for system calls, one for processor stats, and so on) for better management. From here, you set your log file's characteristics in the Log Files tab.

Log Files Performance Log Properties

The Log Files tab lets you manipulate the following properties:

- *Log File Location*—Use this option to set the location of your log files; (C:\PerfLogs) is the default.
- *Log File Filename*—Use this option to name the current log file.
- *End File Names With*—This lets you specify a file extension if you want. Good if you're doing script-based analysis.
- *Log File Type*—Here, the system offers several choices: Binary File, Binary Circular File, Text File-CSV, and Text File-TSV.
- *Comment*—This text is what appears in the performance console.
- *Log File Size*—Use this option to limit your file size.

Schedule Performance Log Properties

The Schedule tab lets you manipulate the following properties:

- *Start Log*—This option lets you specify when logging should start. You can either choose Manually (in which case, you start the log yourself from the shortcut menu) or specify a date and time.
- *Stop Log*—This option lets you specify when logging should stop. You can choose Manually (in which case, you stop the log yourself from the shortcut menu) or specify an interval (in days), or specify a date and time.

Summary

Never underestimate the importance of keeping detailed logs. Not only are logs essential when you're investigating a network intrusion, they're also required for bringing charges against an attacker. Now that you know a bit about them, the next step is to learn how you can use logs to detect intrusions. That's what Chapter 23, "Intrusion Detection," is all about.

Intrusion Detection

IN THIS CHAPTER

Intrusion detection (ID) is a technique that attempts to detect inappropriate activity that originates locally or from the outside. Intrusion detection systems (IDS) techniques include monitoring traffic, security logs, and audit data. This chapter explains intrusion detection and its use.

Types of Intrusion Detection Systems

There are two types of intrusion detection systems. Intrusion detection systems that run on a host to detect inappropriate activity on that host are called *host-based* intrusion detection systems. Intrusion detection systems that examine network data flow are called *network-based* intrusion detection systems.

Host-Based Intrusion Detection

For the network administrator to properly monitor for intrusion detection, he needs to be familiar with the host machine, the network connections to that machine, applications installed on the host machine, and the habits of users accessing the host machine. For example, the network administrator needs to be on the lookout for changes in patterns of network traffic or users logging in at unusual times.

Bearing this in mind, you need a host-based intrusion detection system that not only analyzes traffic in and out of the host computer, but also checks for suspicious activity and for machine integrity. If you use host-based intrusion detection software, you need to load the software on every computer in your network. There are two classes of host-based intrusion detection software—firewalls and agent-based software. You use host-based ID software to detect both inside attacks and attacks from outside of your network. Firewalls are covered in more detail in Chapter 16, "TCP Filtering and Firewalls."

Host-based agents generally report to an ID server that then analyzes the information to detect anomalies in communication for the hosts across the network. Agents might have the capability to monitor changes in user privileges and critical system files. These are features that you should look for in host-based intrusion detection systems. RealSecure is a host and network-based intrusion detection system that you might want to consider for your network.

Network-Based Intrusion Detection

Network-based intrusion detection involves monitoring and analyzing the traffic on a network segment. Generally, this process is accomplished by placing a server's network interface card (NIC) into promiscuous mode to capture all network traffic that crosses into its network segment. Each packet on the network segment is examined. Packets that match a particular signature are examined more closely. A signature is a known attack pattern that includes the following (not all IDS's support all these types of signatures; do your research to determine which IDS is right for your organization):

- *Header signatures*—A network IDS looks for header signatures that combine illogical packet headers. For example, a hacker might send TCP packets across the network with both the SYN and FIN flags set in packet headers, indicating that the sender wants to both start and stop a connection at the same time. These packets could indicate a denial-of-service attack against a machine in the network segment.

- *Port signatures*—The network segment is watched for attempted connections to ports that hackers frequently attack, such as the Telnet port (TCP port 23). If there is an attempted connection to a port that isn't in use by your site, the incoming packets to those ports are indicative of a possible attack.

- *String signatures*—The IDS searches for text strings that might indicate a potential attack.

- *Checksum violations*—These types of signatures include viruses and Trojan horses.

- *File permission violations*—An attacker might attempt to access confidential files in an attempt to test security on local machines.

Network-based intrusion detection systems can be configured to send an alert to an administrator if any signatures are detected on his network.

Both host-based and network-based intrusion detection systems have features that would benefit your network in the detection of intruders. In the end, the best solution is to find a network intrusion system that combines the best features of both. One such product is NetProwler from Symantec. Symantec can also protect your network against malicious code with their network-based, anti-virus package called Norton AntiVirus Corporate Edition. Of course, you will need to research any product before purchasing it to ensure that it is the right product for your organization.

Detection Methods Used by Intrusion Detection Systems

Intrusion detection systems use a number of approaches to detect attacks on networks. Common standard detection methods employed by IDSs include the following:

- Statistical anomaly detection
- Rule-based anomaly detection
- Rule-based penetration identification

Statistical Anomaly Detection

This method forms a statistical profile about what activities look normal on your network. The assumption is that because users are usually creatures of habit, they perform tasks in a standard

23

INTRUSION
DETECTION

behavioral manner. Therefore, current activity is compared to the statistical profile to discover anomalous activity. The IDS flags any activity that looks like an attack (for example, when a user performs an activity that deviates from your established baseline) and then sends an alert to the designated network security administrator.

Rule-Based Anomaly Detection

This method also analyzes the users' behavior. The difference between this method and statistical anomaly detection is that rather than developing a statistical profile, rules for deviation from the normal are created by the IDS. Attacks are detected based on deviations from the rules that were created from previous patterns.

Rule-Based Penetration Identification

This method uses pre-defined rules for penetration behavior, rather than developing rules against past abnormal activities that have occurred on your network. The strength of the rules depend on the expertise of the person(s) who define the rules.

Flaws in Intrusion Detection Methods

It helps to know the limitations as well as the advantages of running an intrusion detection system on your network. Flaws in the three intrusion detection methods include the following:

- What is considered by the IDS to be normal can shift over time. For example, your organization might install a new operating system or a new application on the machines in your network.

- The IDS can take a long time to build the statistical or rules profile that determines normal activity.

- An activity on your network might be flagged to be abnormal when it actually isn't, or visa versa. The IDS can't distinguish between non-threatening abnormal activity and malicious activity. These types of activities are categorized as a false positive or a false negative error.

  A false positive error occurs when the IDS flags an activity as a possible attack when it is actually a legitimate activity. You should try to configure your IDS to minimize these types of errors. If there are too many false positive alerts, your administrator could, over time, come to ignore the IDS output which, in turn, could result in a real intrusion being ignored.

  A false negative occurs when the IDS doesn't flag an activity as a possible attack, but it actually is an attack. This type of error can be more dangerous than a false positive error because it will give your administrator a false sense of security. This is why your administrator must make sure that all updates to signatures and rules are followed through.

Common Threats to Networks and Systems

This section lists a few of the common threats that your intrusion detection system should be able to discover and from which your network and Web sites need to be protected.

Attacks from an Inside Source

Depending on the level of security that disgruntled employees are assigned, they can be one of the greatest potential threats to your organization. They can, for example, install backdoors, alter critical data, or take down your network's system resources. Your organization should have policies in effect to deal with these kinds of situations.

When a disgruntled or fired employee quits or is asked to leave, your place of employment should always change passwords for accounts that can perform administrative functions immediately to try to eliminate a potential future attack against your network. Also, look for unusual accounts that could have been set up for the purpose of performing administrative functions on your network.

Kernel Attacks

Hackers use this malicious, sophisticated form of attack to replace or corrupt programs in the operating system's kernel, which can result in severe system damage. Attackers can accomplish this attack by uploading and installing a rootkit. A *rootkit* is a collection of operating system programs meant to replace actual system programs. That enables the hacker to hide his tracks and enables the hacker to easily reconnect to the system any time he wants.

The primary method of the detection of a rootkit is with the use of integrity assessment software. This type of software takes a digital snapshot of your system(s) and will alert you to any changes to system files. A popular integrity assessment package is called Tripwire. You can find Tripwire's home page at http://www.tripwiresecurity.com/.

Operating and Application Security Flaws

You must keep up on all fixes and service packs for your applications and operating systems. New exploitations for vulnerabilities are frequently being discovered. Exploitations can be used to gain access to other applications, other machines, or to your organization's network itself. Microsoft is releasing new patches all the time. Find them at http://www.microsoft.com/technet/treeview/default.asp?url=/technet/itsolutions/security/current.asp.

23

INTRUSION
DETECTION

Password Sniffing

Hackers frequently use this method of exploitation to guess a user's password to gain access to a particular system or to all of the network's resources, depending on the level of security assigned to the user's account. There are many password crackers that can be found on the Internet. Perhaps the best-known password-cracking tool is called LophtCrack (or LC3) and it can be found at `http://www.10pht.com/10phtcrack`.

Denial of Service Attacks

A hacker will launch this type of attack to deliberately shut down the server or to slow down the traffic going through the server to render the server inoperable for a period of time. The attack intentionally overloads a network service or connection with excessive data that results in that failure.

This type of attack usually doesn't result in direct damage to the system(s) being attacked. If the Web site is a commercial site, however, the damage could be felt in its "pocketbook" because there can be a financial loss due to the downtime of the Web site.

Reconnaissance Scans

Hackers can use a number of tools to scan your network for information that will make their attack successful. For example, they can use ping sweeps, such as SNMP Sweep, to ping a range of IP addresses to discover which machines are active. You can find SNMP Sweep at `http://www.solarwinds.net/Tools/Network_Discovery/SNMPSweep/`.

Intrusion Detection Tools

Listed in this section are some of the more popular intrusion detection systems that you might want to consider if you are planning on installing an intrusion detection system on your network.

BlackICE Defender

BlackICE Defender is a real-time personal firewall for your PC that includes an IDS. It inspects all traffic on your computer to look for suspicious code and activity. When it detects an attack, it automatically blocks all traffic from that source. It performs a back-trace to discover the origins of the attack as well as the hacker's identity. You have the option of logging attacks in case you need to keep a record of an attack. You can find information about this package at:

Network ICE Corporation
2121 S. El Camino Real, Suite 1100
San Mateo, CA 94403
(650) 532-4100
E-mail: info@networkice.com
URL: http://www.networkice.com/products/blackice_defender.html

Cisco Secure Intrusion Detection System (Formerly NetRanger)

The Cisco Secure Intrusion Detection System (IDS) consists of sensing devices (hardware) and a central management console. It's a real-time, network-based IDS that detects unauthorized activity across the network, responds to those events by terminating the suspicious connection, and then sends an alarm to the central management console. You use the management console to perform remote system configuration and to respond to alarms.

Cisco Systems, Inc.
170 West Tasman Drive
San Jose, CA 95134-1619
(800) 553-6387
E-mail: cs-support-us@cisco.com
URL: http://www.cisco.com/warp/public/cc/pd/sqsw/sqidsz/index.shtml

CyberCop Monitor

CyberCop Monitor by PGP Security monitors traffic flowing both into and out of your network from one central console. This IDS includes features like real-time intrusion detection, administrative alerts, prevents unauthorized Web setting changes, and provides protection against the most common attacks, including denial of service attacks.

PGP Security
3965 Freedom Circle
Santa Clara, CA 95054
(888) 747-3011
E-mail: sstephen@nai.com
URL: http://www.cybercop.co.uk/cybercop/monitor/default.htm

Dragon Intrusion Detection System

The Dragon Intrusion Detection System (IDS) utilizes three techniques for intrusion detection.

- A large database of attacks and their corresponding signatures are programmed into both the Dragon network and host agents, including buffer overflows and denial of service attacks.

23

INTRUSION
DETECTION

- The Dragon network and host agents search for anomalies that could indicate an attack. These anomalies include port scans and denial of service attacks.

- All Dragon agents can detect deviations from security policy, which include applications running on unusual ports and unauthorized network services.

The Dragon IDS employs network IDS, host IDS, and firewall security technologies. The Dragon Sensor is a network IDS that monitors network packs for internal and external attacks. The Dragon Squire is a host-based IDS that processes logs from a variety of firewalls, such as Checkpoint and Raptor. The Dragon Server processes all information gathered from both the Dragon Sensor and the Dragon Squire for analysis and reporting purposes. Each of these technologies work together to compensate for inherent shortcomings found in each other.

Enterasys Networks Corporation
35 Industrial Way
Rochester, NH 03866
(801) 972-2192
E-mail: sales@enterasys.com
URL: http://www.securitywizards.com/intro.htm

ICEpac Security Suite

ICEpac Security Suite is a real-time network IDS for local and remote protection for every server, segment, and VPN machine in your network. This suite consists of five components that provide security for your network.

- *BlackICE Agent*—You install BlackICE Agent on every local and remote system to enforce user, group, and enterprise-wide security policies that you set through ICEcap Manager. You can install BlackICE Agent on Windows, Solaris, and Linux platforms.

- *BlackICE Guard*—This component eliminates hostile traffic from a network by identifying and removing attacks from a segment before the attack can be successful.

- *BlackICE Sentry*—You use this component to report suspicious traffic directed against network resources on fast network segments to the ICEcap Manager without the use of costly, hardware-based solutions.

- *ICEcap Manager*—ICEcap Manager provides centralized management throughout the network. Its features include deploying, updating, and managing BlackICE agents, Sentries, and Guards, alerting the administrator about suspicious activity, and logging detected suspicious and hostile activity.

- *InstallPac*—This component is a remote installation tool. You use it to install and update BlackICE Agents and Sentries across the network.

Network ICE Corporation
2121 S. El Camino Real, Suite 1100
San Mateo, CA 94403
(650) 532-4100
E-mail: `info@networkice.com`
URL: `http://www.networkice.com/products/icepac_suite.html`

Manhunt

Manhunt, by Recourse Technologies, identifies common and previous unknown attacks against your network. It does this by employing on-the-fly anomaly detection to detect not only known signatures, but also activity outside of normal or expected protocols. In addition, Manhunt employs statistical correlation analysis to evaluate entire events to minimize false alarms and positively identify a potential attack. After an attack is identified, Manhunt contains the attack and tracks it back to the source, gathering information about the attack and the attacker. Manhunt also has the ability to stop the attack, disconnect the malicious connection, or divert the attack to a honeypot, such as Recourse Technologies' ManTrap system. Honeypots are discussed in detail later in this chapter.

An important feature of Manhunt is its ability to automatically locate the source of the attack—whether the source is local to the network or across the Internet. It does this by identifying the attack path to its entry point, even for spoofed attacks. Manhunt documents the attack so that prosecution is possible if your organization so desires.

Recourse Technologies, Inc.
700 Bay Road
Redwood City, CA 94063-2469
(877) 786-9633
Fax: (650) 568-0598
E-mail: `sales@recourse.com`
URL: `http://www.ruowned.com/products/manhunt/hunt.html`

NetProwler

NetProwler is a dynamic network intrusion detection system by Symantec and is integrated with AXENT's Intruder Alert program. This product combines both host-based and network-based IDSs. Intruder Alert performs enterprise monitoring of network and host security events. Symantec acquired AXENT Technologies, Inc. on December 18, 2000. The combined package includes the detection of hundreds of real-time, common operating system and application attacks, on-the-fly loading of new attack signatures, and updates to keep your system current online.

Symantec Corporation
20330 Stevens Creek Blvd.
Cupertino, CA 95014
(800) 441-7234
Online Service and Support:
http://www.symantec.com/techsupp/news/custserv_ask.html
URL: http://enterprisesecurity.symantec.com/

NFR Network Intrusion Detection (NFR NID)

NFR NID performs real-time network monitoring for known attacks, unauthorized access attempts, policy infringements, and other abnormal behavior. It checks for suspicious activity with both anomaly detection and by checking for known signatures.

NFR Security, Inc.
1395 Piccard Drive
Suite 230
Rockville, MD 20850-4348
(240) 632-9000
E-mail: info@nfr.com
URL: http://www.nfr.com/

RealSecure

RealSecure is a host and network-based intrusion detection system. It features a real-time attack recognition and response system and it compares network traffic and host log entries to the known methods of attackers. Some of the features you can configure are triggering administrator alarms via email or paging for suspicious activities, recording the attack, saving the attack information to a file, or terminating the intruder's connection.

Internet Security Systems, Inc.
6303 Barfield Road
Atlanta, GA 30328
(404) 236-2600
E-mail: http://www.iss.net/cgi-bin/getSGIInfo.pl
URL: http://www.iss.net/securing_e-business/security_products/intrusion_detection/

Methods of Evading an Intrusion Detection System

The most common methods hackers employ to evade an intrusion detection system are covered in this section.

Slow Scans

IDSs can't maintain long-term traffic logs due to the large volume of traffic across the network. This makes it easier for hackers to evade detection because it is difficult for the IDS to detect a potential attack that starts out by slow scanning one port or address at a time every hour or so.

Fragmenting Attack Packets

Fragmentation of packets occurs when a single IP packet is broken into multiple smaller packets. The destination TCP/IP stack reassembles the packet before transmitting it to the intended destination. Most IDSs aren't able to reassemble IP packets and so attackers use tools, such as Fragrouter, to automatically fragment attacks and thus evade intrusion detection systems.

Signature Changes

A number of intrusion detection systems rely on matching signatures. Because attack scripts have well-known patterns, some signature databases consist of the signatures of known attacks that the IDS then compares to current network traffic. Building the signature database in this way makes it easier for an attacker to evade the IDS. All he or she has to do is change the script somewhat so that the signature looks different to the IDS.

Actions Performed over Time

The IDS is continuously updating what it considers to be normal behavior on your system, and changes in network usage patterns are expected. A hacker can take advantage of this possible weakness by performing actions over a period of time that are just slightly outside of what the IDS considers normal. Over time, each of these actions might become accepted by the IDS as legitimate activity, even though when all put together they are really part of an intrusion attempt. This evasion leaves your network open to a serious threat.

Methods of Defeating an Intrusion Detection System

The most common methods hackers can employ to defeat an intrusion detection system include the following.

Flooding the Network

A hacker can attack an IDS by saturating the network with packets. If the IDS can't keep up with the high rate of traffic across the network, it will start dropping packets and eventually completely shut down.

23

INTRUSION
DETECTION

Denial of Service Attacks

Intrusion detection systems are as susceptible to denial of service attacks, such as SYN floods, as any other system. Hackers will often acquire intrusion detection systems that are in use by potential victims. They do this so that they can find packets that will cause the IDS to fail and the attack to continue undetected.

Decoy Scanning

Decoy scanning tools, such as Nmap, can scan your network using hundreds of spoofed source IP addresses. Of course, the hackers' IP addresses are also exposed to the IDS. The problem is that the IDS has to deal with so many different IP addresses, it is difficult to discover which of the IP addresses are the spoofed addresses and which are the real ones.

How to Select an Intrusion Detection System

Choosing an intrusion detection system can be complex. This section covers questions you should ask the IDS vendor.

When considering an IDS, you should consider asking the vendor the following questions.

- How much does your product cost?
- What are the weaknesses in your product? In other words, how might an attacker evade or defeat your product?
- How responsive is your customer service department? How long will it take for you to get back to me when I'm experiencing a problem with your product?
- What level of training and expertise do you presume my IT department has to set up and maintain your product and to analyze the data that the IDS gathers?
- How much training and support can we expect from your company? At the very least, are detailed manuals available?
- What type of expertise do your employees have in the area of intrusion detection and hacker attacks?
- Does your product detect internal abuse by authorized users? How is this accomplished?
- What do you do to stay current with intrusion detection and the latest hacker attacks?
- Can I manage your product remotely?
- Is your product host-based or network-based?
- On which operating systems does your product run?
- Does your product require any special hardware or equipment?
- Can your product be customized to meet my organization's needs and policies?

- What is your product's percentage of false-positives? What about the percentage of false-negatives?

- Which types of auto-response mechanisms does your product employ?

- What method(s) does your product use to alert responsible security personnel?

- How often do you update your product's attack signatures, and how do I go about upgrading them. Is there a cost associated with upgrades for signatures?

- Do you upgrade rules? How often are they upgraded and do you charge for the upgrades?

- What performance issues will your product raise for my network? Will it have any impact on my network's or my host's performance?

- Is a tool for generating written reports to summarize the daily event log included with your product? Describe the tool.

- Can I get an evaluation copy of your product?

Further Reading on Intrusion Detection

The following lists references for additional reading on intrusion detection.

Information Warfare and Security. Dorothy E. Denning. Addison-Wesley Pub Co. ISBN: 0201433036. 1998.

Insertion, Evasion, and Denial of Service: Eluding Network Intrusion Detection. Thomas H. Ptacek and Timothy N. Newsham. Secure Networks, Inc.
`http://www.robertgraham.com/mirror/Ptacek-Newsham-Evasion-98.html#cit2`.

Intrusion Detection. Mark Burgess.
`http://www.iu.hio.no/~mark/lectures/security/SE13.eng.html`.

Intrusion Detection (Macmillan Technology Series). Rebecca Gurley Bace. Pearson Higher Education. ISBN: 1578701856. 1999.

Intrusion Detection: An Introduction to Internet Surveillance, Correlation, Trace Back, Traps, and Response. Edward G. Amoroso. Intrusion.Net Books. ISBN: 0966670078. 1999

Intrusion Detection: Network Security Beyond the Firewall. Terry Escamilla. John Wiley & Sons. ISBN: 0471290009. 1998.

Intrusion Signatures and Analysis. Mark Cooper, Stephen Northcutt, Matt Fearnow and Karen Frederick. New Riders Publishing. ISBN: 073571063. 2001.

Network Intrusion Detection: An Analysts' Handbook. Stephen Northcutt. New Riders Publishing. ISBN: 0735708681. 1999.

New Methods of Intrusion Detection using Control-Loop Measurement. Dr. Myron L. Cramer, James Cannady, and Jay Harrell. `http://iw.windermeregroup.com/Papers/ids_newm.html`.

Practical Intrusion Detection Handbook. Paul E. Proctor. Prentice Hall PTR. ISBN: 0130259608. 2000.

System Design Laboratory—Intrusion Detection. Phillip Porras, Director. SRI International/Computer Science Laboratory. `http://www.sdl.sri.com/programs/intrusion/`.

Honeypots

A chapter on intrusion detection would be incomplete without a discussion of honeypots. What is a honeypot?

Well, has your network been attacked on a few occasions and you want to be able to set a trap for the hackers who insist on leaving calling cards on your network? You *can* set a trap for them with something called a honeypot.

You use honeypot software to simulate one or more network services to make it appear to a hacker as though you are running vulnerable services that he or she can take advantage of to break into your network. Administrators usually set up honeypots on sacrificial systems that run vulnerable services that are most often attacked, such as mail, Web, FTP, or DNS servers that act as bait to lure hackers. Honeypots can give you an advanced warning of an all-out attack on your network because they can be used to log access attempts to your more vulnerable ports. You might even be able to substitute a honeypot system for the target system when your network comes under attack. You can think of a honeypot as a system decoy and booby trap for hackers.

A honeypot can be an important tool in your security arsenal because it can help protect your network from unauthorized access to important data. The honeypot doesn't contain any information that is critical to your organization, but you can make it look like it contains information interesting enough to reel in a hacker. The sole purpose of the honeypot is to make it behave like a real system. In actuality, it is configured to capture details of an attack. Bearing this in mind, you want to make your honeypot look as realistic as possible. The longer you can keep the hackers occupied with your honeypot, the longer you can keep them away from your actual production systems, and the more information you can gather about them. You can use this information to potentially discover who they are, what they are after on your network, what tools they use, and what their skill levels are. This information is also important to help you secure your network against potential hackers.

What can you do to make your machine look hackable? One thing you can do is to install an older operating system on a machine to make it look more vulnerable, like a Windows 4.0

version that either has older or no service packs installed on it. The honeypot makes the hackers believe that they are successful in their attack, without actually allowing them access to critical data. Meanwhile, you can use the honeypot in conjunction with an intrusion detection system to gather as much information as possible about the hackers and the attacks.

The Advantages and Disadvantages of Running a Honeypot System

As with any software system you install on your network, you need to consider the advantages and disadvantages for your organization. This section lists things you should think about when you are considering adding a honeypot to your network.

Advantages

- *An early warning system*—A honeypot can serve as an early warning system that will alert you to hostile activity occurring on your network. Network intrusion systems can have difficulty in distinguishing between benign and hostile traffic. This is where the honeypot steps in. Activity in itself is an indication of hostile activity, because the honeypots should be located on isolated machines that normally are not accessed during the course of the day by any of your users. This means that traffic going into a honeypot system should be looked on with suspicion.

- *Learn techniques of hackers*—You can learn a lot about hacking by watching and analyzing attacks launched against the honeypots. If you want to tighten up security for confidential or critical data, you can set up a system that is similar to the one that holds that data, but that contains bogus information. In this way, you can learn techniques to protect your organization from attacks, and how to clean up after those attacks.

Disadvantages

- Honeypots could lure hackers to your network and cause them to launch further attacks.

- Honeypots add complexity to your network security plan.

- You must maintain honeypots. This means that you must test the honeypots to make sure that they are logging attacks correctly. You must also learn how to respond to new attacks launched against your systems, and to make sure that your production machines are adequately protected against those types of attacks.

- Your honeypot could be used as a launching point by hackers for attacks on your network or other networks. If your honeypots are used in such an instance, your organization could be involved in any legal actions that the attacked parties undertake.

- Ensure that the honeypot system is not involved in any trust relationships, and that it's on its own network segment.

Honeypot Systems

Listed in the following sections are some honeypot systems that you might want to consider if you are planning on installing this type of security system on your network.

CyberCop Sting

CyberCop Sting is a decoy system that employs honeypot technology to direct hackers away from critical machines. It does this by using a single server to simulate a virtual network. This server deflects attacks against your network, and tracks and collects information against intruders, whether they are inside or outside your network.

> PGP Security
> 3965 Freedom Circle
> Santa Clara, CA 95054
> (888) 747-3011
> E-mail: sstephen@nai.com
> URL: http://www.pgp.com/products/cybercop-sting/default.asp

Deception Toolkit

Deception Toolkit by Fred Cohen and Associates logs attacks by hackers. It "listens" for input, looks for unauthorized port usage, looks for known attack patterns, and attempts to get passwords. It also logs what is being done on the honeypot. You can configure the responses for each port that are generally not active on your network to indicate unauthorized use.

> Fred Cohen and Associates
> URL: http://www.all.net/dtk/

Mantrap

Mantrap is a honeypot system that can be configured to catch both internal and external attacks against your network. You configure Mantrap to resemble hosts that reside on your network by having similar IPs, hostnames, file systems, and similar services or servers that reside on your network. It can also mirror your corporate Web site. This honeypot is designed by Recourse Technologies to work with Manhunt, their intrusion detection system.

> Recourse Technologies, Inc.
> 700 Bay Road
> Redwood City, CA 94063-2469
> (877) 786-9633
> Fax: (650) 568-0598
> E-mail: sales@recourse.com
> URL: http://www.ruowned.com/products/mantrap/trap.html

Specter

Specter can simulate a complete system on your network and offers Internet services, such as FTP and SMTP, that appear to be normal to hackers, but are actually traps that are set for them. Alerts can be configured to alert the appropriate administrators. Everything that the hackers do is traced and logged. Specter can detect the hackers while they are still trying to break into your network.

> NETSEC—Network Security
> Munzingerstr. 17
> CH-3007 Bern
> Switzerland
> +41 31 376 0534
> Fax: +41 31 376 0533
> E-mail: info@specter.com
> URL: http://www.specter.ch/

Further Reading on Honeypots

The following lists references for additional reading on honeypots.

Build A Honeypot. Lance Spitzner. http://kracked.com/~felons/pub/security/spitzner-papers/honeypot.html. 1999.

'Decoy nets' gain backers in battle against hackers. Ellen Messmer. Network World. 2001. http://www.nwfusion.com/news/2001/0305honeypot.html.

SDSC's Security Experiment - worm.sdsc.edu. http://security.sdsc.edu/incidents/worm.2000.01.18.shtml.

The Cuckoo's Egg: Tracking a Spy Through the Maze of Computer Espionage. Clifford Stoll. Pocket Books. ISBN: 0743411463. 2000.

Summary

Intrusion detection systems are fast becoming an important tool to secure your network against internal and external attacks. The ideal intrusion detection system combines the best features from both host-based and network-based IDSs. If you suspect your network is being accessed or attacked by hackers, a honeypot might be just the right piece of software to trick them at their own game.

23

INTRUSION DETECTION

Backups and Disaster Recovery

IN THIS CHAPTER

Every system administrator knows the importance of keeping good backups to keep from losing data, but, in the context of security, backups are even more significant. Disasters can take many forms, and certainly not all disasters are natural. Getting paged at 3 a.m. because your company's Web server has been defaced is undoubtedly considered a disaster. When that happens, the first place you might turn are to your system backups. These backups not only allow you to restore your system to its original state, they can also provide evidence of what has changed.

Nevertheless, countless organizations fail to implement a regular backup strategy. Not having a good backup plan can leave a company with no means for disaster recovery and no baseline from which to compare. Backup and disaster recovery is the process of saving data and then later restoring that data. You can take steps to implement a good security policy, secure your system, monitor logfiles, and train your users, but you eventually will have to deal with a disaster recovery.

Throughout this book, we discuss ways of preventing acts of human malice. In this chapter, we will deal with recovery from those acts, as well as recovery from other disasters such as the following:

- *Force Majeure*—Acts of God and nature (volcanic eruptions, fires, floods, earthquakes, hurricanes, and tidal waves) can wipe out entire network operation centers.

- *Innocent mistakes*—You, or authorized privileged users, can inadvertently destroy your Windows 2000 system or overwrite vital data.

- *Mechanical failure*—In this age of inexpensive, mass-produced hardware, mechanical failures are common. For example, perfectly new hard disk drives sometimes crash.

- *Software bugs*—You might install flawed software that damages important data.

When formulating a recovery plan, you should not only consider recovering from natural disasters, but also how you would recover from a security incident. Normally, disaster recovery involves restoring data from a backup tape or other device. However, if a security breach occurred, you might need to backup the server's current state for evidence before restoring a clean backup. If the breach is serious enough, you might be best off leaving the system intact for forensic analysis. In that case, you will need an entirely new server, or at least new hard drives to put in its place. Either way, your backup strategy needs to be planned before an incident occurs. Pre-planning will help ensure that your backup and restore procedures go smoothly.

Planning a Backup Strategy

When planning a backup strategy, you must consider the various situations that would require a backup. Each of these situations has its own special requirements and will require special consideration. For example, if a fire occurs in the server room, you might have to restore to a system that is not identical to the original. As just mentioned, you might also need to take extra precautions in a security breach so that the backup and restore procedure does not corrupt any evidence. Each organization has unique backup and restore requirements, so it is critical to take the time to consider your organization's particular needs.

Part of the backup planning process includes considering the hardware and software that will be used on your network. Although you will have numerous hardware and software platforms, you should make every effort possible to keep your critical servers as standardized as possible. This includes standardizing both the hardware and software used.

Hardware Standardization

The hardware you select for your servers will have a great impact on your backup and restore procedures. You should make every effort possible to use identical (or at least similar) hardware among all your critical servers. Having common hardware makes it easier to restore to different systems and also narrows the field of hardware vendors with whom you must deal. Furthermore, it limits the number of configurations and maintenance procedures you must learn.

Many IT shops find a reputable hardware manufacturer they have had good experience with and stick to using only that company's servers. The benefit of using servers from companies such as Compaq, IBM, HP, and Dell is that each system component is known to work with each other and any individual configuration has been tested by thousands (and perhaps even millions) of users. Moreover, these systems are engineered for high availability and are well worth the extra cost. Finally, most large server manufacturers work closely with Microsoft, and their common server systems have been well tested for use with Windows 2000.

> **NOTE**
>
> Check out Microsoft's hardware compatibility list at `http://www.microsoft.com/hcl/default.asp` to ensure that the hardware you select has been tested and approved for use with Windows 2000.

24

BACKUPS AND DISASTER RECOVERY

Another benefit of using standard hardware is that you can justify keeping extra parts around, such as hot-swap hard drives or motherboards because they can be used on any of the systems. You might also be able to justify having a complete server with a basic Windows 2000 installation that you can quickly put into place when another server goes down (or is taken down). Also make sure any hot-swap hard drives are large enough to be placed in any of your systems. This might require stocking spare drives of multiple capacities and speeds.

Perhaps the most important reason for hardware standardization is that it sets a precedence for planning that can be built on throughout your whole disaster and recovery planning process.

Software Standardization

Software standardization has many of the common elements as hardware standardization. To ensure maximum uptime and minimal restore hassles, you should limit the diversity of software used on your servers. You should also establish a set of baseline Windows 2000 configurations used for each different server role. For example, you might have one baseline configuration for Web servers and another for domain controllers.

You should also keep your common software in a central location so that you can rebuild a new system from scratch if necessary. If you do this, be sure to keep old versions of software around so that you can avoid performing a restore and an upgrade at the same time. For example, if you have one server that is running an older version of a software application, you would want to build a new system with that same version to avoid other problems that can be introduced if performing an upgrade. When purchasing software, consider paying for the full-blown version and not just the upgrades to avoid upgrade problems during disaster recovery scenarios.

One final note that applies to both software and hardware standardization is that you should keep a working copy of your old backup systems. This includes both the backup devices and the restoration software. It is not uncommon for an organization to require the restoration of some very old backups, but not have the hardware or software to perform the restoration.

Backup and Restore Permissions

Windows 2000 has a special built-in group for performing system backups. This group, Backup Operators, has the Backup Files and Directories user permission. This permission allows a user to back up and restore all files on a system, regardless of the file permissions. Normally, users can copy only files they own or can read and restore to those directories where they have Write permissions.

> **NOTE**
>
> By default, the Backup Operators group is empty, although administrators also have the Backup Files and Directories user permission.

Because the Backup Operators account has unlimited access to system files, it should be used carefully and only contain trusted users or system administrators.

Choosing Your Backup Tools

Windows 2000 supports a wide range of traditional backup devices, including the following:

- SCSI tape drives (including DAT and DLT)
- CD-ROM and DVD Recorders
- Optical drives
- Parallel and SCSI removable hard drives
- Standard ATAPI tape drives

To some degree, your choice will be influenced by the type of backups you perform and which backup software you use. Not all devices are suitable for all backup methods and software applications, such as Microsoft Backup does not support backing up to CD-ROM drives. Certainly, if you intend to perform full backups routinely, you should opt for storage media that can handle large amounts of data (such as DAT, DLT or optical disks). This way, you can back up to a single unit rather than splitting your backup across several tapes.

Speed is another major factor in selecting a backup hardware and media. Speed refers to the backup time as well as the restore time. Administrators should remember that the longer the backup time, the longer the restore would take. Also, if a backup job is spread across multiple tapes, tape management becomes more complex, and the risk of one of the tapes being unre-coverable is higher. For large operations, Auto Loaders, Tape Libraries, Redundant Tape Arrays (RAITs), Image backup solutions, Storage Area Networks (SANS), and Network Attached Storage (NAS) solutions might be more appropriate. As storage capacity scales into terabytes, backup solutions must also scale in terms of capacity, reliability, and speed.

WinZip: Simple Archiving

Sometimes, for small jobs, you needn't use automated backup systems at all. For quick-and-dirty backups of files, individual directories, or directory trees, try PKzip or WinZip.

Get PKzip at http://www.pkware.com and WinZip at http://www.winzip.com.

Microsoft Windows Backup

Windows 2000 ships with a very decent backup application appropriately named Windows Backup. To start Microsoft Windows Backup ("Backup"), choose Start, Programs, Accessories, System Tools, Backup. In response, Windows 2000 will load Backup's main interface (see Figure 24.1).

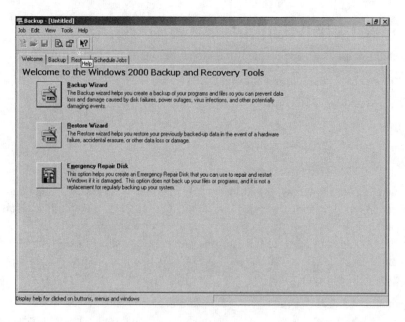

FIGURE 24.1

Microsoft Windows Backup main interface.

Backup's main interface, from the Welcome tab, presents three preset options at startup:

- *Backup Wizard*—A question/response-based interface that guides you through the process of backing up data

- *Restore Wizard*—A question/response-based interface that guides you through the process of restoring data

- *Emergency Repair Disk*—A question/response-based interface that guides you through the process of creating a repair disk

Whether you use these functions or not will depend on what type of backup you're trying to achieve. Certainly, for general-purpose backups and restoration, these wizards are fine. However, eventually, you'll want to more finely customize your backups. To do so effectively, you must have a familiarity with Backup's options.

Windows 2000 System State Data Backup and Restores

Windows 2000 introduced a new concept called the System State data. Windows 2000 requires more components to operate than just the registry. All of the system components Windows 2000 requires to operate are included in the System State data and must be backed up as a single set because they are all dependant on one another. Treating the System State data as a single unit also makes backing up and restoring a Windows 2000 system easier by only having to select the System State data rather than having to locate and select multiple system components. The following components are included in the System State data:

- *The Registry*—All Windows 2000 systems
- *Active Directory Database (NTDS directory)*—Only present on Domain Controllers
- *COM+ Class Registration database*—All Windows 2000 systems
- *System startup files*—All Windows 2000 systems
- *Certificate Services*—Only on present servers with Certificate Services installed
- *SYSVOL*—Only present on Domain Controllers

The Windows 2000 backup tool supports backing up and restoring the System State data. Most third-party backup applications also support backing up and restoring the System State data. It should be noted that administrators should verify their version of any backup applications with their backup software vendor to make sure there aren't any known issues with backing up and restoring the system state data with the version of the backup software the administrator is using. After the initial release of Windows 2000, several backup software vendors released a series of patches that were related to supporting the System State data. Be wary when using freeware or other lesser-known backup products on your Windows 2000 servers.

The only way to really know whether the backup application that is being used supports backing up and restoring the System State data, and to know if your backup media is good, is to perform a fire drill and recover one of the organization's servers in a lab environment. If a fire drill has not been performed since the organization has upgraded to Windows 2000, the restore process should be tested immediately. Without testing the backup media, software, and the organization's disaster recovery processes, the organization can never be sure it will be able to recover when a disaster strikes.

To back up the System State data on a Windows 2000 System with the Windows 2000 Backup tool, do the following:

1. Open the Windows 2000 Backup tool.
2. Click the Backup tab.
3. Click to select the System State check box. Notice that all of the System State components to be backed up are listed in the right pane, as shown in Figure 24.2, and you cannot individually select each component.

One item to note for Active Directory Domain controllers is that you must also select to back up the Winnt\SYSVOL folder. You must also select this option during the restore operation to have a working SYSVOL after the restore. Notice that the Winnt\SYSVOL is also selected in Figure 24.2

24

BACKUPS AND
DISASTER
RECOVERY

FIGURE 24.2
Backing up the System State data.

To restore the System State data, the restore can be performed from the Windows 2000 Backup tool for Windows 2000 Server and Windows 2000 Professional systems. The one exception on restoring the System State data is for Active Directory Domain Controller servers. For Domain Controllers, the administrator must run the restore from Directory Services Restore Mode. To enter Directory Service Restore Mode, do the following:

1. Restart the computer and press the F8 key at the Boot menu.

2. Choose Directory Services Restore Mode.

3. Select the Windows 2000 installation to recover.

4. At the logon prompt, supply the Directory Services Restore mode credentials that were supplied during the Dcpromo.exe process used to add the Domain Controller services to this server.

5. Click OK at the Safe mode warning.

After the administrator is in Directory Services Restore Mode on the Domain Controller, he or she can begin the restore of the System State data, just like any other Windows 2000 system. To begin the restore of the System State data, perform the following steps:

1. Open the Windows 2000 Backup tool and choose Restore.

2. Select the backup media and System State data to restore.

3. Select the Winnt\SYSVOL directory if this server is an Active Directory Domain Controller.

4. Select the advanced option to restore Junction Points and Data if this server is an Active Directory Domain Controller.

5. At the Restore Files To box, select Original Location.

6. Select Start Restore.

7. When the restore is complete, reboot the computer.

The following additional items should be noted when restoring Windows 2000 systems and Active Directory Domain Controllers:

- The drive letter for the `%SystemRoot%` folder for the restore must be the same as when it was backed up. For example, if the original location of the WINNT directory was on drive `C:\`, you cannot restore the WINNT directory to drive `D:\`.

- The `%SystemRoot%` folder must have the same folder name as when it was backed up. For example, if the original folder name of the operating system directory was `WIN2K`, you cannot restore the operating system to a directory named `WINNT`.

- If SYSVOL or the Active Directory databases (NTDS directory) were located on another drive letter, the drives must exist and have the same drive letters before attempting to restore the server. For example, if the Active Directory database was moved to drive `D:\NTDS`, drive `D:\` and the `NTDS` directory must exist before attempting to restore the server.

- Volume sizes do not have to match between the original server and the restore server. For example, the source server's `C:\` drive that was backed up could be 18GB, and the destination server's `C:\` for the restore could be 36GB and the restore will work.

Backup Options

Microsoft Backup lets you specify many options that control your backup's behavior. To reach those options, choose Tools, Options from the main menu. In response, Backup will display the Options window (see Figure 24.3).

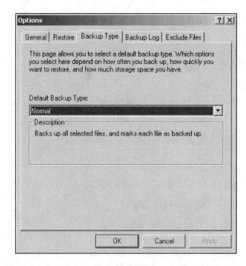

FIGURE 24.3

Microsoft Windows Backup Options window.

Backup provides options in five categories:

- *General*—Options here control Backup's overall behavior, such as notify messages, backing up of mounted volumes, and pre-computing of backup sets
- *Restore*—Options here control whether and how Backup replaces existing disk files when writing restores
- *Backup Type*—Options here control the type of backup that Backup performs (we'll address this shortly)
- *Backup Log*—Options here control the backup log type (if any)
- *Exclude Files*—This is a critical option set because it lets you specify files and file types to exclude from backups (we'll address this shortly)

Let's run through these options now.

Backup's General Options

Backup's general options govern Backup's overall behavior. To locate the General options tab, select Tools, Options, General from within the Windows Backup interface. Table 24.1 lists these options and their functions.

TABLE 24.1   Backup's General Options

Option	Function
Selection Computation	Determines whether Backup computes selection information before backup and restore procedures. This is enabled by default, and you should probably leave it that way. Selection computation naturally takes longer, but the information could be critical. Backup calculates all files and volumes to be backed up and estimates the required space, so this act makes you aware of how much backup media you need.
Use Catalogs on Media	Sets whether Backup uses the media's catalog or catalogs. This is enabled by default. However, you might want to disable this. If you leave this option enabled and deal with partial or damaged backups, you could be waiting a while. In such instances, where Backup cannot find a valid catalog, it builds one.
Verify Data	Disabled by default. I recommend enabling this option, which forces Backup to verify all data written. This, of course, takes a bit longer, but can notify you of errors that Backup didn't catch. Administrators that fail to verify their backups end up being unhappy campers. Note that verifying data doubles the time it takes to perform backups.
Mounted drive support	Enabled by default, this option makes it possible for Backup to select and back up files on a mounted drive. If this option is not selected, Microsoft Backup will only back up the path information and not the data itself.
Removable Storage Alert	Enabled by default, this option specifies that Backup should alert you when you start Backup and Removable Storage isn't running. It is a good idea to select this option.
Import Media Alert	Enabled by default, this option notifies you when suitable import media is available. This is a good idea if you're dealing with Removable Storage. Otherwise, disable it.
New Media Alert	Enabled by default, this option notifies you when new media is inserted while using removable media.
New Import Media Move	Disabled by default, this option specifies that when you install new import media, Backup should migrate it to the backup pool immediately.

24

BACKUPS AND
DISASTER
RECOVERY

Restore

Backup's Restore options specify whether and how Backup replaces existing disk files when writing restores. To locate the Restore tab, select Tools, Options, Restore from within the Windows Backup interface. Backup offers three choices:

- *Do not replace files*—This option will not replace files that exist on the target drive. Microsoft asserts that this is your safest option and that's exactly right. This option is the default and, in almost all cases, it should remain so.

- *Replace file on disk only if disk file is older*—This is slightly less dangerous than always replacing files. However, remember that newer isn't always better. In many instances, older documents, source code, and other files have important, valuable data that you or your users failed to include in newer versions. Files are compared by the last modified date.

- *Always replace the file*—This will replace all files on the hard disk with the files in the backup set. Be certain you really want to replace all the files before selecting this option. Consider backing up the existing state of the server before restoring with this option. This way, in the event the restore does not provide the desired results, you have the ability to get the server back to its original state.

Backup Type

Backup offers five backup types or strategies. To locate the Backup Type tab, select Tools, Options, Backup Type from within the Windows Backup interface. The following backup types are available:

- *Copy backup*—Copy backups copy specified files without marking them as backed up and do not clear the Archive (A) attribute.

- *Daily backup*—Daily backups copy files modified on the same day you perform the backup and do not clear the Archive (A) attribute.

- *Differential backup*—Differential backups copy files created or changed since your last normal or incremental backup, without marking them as backed up, and do not clear the Archive (A) attribute.

- *Incremental backup*—Incremental backups back up files created or changed since your last normal or incremental backup and clear the Archive (A) attribute.

- *Normal backup*—Normal backups back up all specified files and clears their Archive (A) attributes.

Whether you're just now establishing a box or you're backing up an existing system will have a strong bearing on your backup strategy. The preferred and down-and-dirty method is to start with a normal (full) backup and perform either incremental or differential backups throughout the week. However, that's not always the best strategy, and much depends on how you organized the system. The following are some points to consider:

- *Sparingly backup generic and readily replaceable data*—Overzealous and lazy administrators alike sometimes back up everything, every time, often needlessly. Generic and readily replaceable files, directory structures, and software need not be backed up. Good examples are operating system components or any software for which you have the original distribution disks. Backing up such data needlessly eats valuable space.

- *Good organization leads to cleaner, easier backups*—Windows 2000, by default, creates standardized directories for user documents, images, and so on. This, coupled with directory permissions, lets Windows 2000 force—to some degree—where user data ends up. But user conformity plays a limited role here, because users can, and often do, create their own directory structures. Sometimes, these new directories are *beneath* the prefabbed directories, but not always. For the most part, Windows 2000's approach guarantees that user data will be localized, though. *The same is not true for your data.* You, being the administrator, can theoretically put data anywhere, but that is not a good practice. For scripts, policy files, and other custom components you create, establish one directory tree and stick to it. This simplifies backups by centralizing such interrelated files (rather than having them spread out everywhere).

- *Segregation is vital*—Never store (or allow users to store) data files in the same directories as application data. This is especially important to remember when using older applications. In some such applications (Corel, PSP, and so on), the Save and Save As options default to application directories. This behavior is a throwback to Windows 3.x programming conventions. Most new applications don't behave this way, but we're sometimes forced to use legacy applications.

Backup Log

The Backup Log option controls the backup log type you want to use. To locate the Backup Log tab, select Tools, Options, Backup Log from within the Windows Backup interface. Logging options come in three flavors, specified in Table 24.2.

24

TABLE 24.2   Backup's Backup Log Options

Option	Function
Detailed	This option, disabled by default, specifies that Backup should log everything, including fully qualified filenames and directory names. Certainly, this takes slightly longer, but I recommend it except in situations where filenames aren't critical (such as when you're backing up software dependency files).
Summary	This option, the default, specifies that Backup will only log essential events, such as media loading, mounting, and unmounting.
None	This specifies that Backup shouldn't maintain a log.

Whenever possible, always generate detailed logs. System logs are often the only means you have to determine what happened during a particular procedure.

Exclude Files

Backup's Exclude Files function is perhaps the most valuable function of all because it lets you specify files and file types that Backup should omit from the backup regimen. To reach the Exclude Files window, choose Tools, Options, Exclude Files from within the Windows Backup interface. In response, Backup will display the Exclude Files window (see Figure 24.4).

FIGURE 24.4
Microsoft Windows Backup Exclude Files window.

The Exclude Files window is split in two parts. The top pane stores files and file types that Backup will exclude for all users.

Files and file types that Backup excludes by default are as follows:

- ComPlus
- Power Management
- Memory Page File
- Internet Explorer
- Temporary Files
- Client Side Cache
- Winlogon Debug
- Netlogon
- Task Scheduler

Backup excludes files and file types such as these for various reasons. One is that many of these files and file types are transient. Consider temporary files, for example. A majority of temporary files are precisely that—temporary. Examples include `*.tmp` files generated by applications like Microsoft Word. Unless you're really conducting close surveillance on your users, you wouldn't want such files. They often have duplicate and worthless information.

Other files are sensitive in different ways. Page files are a good example. Page files consist of virtual memory areas that either Windows 2000 specifies or that you specify yourself. These files serve as quasi-RAM and serve the same purpose as Unix swap files. Such files can be sensitive in a security context (many applications store sensitive data in memory, including passwords and pass phrases, and with page files, this data gets written to disk). Only in extreme cases where you're searching for suspicious user behavior would you want to preserve such files.

You can approach file exclusion in two ways: choosing registered file types or manually providing custom file masks. To do either, choose Add New from the Exclude Files window. In response, Backup will display the Add Excluded Files window (see Figure 24.5).

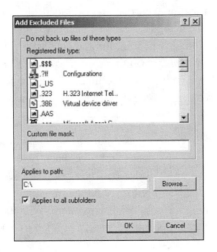

FIGURE 24.5
Backup's Add Excluded Files window.

The Add Excluded Files window provides you with a list of registered file types. This list is essentially the same list you'll find in Windows File Explorer and, in a beefed-up system, typically contains several hundred types (aif, au, wav, zip, and so on). To add such file types, double-click them in the list or hold down the Ctrl key to select multiple items and then press the Enter key.

Otherwise, if you have custom file types to include that do not appear on the registered file type list, add their extensions in the Custom File Mask field. Such custom types consist of file types that the registry doesn't track (because the registry doesn't know about them).

The Exclude Files function is valuable for several reasons. First, it saves you substantial space. Many system-related files (especially those that originate on OEM disks) are basically generic and are replaceable. Caution should be exercised when excluding files after the system has been patched with a service pack or hot fix. If you are excluding files, make sure the patch or service pack installation media is available in the event the system must be reinstalled.

As your system grows, you'll likely create your own file types for storage, scripts, and so on. Many of these files you create will be temporary and insignificant. But exclusions can work both ways. You can either specify a limited set of excluded files and back up the remaining drive, or you can specify a wide range of excluded files and back up the limited, approved sets that remain.

Also, as administrator, the Exclude Files function has special uses. For example, you can differentiate between excluded files for everyone and excluded files for a particular user. This has several applications. First, you can create a backup account with limited privileges that you authorize and instruct to back up only certain, limited data sets. You can also use this function to limit what users can back up, thus preventing media waste. Users with backup privileges might back up anything and everything. The Exclude Files function lets you limit classes of file types across multiple directories, some that users have permissions on and some that users don't.

It should be noted that if you do choose to exclude files, there will not be a complete system image on tape. Although this will save space and time when backing up the systems, it can work against you when performing forensics on a compromised system. In the event the system is compromised, business needs might force the administrators to reformat and rebuild the server without fully investigating the compromised system. Without a complete backup, it will be impossible to reconstruct the compromised system in a lab to perform detailed forensic work after the server is back into production.

Backing Up Your Data

To back up your data, open Windows 2000 Backup and then choose the Backup tab from the main menu of the Windows 2000 Backup window. Here, Backup displays a two-tiered interface for choosing directories and files (see Figure 24.6).

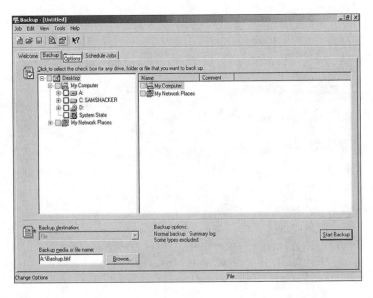

FIGURE 24.6
Backup's Main interface.

On the left side, you navigate directories and, at any time, you can enable the check box that appears next to each one. Enabling this check box chooses the entire directory (see Figure 24.7).

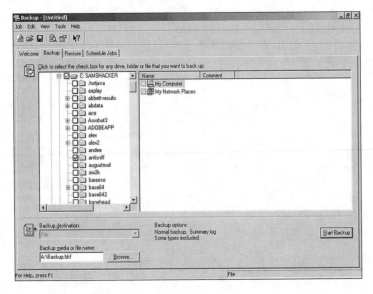

24

FIGURE 24.7
Choosing an entire directory in Backup.

In the right pane, Backup also allows you to drill down deeper, to the file level. To do so, highlight your chosen directory. In response, Backup will show all files in that directory (and for each such file, an enabled check box) (see Figure 24.8).

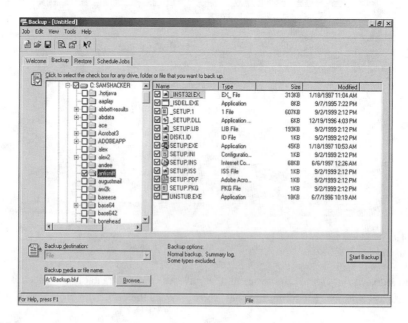

FIGURE 24.8
Backup highlights all files when you choose a directory for backup.

To clear files from the backup list, clear their corresponding check boxes. When you're done, specify your backup's destination in the Backup Media or File Name field. At this point, you're ready to begin.

NOTE

Backup works equally well for FAT and NTFS. However, you should restore to the same type of file system that you backed up, or you will lose data. For example, if the data that was backed up was on a partition formatted as NTFS 5.0, it must be restored to a partition that is formatted as NTFS 5.0.

When you've made your choices, choose Start Backup. In response, Backup will back up the specified files and directories to either a file or tape.

mtfcheck: Verifying Backup Tapes from Scripts

Occasionally, you might want to verify that Backup wrote your data correctly, or even merely erase a tape. In most cases, Backup is sufficient for this. However, if you want to perform these tasks from scripts, use mtfcheck, which is available as part of the Windows 2000 Resource Kit. Table 24.3 lists mtfcheck options and what they do.

TABLE 24.3   mftcheck Options and Arguments

Option	Function
?	Gets onscreen help for mtfcheck.
-e	Indicates that mtfcheck should erase the specified tape. An additional option (l for long) is available, and this forces mtfcheck to zero all data on the tape. You might do this if you want to obliterate the previous data (which mtfcheck will overwrite).
-f[*n*]	Indicates the file number (expressed as n) to restore from the backup tape. You derive this number from a report file.
-l[*label*]	Indicates the label you'd like to assign to the specified tape.
-r[*reportfilename*]	Indicates the file that mtfcheck redirects output to (and its name). If you fail to provide such a filename or specify an impossible filename, mtfcheck directs output to stdout.
-s[*n*]	This indicates the specific set number (expressed as n) to restore from the specified tape.
-t[*tapename*]	This indicates the tape to use and its name, typically tape0, tape1, and so on (similar to tape naming conventions in Unix).

To use mtfcheck merely to verify tapes, use nominal syntax, as follows:

```
mtfcheck -ttape0
```

This verifies a tape's contents. However, you can also use mtfcheck to restore files incisively, too.

```
mtfcheck  -ttape0 -f3 -s1
```

This specifies that mtfcheck should restore the third file from Set 1 on tape0. mtfcheck, therefore, offers a means to handle backup restoration from scripts. However, in certain cases, you might require special utilities for this. For example, suppose you want to back up and restore just your registry. You might consider using regback and regrest instead. Let's briefly cover those now.

regback: Registry Backup

The system registry is a critical component (or series of components) in Windows 2000 without which your system cannot operate. Although you can back up registry components using the Windows 2000 Backup tool, there is also another utility available for this purpose (and which you can use in scripts) exists—regback. regback, available in the Windows 2000 Resource Kit, backs up your registry (even while the hives are open) and run that backup to a file. (regback is not for use with tape drives).

NOTE

Some regback limitations exist. First, to use it, you must belong to a group with Backup privileges. Also, note that regback will not perform overwriting. After it writes a registry backup, that's it. You must direct subsequent regback backups to different files.

To back up your registry now, issue the regback command plus the backup file output name:

```
regback c:\mybackup.bku
```

This will back up your registry in the file mybackup.bku. But perhaps you want more control. For this, regback provides several options that allow you to more incisively specify your backup preferences. Let's cover those now.

regback Options and Arguments

Often, you'll want to back up only a portion of your registry (a beefed-up system's registry can be huge—hundreds of megabytes). Table 24.4 explains regback options and how to use them.

TABLE 24.4   regback Options and Arguments

Option	Function
destination-directory	Indicates your desired directory, the directory where your backup file will reside. You can direct such backups to any disk or share with adequate space.
filename	Your backup file's name.
hivename	Must be a valid subtree (and to use this, you must specify a valid root hivetype).
hivetype	Must either be machine or users.

A fully qualified regback command will contain all four arguments:

```
regback c:\myregbackup\regout.bku users s-1-0000-0000-1234
```

Here, the values are as follows:

- The destination directory—`c:\myregbackup`
- The backup filename—`regout.bku`
- The hive type—`users`
- The hive name—`s-1-0000-0000-1234`

CAUTION

Note that `regback` backups *do* scoop up access control lists (ACLs). This can have an effect on system operation. For example, if you restore a registry backup from a month ago, that restore will carry the original ACLs. Be mindful of this or you might find certain services unavailable and certain users locked out of vital systems.

Also, note that `regback` will not perform half measures. If it encounters insufficient space or a critical error, it aborts.

regrest: Restoring Registry regback Backups

To restore backups created with `regback`, use `regrest`, the registry restore utility. If you used the Windows 2000 Backup tool to backup the registry, use Windows 2000 Backup tool to restore the registry.

NOTE

Some regrest limitations exist. First, to use it, you must belong to a group with Backup privileges. Also, note that `regrest` renames rather than copies files, and all files must reside on the same volume.

Table 24.5 lists `regrest`'s options and what they do.

TABLE 24.5   regrest Options and Arguments

Option	Function
hivename	Must be a valid subtree (and to use this, you must specify a valid root hivetype).

TABLE 24.5   Continued

Option	Function
hivetype	Must either be `machine` or `users`.
newfile	This indicates the backup source file, with which `regrest` replaces hive-name.
savefile	This indicates the name and location to which `regrest` renames the old hive file.

`regrest` syntax, wherein you specify all options, is as follows:

`regrest newfile savefile hivetype hivename`

For example,

`regrest c:\registry1.sav\system c:\registry2.sav machine system`

However, in most cases, you'll do a flat `regrest` for the entire registry:

`regrest c:\.bku  c:\install.sav`

More Backup Strategies

Finally, the following are some rules to remember about backups:

- After each backup, verify that your backup program actually wrote the data correctly. Try accessing random portions of the tape rather than simply reading the headers, just to make sure.
- Don't cut corners on backup media. Cheap or old backup media can lead to poorly written data. Buy quality backup media.
- If anything at all unusual happens during backup, be suspicious, and consider starting again with new media. Even minor glitches can sometimes render a backup useless.
- Make full backups every two weeks or, on critical systems, every week.
- Meticulously label your tapes. Ensure that at minimum, you mark them with description of contents and the date of the backup.
- Store at least one full backup set off site in a safe, dry, cool, location free from magnetic fields, electrical charges, and so forth. Consider getting a fire safe.

Summary

Backups are vital not merely in a disaster recovery context, but they also play a vital role in a security context. If you operate a multi-user system, you *must* make backups. It must be stated that backups offer the ability to recover the system after it has been compromised, but they do not offer an index against which to measure your current file system and possibly detect suspicious changes. To detect a change in the file systems, a file integrity checker is needed. Chapter 10, "Trojans and Backdoors," discusses TripWire, a third-party file integrity checker that will help detect unauthorized files system changes. When a compromise is discovered, the backup might preserve evidence of unauthorized activity that can be used to prosecute the intruder.

SYMBOLS

A

C

E

Hey, you've got enough worries.

Don't let IT training be one of them.

Get on the fast track to IT training at InformIT,
your total Information Technology training network.

 | **www.informit.com** | **SAMS**

■ Hundreds of timely articles on dozens of topics ■ Discounts on IT books from all our publishing partners, including Sams Publishing ■ Free, unabridged books from the InformIT Free Library ■ "Expert Q&A"—our live, online chat with IT experts ■ Faster, easier certification and training from our Web- or classroom-based training programs ■ Current IT news ■ Software downloads ■ Career-enhancing resources

InformIT is a registered trademark of Pearson. Copyright ©2001 by Pearson.
Copyright ©2001 by Sams Publishing.

Other Related Titles

Maximum Security, Third Edition
Anonymous
0-672-31871-7
$49.99 US/$74.95 CAN

WSH and ADSI Administrative Scripting
Gerry O'Brien
0-672-32250-1
$39.99 US/$59.95 CAN

Microsoft Active Directory Administration
Kevin Kocis
0-672-31975-6
$39.99 US/$59.95 CAN

Microsoft Windows 2000 DNS— Implementation and Administration
Kevin Kocis
0-672-32200-5
$39.99 US/$59.95 CAN

Teach Yourself Windows 2000 Server in 24 Hours
Barrie Sosinksy and Jeremy Moskowitz
0-672-31940-3
$19.99 US/$29.95 CAN

Peter Norton's Complete Guide to Windows 2000 Professional
Peter Norton, John Mueller, Richard Mansfield
0-672-31778-8
$39.99 US/$59.95 CAN

Maximum Linux Security, Second Edition
Anonymous
0-672-32134-3
$49.99 US/$74.95 CAN

Microsoft Windows 2000 Server Unleashed
Todd Brown and Chris Miller
0-672-31739-7
$49.99 US/$74.95 CAN

www.samspublishing.com

All prices are subject to change.